Labor's Lot

Labor's Lot

THE POWER,
HISTORY,
AND
CULTURE OF
ABORIGINAL
ACTION

ELIZABETH A. POVINELLI

THE UNIVERSITY OF CHICAGO PRESS • CHICAGO AND LONDON

Elizabeth Povinelli is assistant professor
of anthropology at Cornell University

The University of Chicago Press, Chicago 60637
The University of Chicago Press, Ltd., London
© 1993 by The University of Chicago
All rights reserved. Published 1993
Printed in the United States of America

02 01 00 99 98 97 96 95 94   2 3 4 5

ISBN: 0-226-67673-0 (cloth)
ISBN: 0-226-67674-9 (paper)

Library of Congress Cataloging-in-Publication Data

Povinelli, Elizabeth A.
  Labor's lot : the power, history, and culture of aboriginal action
  / Elizabeth A. Povinelli.
      p.   cm.
  Includes bibliographical references and index.
  1. Australian aborigines—Australia—Cox peninsula
(N. T.)—Economic conditions. 2. Australian aborigines—
Australia—Cox Peninsula (N. T.)—Land tenure. 3. Austra-
lian aborigines—Australia—Cox Peninsula (N. T.)—Ethnic
identity. 4. Belyuen (australia)—Economic condi-
tions. 5. Land use—Australia—Cox Peninsula
(N. T.) 6. Hunting and gathering socieities. I. Title.
GN667.N6P68   1993
306'.089'991509429—dc20   93-2511

⊗ The paper used in this publication meets the minimum
requirements of the American National Standard for Information Sciences—Permanence of Paper for Printed Library
Materials, ANSI Z39.48-1984.

To
Susan Louise and the Voice Dolls

Contents

List of Maps and Tables ix
Acknowledgments xi
Foreword xiii
INTRODUCTION 1

PART ONE • SETTING UP LABOR-ACTION: LEGITIMATE LAW, IDENTITY, HISTORY 21

CHAPTER ONE
Legal Entanglements
Aboriginal Action and Identity 23

CHAPTER TWO
Positioning Aborigines
Precolonial, Colonial and Postcolonial Aboriginal Pasts 64

PART TWO • ASSESSING LABOR-ACTION: DREAMING, DEVELOPMENT, KNOWLEDGE/POWER 131

CHAPTER THREE
Labor's Lot
The Construction of Human Bodies and the Countryside 133

CHAPTER FOUR
"Today We Struggle"
Contemporary Hunting, Fishing, and Collecting and the Market 168

CHAPTER FIVE
"Being There"
Dreaming and Development as Political Frames for Land Use 203

CHAPTER SIX
The Assessment of Cultural Identity and Political-Economic Practice
A Conclusion   239

Appendixes   253

Notes   273

Works Cited   297

Index   321

Maps and Tables

MAP ONE
Coast of the Northern Territory from Port Keats to Port Darwin
61

MAP TWO
The Historical Location of non-Aboriginal Activity on the Cox Peninsula
69

MAP THREE
Trips Made from the Belyuen Community to Regions of the Cox Peninsula
206

MAP FOUR
Northern Territory Land Use Plan, 1990
213

MAP FIVE
Ownership of Land in the Darwin Region in the 1880s
226

TABLE ONE
Comparison of Women's Use of Six Mangrove Regions
59

TABLE TWO
The Contribution of Bush Foods to the Belyuen Diet
177

TABLE THREE
Monetary and Caloric Values of Foods Purchased from Grocery Markets
179

TABLE FOUR
Temporal Aspects of the Belyuen Aborigines' Hunter-Gathering Activity
182

TABLE FIVE
A Gender Comparison of the Difficulty of Hunter-Gathering Activities
184

TABLE SIX
Distribution of Income for the Purchase of Alcohol
193

TABLE SEVEN
Notable European Economic Activities in Tropical Northern Territory
219

TABLE EIGHT
Lapsed Time Spent Hunting and Gathering Foods and Materials
228

Acknowledgments

This book is a meager representation of the depth of thought, skill of living, and verbal imagination of the men and women who live at Belyuen. I thank them for helping make this book possible, for deeply influencing how I think about myself and my community, and for the delight of their company. In particular I wish to acknowledge the help of Betty Bilawag, Marjorie Bilbil, Ruby Yarrowin, Agnes Lippo, Alice Djarug, Maggie Timber, Ann Timber, Henry Moreen, and the deceased mother and grandmother of Raelene, Jason, and Zoe Singh. I am also grateful to Lorna Tennant, John Singh, Lenny Singh and the other members of the Belyuen Community Council who provided support and a place to live in the community during my various stays, ten months in 1984–85, the summer of 1987, fourteen months from January 1989 to March 1990, and July 1992.

Other people and organizations have contributed to the research, writing, and form of this book in a variety of ways. I would like to thank the librarians at the Australian Archives in Darwin, especially those in Special Collections, at the Mitchell Library in Sydney, and at the Elkin Collections housed at the University of Sydney. The Northern Land Council and the Aboriginal Areas Protection Authority provided a critical political framework for my thinking. My trips were graciously funded by the Thomas J. Watson Foundation, Sigma Xi, the Scientific Research Society, the National Science Foundation (grant BNS-8814363), the Australian Institute of Aboriginal Studies, the Yale Williams' Fund, and the Yale International and Areas Studies Grant. Camille Ward drafted several of the maps appearing in this book. T. David Brent, senior editor, and Jean Eckenfels, senior manuscript editor at the University of Chicago Press, provided the good guidance that made publishing this book a remarkably painless process. Francesca Merlan, Frank McKeown, David Parsons, Ian Grey, Adrienne Haritos, Bill, Djidjila, and David Turner, Maria Brandl, Ros Fraser, Patrick McConvell, and Michael Walsh have offered critical perspectives on anthropology, social issues, land rights, and language. Hal Scheffler, Micaela di Leonardo, Fred Myers, Don Donham, Bruce

Knauft, Bill Kelly, Vicky Burbank, and Bradd Shore provided critical and insightful commentary on the form and substance of this book through its many drafts. Siobhan Somerville, Bruce Hainley, and Lisa Cohen provided stimulating conversation which, although more indirectly, as importantly shaped this book's form and content. Ada Fall and her descendents provided an imaginary genealogy necessary for me to begin writing. Susan Edmunds's companionship and thinking on twentieth-century American women's literature has been central to my writing and thinking in this book and has provided the means for me to finish writing, at least for now.

Introduction

This book aims to demonstrate the dialectic engagement between an Australian Aboriginal community's understandings of the productivity of their action and identity—how speech and sweat are seen to affect a sentient landscape and a hostile government, where intentionality lies, how indigenous actions are or should be differentiated from those of other ethnic groups—and historical and present-day state discourses on hunter-gatherer economy and society.

The Belyuen community is located in the middle of the Cox Peninsula, Northern Territory of Australia (map 1) and is composed of roughly 200 people from a variety of coastal Daly River language groups, mainly the Wagaitj and Beringgen.[1] Belyuen Wagaitj-Beringgen and Darwin Laragiya have been engaged in a land claim for the Cox Peninsula region since 1976. Western models of productivity, traditionality (and history), and cultural identity play a significant role in the way the claim has been evaluated.

In contemporary Australia, the meaning and value of what Aborigines do and say is often a site of intense struggle. Aboriginal practice—Aboriginal action and the interpretation of that action—is a symbolic landscape read in alternate, usually competing ways by various Aboriginal and Euro-Australian groups and is used to construct and interpret both their identities. This "reading of action" is embedded within historically changing fields of power and value (Bourdieu 1991; also Appadurai 1986), which in the past included often horrifically violent legal and extralegal confrontations in the outback and now includes socially liberal land rights legislation for Aborigines in the city and countryside.

At various points in history and with various cultural perspectives, a society makes a claim about how "truth" can be discovered, recovered, or uncovered and what value such truth has; this includes some form of domination.[2] Belyuen Aborigines and observers such as myself make claims about how to judge the authenticity of a group's knowledges and practices; we attempt to discover which events are meaningful and valuable and which are not. The "truth" of how humans relate to the land, or countryside, is highly contested in regions of Australia where colonial and postcolonial violence was focused on Aboriginal inhabitants. Therefore, while this ethnography focuses on the Belyuen Aborigines' effort to produce themselves and their identity in contemporary Australia, I also discuss their struggles' effect on other Aboriginal groups in the Darwin region. Other Aboriginal groups may disagree with the form of this struggle. The Wadeye ("Port Keats," an Aboriginal community south of the Daly River) Murinpatha and Beringgen may view the patrilineal group's relationship to an "estate" (see Stanner 1965a) as superior to the joint rights and duties of all other peoples in relation to that piece of land (see Barber 1987). Some Laragiya living in Darwin may also disagree with Belyuen ways of relating to country. Finally, Belyuen Aborigines themselves may disagree with how I understand their relationship to country. Because of these conflicting views and the real political intersections they entail (see Brandl and Walsh 1983; Merlan 1991), I highlight how knowledge is "performed" in specific social situations; that is, how truth is presented and contested, including my role in this process. Because Belyuen Aborigines and Euro-Australians use the same regions, often the same places, I highlight the conflicts and connections between groups in the Cox Peninsula as they have entwined, adapted, and unraveled over time.

The relevance of Belyuen land use is not confined to the Cox Peninsula. Today symbols of "Aboriginality" are cornerstones to an ongoing construction of the Australian nation-state (Beckett 1988; Lattas 1990). Even indigenous symbols of Aborigines' struggle against the nation-state, Sally Weaver notes, can be incorporated into the "political culture" against which they act (1984, 184). For instance, the names of and the mythic stories and artifacts associated with places where Aborigines hunt and the quantity of foods they find are matters of knowledge, status, and secrecy, not only within an Aboriginal system of power and law, but also within the larger political economy of the region. The Northern Territory government takes an active role in encouraging tourist outfits and fisheries to take advantage of known and available scenic and productive hunting grounds, some of which lie on the Cox Peninsula and are used by Belyuen families. This is a common pattern throughout the continent. Many who have seen the videos and films of Uluru (Ayers Rock in Central Australia) made by the Australian tourist industry would probably agree with Julie Marcus that "the rise of Ayers Rock as a central and dominating national symbol has led to the appropriation of this important Aboriginal sacred site by settler Australians, and to the incorporation of an etiolated form of the Aboriginal meanings of the Rock into a rapidly developing settler cosmology" (1988, 5–6; Layton 1989; Hamilton 1984).

The national imagery of Aboriginal action works into indigenous self-construction insofar as it must be resisted, accepted, or ignored—a form of action in and of itself (see Morris 1989; Trigger 1992). But national imagery is reworked through and read against local perspectives on social action. For example, most of my discussion comes from middle-aged and senior Belyuen women's views of their social practices, views which at times can be read as part of the larger community's performance of self-identity for a Western audience and at other times as a dispute among community members—young and old, men and women—about what constitutes "proper" social action. This contextual "mixing" and "straightening"; of social action and cultural identity is a central concern of the book.

The book itself arises from my deep dissatisfaction with current portrayals of Australian Aboriginal economic labor and of hunter-gatherers' labor more generally. For historical reasons, the economic activities of Aboriginal Australians have been apprehended and described outside of the cultural (and often the political) fields in which they reside—if they have been described at all. Historical reasons for this theoretical partition include Western models of economic and cultural evolution, colonial disruptions of Aboriginal life which set conditions for ethnographic work, and the legal and political frameworks in which Aboriginal action and ethnographic inquiry are evaluated; a context of particular importance today is the Land Rights (Northern Territory) Act, 1976.[3] By demonstrating the deep interconnections among everyday economic activity, cultural meaning, and social identity—the articulations of power, identity, and action in Aboriginal Australia—this book is an effort to challenge the theoretical divide between Aboriginal culture and economy and the descriptive relevance of "the subsistence economy" (cf. Lee 1988; Ingold 1988; Woodburn 1982).

ORGANIZATION OF THE BOOK

My dissatisfaction with current portrayals of contemporary hunter-gatherer societies has led to the specific organization of this book and to the theoretical frame underlying it. The book is broken into two parts, and, in some respects, it addresses two divergent topics. On the one hand, I discuss the conflicting understandings of Belyuen Aboriginal cultural identity and socioeconomic history in the context of contemporary liberal Australian land rights legislation; on the other hand, I examine competing frameworks for understanding Belyuen labor-action, its value, and its effects on landscapes. Part 1 examines the legal and historical web within which Belyuen Aborigines currently find themselves, and the effect of these legalities and socioeconomic histories on the way that they and

Euro-Australians now assess "Belyuen" cultural identity and economic practice. Chapter 1 concentrates on how social theory about Australian hunter-gatherers, especially its separation of their "complex" sociocultural beliefs from their "simple" economic practices, has underwritten contemporary land rights legislation and has provided many artificial and insurmountable legal and political hurdles for Belyuen Aborigines' attempts to gain rights to local lands. Chapter 2 examines the complex socioeconomic history of local Belyuen Aborigines. It shows how historical portraits of their origins and practices constrain the possible ways Belyuen Aborigines can now present themselves as authentic cultural subjects. Both chapters concentrate on the role that Belyuen women's speech practices play in the production and mediation of these legal and historical discourses. Part 2 looks at how Belyuen Aborigines and the Australian government differently assess the productive power, value, and potential of hunting and gathering labor-action. In this second half, I compare local cultural notions of how labor-action productively affects the sentient landscape and the social group (chap. 3) to conflicting Western measures of local hunting and gathering action—including the productivity of Belyuen hunting and gathering (chap. 4)—and Western discourses on development—including Belyuen Aborigines' spatial use of the Cox Peninsula (chap. 5).

I have organized the book in this way for two broad reasons. First, I intend the division to be both argument and evidence of the simultaneous but independent structuring of cultural identity, economic practice, and legal assessment. Relatedly, I wish the two parts to show a common underlying conflict between Aborigines and non-Aborigines over who will have authority to *link* practice and meaning and thus produce value, power, and authority for the self and social group. In summary, in part 1, I show how Euro-Australians and Belyuen Aborigines struggle over who will link socioeconomic histories, cultural identities, and their legal meanings; in part 2 I show how these same actors struggle over who will link labor-action, social health, and productivity. Thus, much of my discussion, while presenting the facts of histories, economies, and laws, focuses on *how* various social histories, cultural identities, and economies are legitimately linked (or fail to be linked) to dominant forms of economy, power, and law. Second, I intend the division of the book into discussions of authenticity and productivity to reflect the real sociological position within which contemporary Belyuen Aborigines find themselves. Assessment of Belyuen practice and identity—indeed the practices and identities of many contemporary Australian Aborigines—occurs along two often contradictory lines. As I discuss briefly below and in detail in chapter 1, issues of Aboriginal cultural identity and social history are assessed according to one set of criteria (traditionally and change; see

Merlan [1992] for an important critique of this practice), while their economic practices are assessed according to another (productivity and economic ecology; see Wilmsen [1989a] and Myers [1982a] for critiques of these approaches). This partitioning of Aboriginal social life continues despite the fact that most Aborigines, Aboriginal advocates, and even Aboriginal opponents have long realized that Aboriginal culture and economy are linked in local thought and in national law and policy and that it is far more important to understand the *mechanism* by which practice and identities are linked (in an Aboriginal and a non-Aboriginal arena) than to identify what constitutes the unchanging substance of these identities and practices. In short, I hope to show that the constitution and legitimation of cultural identities and social histories are productive enterprises even as economic productivities can have authentic and unauthentic, empowering and disempowering forms. Those with a greater interest in one half or the other of this productive enterprise can suitably tailor their reading.

POLITICAL-ECONOMIC AND INTERPRETIVE ANTHROPOLOGY

My discussion of the dialogical and contested nature, value, and meaning of action intends to critique and nuance theoretical issues in political-economic and interpretive anthropology. In postcolonial north Australia, where most Aboriginal groups have had some if not extensive dealings with the Northern Territory government and the Aboriginal-run Northern Land Council and where many groups continue to draw important economic and cultural resources from surrounding landscapes, the form and meaning of the Aboriginal bush food economy (their cultural economy) must be studied in a more complex cultural and political-economic framework than that offered by our current choice between a forager or class model.[4] Belyuen Aborigines do not just live off the land, they live in and with a living country; that is, they interact with it according to culturally defined guidelines for how the landscape will react to and assess their actions. In addition, they live under a Western gaze: how they act is apprehended by a Western political-economic framework and is assessed by Western models of productivity. Aboriginal economic action is, therefore, neither an enclave of subsistence production nor a peripheral outpost of capital penetration. It is part of an ongoing production of the group—its economic, cultural, and political well-being—drawn from the multiplicity of cultural and political-economic discourses and resources that Aboriginal people find in their lives.

In the following I introduce several subtending issues in political-economic theory that affect how Aboriginal labor-action is framed and assessed by colonial law and classic Australian social anthropology, issues on which, I hope, this ethnography sheds new light. Political-economic anthropology has paid critical attention to issues of power, history, and ideology in the construction and reproduction of social groups within regional and national contexts. But the concepts of intentional labor and productivity that underpin many discussions of power and history may be used by dominant social groups and imperialist states to undermine the meaning and importance of indigenous labor-action. That is, Western notions of labor, most fully described in political-economic theory, are an interpretive endeavor to understand the human social organization of labor and wealth and a discursive tool that can be deployed on behalf of or against non-Western peoples; they do not a priori describe indigenous labor-action, because they do not view labor-action outside the West's own cultural frames.[5] Properly, it is Belyuen labor-action, its histories, and discursive uses that this ethnography explores, not the Aboriginal economy or foraging mode of production. But because these latter models contest Belyuen claims about the productivity of their labor, it is critical to discuss these views, if only briefly, in this introduction.

It would be hard to image an outlook more at odds with Belyuen understandings of the mutual constitution of humans and country than that of the emerging Western manufacturing and imperialistic nations of the eighteenth and nineteenth centuries. Political-economic theories and the new scientific philosophy that accompanied them attempted to understand emerging socioeconomic and political formations by rejecting any notion of a "country that listens" or "an object that behaves willfully." Although often disagreeing among themselves, such diverse thinkers as Boyle, Locke, and Hobbes attacked alchemic understandings of nature and society as uncomfortably animistic in their outlook (things were too alive), offering as a replacement a mechanical view of human action and nature (see Alexander 1985; Shapin and Schaffer 1985; Adas 1989). The New Science, which social sciences were increasingly to imitate as a source of legitimacy, sought not only to overturn a previous alchemic understanding of the living world, but also to establish a way of seeing the natural mechanical order as liable to human manipulation. According to the New Science, because objects lack the distinguishing features of human life—will and reason—they are perfectly manipulable and the results of this manipulation perfectly calculable. This calculation progressed from the almost sweet naivete of Locke, wherein people owned things to which their labor was added, to a draconian Taylorism in which even a worker's fleeting memory of a loved one was a calculable theft of the capitalist's potential property. Efficiency became all. Advanced modes of production, marked by a complex division of labor, allowed human efficiency, and therefore human productivity and "wealth," to soar as it created vast human economic inequalities (Engels 1958).

While natural philosophers were extending the mechanical or geometrical model to explain natural and market forces—from the movement of the planets to the action of the assembly line (cf. Ian Shapiro 1986, 23)—they were uneasily holding the divide between natural objects, animals, and the human subject. Natural and enlightened philosophers differentiated humans from natural objects and animals not in their biological, physical, or mechanical aspect, but in the former's capacity to reason, speak, and exchange (words and goods) at will, and to make the world around them. For these traits to be characteristic of human beings, natural philosophers and classical political economists had to refuse them to nonhuman beings and things; and they also had to discredit those people who believed otherwise. The latter was done by temporalizing a counter-discourse in two interlocking ways: (1) people who believed otherwise were primitive in their thought and reflected an earlier point in philosophical or scientific thought, and (2) the mode of production that allowed the human subject, and correlatively the productive subject, to emerge most fully (and thus oppose itself to emerging objects) was temporally progressive in nature. Thus the infamous four-stages theory in which a "society 'naturally' or 'normally' progressed over time through four more or less distinct and consecutive stages, each corresponding to a different mode of subsistence" (Meek 1976, 2; Williams 1986). The four-stages theory, modified in ways I discuss below, reemerged in Marxist anthropology as the history and articulations of modes of production, a history that at its end united primitive and advanced communisms (Donham 1990, 16; see also Meillassoux 1973).

Western philosophers' disagreements, while significant within the tradition, are less important from an indigenous viewpoint than their shared view that humans had a unique capacity to make, in an intentional way, the world around them, a capacity that distinguished them from dumb animals and insentient objects. These philosophers believed that a society's mode of production and reproduction either deeply influenced or determined a society's corresponding social, cultural, and political institutions. In the first instance, and critical to this study's discussion of Aboriginal labor practice and Western legal and economic assessments of it, the unique human capacity of intentional making became "the bedrock for the analysis of property" (Tully 1980; see also Shapiro 1986; MacPherson 1962) and value. Of course this bedrock of value was shaken when Marx made quite clear the revolutionary potential of a labor theory of value. In the century that followed Marx's writings, political-economic concerns about the creation and distribution of wealth across social groups or classes were displaced by a neoclassical theory of economy that rejected labor as the key determinant of value and turned instead to endless and rigidly scientific measurements of utility, supply, and demand. But property itself and, more important, the relation of the nation-state to indigenous property, was first informed and continues to be underwritten by the notion that the action of intentional subjects has the power to transform mere objects and landscapes into things of value (see Wilmsen [1989a] and Williams [1986] for African and Australian cases). From a perspective of classical political economy, "Fourth World" hunter-gather peoples neither sufficiently produce (or differentiate) themselves as subjects in relation to natural objects and animals nor are they sufficiently productive in terms of transforming objects and animals into depositories of value. At most they "own" (because they in some way make) the things they hunt and gather but not the land on which they pursue these practices. Tim Ingold's recent *Appropriation of Nature,* returns to Marx's writings to offer a powerful critique of the way that hunter-gatherer peoples have been denied intentional action and full subjectivity. But in doing so, he returns to critical Western notions of the divide between human subject/agents (gatherer-hunter), nonintentional animals (predator/prey), and objects (insentient things). The hunter-gatherer remains a "self-conscious agent, confronting a world of plants and animals from which he or she selects those that will furnish suitable raw materials for consumption" (Ingold 1987, 3). This description does not fit Belyuen understandings of the relationship between human laborers and the nonhuman world.

While contemporary political-economic anthropology has made invaluable contributions to our understandings of the power of the capitalist state in casting, constraining, and transforming noncapitalist—often described as 'precapitalist'—modes of production in terms productive to itself (e.g., Mintz 1985; Roseberry 1983), it has yet to question the hegemonic employment by the state of political-economic notions of work, leisure, subject, and object. What are the limits of critical notions of labor and action in different cultural contexts? What is labor and where is the laboring subject to be found? A justifiable criticism, it seems to me, of many political-economic studies is that local concepts of labor-action, when viewed through foundational Western notions of economic action, are seen to be about something else or serving some other social function; for example, they are believed to be moral arguments or religious motifs. But in the case of Belyuen Aborigines their discussion about labor's and language's effect on the countryside are about labor and language; they are challenging whether the productivity of their action can be assessed and represented by models that do not account for the reaction of sentient objects to their presence and the effects of those sentient objects on their bodies and social constitution through time.

While Western intellectual theory shifted from a political-economic to a neoclassical, or economic, paradigm of value, Western colonial law and policy were critically informed by progressive notions of the four-stages theory and by a corresponding notion of the evolution of property. An evolving framework that began with the early Australian colony (discovered in 1770, first colonized in 1788, Port Darwin established in 1869) colonial law itself evolved within the reign of political-economic theory (it is doubtful that the later, neoclassical paradigm would have better suited indigenous peoples during the colonial period). For instance, the settlement of Australia as *terra nullius* was justified by reference to the productive practices of its indigenous peoples. The Aboriginal economy was claimed to be too primitive to have evolved a notion of property *in land* (Williams 1986); far from it, settlers hardly granted indigenous people full subjectivity—although they probably were aware that Aborigines thought of themselves as subjects owning the land (Williams 1986).

There is a deeply interwoven and reinforcing dialogue not only across colonial, national, and international law and the principles of political economy, but also between these and classic Australian social anthropology insofar as the latter was born out of an interest in the comparative nature of law in supposedly nonmodern societies (Gluckman 1955, 1962). Contrary to popular views that noncapitalist societies had no political or social regulation, social anthropologists sought to demonstrate how social (especially kinship and marriage) and religious (often ritual and witchcraft) institutions regulated individual and group rights and duties to land and things. In Australia, under the tutelage of Radcliffe-Brown (1952), W. E. H. Stanner (1965a, 1965b, 1966, 1979) in a series of highly influential essays, argued that while Aborigines' economic practices were regulated by the changing seasons (i.e., were environmentally determined), their land-tenure and social practices were organized by complex philosophical notions known as "the Dreaming" (see chap. 3 below). Corporateness, and the corresponding regulation of individual and group rights and duties to places, was found in religious sanctioned "estate groups" (a patrilineal totemic clan) who were the landowners (see Radcliffe-Brown 1930–31; Hiatt 1962; Stanner 1965a). Taking a progressive if not radical position for his time, Stanner argued against the notion that a society's mode of production determined its cultural institutions.

While today this distinction between the regulatory effects of cultural beliefs and those of economic practices presents a problem for indigenous property law (see chap. 1), Stanner was writing to an audience that saw no regulation or organization *at all* in the "aimless wanderings" of indigenous peoples. At the height of the colonial period, Australian Aborigines caught the imagination of Western readers on the trail of the exotic, readers looking for new puzzles to find and to unravel in the world of culture and society. Early ethnologists and popular writers described Aborigines as, by day, Pleistocene foragers scattered across the landscape grubbing out a living and, by night, ecstatic savages dancing in fire-lit revelry. Aborigines were popularly portrayed as having *no* constraints or inhibitions other than what the environment provided them.

When Stanner presented Aborigines as serious students of human organization who had devised a social structure of "surprising complexity" and were using it to "sing" the world into being (1979b, 33), his findings contradicted legal and popular opinion that Aborigines lacked any sense of proprietary interests in their land. It is, perhaps, deeply ironic that in order to present the proprietary interest of Aborigines, Stanner felt he had to demonstrate that economy and culture could be unhinged and that each differently influenced the shape and function of the social group. He had to argue forcefully that Australian Aboriginal groups provided a unique and startling set of socioeconomic and cultural contradictions to a still-influential four-stages theory. Even if Aboriginal groups had the "rudest" of economic practices, they nevertheless had complex social systems that supported a rich conceptual system he popularized as "the Dreaming" or "the Dreamtime." But correspondingly, although Aborigines' "metaphysical outlook" allowed them to see a oneness and "a unity" between "two persons, such as two siblings or a grandparent and grandchild; or a living man and something inanimate, as when he tells you that, say, the wollybutt tree, a totem, is his wife's brother" (1979b, 25), their economic outlook was "direct" and unmediated, influenced as it was by the relentless, rhythmic, change of the seasons.[6] Aborigines were led from hill to dale by "the seasonal food supply"; the creative side of Aboriginal life was "concentrated on the social rather than on the metaphysical or the materials side" (Stanner 1979b, 33). Ronald Berndt, whose views, as we see later, are thought to have influenced the writing of the Aboriginal Land Rights (NT) Act, 1976, also claimed that Aboriginal social life had two distinct parts: a direct empirical side consisting of social rules for regulating human activity and land use and a symbolic, nonempirical side that consisted of an "additional *quality* which the bare social relationship itself did not define" (1970a, 1). This latter side was the spiritual, totemic relationship—expressed in myth and rite and formally outside of historical intrusion—that existed between human groups and a stretch of land that was their "country." Pragmatic everyday interactions between a stretch of country and a group of people were treated as a side issue to the exegesis of the "deep meaning" and "spirit" of myth. Posited as direct and unmediated, the practicalities of economy paled in comparison to the elaborations of myth and totemism. In early portraits, events that occurred during the colonial and postcolonial upheaval were seen to sever this totemic anchor of Aboriginal social life.[7] Later legislation would further exacerbate the division between economic and cultural practice to the point that the effect of labor-action and economic practice on the spiritual/totemic relationship between human groups and the countryside was denied. Early political-economic theory postulated that laboring subjects created proprietary interests in things and that the mode of production determined the level of those proprietary interests. And colonial law settled Australia as *terra nullius* based on this assumption. But today current land-rights legislation has swung full circle, denying virtually all correlation between laboring subjects and proprietary interests.

Later portraits in popular art, film, and writing have developed the earlier Dr. Jeckyll/Mr. Hyde portrait. In *The Last Wave,* for example, viewers discover that the innocuous fringe dwellers they see roaming the byways of Sydney carry on complex and powerful Stone Age rites in the nightlike darkness of the sewers. As opposed to other hunter-gatherers, Australian Aborigines' culture and economy were portrayed as unevenly articulated and therefore easily disarticulated. Their "foraging" way of life may not be powerful enough to withstand civilization's onslaught, but Aborigines' social and ceremonial complexes survive intact alongside, or figuratively and formatively below, the apex of Western civilization: the modern Australian metropolitan city. The architecture of this "Aussie" city, according to Andrew Lattas, is itself based on Western views of Aborigines "as supremely spiritual beings (beings who inhabit the mythic space of dreamtime) and yet also as beings who have most successfully adapted to the material requirements of their extreme environment" (1990, 53). Belyuen and other Aborigines live the legal implications of these anthropological theories and popular representations of Australian hunter-gatherer cultural and economic practices.

There are, therefore, two ways in which Aboriginal action is assessed in contemporary Australia and, more generally, how hunter-gatherer action is assessed worldwide. On the one hand, when the Aboriginal economy is the focus of study, it is assessed according to notions of productivity based on Western notions of what happens when intentional subjects labor in an insentient environment. Work is measured—the values it produces and the leisure it affords. On the other hand, when Aboriginal proprietary interests are the object of study, the productive relationship between laboring humans and the laboring environment is pushed to the background if not excluded outright. The rich symbolic/interpretive studies of Aboriginal conceptions of land are artificially and quite unproductively isolated from studies of Aboriginal land use. This ethnography attempts to demonstrate the falsity of both moves and their effect on what options Belyuen Aborigines have to challenge the nation-state's control of regional lands. It does so by drawing together cultural notions of labor-action and the political economy of its interpretation.

The importance of studying non-Western notions of productivity and their discursive uses lies in the need for a countervoice to the hegemonic frame of Western economic policy. When those of us interested in the political consequences of human labor and action in complex societies (which this study assumes includes the Fourth World) treat a counterdiscourse of labor-action as something other than what values are produced when humans act in the world, we contribute to the state's domination, delegitimization or, worse, contextualization of indigenous knowledges as primitive (or irrelevantly subaltern) in one way or another. When discussing Aboriginal notions of land and labor I am often asked if I believe in them. Or how can I believe that non–human beings act as agents and are sentient, much less base economic policy (though it seems we might be able to base political policy) on such a belief? Certainly this question was one of the motivations for the emerging political-economic and New Science paradigms of the eighteen century. How could a manufacturing base be built if objects might at any time act according to their own intentions? At best we can endlessly debate the intentional nature or mental capacity of primates, dolphins, and elephants. But a rock? Obviously these questions are misleading. Of course we find it hard to believe rocks listen when the very conditions of the Western cultural and material world are discursively underpinned by the refusal of this fact. But if, at best, we can only hold our disbelief in abeyance then we should do so in order to demonstrate (1) that the cultural underpinnings of political-economic approaches to the study of human societies mandate a certain way of assessing human action in relation to land and things, (2) that these ways of assessing action are now entangled in dominant government institutions such as law and economic policy and are used to discredit indigenous perspectives, and (3) that other cultural notions of labor-action and their relationship to knowledge and power are about something else only insofar as Western notions are as well; each makes an argument about what values are produced when humans encounter nonhuman things.

In order to examine these three points, this ethnography draws from political-economic anthropology (in its focus on work and its effect on people and things including the work of the countryside in the constitution of the human group and the work of politically dominant groups to constrain the possible expression of Aboriginal labor-action) and on the historical and discursive uses of competing notions of labor-action. But this study also investigates how conflicts between Belyuen Aborigines and

Euro-Australians over the productivity of the human-country encounter are about divergent epistemologies and the social and legal apparatuses that support them. Rather than investigating two alternative ideologies of work that can be resolved by reference to a material reality, this study shows that material reality emerges from ways of knowing it and ways of understanding labor in it. Therefore, while drawing from Foucault's (1973, 1990) insight that particular forms of knowledge are an aspect of Western power and domination, this study also attempts to demonstrate the power of Fourth World knowledge to resist domination. This is not to say that indigenous knowledge systems are immune form hegemonic domination. As I discuss throughout this text, Belyuen forms of resistance are often reconstituted by the state as a symbol of its own productivity and social cohesion. Foucault's pessimism about the resistant potential of alternate knowledges is, therefore, well taken, but the deployment of counterdiscourses by groups neither fully within nor fully without the nation-state needs to be acknowledged.

Along with examining the multiple motivations and values of Belyuen labor, this book examines Belyuen Aborigines' history of "work" and the descent, articulation, and transformation of power over time. My discussion of the histories and cultures of "work" in an Aboriginal community—the struggles that occur over a definition and understanding of human labor-action—crosses broader issues in history and anthropology. As others have noted, current "anthropolog*ies* and histor*ies*" originate in older theoretical wars between cultural ecology and symbolic anthropology (Ortner 1989), two fields that have critically, and divergently, informed studies of Australian economic and totemic life. In one model of cultural and political-economic anthropology "events" are seen to alter "experience," the "concatenation of structure and event" is seen to be "a constant process, one in which culture is constantly being shaped, produced, reproduced, and transformed by activity (Roseberry 1989, 43), and "cultural differentiation, . . . social and political inequalities . . . and historical formation of anthropological subjects" are seen to occur within processes of uneven development (Roseberry 1989, 13–14). In structural history (also called "emic history" [Ortner 1989] and "analytic practice" [Comaroff and Comaroff 1991]), drawing from Lévi-Strauss and early Marxian traditions, theorists seek "to show the way in which the impact of external forces is internally" and culturally mediated, reinterpreted, and transformed (Ortner 1989, 17; see also Sahlins 1985). On the one hand, culture is constantly manipulated and reformed by historical forces and, on the other hand, culture constantly mediates these forces for the social group.

In this book I argue that economic and cultural action *and the identities they produce* are the processes of association from which Aboriginal identity and history emerge, but they are also objects of assessment within, evolving, uneven power relations. In this book Aboriginal action is a symbolic and historical statement; it argues, perhaps like the Polynesian lineage (Sahlins 1985) that objects, places, and peoples involved in action can be linked in a certain form (a hunting group, an exchange, a narrative plot, a dialogue). Likewise, in contemporary contexts, rent, wage labor, and commodity rights are arguments lodged within economic practices about how people should associate together and view things. But the state plays a critical role in framing some questions (What is the relevant social formation for land tenure? Are people's economic practices productive? What is the link between economic practice and cultural identity?) as the arguments that people are trying to answer (Donham 1990, 211; Jasanoff 1990) and in vesting certain social and ethnic groups with the authority to answer these questions (Comaroff and Comaroff 1991). Belyuen Aborigines play with the terms of economic, cultural, and historical arguments, but they are also cognizant of the multiple ways in which *resistance* is rearticulated into dominant relations of power. History, then, neither dictates cultural forms or is subsumed by them, but rather emerges in processes of social action and association, including various social ways of organizing memory, and their institutional supports.

A history of indigenous labor-action and its relation to power must, therefore, entail local discourses of action and the apparatuses of power that accompany their assessments. Anthropologies and histories and cultural and political-economic approaches must account for the complex entanglement of cultural expression in local, national, and international political economies and for the competing discourses on labor-action within and between Aboriginal and Western communities. Local culture becomes an object of the national and international economy the moment state government sees it as a commodity. The political economic becomes part and parcel of the power of symbolic knowledge when we recognize that, rather than objective and neutral truths, legal and economic principles are originary Western notions for understanding human relations to themselves and to the nonhuman world.

WOMEN, LABOR, AND THE LAW

The insights this book offers in the areas of law, anthropology, and political economy are directly related to the gendered nature of my fieldwork. In main this study presents senior Belyuen women's discussions of their and their families' labor-action and place in the countryside. While Aboriginal women's perspectives on land issues and labor have been neglected in social anthropology's focus on corporate group structure and, more recently, the law's focus on the same (Jacobs 1989; Hercus 1989; Bell 1984–85), this work does not present the corporate nature of women's practice such as has been shown by Diane Bell (1983, 1987) and Catherine Berndt (1954, 1965). What then makes gender a critical component of this analysis?

It seems to me that three issues predominate. First, as I noted above, a critical mass of my knowledge about and understanding of labor-action comes from my relationship with senior Belyuen women. And Belyuen women's knowledge of the countryside, as men's and women's knowledges in most Aboriginal communities (Bell 1987; Hamilton 1980–81), is "gendered" in the sense that it is framed by practices and cultural texts that, though not wholly, are largely produced and circulated within the group. That is, the cultural texts and practices women engage and manage structure their knowledges in certain ways. Therefore, what I know is due to our mutually acknowledged similarity of gender and the orientation to social institutions and cultural texts that it provides. But, in an equal way, my position as a relatively young white American woman (i.e., my age—I was twenty-two when I first arrived at Belyuen in 1984—race, and national identity) structurally denies any collapse of what I know and what they know as women—a point we have made at several important junctions during my stays in the community (see also Narayan 1989). And, perhaps in an overly cautious caveat, I and they learn more from men than we normally do or can admit; in other words, the kind of radical epistemological disjunction that some authors describe between Aboriginal men and women flies in the face of cultural, conversational, and economic overlap, interinvolvement, and exchange. To elaborate, while most of my knowledge about "Belyuen" ways of thinking about labor and land comes from a group of senior Belyuen women whose ideas and understandings are complex and nuanced, and while they spend much of their time in female groups, I have, since coming to Belyuen, lived with a dozen different families on the community and outstations in the region, families that include very talkative and insightful men. And women talk with and listen to these men; their knowledge comes from discussions they have had with husbands, fathers, and uncles, and from, in some limited cases, experiences they have had in male ceremony.

A second way that this ethnography is gendered relates to the emphasis Belyuen women place on the processual nature of human-human and human-land relationships. But to what extent this is an artifact of gender remains unclear. Is Belyuen women's emphasis on the ongoing emergent nature of human relationships to land unique to their conversational and socioeconomic practices and opposed to the way that Belyuen men think and talk about the same? Did the canonical works on Australian Aboriginal social relations and land tenure systems prioritize patrilineal and matrilineal corporate groups because of a reliance on Aboriginal men's accounts of the way things worked or because of the orientation of social theory at the time?

The position I give women's voices is not supplemental in the sense of supplementing Belyuen men's emphasis on the corporateness of the descent group in relation to land. Rather, I intend Belyuen women's views to undermine existing accounts that exclude day-to-day economic processes when discussing human country relations in Aboriginal Australia, especially those studies that focus on male corporateness in ritual and descent (but see Myers [1986] and Sutton and Rigsby [1982] on the processual nature of male relations to land). In short, I propose women's views to be at least as central to how we understand Aboriginal people's organization in and understanding of the countryside. I do so even while holding open the possibility of, and commenting upon what I think are relevant, differences in male and female viewpoints on labor, language, and land. There does seem to be a tension between Aboriginal men's emphasis of patrilineal descent and women's emphasis on processual relations (such as conception), but this may have more to do with the entangled nature of Western and Aboriginal discourses on law and property than some Urgender difference (Hamilton 1982). Moreover, while there are tensions between senior male and female accounts of how and why the mythic countryside reacts to different social groups, on the one hand, neither Belyuen men nor Belyuen women can rely on a discourse of totemic descent, as it is normally understood, to ground their relationship to Cox Peninsula lands (both men and women are living on land not normally considered their matrilineal or patrilineal estate), and, on the other hand, there are important common themes in both groups' discussions. Thus it is the discursive potential and problems both men and women face in grounding their rights to land in their labor-action that this ethnography addresses. Rather than finding some set of final differences between men and women—biological, historical, cultural—this ethnography discusses how economic practice, history, and culture are gendered in some instances and generalized in others for social and political reasons.

Finally, this ethnography is about gender insofar as a woman's voice is a marked perspective, both because a social group's voice represents a certain window on community life and because a woman's voice is generally marginalized. In theory, men's views are as partial as women's. But in practice, men's voices are not received as partial in the same way women's are in some quarters of the legal and anthropological forum. If, at times, this ethnography seems to be framing women's voices as *the Belyuen voice* it does so (1) to examine playfully the continuing impossibility of such a representation, (2) in spite of the fact that I note the complex overlap, conflicts, and contradictions of various identities summarized as female, and (3) because in some instances women's views *are* the Belyuen voice as it is presented to the non-Belyuen world.

NOTES ON TRANSCRIPTS

The book makes significant use of transcribed conversations among Belyuen women and between these women and me. It does so for several theoretical and methodological reasons. First, the transcripts are sometimes used to make a specific point about Belyuen "ways of speaking" and ways of negotiating power and constructing identities.[9] Although, in this book, most of my discussion of Belyuen ways of speaking centers around a classroom conversation about Belyuen "family history," my arguments are based on a much larger data base of recorded and transcribed conversations.[10] Part of Belyuen speaking practices is the avoidance of names of living and deceased persons, especially in relationship to quoted speech. I, therefore, used pseudonyms in my transcripts. Second, the transcripts are intended to work against the reifying tendencies of this monograph as are the other textual pieces I splice into the narrative, including exploration texts, land claim transcripts, and excerpts from popular fiction. While such practices do not promise to be the cornerstone of countervoicedness (Terdiman 1985) or to avoid the problem of authoring other people's lives (Marcus and Fischer 1986; Gelder 1991), they do, in my opinion, most clearly point to the authoring (Clifford [1988, "Identity in Mashpee," 277–348] succeeds, I think in doing this). My purpose is not to deny my authorship, but to show the discursive work of identity and knowledge construction and its play in everyday life. Or, as Edward Said has written, to show the discursive and "historically constituted" relationship "between cultures and their adherents" (1983).

NOTES ON HUNTING DATA

The data I present in chapters 4 and 5 were collected during fourteen months in 1989 and 1990, part of which time I spent at outstations on the north and southwest coasts of the Cox Peninsula. In addition to this work, during my first stay at Belyuen in 1984–85, I went on eighty-five recorded foraging trips and spent the dry season at an outstation on the west coast of the Cox Peninsula.[11] During a short visit to the community from 12 June to 13 July 1987, I went on another seventeen recorded foraging trips and again spent the weekends at outstations on the west coast. In 1989–90, I recorded 532 foraging trips made by Laragiya, Wagaitj, and Beringgen to sites on the Cox Peninsula and in the Port Patterson area. I was present on 282 of these trips, which provide most of the data I present below. Measurements of gross food weights were made by hand scales or, in the case of the larger sea and land mammals, by measurement and comparison to previously recorded weights of the species. In figuring food composition tables, I have followed Betty Meehan's (1982) and Jon Altman's (1987b; see also Thomas and Corden 1977) standard conversion tables for figuring the values of flesh and kilocaloric gains. In addition, the Human Nutrition Unit, Department of Biochemistry, University of Sydney, analyzed several species of shellfish, vegetable, and crustacea that Vic Cherikoff gathered with Belyuen women and me in 1985 and 1987. Finally, I often use the term "hunting" in the local sense of seeking out foods and materials.

Because of the Belyuen community's size and the high number of foraging trips conducted on the Cox Peninsula and Bynoe Harbour Islands per year, I limited the number of families for whom I recorded a comprehensive foraging diary and amassed whatever other data I could from persons outside of them. Two families are completely unaccounted for; another two families provided data in some areas (e.g., outstation composition) but not in the day-to-day collection of foods. I also sought to record a representative sample of data from each language group at Belyuen (Emiyenggal, Menthayenggal, Marritjaben, Marriamu, Wadjigiyn, and Kiyuk) in order to analyze differences between language-group identity and land use. The data are based around a core group of thirty adults. An average food-collecting group consisted of six women from the forty-five to seventy year old range, three younger women eighteen to forty-five years old, and seven children (newborn to 18 years old, with most of the children between three and ten). Often with these women were two or three men, either a husband of one of the younger women or the young adult sons of an older woman. As in other Australian Aboriginal communities, women and men tend to socialize and hunt in separate groups. Sea hunting and shooting groups are typically composed of five men between twenty and forty-five years old. Data concerning offshore hunting are based on my observations of the catches of three harpooners, on discussions with them, and on ten trips on which I accompanied them.

In an economic analysis, there are obvious advantages and disadvantages gained by focusing on a group of more than forty persons. On the one hand, there is little quantitative research on the food-collection practices of small-scale settlements in Australia.[12] Most research on communities of this size examines the economies of pastoralists or agriculturalists, groups in which the food and capital transactions are larger or more centralized (see, e.g., Young 1988). Few researchers have examined how residents of small communities allocate their time between the settlement and the bush or the relative contributions of market and bush foods to the local diet (but see Anderson [1982] for one such study). On the other hand, dealing with a large population, one cannot hope to measure the consumption of each and every person and thereby establish precise comparisons between levels of market and bush food consumption for individuals or households. Both the wide range of foods that are collected in often minute quantities and the social constitution of the Belyuen household permit far too many people to travel through far too many households for one to have any assurance that foods bought or gathered by one household are eaten by it or a stable number of relatives. Further, one cannot be present on every trip that originates from the community or on every trip a particular subset of persons makes. Social and foraging groups fracture and realign themselves throughout the year so that the group hunting (or going to the store) together today will not be the group desiring to hunt together tomorrow.

In addition to social realignment, the community's position in the day-to-day politics of the region realigns group composition because of political and economic imperatives: government officials arrive to discuss self-government proposals with some and ethnobotanical researchers arrive to work with others. Welfare workers travel from Darwin to discuss health issues with young and old people and land claim lawyers and anthropologists fly in from the south and siphon off the knowledgable and the talkative. I have played all of these intruder roles as well as that of the nominal white female insider. I have motivated, impeded, and tinkered with the timing of food-gathering trips as have all of the people I mention above. Moreover, my own productive skills are included in the data I present, on par with other adult Belyuen women.

The point is that, with or without my presence as an anthropologist, there are diverse "intrusions" into the "foraging moment." All are instances of the interpenetration of Aboriginal communities within the regional and global polity, of the "mixed" nature of identity (Belyuen, Aborigine, Australian) and of the fissures and fractures of *communitas* (Turner 1969). The ethnographic literature that focuses on precolonial Aboriginal regional trade networks, ceremonial exchange, and inter- and intragroup land politics suggests that such nonforaging activities were always occurring and always influencing where and why people were hunting for specific foods.[13]

part one

SETTING UP
LABOR-ACTION:
LEGITIMATE LAW,
IDENTITY,
HISTORY

1 Legal Entanglements
Aboriginal Action and Identity

> The task for this subtrend in the current experimental moment is thus to revise conventions of ethnographic description away from a measuring of change against some self-contained, homogeneous, and largely ahistorical framing of the cultural unit toward a view of cultural situations as *always* in flux, in a perpetual historically sensitive state of resistance and accommodation to broader processes of influence that are as much inside as outside the local control.
>
> —Marcus and Fischer on Raymond Williams (1986, 78)

ACTION AND IDENTITY

This chapter introduces some issues in the study of indigenous hunter-gatherer productivity and identity and their political and legal implications. These issues serve as a general introduction to how Belyuen Aborigines produce themselves and their identities within the context and discourses of the contemporary Australian nation-state, topics I explore in detail throughout the rest of the book.

Belyuen is located on sixteen square miles of Aboriginal freehold land roughly in the middle of the Cox Peninsula. It is composed of families who identify themselves both as members of specific Daly River language groups (in main, Wadjigiyn, Kiyuk, Emi, Mentha, Marriamu, and Marritjabcn) and as the "Belyuen mob"; which identity a person chooses in a given exchange is based upon the audience, the context of the query, and the motivation of the identification (see also Sutton and Rigsby 1982; Barker 1976). With a few exceptions, these groups have lived on the Cox Peninsula at least for the last 110-odd years, but, when asked in formal hearings, will not claim the identity of "traditional Aboriginal owners" of the countryside in which they live. They reserve this label for the Laragiya. Most other coastal Daly River Wagaitj and Beringgen families live at Wadeye, the Daly River Mission, and outstations within the Daly River region. Most Laragiya in the Northern Territory live in the greater Darwin region. There is no other significant Aboriginal presence on the peninsula.

THE FOURTH WORLD IN HUNTER-GATHERER STUDIES

Indigenous groups (the Fourth World) share many common problems when trying to define their property and human rights.[1] The special problems of hunter-gatherers within the Fourth World have been the subject of much commentary in recent years. Several of their difficulties merit attention here. Perhaps most important, a historically negative Western assessment of hunter-gatherer economies is rooted in the very liberal state that evaluates indigenous claims to traditional lands. It is only now fully emerging how deeply the liberal capitalist state has itself been defined in opposition to Western constructions of "hunter-gatherers"—the archtypical primitive—and therefore how difficult it is legally and economically for that state to make a fair assessment of Fourth World hunters', fishers', and collectors' claims to traditional lands or their notions about land-use and labor-action. Barbara Hocking, a jurist, writes that while European colonizers were able to recognize the native title of "communities with obvious inhabited villages of a permanent nature," they were not willing or able to concede the proprietary rights of hunting and gathering peoples whose economies were thought to be deeply antithetical to their own (1988, 12–13; see also Wilmsen 1989b, 4–5). Even when states grant land to indigenous groups it often, in effect, establishes a further dependency relationship between the group and the nation-state (see Peterson 1985). Moreover, the use of 'indigenous identity" as a political discourse for group rights to land, like ethnicity, structures as much as it allows identity to serve a political agenda (Chicago Cultural Studies Group 1992; Hendrickson 1991).

Exciting theoretical and applied issues are now being explored in the area of indigenous human and proprietary rights (Wilmsen 1989b; Berger 1986; Dyck 1985). Outside the academy, the Otherness of indigenous economic and cultural practice has caught the imagination of the world press and such global personalities as Jane Fonda and Sting—biodiversity and cultural diversity are portrayed as the complimentary and necessary features of a healthy, evolving planet. But discussions of the Fourth World have as yet failed to describe adequately the dense network of economic, political, and cultural motivations that account for indigenous practice (in particular indigenous struggles to produce economic and cultural well-being in the postcolonial nation) or to theorize the relationship between the productivity of indigenous practice and the production of cultural identity. In part this is due to a broader theoretical legacy in the social sciences in which cultural and political-economic approaches have been opposed, often hostilely.[2] As a result the deep enmeshment of both aspects of lived experience has been lost and an "applied hermeneutic" of Aboriginal labor-action has yet to be developed (Myers 1988b, 276).

A second impediment to the ongoing discussion of Aboriginal practice and identity is current models of hunter-gatherer productivity. In *Capital*, Marx ([1887] 1987) describes "the bodies of commodities" as combinations of two elements: matter and labor. Useful labor congeals (or is "embodied") in the object and, in the process, qualitatively transforms common articles into socially valuable things. Human labor is differentiated from other nonhuman and chemical actions, not simply in its organization and transformative ability, but also in its intentionality: human subjects fix in their minds images of the transformation about to occur before they fix their labor onto objects. To appropriate the products of peoples' labor is then effectively to snatch products of their mind extended into the world and parts of their bodies lodged within the object.

Marx's discussion of intentionality and the transformative power of productive labor draws on the very view it critiques: the classical political-economic models of the role played by productive labor in the creation and transformation of self-knowledge, property, and history. In social theory after Locke, productive labor is that which fixes itself to objects, transforms them, and in the process provides laborers with proprietary rights and self and social understanding. The nonproductive, appropriative labor of hunter-gatherers (crippled by its mode of subsistence production) has thus been portrayed as unable to coagulate fully in things or landscapes and as too closely aligned with nature's will. Dominated by nature—thrust along by the changing of the seasons or tides—hunter-gatherers neither fix in their minds alternate images of the ecological landscape, nor permanently fix upon landscapes their labor. In Locke's well-known dictum, "original man" only owns the "Acorns he pickt up under an Oak or the Apples he gathered from the Trees in the Wood" because at least within these objects "something was annexed."[3]

In an effort to critique how hunter-gatherers have been situated in Western theories of labor, Tim Ingold (1987) has recently and forcefully questioned the association of productive labor with transformative processes, arguing instead that "intentionality" (Marx's architect as opposed to his bee) is the key characteristic of productive labor. According to Ingold, the opposition of transformative and appropriative labor-action should be seen as a subset of human productive-intentional labor more generally, for hunter-gatherers like the rest of productive humankind, he claims, act *on* the world rather than *interact* with it. In his model, productive-intentional action would characterize "immediate return" and "delayed return" societies.[4]

The lot Australian Aborigines project for their and the mythic countryside's labor neither simply opposes nor simply supports the several complex strains of Western theories on hunter-gatherer's labor-action and its productive potential. Notions of congelation, transformation, and intentionality are equally important in the vine jungles of Aboriginal north Australia as in the texts of classical political economists and of more recent theorists, but their meanings and values differ in interesting ways—ways I explore in detail in chapter 3. But when Aboriginal economic activity has been described it is through models developed in the West with little regard to how local notions of labor or of the country as "subject" (Munn 1970) might alter our understanding of Aboriginal action. Instead, the material side of Aboriginal life is often described as direct and unmediated and as apprehensible by a model first developed in the eighteenth century that examines productive and nonproductive labor as it arose in the European factory; namely, capital wage labor. For example, Marshall Sahlins's by now well-discussed and critiqued "original affluent society" essay argued that hunting-gathering was a relatively leisurely "Zen way" of life based on comparisons of people's work and leisure times (Sahlins 1968; see also Bird-David's reappraisal 1992 and Povinelli 1993). Subsequently, several ecological schools have researched more extensively the work-leisure ratios of various hunter-gatherer societies.[5] But notions of work and leisure fail to describe a system in which "just sitting" in the countryside produces health and productivity for the human group and the land.

While several works have attempted to "identify or conceptualize the basic . . . units and characteristics of 'hunter-gatherer society'" (Myers 1988b, 267; see also Ingold 1988; Woodburn 1988; Meillassoux 1973), I know of no major study that has focused on hunter-gatherers' perceptions and discursive uses of the productive power of their everyday action. Moreover, recent forays into metaphor theory as a method of articulating hunter-gatherer culture and economy fail to account for other, often primary, tropic relations. Australian Aborigines' cultural economy is neither bank nor basement sale as described, respectively, in Bird-David (1990, 1992) and Lee (1988, 1992); perhaps, more appropriately it is a series of metonymic associations between humans and places. In any case, positing grand metaphorical tropes for diverse associative practices misses "a more natural and logical path of engagement with empirical facts of perception, with nuts-and-bolts experience, with mystic and scientific insight, . . . and with yet other dimensions of experience" (Friedrich 1991, 54).

For Belyuen Aborigines hunting-gathering is an activity and a discourse; it is a form of production in the fullest cultural and economic sense of this term, generating a range of sociocultural meanings and political-economic problems and rewards. Hunting and gathering grounds Belyuen Aborigines' relationship to the Cox Peninsula and, vis-à-vis other ethnic groups in the region, defines their Aboriginality. Aboriginal notions of work, labor, history, and authenticity are assessed and, in many ways, forged by hunter-gatherer discourses and by Western law, but Aborigines' real-life activities and dialogues also critique and challenge the reified categories of "hunter-gatherer theory" and produce an identity not in anyway reducible to them.

Projects that measure Aboriginal action, assess its products, and determine its meanings often erase an earlier struggle over what will count as productive activity and what that activity can produce. For example, one of the motivations of liberal anthropologists is to make visible the productivity of indigenous people and to bring "into sharp focus the artificially created polar nodes—rural and urban—of what is and has always been, in its operation, an integrated system" (Wilmsen 1989a, xi–xii). Development economists look at a related set of issues: For a certain population size based on a certain economic form, what is the appropriate land area necessary for a group's reproduction? But rather than the question of how much space is needed for a certain population, local Belyuen Aborigines might ask how much space is needed for the expression of the mythic countryside. Critical to this expression is its continual interaction with Aboriginal people, an interaction not amenable to measurements currently employed in hunter-gatherer studies. Part of the Belyuen Aborigines' struggle is, therefore, to redefine the meaning of productive action. This struggle, however, is not unidirectional: it is not carried out against an ever-present and all-evil white population. Relations among competing Aboriginal groups—their sometimes differing views of land use—and between them and various non-Aboriginal Australians often hinder any one group's ability to compete against the others.

Alongside peoples' struggle to define action is their struggle to link productive action and cultural identity (see Povinelli 1993b). Belyuen Aborigines articulate their use and management of the Cox Peninsula with their cultural identity and land aspirations. Again the results of this vary and depend in good part on the composition and context of the audience. A good example of the contingencies Belyuen Aborigines face when linking their cultural identity to economic actions is their own and others' representations of their *legal* status—their rights from a non-Aboriginal perspective—as a migrant group. Their migrant status has political implications within the Aboriginal population of the Top End of the Northern Territory and between Anglo and Aboriginal groups.

While Aborigines have long been "a people with politics" (see Sutton and Rigsby 1982; Hiatt 1986; Myers 1986), specific national and regional legislative acts have affected the form of intra-Aboriginal relations as well as relationships between Aboriginal and non-Aboriginal groups.

One such context, interlacing this book's writing and informing the pragmatic goals behind its theoretical approach, is the ongoing Kenbi Land Claim. I discuss certain aspects of this claim below, forecasting arguments addressed more fully in later chapters in order to describe, first, why, from an Aboriginal ideology of mythic welfare, a hunting-gathering discourse is a good way of influencing Aboriginal politics. I then examine the problems Belyuen people face and the potential benefits that exist when they move this local Aboriginal discourse to a national political arena, specifically into interethnic discussions of land ownership.

The following skeletal description of the land claim is important to this book's general aim of exploring Aboriginal action and identity in the contemporary nation-state for several reasons. First, land-rights legislation, whether one supports it or not, is a significant piece of social legislation in the Fourth World's ongoing struggle for the recognition of their rights as indigenous peoples.[6] It has had an important effect not only on the political-economic viability of Aboriginal groups, but also on the cultural construction and reception of their identity (see Merlan 1991; Peterson 1985). Aborigines who participate in a land claim are usually forced to enter the national symbolic (Bhabha 1990) and to articulate various regional and national discourses on Aboriginality with their own local understandings of action and identity (Beckett 1988). Second, the specific wording of the Aboriginal Land Rights (Northern Territory [NT]) Act, 1976, provides a political and cultural mandate from the nation-state for a certain type of Aboriginal social organization, a mandate that deserves some discussion here. The Aboriginal Land Rights (NT) Act, 1976, is not the only piece of legislation affecting Aboriginal social organization and cultural identity.[7] But the act is that which has most significantly defined Belyuen Aboriginal relations with the Western legal systems for the last twelve years.

ECONOMIC ACTION AND THE "TRADITIONAL ABORIGINAL OWNER"

Land commissioners, Aboriginal-run land councils, and traditional Aboriginal land claims stand in a synergistic relationship that owes its existence to the Aboriginal Land Rights (NT) Act, 1976. Aboriginal-run land councils were established to administer Aboriginal land and to act on the behalf of traditional Aboriginal land owners.[8] The land commissioner accepts applications on behalf of Aborigines "claiming to have a traditional land claim to an area of land available for such a claim" and ascertains "whether those Aboriginals or any other Aboriginals are the traditional Aboriginal owners of the land" (Neate 1989, 16).[9] In the act, "traditional Aboriginal owners" are

a local descent group of Aborigines who—
(a) have common spiritual affiliations to a site on the land, being affiliations that place the group under a primary spiritual responsibility for that site and for the land; and
(b) are entitled by Aboriginal tradition to forage as of right over that land.
[Sec. 3(1)]

Ian Keen has described the relationship between the definition of "traditional Aboriginal owners" and "the 'orthodox model' of Aboriginal land tenure" (1984, 25). In particular, Keen draws out the connections between the act's use of the phrases "local descent group," "common spiritual affiliation," "primary spiritual responsibility," and "to forage as of right over the land" and Berndt and Berndt's (1964) discussion of the differences between Aboriginal landholders and land users (see also Radcliffe-Brown 1930; Stanner 1965a). Landholders were posited to be an exogamous patrilineal descent group (or "clan"). In contrast, land users (bands or "hordes") were thought to be a looser confederation of families ("the residential unit was thought to have been almost identical in membership to the patrilineal totemic clan, give or take a few women" [Merlan 1981, 135]) actually living on and using the clan territory. Landholders were a social group defined by their spiritual ties to a stretch of the countryside, while land users were defined by their economic interests in it. As numerous authors have noted, the "orthodox model" fails to account for the "demographic and political dynamics of Aboriginal landholding groups" (Keen 1984, 27; Gumbert 1981; Hiatt 1984), for noncognatic methods of affiliation to sites such as conception (Hamilton 1982; Myers 1986), or for "the practical relationships between land using local groups and the larger social system" (Myers 1986, 20).

The historical evolution of anthropological theory on Aboriginal land tenure is loosely reflected in land commissioners' evolving interpretations of "traditional Aboriginal land owners." Their interpretation of what is a traditional owner—in which the commissioners seek to reflect the dynamic, flexible, and regionally defined nature of Aboriginal land tenure has expanded from an early, narrow meaning of a member of a patrilineal clan to, in some cases, a broader, encompassing meaning of a member of an "owner group," a "manager group" and, potentially, a "language group."[10] The expansion of the phrase's referent does not mean that "anything goes" (Maddock 1983, 217). The specific wording of the act has ruled out claims on the basis of need, restricted what land can be claimed (it must be unalienated and have or be near a sacred site), and, important to my discussion here, made extant knowledge of the land a critical criterion for assessing a person's rights to it.[11]

Not yet fully discussed but equally important to the assessment of a group's claim to land is the Aboriginal Land Rights (NT) Act's subtle contrast between totemic/cultural and economic sides of Aboriginal life. At the surface this is not apparent; after all the act makes specific reference to Aboriginal foraging. But the contrast is found in how cultural beliefs and economic practices are disarticulated as categories. While the existence of spiritual beliefs and responsibilities is generally assumed to imply the complimentary entitlement to forage as of right, the opposite does not hold: the entitlement to forage has had little effect on whether a land commissioner is convinced that a group has a common spiritual affiliation to or the primary spiritual responsibility for a site. For example, Mr. Justice Kearney limits his discussion of the Jawoyn entitlement to forage to a short summary of what bush foods they may collect (Kearney 1988, 20). In an earlier report Mr. Justice Toohey set the stage for such brevity by stating, "It would, I suppose, be surprising if a group with primary spiritual responsibility for land did not have an entitlement by Aboriginal tradition to forage over the land" (1982b, 43). Foraging activity can have an effect on how the land commissioner views a group's strength of attachment to the land,[12] but its absence does not cripple a group's claim to country. In the best cases, the land under claim is a "happy combination for the claimants of places of significance associated with country well suited for hunting and foraging" (Toohey 1982a, 36). But where such happy coincident is not found, Toohey's former comment is generally the norm; foraging is in a necessary but subordinate relation to Aboriginal social and cultural expressions of land attachment.[13] As I discussed in the Introduction, the imbalance to how the two "sides" of Aboriginal life are weighed in land claim hearings has historical roots in popular and anthropological models of Aboriginal social life.

PROBLEMS WITH PRACTICE AND WITH AUDIENCE

In order to understand Belyuen Aborigines' descriptions of their productive encounter with the landscape during everyday hunting-gathering activities, these accounts must be read in light of but not be reduced to the legal entanglements with which people now wrestle. As I show in due course, their hunting-gathering activities have provided them with a way of attending to, reenacting, and ensuring the physical, mythical, and emotional production of the environment, the human body, and the social group in the midst of sometimes horrendous historical upheavals and dislocations. But the meanings that the Belyuen draw from such encounters and the uses they make of them (labor's lot) interact with the Australian government's understandings of the productive potential of hunting and gathering and with the legal significance granted to "foraging" activity.

The problems Belyuen people face when using their economic practices to articulate their rights to and responsibilities for places are twofold. First, a cost-benefits analysis which is used to assess need, reveals that their practices are not highly productive, although they are economically significant (see chap. 4).[14] Second, although quite effective at producing a locally coherent social group and influencing the actions of regional Aboriginal groups, foraging and its associated activities have only been partially effective in influencing the course of a local land claim. First, let me introduce why foraging discourse is a good way of influencing Aboriginal politics at a local level.

Persuading the Local Group

For Belyuen Aborigines, the health of the countryside and of human groups depends upon the mutual, positive action of each on the other. Why this is so will be well-attested by the end of this book, but in summary: places are perceived as sentient-like beings or as filled with those beings. Mythic vistas and ordinary jungle patches absorb and evaluate the physical sounds and smells, the ceremonial names and social identities of the people who walk through them. If the countryside does not recognize the language and sweat of persons, it inflicts them with bad luck, or worse, mental and physical disease. Aborigines also judge the relative merits and absorb the mythical aspects of different places; for instance, they may have a patrilineal or matrilineal totem from a place (*durlg*),[15] a conception Dreaming from a site (*maroi*), or they may share a name with a site (*ngirrwat*), which for Daly River Aborigines establishes a totemic-like relationship between person and place (Elkin 1950; Falkenberg 1962).

While totemic systems and ritual activity have received most of our attention as the ways in which Australian Aborigines articulate rights to land, Belyuen Aborigines use hunting, fishing, collecting, and just plain sitting in the countryside as methods to position their rights vis-à-vis sites. They use hunting and gathering to position their rights, first, by grounding their mythic knowledge in their foraging practices and, second, by challenging others to show the same level of intimate knowledge that they have of the countryside. They ground their knowledge by discursively linking mythic and economic practices and interrelating the key role of language and sweat in both. Let me summarize.

The grounding of mythic knowledge in everyday practice occurs in a variety of settings I examine throughout this book: day-to-day conversations, formal ethnohistorical interviews, and sacred site registrations. In each, when Belyuen Aborigines talk about a site's character ("What kind this one"), it is quite common for them first to describe their knowledge of a site, such as, "That's Kookoburra Dreaming, it's a bird, it's cheeky [temperamental], got to paint up and carry smoking sticks under the arm," and second to close their statement with something like, "I know this because my mom and dad all a time told me when we were walking by here on our way hunting" or "When I was here hunting I saw it do (such and such) and knew myself it was true."

The interpenetration of economic and cultural activity is further elaborated through the power Aborigines grant sweat and speech over the disposition of the countryside (speech and sweat being an element and byproduct of both ritual and economic activity—see also Merlan [1981] for a discussion of language identity and land politics in Aboriginal Australia). Aborigines act on the assumption that entities inhabiting the countryside "smell" and "hear" their physical and verbal activity and that these beings "come out" or "send out" agents in the form of climatic changes, an abundance of foods, spirits of possession, and sicknesses in order to communicate their reactions to a human presence. Moreover, speech and sweat are seen to penetrate people and places: speech goes in the human ear and travels through the air, sweat comes out of the body and sinks into waterholes (the earth's pores or ear channels). Local people's language and sweat are seen to make the country "sweet" and productive and willing to give its produce. Foreign language and sweat block communication and cause the country to withdraw its life and products ("to dry up") and to act violently toward an unfamiliar group.

Given the critical role that language and sweat or speaking and acting in the countryside play in the maintenance of its life and productivity—a role I explore in detail in chapter 3—it is not surprising that foraging is a key way that Belyuen Aborigines articulate their rights to the Cox Peninsula countryside. First, daily activity in the countryside provides a regular and constant supply of both substances. Second, regular landed activity provides Belyuen families with the means of documenting the beneficial quality of their action.

Because of the importance of everyday landed activity to human-land relations, Belyuen people are constantly querying why an event occurred during a hunting trip. Does it have meaning? Why, for instance, did a dove cry out like a small child while we were digging yams? Or why does so-and-so woman always have good luck collecting crabs in the Madpil mangrove? Many events end up being nothing, meaning nothing—the bird cried for its own reasons. But many events have significance later. Because no one can know what will be useful or meaningful "down the track"—and I mean this metaphor to strike in time and in place—local people's strategy is to note all events, comment on their possible significance ("Mmm, auntie might be something"), and then wait to see if some connection develops between one event and another: a bird's cry and a death, for instance (see also Povinelli 1993a). The strategy Belyuen Aborigines have for foraging knowledge mirrors the one they have for foraging foods: gear the trip for one or two foods (crab and fish) but keep your eyes open for anything that may hop, crawl, or fly by (wallaby, goanna, goose).

Of importance here is the constant nature of the Belyuen people's story retrieval from the countryside; they are constantly finding "stories" (*mal*, also "word," "language") during everyday hunting trips. The story might describe the discovery of signs left in the environment by a deceased relative; one such story recounts how a deceased man left five brightly colored pebbles lined up on a log for his widow to find while she was hunting sugarbag (indigenous honey). He put the five stones there to let her know his desire that she and their five children continue camping at a nearby site. A story may be made of more mundane origins, such as the antics of a day's fishing trip. But people muster all such events when evaluating who "has the stories" for a place (see also Hiatt 1982).

Belyuen Aborigines are not gullible innocents who believe that all unusual events point to an ancestral origin. W. E. H. Stanner noted that the Aboriginal belief in the "'magnificence of life' was shown by the intense, one could almost say obsessive, preoccupation with the signs, symbols, means, portents, tokens, and evidences of vitality"; but he also warned that "there were many things in the environment that were just things, themselves only and no more, without import, standing for nothing" (1965b, 217). Sorting out which event is meaningful and, relatedly, which version or interpretation of an event is "true" is critical to Belyuen speakers. For, although Aborigines generally agree that human social identity (sex, age, kin, and language affiliation) can upset or soothe mythic sites and they agree that mythic sites can communicate pleasure and displeasure by emerging or submerging in the form of a natural product or climatic change, *which* reaction a place is communicating, if it is communicating anything at all, is highly political and is negotiated in people's conversations based on their experience of the country.

In disputes over rights of access or, as I show here, over who has preeminent *legal* authority over land, Belyuen Aborigines challenge others to show the same level of intimate and everyday knowledge that they possess. When issues of land use or development arise, Belyuen women and men constantly circle around to questions such as Who goes out and hunts in the countryside? Who maintains outstations? Who has the mythic and everyday stories about the life of the country? What are the effects of people's language and sweat on the productivity of the countryside? All these issues are part of the local method of determining persons' rights and duties for the country. Obviously, spending time in the surrounding country can favorably affect how persons can answer many of these questions and how speakers compare in their knowledge of the names of sites, the practices associated with them, and the reactions of the sites to different groups of people. But we remain with the question of whether this practice is advantageous given the current legal and political environments in the Northern Territory and in Australia more generally.

From a local viewpoint the Belyuen discourse of hunting and gathering is advantageous for two reasons. First, rooting one's authority in one's knowledge and use of the countryside is a very effective strategy for small-scale communities like Belyuen in which no centralized authority or "big man" holds sway. Second, because local Aboriginal groups (Laragiya *and* Wagaitj-Beringgen Aborigines) generally agree that language and sweat can have a powerful effect on the life and productivity of the countryside, the Belyuen's discourse on hunting and gathering has proven a very effective tool for intra-Aboriginal land conflict. In order to demonstrate how Belyuen Aborigines use conversation to frame hunting action's effect on social identity I leave for a moment directly addressing land rights and instead describe some ways the Belyuen organize who speaks and what stories are told in local contexts and then how these principles effect interethnic discussions of land.

Conversational Practice and Social Group Identity

The struggle of the Belyuen Aborigines to produce themselves and their identities in the contemporary nation-state (an unreliable social order that at various times appropriates, contests, and supports their efforts) centers *in the community* on talk. Belyuen persons pay critical attention to talk, that is, in how people speak to one another and what they say or do not say in their day-to-day personal interactions (see also Haviland 1991; Liberman 1985; Sansom 1980). People draw from their own conversations and their observations of other peoples' conversations their understandings of social group identity. While actions as well as people speak to the Belyuen, they do not speak louder than words. Or, both actions and words must be carefully inspected for their inner meanings, as the possible meanings of an event must be held open until new information emerges down the track: why certain birds appeared at a hunt site, why an old man left a meeting, why a senior woman brought up a particular story during a conversation.

Belyuen "ways of speaking" are like other Aboriginal groups whose speech practices have been studied (Sansom 1980; Liberman 1985); they favor indirect conversation (Stubbs 1983; Gumperz 1982),[16] and they avoid "hard" talk (Brenneis 1984, 73–74).[17] They see words as substantive things, able to wound and heal. Their ways of speaking reflect their mythic and economic practices insofar as both depend on careful observation of the extant form and context and the historical and mythic environment of an event to understand its "inside" meaning and purpose. People come to conversations with social histories, but they can radically change those histories by convincing others of new ways of seeing how events can fit into accepted cultural patterns.

Belyuen Aborigines' heightened awareness that the outside form of talk, its pattern and purpose, hides as it reveals an inner pattern, purpose, and meaning is not limited to inter Aboriginal interaction. Belyuen men and women impute the same "trickiness" to Anglo-Australian talk, and they orient their conversational praxis thusly. Belyuen Aborigines use their conversations to frame symbolically economic interdependence as a moral duty (Scott 1985); and they often complain that Anglo *tjeingithut* (shut up ears, deafness) makes their task doubly difficult in interethnic conversation. Although heard by the deaf, Belyuen Aborigines know that what they say has an important effect in how they are assessed by government officials and private researchers. Further, they know that their disputes with the government over the meanings of Aboriginal action and cultural identity do not occur on a level playing field either in a political-economic or conversational sense (see chap. 2 below).[18] No matter how Belyuen women assess and represent their own and their families' practices over the last 150-odd years, they must balance the social and political contexts in which their memories arise and the cultural and social work to which those memories contribute. Moreover, women know that the Aboriginal histories they describe and the actions they represent may contribute to governmental and private attempts to restrict the movements of their minds and bodies. During the Kenbi Land Claim, a senior woman who had participated in its preparation over the years and who had seen other land claim hearings reminded her age-mates,

> *You gana see. You gana look, im look you hard that man [land commissioner]. Im listen hard what you gana say. Then im think: what everybody been say, right back, dead people where they been write im down, words blei im. Im think hard now what kind that story, im straight or im turn turn. Finished then. We win oh, or we lose. Maybe that man can understand people, maybe nothing; might he caan listen. You gana think hard what you gana say.*

> You are going to see [what I mean]. You are going to see, he looks intently at you, that man [the land commissioner]. He listens intently to what you will say. Then he thinks: what did everyone say, even in the past, even what now-deceased people said that was written down, their words. He thinks hard, What kind of story was I told, was it consistent or inconsistent? That's it. [Based on what he thinks] we win or we lose. Maybe that man understands what Aboriginal people say, maybe not; maybe he is deaf to our words [maybe he cannot understand us]. You're going to think seriously about what you're going to say to him.

Who speaks is an essential part of what story is told and, therefore, what part of history and experience are passed on to others. For conversations between Belyuen Aborigines, three principles seem to account for how women interactively gain and relinquish rights to tell a narrative about a mythic site or historical event: *being straight for* a story or event, *being there* during the occurrence of a story or event, and *being part of* the story or of the social group which is the occasion for the storytelling. These are not the only items included in the organization of conversations, but they seem to be some of the most important ones. Each principal indexes the association of the speaker with the event. "Being straight for" a story or event means that the person or a close relation is personally connected in it. Perhaps the person has a Dreaming from the area that the story describes or the person's mother or father was the main protagonist of the story. To be straight for a story is to have the "inside story" and to have the right to place it "outside" or not. "Having been there" gives a person the right to take a turn or to refuse it and to allow others to tell the story or to block its recitation. People who were not physically at an event or not closely related to the persons in the story (i.e. cannot claim to "be part of") must defer to others.

Conversations about how a mythic being acts in relation to historical persons are highly politicized moments that comment upon the relations among persons and between persons and landscapes. As people interactively decide who will and should speak, based on their different experiences and social roles, they are enunciating how people are related to a narrated event and establishing relationships between speakers in the act of narration and to the setting of the narration. Narrations of the past and of persons' relationships to the past become the ground of future discussions and negotiations. We can see some of these social processes occurring during the school history lesson. The right to put a story "outside" became the focus of the conversation.

There are two education centers on the Belyuen community: the Belyuen School and, on a crest behind it, the adult education building (also called "Home Management" and "The Women's Center"; see Povinelli 1991). Belyuen women use the adult education building for meetings, for linguistic work, and for other women's activities. A few days before the recording of the following conversation, the new male headmaster of the school asked Joan Ela, the adult education assistant, if the older women would come down to the school and tell the children about "family history." Family history is a phrase Belyuen women have heard for various activities: doing genealogical work, describing traditional activities, and locating patrilineal and matrilineal estates.

At the beginning of the recorded conversation, Mary Eladi, Emily Nela, Claire Mamaka, Jean Ziya, and Catherine Burga (ranging in age from fifty-five to seventy years old) have just come into the school lot with approximately thirty school children, four young female adults (including myself), and the school teachers. Joan Ela sits to one side of the older women "to help them" and Deborah Zirita, a young Belyuen woman who is an assistant educator at the school, conducts the interview. Joan Ela's role as a helper includes conveying to the women what kind of story the schoolteachers want. Like any social event in the Belyuen community, there are a number of other residents sitting around and listening to the older women, but there are no Aboriginal men present.

After discussing the historical topics the schoolteachers thought appropriate for the school lesson—telling the children about old Aboriginal camps on the coast[19]—older women moved off to one side and among themselves described how a *therrawin* (E; *durlg*, B; Rainbow Serpent Dreaming)[20] drowned a young woman. The conversation began with several of the women stating that they could not tell the story (could not put the story "outside"). Emily Nela, for instance, a renowned storyteller, says that she cannot tell it because she was not "there" (at the place it occurred); she only heard the story from someone else.

YOU CAN RUN (6 February 1989)

Speakers in order of appearance
me: Mary Eladi (father Wadjigiyn, mother Emi) born circa 1927
bp: Beth Povinelli (Italian-American) born 1962
en: Emily Nela (father and mother Emi) born circa 1925
cm: Claire Mamaka (father Marritjaben, mother Marriamu) born circa 1930
je: Joan Ela (father Marritjaben, mother Marriamu) born 1943
cb: Catherine Burga (father Marritjaben, mother Marriamu) born circa 1920
dz: Deborah Zirita (father Emi, mother Marriamu) born circa 1950

me: *dæt wan naw dæt lIt>l gerl stari dei ben teling yu*
that is the one now, that "little girl story" they were telling you

bp: *dæt da wan*
that's the one

me: *yeh*
yeh
[noise]

en: *now ai kent tel ai kent tel*
no I can't tell it I can't tell it

[noise]

bik>z ai never ben der samb>di tel mi stari
because I was not there somebody told me the story

cm: [ziyesta] sh>d bi her end tel shi nowz
Ziyesta [personal name] should be here and tell she knows
[noise]

je: nat eni mama now yuz howldImbet g>tz Im gana helpImbet <u>Pugali</u>
(Marr) no momma, no use holding back, your <u>cousin</u> [en] will help tell the story

en: <u>mal:thena menggin</u> (E)
<u>tell him the story, cousin.</u>

Mary Eladi notes that the "little girl story" is the story that I had asked the women about after the formal part of the history lesson had ended. My half-remembered version (from my first visit in 1984) was that a young woman was eaten by a crocodile as she swam across a narrow channel at the bottom of the Port Patterson Islands. Throughout the first part of the conversation no one makes an attempt to tell it, and I, wary of the social conundrum I had brought up, say "leave it" (forget it). Mary closes the exchange with a "hard" response ("I don't like telling this kind of story all the time").

bp: <u>tjemela tjemela</u> (E) tel thæt stari wer thæt w>mæn Im ben swIm akras en thæt
<u>mo's fa's sister</u> tell that story where that woman swam across that

krakadail Im ben itIm yu sæbi
crocodile ate her, you know

cb: wat-Im dæt krakadail
what's this, that crocodile

cm: hahaha
hahaha

bp: langa langa wat-Im meibi aim rang
at at what-this maybe I'm wrong

me: wer le
where's this

je: wen dei ben swIm akras
when they swam across

bp: yeh
yeh

me: ah yeh dæt tjen>l ailend
ah yeh that Channel Island

en: dæt <u>wulmarr</u> wei?
that <u>Wulmarra</u> [place name] way?

me: *this wei ar thæt?*
     this way or that?
en: *now mar dIs wei*
     no more this way
je: *this wei einlt*
     this way isn't it
cb: [faint]
je: [faint]
me: *nymbeka (B)*
     Nym [personal name]
cm: *n>thing naw Im caan rimember*
     nothing now, she can't remember
bp: *owkei livIm then*
     okay leave it then
cb: *ai farget naw dærr>n lang taim ai caan rimember*
     I forget that now that story, long time, I can't remember
bp: *livIm*
     leave it
     [noise]
me: *ai now mar laigIm tel-Imbet thIs kainda stari ala taim*
     I don't like to keep telling this kind of story all the time.

A few minutes later, describing the reef that connects the Port Patterson Islands, Mary Eladi brings up this story again.

dz: *wulmarr Im ather said Indiyen*
     Wulmarra is on the other side of Indian [Island]
je: *haw bIg naw kanayi bandjik (E)*
     how far does the reef extend?
en: *kagow kanayi wunthu therrawin (E)*
     It goes right to the Rainbow Serpent.
me: *dæt wan naw dæt lIt>l gerl stari thei ben teling yu*
     that is the one now, that "little girl story" they were telling you
bp: *thæt tha wan*
     that's the one
me: *yeh*
     yeh.

Claire Mamaka then comments on Grace Ziyesta's absence—she should be with this group of women because she was there and knows the story.

Joan Ela next asks for her father's sister, Catherine Burga, to tell the story, assuring her that Emily Nela will help. Emily, in turn, asks Catherine to "tell the story, cousin" and is refused. Finally we begin to hear the story as Emily tells Deborah Zirita, a young Emi woman, how, in the 1940s, two women ran away from the Banagula Daly River estate; Emily Nela starts by telling that part that she witnessed.[21]

en: *aa ai ben dir wen Im ben r>nawei gat det mai anti naw mait bi*
        [noise]
        aa I was there when she ran away with my aunt, now, might be

cm: *yeehh*
                                         yehh

en: *Im ben r>n awei gat dæt wulgamen hu mama K>nel ala Mægi*
        she ran away with that old lady, who? mother-Kunnel [personal name], all the Maggies

me: *mægi Im neim*
                           Maggie was her name

bp: *dæt da wan?*
        that's the one?

en: *Im k>zln bla yu*
        she's your cousin [to Mary or Joan]

me: *yei*
            yeh

dz: *narthern lend kawsIl gata mep æsk mab mep*
        [to bp] Northern Land Council has a map ask that mob for a map

The women then figure the kinship and affinity existing between the persons in the story and the people telling it.

cb: <u>*menggin ngaingow*</u> *(E)*
        <u>she was my cousin</u>
        samb>di ben r>n >p dem tupela
        somebody ran up those two women

en: *mama dædi* <u>*kumanye-werra*</u> *(E) ble yer father*
        momma <u>they were standing there might be</u> with your father

dz: *yeh dæd*
                                         yeh dad

en: *bli nInmi father Im ben r>n awei fr>m Im father Im ben j>s gItlmIm fram bainagula mai*
        from your and my father, she ran away from our father; he got her at Bainagula my

> *kuntri aliya, Im ben j>s kleim Im. "yu mirrid" dæt mai father.*
> *"nu wan," yu mirid gat*
>
> country, all of them, he just claimed her: "you married" that's what my father said, "no one" [she said], then you are married to
>
> *mai father, Im never ben laikIm mai father si*
>
> my father. She never liked him my father see

me: *dæts wai Im ben r>nawei*
    that's why she ran away

en: *dasawai hev tu, wai Im ben r>nawei fr>m Im naw Im sei that mama ben y>ng dæt leidi*
    that's why she had to, why she ran away from him, now, he said that "momma" had been too young for him

> *Im ben r>nawei mai father bla yInmi father Im never ben laikIm Im mai father tu y>ng*
>
> she ran away from my father, from your and my father, she never liked him, my father, she was too young for him
>
> *Im ben hev tu r>nawei Im ben hev tu r>n awei na*
>
> she had to run away, she had to run away from

je: *dæt pleis naw*
    that place now.

It is in fact, Joan's father from whom the woman is running, and it is her classificatory cousin who drowns. Joan takes over and starts the action of the story. She effectively puts the story outside: the two women were cross-cousins (*menggin,* E) and as they swam across the channel heading for a small island something "like a Dreaming" came up from the water.

en: *wel Im-ben r>n awei fr>m Im naw*
    well she ran away from him now

je: *Im ben teikIm edja (E) tupela mipela*
    she took sister, my two sisters

en: *Im ben frait*
    she was frightened

je: *ben trai r>nawei akras pleis tu get tu lang ailend*
    she tried to run away across the harbor to get to long island

bp: *land lang wei*
    long long way

je: *hmm dæt taid Im ben j>s laik k>m In laik dæt*
    hmm that tide it just, like, came in like that

cb: *mmm*
    mmm

je: *m>sta ben samthing laik drimIng*
must of been something like a dreaming

me: *tupela ben swIm Im ben swImswIm b>t dat gerl dIdent wana gu bek ai danow wai*
those two women swam, they swam and swam but that girl didn't want to go back I don't know why

dæt gerl ben singing awt far help naw, help mi meit, help mi, kam bek an yu help mi
that girl was calling out for help "help me mate, help me, come back and you help me,

help mi   meit   nathing na
help me mate"   nothing now

en: *help help help   dja—(E)*
                                   "help help help" goodness

me: *dæt gerl never ben gu bek pikIm >p Im*
that girl never went back to pick her up

en: *ben sei wel Im ben laikadjet laidjet misis [personal name] krul gerl*
she said   well she was like that   [personal name] cruel girl

wel Im ben hev tu lök bek fInIsht naw Im fInIsht
well she had to look back, finished now, she was finished

bp: *Im ben laik dæt therrawin (E) wi ben lök?*
It was like that <u>Rainbow Serpent</u> we saw?

me: *mmm hn dei ben meitz*
mmm and they were mates.

   Clearly the speakers attempt to get the correct person to tell the story of the *therrawin*. For example, Claire Mamaka states that Grace Ziyesta "should be here" to tell the story. Joan and Emily also try to get Catherine Burga, Joan's father's sister, to tell the story, but she refuses. Significantly, Emily begins by telling only the part that she witnessed and outlining the various kin relations the actors had to each other and to her. It is Joan, related to a principal character in the story, who actually places the story outside. Mary and Emily, good storytellers, take over and finish the story.
   Whereas before, at the very beginning of these exchanges, only Ziyesta was said to know this story, suddenly everybody knows and can tell it. The young woman left the Banagula camp with her cross-cousin and traveled north toward Darwin. When they reached the northern shore near the Port Patterson Islands, they decided to swim to the nearest island. The women swam and swam, says Mary, but one of the young women

began to cry out for help while the other kept swimming toward the island. This is an incredibly moving and disturbing point in the story. Over and over Mary, in a slow monotone and with Emily echoing her, says the struggling girl cried out for help, for her mate to come back and help her. Mary finishes her turn by describing how the first woman never looked back. There are intimations here and in other occurrences of this story that a cleverman had "sung" the young woman and made her *tjeingithut* to the cries of her cousin. Emily changes this ending slightly—when she did look back her mate was gone. As if the listeners failed to hear this before, Mary repeats, they were mates, *menggin,* "wives" to each other, kinsfolk who are supposed to have a close, playful, and endearing relationship. Mary and Emily are *edja ngirrwat* (E, same-named sisters). Moreover, they are both Emiyenggal (although Mary's mother was Wadjigiyn), close in age (born ca. 1927 and 1925, respectively) and "looked the same" when they were young and so were always paired during ceremonies and corroborees. They are also recognized, along with Grace Ziyesta, as the most fluent storytellers at Belyuen. The various relationships that exist among women—kin, age, language, and community affiliation—are all drawn into a story ostensibly about the threat of certain mythic creatures to all women.

This story demonstrates something beyond local ways of speaking. Social identity emerges inasmuch as it predetermines the interactions between women. At a minimum, Belyuen listeners ask Who spoke, what relationship does she or he have to the context of the story, to the place where the story occurred, and to the rest of the social group? But conversations can also change a person's relationship to land. People can use talk to make a claim over a place or an experience (Sansom 1988b) by invoking "a range of 'facts' to establish new attachments to other land" (Sutton and Rigsby 1982, 167) or by "discovering" new Dreamings in the countryside (Myers 1986) that redefine persons in relation to each other.

This story, and numerous other conversations like it that have as their topic human relations as mediated by land, orients people toward a type of action (hunting and camping in the countryside) and a type of relation to the past, one of kinship between people and events plotted in the landscape (see Munn 1964, 1970; Myers 1986). Belyuen families' use of residence, shared experience, and sentiment to articulate land attachment is similar to other Aboriginal groups. Having come to the Docker River settlement from a variety of places, Aboriginal people living there ask not who belongs there "*instead* of someone else . . . [but] who belonged there *more* than someone else" (Woenne 1974, 54). "Whose Settlement— whose 'country'—is Docker River? By what rights? Which people are Docker River People? In terms of which criteria? And relative to which social and territorial contexts?" (Woenne 1974, 56). Fred Myers similarly notes that for Pintupi men knowledge of the Dreaming or of the Law and an "ontological orientation to experience of the physical environment" is one source and basis of their authority over it (1982b, 90; see also Munn 1970; Hiatt 1982, 1984; von Sturmer 1978). The crucial aspect of place and sentiment to narration is also shown in the story of the two cousins. I first heard the *therrawin* story on a fishing trip near the island where the event happened, ind I heard it again when traveling around the area with senior women in preparation for a site survey. Several senior women described the site to Joan as "your place," not in the sense of the law's definition of a "traditional owner" but in the sense of Joan having an important orientation of kinship to a traumatically (at other places, joyfully) marked site in the countryside.

Because stories like the *therrawin* have many possible meanings and avenues of kinship, conversations do not simply describe people's relationship to sites, they argue for them. The political use of stories about mythic reactions to human groups is shown in the following conversation that took place on the north coast of the Cox Peninsula. Jean Ziya, the storyteller who is Emiyenggal and has lived on the Cox Peninsula most of her life, describes how the wave-hand of the *kanggalang* Dreaming (Blanket Lizard Dreaming at the Bridjibin site) emerged (*nungguka-manthenaiyi,* E) and threatened to drown a boatload of land claim researchers and Beringgen, Wagaitj, and Laragiya Aborigines from Belyuen and Darwin, but submerged when a Belyuen senior woman talked to the Dreaming. The people in the story were in a small boat off the shore of a northern island in the Port Patterson chain near the mythic *Kanggalang* site. Jean Ziya mentions by name or age several people who were there, including Maria Brandl, one of the original researchers for the Kenbi Land Claim, and *wulgamen* (old woman), a now-deceased Kiyuk woman widely regarded as the expert on the Laragiya language and on Laragiya sites in and around the Cox Peninsula. The old Kiyuk woman learned about the region through her own experience and from her deceased second husband, a senior *danggalaba* Laragiya. Notice that Jean Ziya, the storyteller, never says whether the old Kiyuk woman used the Laragiya language. Instead, Jean foregrounds the importance of local knowledge for settling down the local mythic landscape. Kabal is the name of one of the Port Patterson Islands.

BRIDJIBIN (31 March 1989)

Speakers in order of appearance
jz: Jean Ziya (father and mother Emi) born circa 1935
en: Emily Nela (father and mother Emi) born circa 1925
gz: Grace Ziyesta (father Marriamu, mother Menthayenggal) born circa 1930

jz: *yu tel thIs bet wer wi went Kabal wi dIdent gow ner thæt pleis*
you tell this Beth, when we went to Kabal, we didn't go near that place

en: *<u>abana</u> (E)*
<u>who is that</u>

jz: *b>t dei ben sIdawn kwait ferst taim eh dei ben*
but they traveled undisturbed for the first part, eh they

gz: *mmm*
mmm

jz: *sIdawn kwait dei ben sIdawn na kwait dei ben sIdaaawn kwaiait efta dæt Im ben*
traveled quiet, they traveled undisturbed they traaaveled quieeet, after that her [Dreaming]

<u>nungu kamanthenaiyi</u> (E) tharr>n Im ben muv naw la aliya
<u>finger emerged</u> that Dreaming's, she moved now toward all of them

gz: *langa <u>wik wik</u> (B)*
in the <u>fresh water hole, fresh water hole</u>

jz: *dæt da wan naw*
that's the one now

gz: *<u>wik</u> (B) Im ben kam awt*
the Dreaming came out of <u>the freshwater hole</u>

jz: *en maria brandl Im ben lök*
and Maria Brandl, she saw it

gz: *maria Im now*
Maria, she knows

jz: *kamantheni (E) Im ben wanIm naw bilanga drawnIm naw aliya Im ben fraiten*
<u>the Dreaming emerged,</u> it wanted them, it wanted to drown them, they were frightened,

alidja dæt wulgamen Im ben tak le Im naw hn Im ben gow dawn na dæt <u>nunggu</u> (E) le Im.
all of them, that old Kiyuk lady, she talked to the Dreaming now, and it submerged now, those <u>fingers</u> of it submerged.

Stories like Jean's have a pedagogical and political purpose. They are significant not only because the speaker and I can use them to demonstrate that human language and sweat have the capacity to upset a sentient countryside, but also because speakers and listeners can use these everyday events to demonstrate who knows of this capacity and who can control its effects. In other stories Jean describes local Belyuen Wagaitj and Beringgen, including the above *wulgamen,* as having resisted researchers' desires to get close to the dangerous Dreaming. Through such statements as "we sebi [know]," "they been force im [the old lady]," and "maybe that other mob no more sebi [does not know] im danger [its dangerous]" Belyuen women position their experience of the Cox Peninsula as providing the kind of knowledge that *should* provide them with respect and authority over action in the region. And they prioritize experiential knowledge obtainable from their everyday practice. What does the Blanket Lizard do, what is likely to upset it, what is likely to calm it down? Jean answers these questions without foregrounding the competitive relationship between Aboriginal groups, here between Belyuen and non-Belyuen Aborigines. Rather, she lists the events of the trip and creates a rich visual scene of what happened. But the social conflicts are clear to listeners even slightly familiar with the politics of the region. Maria Brandl works for the Northern land Council on the Kenbi Land Claim; she, Darwin Laragiya, and Belyuen Wagaitj and Beringgen were on a mapping exercise near the Port Patterson Islands. In such highly politicized contexts and narratives, Jean, like the old Kiyuk woman before her, avoids stating who can or cannot manage the regional countryside, choosing instead to demonstrate this: the *Kiyuk* woman *ben tak le im* ["talked to the Dreaming"].

The power of stories such as Jean's lies in three areas. First, they *suggest* who has the mythic knowledge of and therefore rights over the surrounding countryside: if the old Kiyuk woman knew what to do when confronted by the upset Dreaming, she must know the story about it. Second, Jean demonstrates Wagaitj and Beringgen ability to associate events with meanings, here a Dreaming's reaction to foreign sweat and language. Relatedly, stories such as Jean's map the historic association of Wagaitj and Beringgen to various stretches of the countryside. On the Cox Peninsula, Dreamings that are located close to the hunting grounds and outstations of Belyuen families are said to understand Laragiya, Batjemal, Emiyenggal, Menthayenggal, and a "little bit of Marriamu." As one moves to Dreamings on the outer edge of where Belyuen families have historically used the country, Dreaming sites are said to understand only Laragiya and, for some, a little Batjemal. The country's linguistic competence becomes the index through which groups rank each other's competence to mind the country. Finally, Jean's story and others that resemble it shift the emphasis on knowledge from a mythic to an everyday canon of stories about the reciprocal and intentional effects of people's and country's activities. Residing in a place achieves a sense of community (Sansom 1982, 1988*a*) around the everyday mythic encounters that local people have. Women's subjectivity—who they understand themselves to be and what role they play in the community—emerges from and reinforces the strategic grounding of knowledge in land activity. Moreover, from a political pragmatics, residing in or traveling from place to place also allows people to increase and nuance their cultural encyclopedia. This, in turn, provides them with richly detailed stories to back up their own or to dispute others' claims about how places are related to people. Referring to the modern mythic adventures that they or their relatives have had, Belyuen men and women claim that "we got that story now for this Delissaville area" (indicating the Cox Peninsula, Bynoe Harbour, and Port Patterson regions).

Disputes people have over the meaning of events that occur in the countryside have very different political and sociological consequences when held within and without the community. An example of how persons in the community joust over and negotiate knowledge (and through knowledge, power) is seen in an earlier part of the school family history lesson.[22] Older Belyuen women were discussing the Cheeky Yam, a mythic old woman who travels up and down the Bynoe Harbour; when a boat crosses her path with young men and women, the Cheeky Yam will emerge from the water and try to sink the vessel.[23]

In the segment of conversation below, women engage in a common conversational routine (see App. 1, part B). While discussing the country, they challenge each other's knowledge of the correct names and locations of Dreamings and the correct practices associated with them. Belyuen women say that this type of conversation is good because it allows them to "straighten up" the countryside and it allows the countryside to hear them talking about it. Discussing the correct topography is necessary if the memory of it and, through memory, the well-being of the country are to pass to the next generation. If the cultural topography is scrambled, people might accidentally walk near or over a dangerous mythic site. When the intentionality of the actor is not a factor in a mythic site's reaction to the actor, the knowledge people gain during negotiations like the one below are, from a pragmatic standpoint, very important.

While reading this short segment it is important to remember that, although these women are disputing each others' and my own knowledge, and thereby establishing power relationships among themselves, they are all part of the Belyuen group. Whether they call the Cheeky Yam *minthene* (B) or *wila* (E), or even *gulida* (L), Belyuen Aborigines seek the name of and appropriate behavior for a site within their own group. Moreover, in her second statement, Mary Eladi roots Belyuen knowledge in a Laragiya origin—local people's knowledge comes from a traditional source. (In the first part of the conversation, women are discussing what Dreamings are found in the Belyuen water hole. Dreamings include the *kenbi* [didjeridoo] and the *koinme* [mangrove stick].)

Chapter One

CHEEKY YAM (6 February 1989)

Speakers in order of appearance
me: Mary Eladi (father Wadjigiyn, mother Emi) born circa 1927
dz: Deborah Zirita (father Emi, mother Marriamu) born circa 1950
je: Joan Ela (father Marritjaben, mother Marriamu) born 1943
sm: school master (Euro-Australian) born circa 1950
jz: Jean Ziya (father and mother Emi) born circa 1935
cb: Catherine Burga (father Marritjaben, mother Marriamu) born circa 1920
en: Emily Nela (father and mother Emi) born circa 1925
bp: Beth Povinelli (Italian-American) born 1962

me: *Yeh dæt de <u>kenbi</u> (B/E) naw thærr>n <u>durlg</u> (B) Im got <u>kenbi durlg</u> (B) hn ding*
yeh that is the <u>didjeridoo</u> now in the water hole. It has a didjeridoo Dreaming and, thing, <u>koinme</u> (B) <u>mangrove stick</u> Dreaming

dz: *dæt dæt mait bi dæt tjen>l-Im kam awt dIferent seikred saits*
that that might be that channel, the tunnel comes out to different sacred sites

me: *yeh Im gat a driming dæt mangow dæt mangrowv wan tri an dæt bambu naw*
yeh, it has several Dreamings: mango, that mangrove tree and that didjeridoo now,

lat driming In dir. dei sei dæt leragiya pip>l naw fr>m dIs water naw Im gow rait
all those Dreamings are in there. Laragiya people say that from this water now, the Dreaming goes right

thru naw kam >p le ailend evirwer, endiyen ailend, duw>n, mm kam awt dIsaid le,
through and comes up at the islands, everywhere, Indian Island, Duwun, the Dreaming comes out this side of

wat Iz Im neim
what's it's name

je: *bridjIbIn*
Bridjibin

me: *bridjIbIn wei streit, <u>yuwei</u> (E), streit ahed le Milik dæt ailend der naw Im kam awt*
Bridjibin way straight, <u>yes</u>, straight ahead to Milik, and it comes out there at that island

derye dæt water fr>m ir gIv It langa
from here the water hole goes to there

LEGAL ENTANGLEMENTS 49

sm: *yu kIdz ar biying tu noizi bi kwaiyet pliz*
you kids are being too noisy be quiet please

me: *Im kam le dæt driming dIsaid la Bainow Harbar wei dæt wat-Im dIswan*
it extends from here to that Dreaming this side of Bynoe Harbour way, what's its name,

bobot awa yuwa (E)
thing of the beef-class there?

je: [faint]

me: *wila (B)   awa (E)   wila (E)   yeda minthene (E)*
Cheeky Yam of the beef-class, Cheeky Yam, look, Cheeky Yam

cb: *yu (E/Marr)* [faint]
yes
[noise]

je: *tak y>ng gerlz*
talk to the young girls

me: *wel laik sam kId dei gow dawn der evritaim la*
well like some kids they go down there everytime to

en: *eh lIsen stari der abi tel-Im*
[to children] hey, listen to the story Abi [me] is telling

me: *aa dæt pleis wat dIs pleis aaa buwambi*
aa that place what this place, aaa, Buwambi

cb: *y>koi (E/Marr)*
you're right

dz: *bawmbi*
Buwambi

me: *yeh dei al taim gow dawn der dæt kId ye now hn mait bi dei now mar sæbi dæt*
yeh, they go down there often, those kids, you know, and maybe they don't know that

meiyidjem (B) awa ngarrawaka minthene (E) wel Im gow dawn
the beef-class Cheeky Yam well it can sink down into the sea

dz: *yeh yeh*
yeh yeh

me: *wel Im gow dawn*
well the Cheeky Yam can sink

dz: *Im laik a a waild laik a*
it is like a a wild like a

me: *walid yem <u>yena</u> (E) Im driming tharr>n djiki yem naw*
wild yam is <u>there,</u> she's a Dreaming, that <u>Cheeky Yam</u> Dreaming now

en: <u>*minthene*</u> *(E) naw*
<u>Cheeky Yam</u> now

jz: <u>*wila*</u> *(B)*
<u>Cheeky Yam</u>

bp: *mimi?(E)*
pumpkin yam?

me: <u>*wila*</u> *(B)*
<u>Cheeky Yam</u>

en: *now mar dæt n>therwan*
no that other one

jz: <u>*minthene*</u> *(E)*
<u>Cheeky Yam</u>

cb: *yeh*
yeh

jz: *yu sei m <u>minthene</u> (E)*
you say <u>Cheeky Yam</u>

je: *dæt manster dæt wi ben show yu dæt dei, yeh <u>therrawin</u> (E)*
that monster we showed you that day, yeh <u>Rainbow Sea Serpent</u>

en: *nat <u>therrawin</u> (E)*
not <u>Sea Serpent</u>

dz: *hm gata aa laika leig thIs mab wulgamen sæbi thei tel yu the wan naw kalIm <u>minthene</u>*
it has a, like a leg, this bunch of old ladies know they can tell you the one, you call it

<u>*minthene*</u> *(E) ar <u>wila</u> (B).*
<u>Cheeky Yam</u> or <u>Cheeky Yam.</u>

As this segment suggests, Belyuen persons pay attention not only to the content of knowledge, but also to its formal presentation. Belyuen women and men evaluate a person's knowledge with a fairly stable set of criteria: Is a person able to say what they know in a "straight way"; that is, in a topographical sense, is a person able to line up the country in the correct order? Above, women noted the direction that a mythic creature traveled: "it comes out," "it goes right through," "Bridjibin way straight going straight ahead to Milik." Belyuen men and women emphasize content and order, and place and seriation in their discussions of the countryside. Stephen Muecke has likewise argued, "Song-cycles are also likely to work with memory in that they progress nomadically, going from place to place.... Knowing the performance text thus means to also know the country" (1988a, 48). Reciprocally, not knowing the order of site names and related stories is an indication that a speaker does not know the country and is, therefore, a dangerous entity in it. Because of the dangerous implications of persons' lack of knowledge about places, people repeatedly challenge each other in conversations. From these challenges comes a consensus on "the real story" and, subsequently, a narrative of the country's cultural topography; or, where no consensus emerges, there is a postponement of this narrative order until a further event or person can clarify the issue.

Even though the historical body of knowledge is constantly negotiated and its political and social context is recognized as critically influencing what part of that knowledge is revealed, the actual body of mythic and historical knowledge itself must not appear to be effected by political or social context. By social I mean what particular people know at particular times as opposed to actual knowledge, the "true story," which Belyuen Aborigines say exists though they may have access to only a part of it. What is known must appear to be uninvolved in the political context of its emergence, even as it is being negotiated and brought forth in the context of speaking.[24] Therefore, the further speakers move from their social center (which in a given context of information gathering might be their close or more distant Belyuen kin), the less open will the negotiation of knowledge be until, in land claims or site surveys, negotiation is silenced in the company of non-Aborigines and an illusion of community consensus is projected. Or, more correctly, the community's agreement at an interethnic level is not an illusion but the real status of community knowledge in this social context. This is not surprising given the contradictions between the power Belyuen persons draw from knowledge and the current structure of Aboriginal social legislation. Among the Belyuen, knowledge of the countryside is a source of power insofar as it is unevenly distributed; researchers must go to older women at Belyuen because they are the ones who know the past and the mythic countryside and the women derive economic benefits from their visits.[25] But to the community as a whole, knowledge is a powerful resource insofar as it is evenly distributed. In a land claim hearing it is *a group* that must show "common spiritual affiliation" to sites on the land if a grant of land is to occur, although commissioners acknowledge the differences that age makes in what people know.

These principles for speaking—who speaks, the ontological orientation of speech, and the contextual basis of negotiations over knowledge—play a significant role in how various Aboriginal groups are assessed during land claim hearings (see also Eades 1991). Let me give an example from the Kenbi Land Claim for the Cox Peninsula, Port Patterson, and Bynoe Harbour regions. The Kenbi Land Claim was submitted in 1979 and has dragged through the courts since then. In 1989 the petition was finally heard. During the hearing, Lorna Tennant, a Wagaitj woman who has an outstation on the west coast, described to the land commissioner what happened when a group of foreign Aborigines traveled by *Wariyn*, the Old Man Dreaming and by *Wutwut*, the Frog Dreaming. Bagamanadjing (here Bakamanadjing) is the site of Lorna's family camp.

> LORNA TENNANT: Anyway, that day it was day like this and sunny, no cloud in the sky and that, and the boys came around—Rex came around to visit his sister—and after they left you could see clouds starting to form up in the sky and you could see where the clouds were forming; it was just forming around the Bakamanadjing area and it started raining them. It started raining out here just outside of Duwun out here and then it came back around it just circled around Bakamanadjing and Wutwut area. That is the only area, but behind that it was just sunny.
> . . . Well, Rex did not know anything about it by coming past Wariyn. I think on Friday a lot of the ladies got painted up and that to go and pay their respect to Wariyn, whereas these boys did not, because they did not know the country and they were from Kormilda or from other places, and Wariyn smelt their sweat—different sweat—it is not from, you know, he did not know them, and because of that they did not pay respect and got punished for it by putting that wind and rain there just around us.[26]

Lorna's story is typical of the way in which Belyuen people politically contextualize events that occur during their everyday hunting and collecting activities. She and others can interpret the meaning of the climatic change as marking her group as a familiar and the other group as a foreigner to the countryside because she and her family are the people who regularly camp at Bagamanadjing. Moreover, following Fred Myers, the political setting of her narrative is one of the "various means [that] exist by which individuals make claims of identification with the 'country' and assert it as their 'own'" (Myers 1988a, 65). Lorna Tennant's story is consistent with other Belyuen speakers' practices in that it attributes a site's upset to a foreign groups' sweat and language. Other stories tell of Belyuen Aborigines' sweat and language calming a site. Unless someone knows the site better than the speaker or can supply a different culturally appropriate interpretation of the events, there are few other as persuasive ways to dispute his or her words.

Generally, then, Wagaitj and Beringgen undermine other Aboriginal groups' claims to the Cox Peninsula in three ways. First, they wait for a public display of another groups' ignorance and then comment upon their "bitsidup stories" (mixed up, misshapen). Second, they describe the character of countryside in an intimate way, indirectly commenting upon the other groups' distance from the day-to-day needs of the mythic and physical environment. In a third and related tactic, they describe a site's reaction to the competing group, again indirectly challenging that group to deny the story; the other Aboriginal group cannot respond if they do not reside in the region as regularly or know the sites as well. Among themselves and afterwards, Belyuen Wagaitj-Beringgen note this lack of response with "im never say anything" or, Belyuen women say, *emimal werre piyamal* ("what talk, might be no story [for this place]"), using code-switching as metacommentary for the other group's lack of a "language" (knowledge) of their own.

Several benefits accrue to Belyuen Aborigines from these discursive practices. The Belyuen Wagaitj-Beringgen strategy of grounding their authority over the Cox Peninsula in knowledge derived from land usage is supported by the Land Rights Act in so far as the act looks to a group's extant knowledge when determining ownership issues. But, and this is most important, Belyuen Aborigines perform their rights and duties over the Cox Peninsula region without claiming the title "traditional Aboriginal owner"—an outright claim, on one hand, with which Belyuen Aborigines are generally uncomfortable and,[27] on the other hand, which would create a serious if not irrevocable social and political rift between the Wagaitj-Beringgen and the Darwin Laragiya.

Life-Styles, Knowledges, and the Law

While the Belyuen Wagaitj-Beringgen's ideology of land use and land welfare is politically effective in manipulating Aboriginal groups it is far less successful in manipulating the Australian legal system. But it is not completely unsuccessful and it is interesting why this is so.

For Aborigines and anthropologists tired by the grueling process of land claims and site registrations, it is hard to remember at times the relative youth of the Aboriginal Land Rights (NT) Act, 1976. Only sixteen years old, the act, a legal discourse on Aboriginality, is still in the process of being interpreted by indigenous peoples, their advocates, and their opponents. Over the last sixteen years the act has gone from being narrowly interpreted as applying only to patrilineal clans to being broadly interpreted as, at least potentially, applicable to an entire "language group" (a group whose constitution, like the clan, presents some sociological problems).

Over the last sixteen years, the Belyuen Wagaitj-Beringgen have watched and participated in this interpretive process that has affected how they understand and present their rights to the countryside. In particular, they have seen the claimant group change three times. In 1976, a collection of Belyuen Laragiya, Wagaitj, and Beringgen families from various clan affiliations were listed as claimants for the Port Patterson Islands (Duwun of Lorna's story being the northern-most island, the Blanket Lizard Dreaming of Jean Ziya's story being located north of it). When later research showed that the entire Cox Peninsula, Bynoe Harbour, and Port Patterson regions could be claimed, the petition was resubmitted in 1979 with a much smaller claimant group: the Laragiya *danggalaba* or crocodile clan, then only ten people. But the claim book itself was not called "The *Danggalaba* Land Claim" but "The *Kenbi* Land Claim" (*kenbi* is the Wagaitj term for crocodile). This linguistic code switching reflected the authors' dilemma: given the structure of the Land Rights Act and how it was then being interpreted, the authors believed that they could not list Wagaitj and Beringgen as claimants and yet they sought to acknowledge the central, historical role Wagaitj and Beringgen played in the Cox Peninsula region. The Kenbi Dreaming lies in the Belyuen water hole and it is the underground spokelike waterways through which Beringgen and Wagaitj sweat is "given to" the entire land claim region, though the authors did not comment on this later point.

Because of the proximity of the claim area to the Darwin Township and because of the generally adversary position taken by territory government to all Aboriginal claims, the Northern Territory disputed the legality of the Kenbi Land Claim on a number of grounds. For the next ten years the claim moved slowly through the courts. In 1988, when it was clear that Aborigines were going to win the court battles, the Northern Land Council reopened research to see how the *danggalaba* clan was doing. This clan, as it was then thought to be constituted, was not doing very well. Core claimants had died, had had crippling seizures, or knew little about the land under claim for historical reasons (one young woman had been removed from her parents when she was just child). In addition, non*danggalaba* Darwin Laragiya, newly aware of their political rights, argued that they should be included as claimants no matter their lifestyle, known clan affiliation, or knowledge of the claimed country—which in many cases, for historical reasons, was limited.

The issue of the life-style of Aboriginal claimants has been addressed directly by the land commissioners. In the act, "Aboriginal traditions" are defined as: "the body of traditions, observances, customs and beliefs of Aboriginals or of a community or group of Aboriginals, and includes those traditions, observances, customs and beliefs as applied in relation to particular persons, sites, areas of land, things or relationships" [sec. 3(1)]. The body of Aboriginal traditions is recognized in land claim reports as an evolving set of beliefs and practices. For instance, in his report on the Jawoyn (Katherine Area) Land Claim, which, like the Kenbi Land Claim, was for an area close to a city center, Mr. Justice Kearney noted that the effect of "non-Aboriginal settlement of the Top End in the late nineteenth century, and later dislocations of World War II in the north" seriously disrupted "Jawoyn traditional life and culture" (1988, 20–21). He, nonetheless, recognized a body of Jawoyn traditions and found for the Jawoyn traditional owners.

These legal insights are often lost, however, in the news media where Aboriginal practices or "life-styles" are political volleyballs used to frame government stances on land claims. So the argument goes, if urban and suburban Aborigines have life-styles that look like those of their average Anglo-Australian neighbors, then they are asking for special rights based simply on race (Hocking 1988, 5). Other representations of northern Aboriginal hunters have also made the life-style of urban Aborigines a potential impediment to their land aspirations. Many authors have stated that Aboriginal culture and economy have survived the colonial and postcolonial period in the northern outback because the natural environment was unsuitable for large scale pastoral and agricultural enterprises (Davidson 1980; MacKenzie 1980). While such descriptions evoke a positive image of the sturdiness and resilience of Aboriginal culture and society, they also contain a suppressed negative image that works against urban Aborigines' fight for land. They entrench the perception that Aborigines' past and future are linked to certain environments and practices and call into question the "authenticity" of urban- and commodity-oriented Aboriginal practices (Beckett 1988; Peterson 1985, 1991).

How Aboriginal performances of knowledge and identity are assessed is tied to their varying degrees of association with Anglo culture and economy. Aboriginal speakers are given greater or lesser authority depending, in part, on the perceptions of an Anglo listener: Is the Aboriginal narrator of "full blood" or "mixed" parentage? What was the means by which the knowledge was acquired? Knowledge is not assessed in and of itself, as the act might suggest it should be (Does the claimant have it or not?) but is implicated in its origins. The cultural organization of learning is itself on trial. For instance, can knowledge be of a traditional sort if it is mediated by Western technologies and educational praxis?

Laragiya men and women who live and work in Darwin, who read, write, and speak fluent English, and who are knowledgeable about Aboriginal and Western law face a different series of questions about their cultural encyclopedia than do Belyuen Wagaitj-Beringgen, although all groups have participated in a dialectic of self whereby the acquisition and performance of knowledge is mediated by, as much as it is in competition with, the Australian nation-state. Nevertheless, because of their social appearances and positions, Laragiya are often charged with having gained knowledge on traditional matters from books rather than sage elders. So gathered, the knowledge loses value to many Western listeners. The spe-

56   *Chapter One*

cific hope of adversaries to the Laragiya land claim is that their knowledge will lose its value in the eyes of the land commissioner. Mr. Hughston, counsel for the Northern Territory Government which challenged the Kenbi Land Claim, used just such a strategy in his examination of Bill Risk and Richard Barnes, two knowledgeable Laragiya men who make their home in Darwin. Hughston suggests that Billy Risk learned what he knows from the Kenbi claim book; namely, he learned through a written rather than an oral medium.

>   MR HUGHSTON: All right. Have you ever read the claim book?
>   BILL RISK: I have not read right through, no. I have just—like I say, I have looked at parts of it, that is all.
>   MR HUGHSTON: All right. You are interested now, are not you, Billy, in learning about the land claim: country, sites and dreamings? Is that right?
>   BILL RISK: I have always been interested in our country.
>   MR HUGHSTON: Well, when did you first become aware that there was a land claim book?
>   BILL RISK: Probably about three years ago.
>   MR HUGHSTON: Three years ago. And did you believe that would contain information about this land claim area, the sites and the dreamings?
>   BILL RISK: No, I did not. What I believe the book contained was just sort of technical information about the claim.
>   MR HUGHSTON: Right. Is that still your belief? That the land claim book just contains technical information about the claim?
>   BILL RISK: Yes, I think so.
>   MR HUGHSTON: It is a fairly thick book, is not it? You have not had sufficient interest to read the thing from cover to cover to see what it is about?
>   BILL RISK: What I have looked at is the front parts of the book.
>   MR HUGHSTON: Yes.
>   BILL RISK: And if there is any parts in there that I want to read, I read them.
>   MR HUGHSTON: All right. Well, how did you know that there were parts in there that you wanted to read?
>   BILL RISK: Because I looked at the front part, the index part.
>   MR HUGHSTON: Yes. Well, what about the site map. Have you seen the site map?
>   BILL RISK: Yes.
>   (Kenbi Transcripts 1989–90, 2391)

Hughston asks Richard Barnes the same general series of questions about reading the claim book. He then suggests that Barnes "cheated" by learning some of what he knows from anthropological and linguistic documents.

> MR HUGHSTON: All right. Have you also read anthropological and historical texts to try and find out more about the Larrakia [Laragiya].
> RICHARD BARNES: I have read—I have read word lists. I have seen word lists which I got from the Institute of Aboriginal Studies on language. They are a lot of words that Uncle George was giving me that I recorded and there are others that he could not remember. And he asked me to get some—get the stuff from Canberra, because he gave it to somebody before. And so I got a copy of a word list of Larrakia words, and—with the object of trying to learn some more from that.
> MR HUGHSTON: All right.
> RICHARD BARNES: It is a bit difficult, though, to learn from the list itself.
> MR HUGHSTON: But are you saying that you have not read anything else in terms of anthropological or historical texts to find out more about the Larrakia?
> RICHARD BARNES: I have read the stuff in the—I cannot recall reading anything else, no.
> MR HUGHSTON: All right. Would it be fair comment to say that most of your knowledge about the Larrakia and about the claim area comes from having read these materials?
> RICHARD BARNES: I put the—I put the information in two classes. The stuff that I read I put in one area as information that somebody else has recorded. And the stuff that is told directly to me, I give that a higher classification in my mind. Simply because it was transferred direct.
> (Kenbi Transcripts 1989–90, 2424–25)

Anglo-Australians are not the only ones to evaluate the origins of knowledge when evaluating its "worth." Older Belyuen women, for instance, distinguish between a knowing based on having seen and participated in an event ("got it inside," "having been there") and based on secondhand accounts such as reading or hearing about it. However, they do not—as did the Northern Territory Government in its cross-examination of Bill Risk and Richard Barnes—tie the authenticity of knowledge to the technological means by which it is first obtained or with which it is remembered. Indeed, the recording of older people's stories allows knowledge to reach and "go inside" listeners. Often, when the source of a person's information is in question, Belyuen Aborigines assess knowledge based on the speaker himself, "what kind im," and the sense that his or her claim makes in a communitywide network of knowledge about places and peoples.

Nevertheless, it was in such a racialized climate of knowledge that, at the beginning of the 1989 hearing, the Laragiya language group was presented as the new claimant group. By this time, Belyuen Wagaitj-Beringgen began to question seriously the direction the claim was taking. Over the ten years of litigation (1979–89), many older Aboriginal people with personal and totemic affiliations connecting Laragiya, Wagaitj, and Beringgen groups had died. As the years passed, Belyuen Aborigines also began worrying that their rights in land would not be protected by the land claim process if they were only recognized as "squatters," a term used inside and outside the community, often as a query. ("We migrants, oh?" or "What we, Beth, squatters?") The Land Rights Act has provisions to protect so-called nontraditional owners who were living on land that is subsequently claimed (see Neate 1989, 200–201). Be this as it may, Belyuen Wagaitj-Beringgen had watched a very complicated and uncomfortable relationship unfold between Finniss River Maranunggu (also historically portrayed as "migrants") and the Kungwarakany traditional owners which in the end saw the Maranunggu leaving country for which they believed they held ceremonies and rituals. The Kungwarakany like many Laragiya had spent much of their lives in urban and suburban Darwin settings (see Layton and Williams 1980). The parallels between the Maranunggu and Kungwarakany case and the Belyuen Wagaitj-Beringgen's own position were striking and remarked upon by everyone. The Belyuen constantly pointed out to their advocates, including me, that the countryside reacted productively to them, they had the stories for it, knew how to use it (where to go and where not to go), and had been given conception Dreamings throughout the region. However, feeling assured that they would not be forced off the Cox Peninsula, Belyuen Beringgen and Wagaitj agreed not to press their claims separately and to participate in the hearing as its key witnesses on behalf of the Laragiya. They were formally presented as the "holders of traditional knowledge" for the Laragiya—as regents of a sort.

A land claim hearing is itself broken into two parts; the first is called the traditional evidence, during which time Aborigines describe why they are a descent group, show the commissioner various sacred sites and camping sites, and perform pertinent ceremonies. The second part of the hearing is called the detriment, during which time the government can present reasons why, no matter if there are traditional owners, the claim should not be granted: they usually point out the detrimental economic effect a successful claim would have on Northern Territory development.

During the hearing in 1989, Wagaitj-Beringgen witnesses followed the discursive strategies I discussed above: they grounded their mythic knowledge and their ties to the land in their use of the countryside. At every site the legal entourage went, Belyuen men and women described their foraging practices, their outstations, and the mythic adventures that happened to them while they were using a place. For example, they told how they had seen *letharrgun* tracks in the sand and how in the middle of a crab-collection trip they had heard the low, pulsing cries of the *munggarra* Dreaming (a Snot Nose Dreaming), and how economically important foraging was to the physical health of the community: "Maybe we starve like African people, if white people take this country." Laragiya practice and knowledge, even where significant, was often lost in the tide of Belyuen evidence. An important incident that occurred at one site, Binbinya, during the land claim shows the potential benefits that this discursive strategy held out to Belyuen families.

Binbinya is a hunting ground on the west coast of the Cox Peninsula just south of where Lorna Tennant described seeing the wind storm from Bagamanadjing. It includes a small beach that lies between a long mangrove, an estuarine creek, and a wetlands swamp. In the nearby swamp, men hunt feral pigs and cattle and women hunt freshwater turtles. But the site is most often used by women for crabbing and fishing (table 1). Its use is typical of how people hunt in enclosed beaches and the inland regions that surround them. People tend to hunt at such sites, perhaps cook the foods collected there, and then move to an open area for the day or return to the Belyuen Community. Senior women have spent a good amount of their life in the Binbinya mangrove collecting crab, shellfish, and bait. Many have lived at its coastal outstation at some point in their lives.

While bush foods collected at Binbinya and other sites throughout the Cox Peninsula represent only about 12 percent of the total Belyuen diet, they are, nonetheless, economically significant in two ways I elaborate in chapter 4 below. First, they provide an important supplement to the poor grocery diet, composed mainly of sugars (and alcohol), fats, and refined grains (primarily white flour). Second, sea products and other bush foods provide needed calories during periods of scarcity on the community. Most Belyuen adults receive some form of government welfare benefit. On alternate weeks, unemployment and social security benefits are dis-

TABLE 1
COMPARISON OF WOMEN'S USES OF SIX MANGROVE REGIONS

	Fish (kg)	Snails (kg)	Crab (kg)	Trips	Calories Obtained
Bitbinbiyirrk (E)	—	607.2	—	11* 6	102,009.6
Binbinya (W)	203.8	89.8	175.7	19* 3.5	328,219.5
Belurriya (N)	104.1	—	—	7* 9.5	114,093.6
Madpil (E)	61.7	48.6	147	66	150,759.3
Bemandjeli (N)	136.6	70.3	34.7	53* 1.3	178,615.5
Bagadjet (W)	14.5	159.3	334.2	21* 3.1	213,597.7

tributed, the former mostly to young and middle-aged men and the latter mostly to older women. Although, in general, each group spends their money on different items (men on alcohol and women on foods and household goods), both groups spend it quickly, which create bimonthly cycles of scarcity (cf. Altman 1987*b;* Coombs, Brandl, and Snowdon 1983; Povinelli 1991). At these times, bush foods provide an important supplement to people's diet.

Having said this, however, hunting-gathering does not carry much weight from a developmental perspective (this is an important point made during the detriment side of a land claim hearing; see chapter 5). During detriment proceedings, both sides present what they believe would happen if their claims are not granted. The Aboriginal-run Northern Land Council has argued that losing the Cox Peninsula would cause Belyuen Aborigines serious economic hardship (Povinelli 1990b). The Northern Territory government, with the aide of elaborate land-use and development plans (see map 4), argues that a land grant would seriously jeopardize the long-term economic welfare of the Northern Territory. Because of Western literature's emphasis on the subsistence role rather than on the productivity of hunts (the production of social cohesion, the communication with the mythic countryside, and the gathering of healthy foods for the human body) and because of the significant contribution of grocery foods to the Belyuen diet, the Northern Territory government is able to portray Belyuen hunting-gathering practices as insignificant in light of their own plans. Of particular interest to Northern Territory government developers is the north coast with its long white sand beaches and the west coast with its deep sea lane, perfect, they claim, for a deep sea port and an onshore oil refinery (with Binbinya and several other Dreaming sites in the way).

What political benefits the Belyuen Aborigines accrue from their foraging practices are also not clear from the vantage of the first half of the land claim hearing, during which evidence is given to determine traditional owners. However, the standards used to gauge Belyuen environmental practices in the traditional evidence oppose the standards used to measure them in the detriment hearings. While Belyuen families' use of sites like Binbinya can be portrayed as economically insignificant, the nonproductive time people spend in the bush provides them with something potentially more valuable than the foods they collect. But so far only potentially. Peoples' failed attempt to extend an effective intra-Aboriginal strategy to a national interethnic context can be seen in how traditional evidence given at Binbinya helped shape the course of the land claim hearing.

An event that had a significant effect on the course of the hearing occurred while traditional evidence was being given at the Binbinya creek.

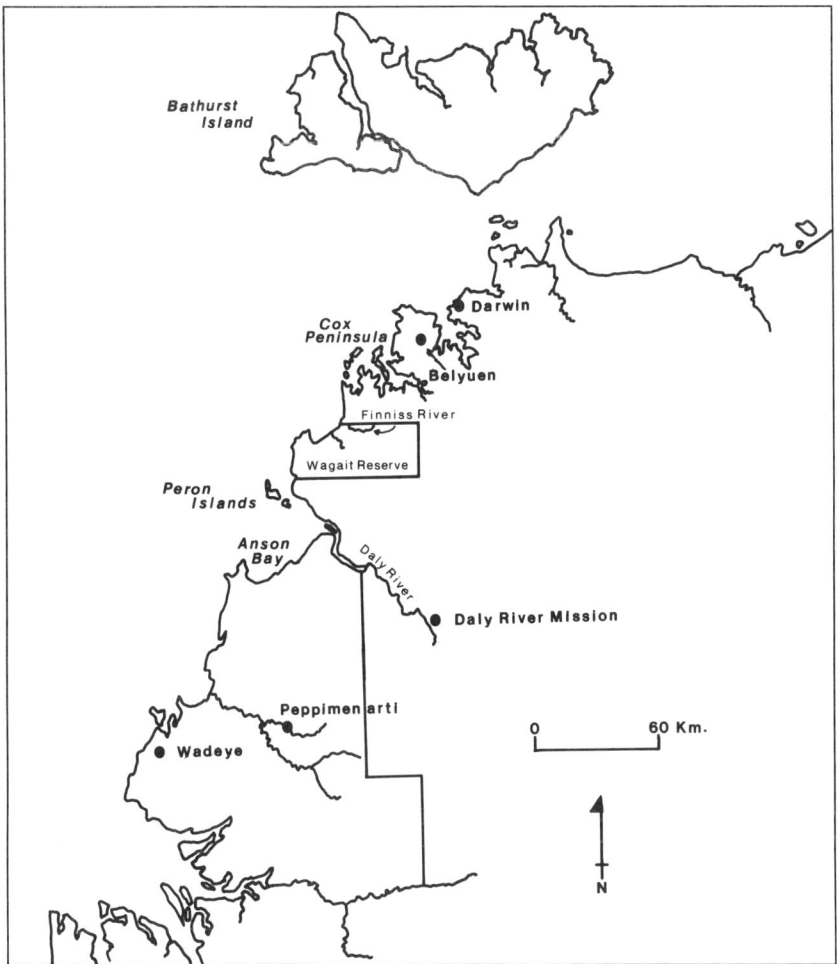

Map One: Coast of the Northern Territory from Port Keats to Port Darwin

As Lorna Tennant noted above, the *Wutwut* or Frog Dreaming is in the mouth of the Binbinya estuarine creek. There are several vantages to *Wutwut*. One can see it from the Bagamanadjing outstation, one can travel to it through the Binbinya mangrove, or one can approach it from the sea by boat. Because the land commissioner wanted to get a good look at the site, he ruled out the Bagamanadjing aspect. Access through the mangrove was ruled out because of the mud. Therefore, the commissioner decided to take two senior Wagaitj women and a senior Beringgen woman in his boat to the *Wutwut* site. These women had led much of the traditional evidence. And as they traveled, the women told several stories about hunting crab in the Binbinya mangrove, listening to the *Wutwut* frog "sing" while they hunted, and watching it send out winds in the manner that Lorna Tennant described above. Whether luck or divine providence, the commissioner's selection of women for the trip was important.[28] Men collect crab far less frequently than women do; women were able to make mythical action seem an everyday event. When the judge's boat arrived at the site the women became upset; they were sure that *Wutwut* had moved. This "shift" meant that something was wrong. Sure enough, all the women said that the sweat of foreign people (implicating whites and newly arriving non-Belyuen Aborigines) were upsetting the mythic countryside. They argued that the *Wutwut* Dreaming never acted this way when surrounded by Belyuen people. The women told the land commissioner's pilot he would have to turn the boat around quickly before they all drowned and the *Wutwut* rock cracked asunder. "More better we lose the case than kill im" was how they justified their actions to me later. Strongly impressed by the deep responsibility these women and other Belyuen families felt about the mythic countryside, by the amount of time people spent in the countryside (note, not the productivity of that time), and by their knowledge and attachment to sites, the land commissioner informed the Northern Land Council either to investigate the Wagaitj-Beringgen as potential claimants or to risk a separate claim mounted by his own lawyers. At this point, Belyuen families seemed successful in moving a locally effective ideology of land use and welfare to a national legislative context.

In February 1990, however, the same Aboriginal land commissioner found that no Aboriginal group could be legally recognized as a traditional owner. In Australian land litigation, however, the appropriate epigram is All is well that never ends. The claim is back in the courts on appeal. In summary and in preparation for the following chapters, the problem of hunter-gatherer productivity is several. From the perspective of Western development and foraging theory, hunting-gathering productivity is a misnomer: it is economically devalued in even its purest form and theoretically constrained as a mode of subsistence rather than an advanced mode of production. While Belyuen hunting and gathering does play a critical role in the local diet, we will see that it produces too much leisure for an area so close to Darwin. From a legal vantage, no matter how hunting-gathering contributes to local cultural, economic, and sociological well-being, it cannot produce what the Land Right Act demands: a local descent group. But perhaps most ironically and tragically, the deep strength of attachment and responsibility that the Belyuen Wagaitj-Beringgen have gathered during their hunting and gathering activity and the current form of land rights legislation has produced the seeds of the Laragiya people's own estrangement: the Wagaitj-Beringgin's intimate knowledge of the countryside has undermined the options and strategies the Darwin Laragiya have found to relate to lands they were deprived of in the earliest point of colonial history.

The rest of this book examines in more detail conflicts between Euro-Australian and Belyuen understandings of Belyuen actions and identities within the contexts of their everyday lives, contexts that include mythic action, social violence, and the relaxing rhythms of the sea. I do not return in any length to a discussion of the Kenbi Land Claim until chapter 6; rather I allow it to hover in the background—annoyingly, persistently, suggestively—as it does in the lives of people living at Belyuen and in Darwin.

2 Positioning Aborigines

Precolonial, Colonial, and Postcolonial Aboriginal Pasts

ANSON BAY

On the shores of Anson Bay
In the tropics far away
Where the oceans murmurs sweetly
Of its secrets night and day;
There inimitable beaches
Strewed with shells of varied features
Fringed with forest bright and gay.

There the stalwart native's roam
And they makes the woods their home
Here nature bounteously give
Free to all the tribes who live
Soon thy peaceful shores will see
Others come across the sea
Eager to escape the strife
Of a strenuous city life.

I must leave thee Anson Bay
To the South must haste away
But I'll ne'er forget the pleasure
Of thy brilliant winter weather
Of thy wild unbounded life
Free from politics and strife
What a place for one to stay!
On thy shores sweet Anson Bay.[1]

—James Harvey

INTRODUCTION

History is one set of actions turned on or toward another, a present work ordering and making sense of a past event. A "discourse on time is in time."[2] Our constructions of the past contain and control actions in an unruly present (Roseberry 1989). To make sure that people do not make any old claim about who they are and where they come from, pasts are used to sort truths from fictions, legitimate from illegitimate statements— they regulate the possible paths of a social history as they leave traces of other means by which social groups have been controlled. I use historical records below to examine three aspects of social control, first, how historical narratives have positioned Laragiya, Wagaitj, and Beringgen groups in social, cultural, and physical landscapes. Using colonial and postcolonial records (ca. 1839–1940) and my present-day discussions with Belyuen women, I demonstrate, in the first section the diversity of discourses and practices through which Aborigines from Darwin to the Daly River have been assessed and represented as authentic and corrupt cultural subjects and as belonging to specific tracts of land. In the second section I examine what physical and economic means were used to regulate and control Aboriginal movement and action, using as my source the recorded social and economic practices of Aborigines dwelling on the Cox Peninsula, 1870–1945. I end the chapter with a discussion of how Belyuen women conversationally negotiate these various Aboriginal pasts, control and manage their present cultural identity, and what motivations they have for doing so.

The representations and practices of coastal Darwin to Daly River Aborigines are, of course, intertwined if not causally related. Thus, I examine the various ways in which Western understandings of indigenous action affected what Aboriginal groups were doing and where they were doing it from the early colonial to the post–World War II period. This historical "positioning" of regional Aboriginal groups in physical, economic, and cultural spaces are palimpsests through which current political assessments of Belyuen action and identity are made. This chapter intends, therefore, to turn on the past in order to reestablish the legitimate nature of Belyuen Aborigines' present-day representations of their practice or, at least, to reentangle the past in such a way as to cause it to loosen its coherent narrative grip on what the Belyuen families and their ancestors were and are "really" doing.

HARBINGERS OF REVOLUTION

Positioning the Precolonial Aboriginal Past

Euro-Australian and Aboriginal-inspired portraits of the precolonial, colonial, and early postcolonial periods move from seemingly nostalgic descriptions of "the good olden days" to searing, violence-laden descriptions of the "cowboy time" or "wild time" when Europeans and

Aborigines battled for control over lands and their lives (Trigger 1992, 17–37; Lyon and Parsons 1989, 9; see more generally, Rosser 1990; Reynolds 1987).[3] As have their set of interests, Euro-Australian understandings and representations of the Aboriginal cultural subject has changed from the "first landing" to the present-day. Discussing Australia's construction of a national image and identity, Richard White notes that changing "European attitudes to, and curiosity about, man, nature and science" caused the portrait of indigenous people to change from a 17th century evaluation of Aborigines as a physically grotesque and commercially valueless group to an 18th century interest in them as natural reserves for the development of social theory (1981; see also Reece 1974, 62–103; Hamilton 1990).

In the late nineteenth century when Port Darwin was being established, Western portraits of indigenous north Australian peoples were motivated by an emerging discourse on the origins and legitimate forms of the nation-state. Australian nationalism not only drew on images of the "jolly bushman" and "Aboriginal outback" (White 1981; Carroll 1982), but it interpreted Aboriginal action in that outback as conforming to developing notions of national history and folklore. Important to this was the notion of "nation-ness as linked to a private-property language" (Anderson 1990, 67). Francesca Merlan (1981, 135) has shown how the "one language–one tribe" (the nation-state adapted to the "primitive" form of the tribe) model was incorporated into early anthropological theory on Aboriginal land tenure.[4] Radcliffe-Brown, according to Merlan, argued that "tribes" were patrilineally defined clans "bounded and distinguished" by a language and name (Merlan 1981, 135; see also Radcliffe-Brown 1930; and Stanner 1965a).[5]

But while language was an important determinant of where in the landscape early colonists, government officials, and ethnologists placed Aboriginal groups, Aboriginal ritual and economic practice also affected how Europeans assessed the group's cultural viability and, therefore, its anthropological and scientific value as well. The cultural and economic practices of Laragiya, Wagaitj, and Beringgen *produced* their identities for Euro-Australian observers even as Anglo representations were producing formal and informal policies that would change the actions of these Aboriginal groups.

A problem colonial observers faced, then, was how to assess ritual and economic practices: what constituted *knowing* a real Aboriginal subject. Drawing on the French school of discursive history,[6] King and McHoul have argued that "white knowledge of Aborigines" consisted of a method of locating Aborigines and rendering familiar a population "always potentially outside white discourse—and therefore outside official knowledge and control" (1986, 24).[7] In the material I present below, a key to how Western observers located and controlled Aborigines was their assessment of the relative "mixture" of local Aboriginal economic and cultural practices with the nonlocal (with Europeans and other Aborigines). This means to knowledge put investigators in a paradoxical position. Genuine knowledge of an Aborigine could be obtained only through the unknowable: What had indigenous Australians' economic and cultural practices been like before Europeans first set shore? In the Darwin–Daly River region this pure form was posited to have existed sometime before the 1869 founding of Port Darwin.[8]

Sailing past, exploratory accounts

The problem with locating precolonial Aborigines is one of time as well as one of space: When and where does one begin to look for the "olden days" in the multiple conceptions and structures of history? (See Sahlins 1985.) Belyuen Aborigines say that people had, in their words, "a strong culture" in the "olden days" before Europeans arrived. Then the wallabies were plentiful, the water was sweet, and the air was filled with the high screech of cockatoos. In the olden days, hunting trips were not interrupted by the dull background roar of planes flying in and out of Darwin, by four-by-four Toyota engines and radios, and by police looking around the bush for dope farms and "rebels."[9] People still cared about the corroborees and ceremonies, believed in the Dreamings, looked after the countryside, and were healthy because of it. According to Belyuen Aborigines there was no sickness in those days; there was none of the alcoholism or high blood pressure that now kills men and women before they reach their mid-fifties. "I think about it a lot," says Joan Ela, a woman in her mid-forties whose husband and brother-in-law both died of stress-related heart troubles. "Before, *they* drank just water, sweet from the ground, maybe with a little wild honey mixed in it. They were never sick, before, you know, that whiteman came."[10] Moreover, according to Joan and others, in the olden days people knew more about the cultural topography of their paternal and maternal countries and were able to live and travel freely within them.

If these activities and knowledges were characteristic of the "olden days before the whiteman"—a question I explore in detail later in this chapter—they were performed a long time before Joan's life or even the lives of her parents. Perhaps they occurred in the lives of her great-great grandmothers and grandfathers. But as early as 1805 Nicholas Baudin, the captain of a French cartographic mission in the South Seas, had already sailed past Cape Dombey and the Peron Islands (1974; cf. Peron 1809; see map 1). If he contacted Aborigines in the area (he does not report doing so), he might have introduced the diseases that, many say, radically changed the relationship between the Daly River and Cox Peninsula groups and the countryside.[11] Surveying the same coast in 1819, Philip Parker King saw and was seen by natives off the Port Patterson area (King 1827). In the 1830s, the Australian explorer J. L. Stokes was traveling around the northwest coast of Australia, from Port Essington to the Victoria River. In 1839, he reported influenza "raging among the natives" around Point Emery in the Port Darwin area (Stokes 1846).[12] At the mouth of the Victoria River Stokes notes:

> We learnt from the party at the boat that a large body of the natives had been down watching their movements, and apparently intending if possible to surprise them. Though they had approached very near, they would not have been seen but for a shooting party, which got view of them from an overlooking height, crawling along the ground with evident caution. They were probably the same party we encountered higher up, and had traced our trail backwards, in order to see whence, and in what force we had entered their territory. Little did they imagine, as they gazed upon our small party and its solitary boat, that they had seen the harbingers of an approaching revolution in the fortunes of their country! (1846, 89)[13]

Today, Belyuen Aborigines locate Marritjaben country—where Joan has a patrilineal totem (*durlg* Dreaming)—just north of the Victoria River on the coast near Cape Dombey. Other Belyuen residents have many paternal and maternal totemic links to coastal lands between these points and north to the Finniss River.

As seems common to exploration texts of the time, Stokes' book has scattered references to indigenous groups he met or briefly sailed by, including the visage and character of the inhabitants and their conduct: whether they carefully watched his ship or immediately fled into the surrounding bush. Stokes does not mention seeing natives between Port Patterson and the Victoria River. But not seeing people did not assure Stokes of their absence. He often notes finding traces of Aborigines where he landed (remains of "feasts" and old camps). Moreover, "natives" were tricksters, able to appear and disappear quickly. Note the description of "wild Aborigines" by one of the first settlers in Darwin: "The natives [Laragiya] were always alert for trouble and could disappear swiftly if there was any available cover. . . . Natives . . . disappeared like magic" (Kelsey 1975, 79).

Explorers saw native inscrutability as evidenced in their potential for hostile resistance to Western colonization. For instance, when Stokes met a group he was never sure if they were acting in a friendly or hostile manner. Landing at Point Emery (near Darwin) he notes how friendly the natives seem to be; they even go so far as "presenting themselves without spears." But Stokes attaches a footnote to this observation, and it is one

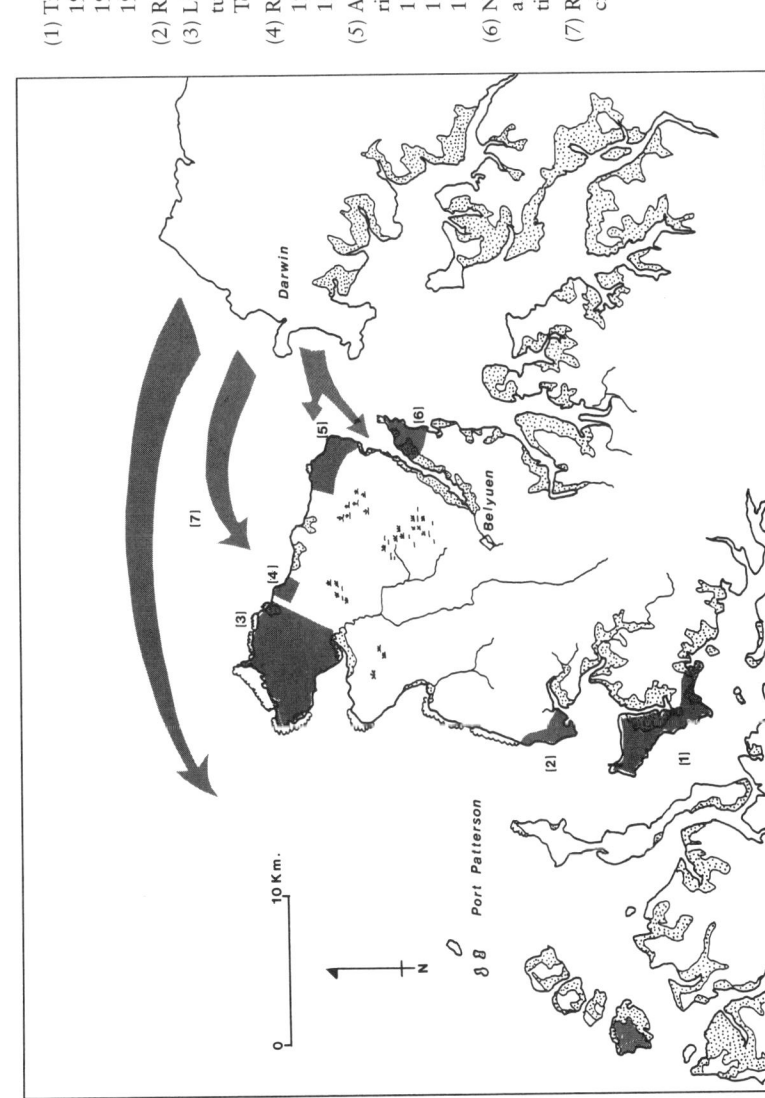

Map Two: The Historical Location of non-Aboriginal Activity on the Cox Peninsula

(1) Tin Mining 1880s, Gravel Mining 1960s–1980s, Pearl Shell Industry 1980s–190s, Residential Squatting 1970s–1990s.

(2) Residential Squatting 1970s–1990s.

(3) Lighthouse 1880s–1990s, Agricultural Plantation late 1920s–1940s, Telecom 1970s–1990s.

(4) Residential and Tourism 1930s–1950s, Cooperative Residential 1980s–1990s.

(5) Agricultural Plantation 1880s, Agricultural 1920s, Army Installation 1940s. Residential Development 1970s, Pub and Tourism 1950s–1990s, Radio Australia 1960s–1990s.

(6) Naval installation 1930s. Pastoral and Tourism 1950s. YMCA, Residential, and Tourism 1970s–1990s.

(7) Recreational Boating and Commercial Fishing 1860s–1990s.

of the earliest examples from the Darwin–Cox Peninsula region of the suspicion with which Euro-Australians regarded the Aborigine: "Speaking of natives appearing without spears, reminds me to mention for the information of future explorers, that their arms are always near at hand. They even trail them sometimes between their toes, a fact which travelers should ever bear in mind" (1846, 19).

The European perception that the Aboriginal personality was uninterpretable and, therefore, unstable in relation to the colonization process—varying wildly, at one moment pleasant and noble and at the next criminal and savage—persisted throughout the late 1800s and early 1900s as some Aborigines took to bushranging and banditry. "All the folk wisdom of the frontier was confirmed. Even apparently civilised blacks could not be trusted. Given half a chance they would revert to a savagery rendered more dangerous by a veneer of sophistication" (Reynolds 1987: 78).

The Foucauldian flavor of Stokes's observations (surveillances) is not surprising given that the Australian nation was founded as a penal colony in the 1780s and developed police tactics like other nations during the industrialization period (Hughes 1986; Foucault 1979). Yet, in the north of Australia during the surveying years, explorers were not the only ones watching for telltale signs of human activity and intentions. Whether or not Joan's specific ancestors saw the billowing sails of Baudin's, King's, and Stokes's ships, Aborigines living in the region were soon on the lookout for the white sails of merchant and exploratory vessels. If "indigenes" were always potentially deadly tricksters, then so also were Anglo settlers and merchants whose sails might, on one day, carry with them food and goods and, on another day, police or settlers with an intent to kill. Indeed, some Europeans reveled in their roles as tricksters, hiding guns under their breeches, lacing arsenic in gifts of flour. But while Aborigines, Europeans, and, later, Chinese had to watch, listen, and learn quickly of the disposition of the other, most historical documents portray only the colonists' drive to understand the personalities and practices of local Aborigines and Asians (Hamilton 1990).

The early commentary on the cultural and economic practices of Aboriginal groups from Darwin to the Daly River was soon supplemented and amended by the descriptions of settlers, government officials, and ethnologists who lived in or studied the area.[14] They would elaborate on the place and personalities of the Darwin, Cox Peninsula, and Daly River Aborigines.

Settler Days

Ten years after the founding of Palmerston (Port Darwin), the *Northern Territory Times and Gazette* (3 May 1879) reported, "Our native tribe, the Larrakeyahs ... invited their brethren from the Peninsular—the 'Waggites'—to meet them at their Congregational Union." It is one of the first mentions of an Aboriginal presence on the Cox Peninsula (then the Douglas Peninsula). Since this time Wagaitji (Wogites, Waggites, Wargites, Wagitj, etc.) have been reported to be living, hunting, and conducting ceremony on the Cox Peninsula and Bynoe Harbour–Port Patterson Islands. The earliest literature disputes on whose land they are living. These disputes occur, however, within accepted temporal and spatial frameworks for understanding Aboriginal action. In these early works, authors move indigenous groups across landscapes as they would pieces on a chessboard. The countryside's physical or mythic constitution is not transformed by time, practice, or the movement of peoples across territorial boundaries, as Belyuen people believe it to be (see chap. 3). It is assumed to be a fairly stable background on which Westerners can draw tribal borders—although there is significant disagreement about which Aboriginal group owned which land.

In a popular work, *The Australian Race,* Edward Curr quotes his brother Montague Curr that "Larrakia" land is "in the neighborhood of Palmerston" (Port Darwin) and that "Waggite" land lay "to the westward of Palmerston, across the harbour, and extend to the Daly River, and perhaps beyond" (1886, 249).[15] In the same volume, Paul Foelsche, the police inspector of Port Darwin from 1870 to 1880 and an amateur ethnologist, posited, "The country of the Larrakia extends along the coast from the mouth of the Adelaide River, west to Port Patterson, and stretches about twenty-five miles inland" (Foelsche 1886, 250).

T. A. Parkhouse, ethnographer and Port Darwin government official, took a stance between Curr and Foelsche regarding the traditional territories of the Wagaitj and Laragiya. In his writings and maps, the Cox Peninsula floats as a "neutral zone" between the Laragiya and the Wagaitj, whom he claims detest one another (1895, 638). Parkhouse does not comment on the quality of Laragiya society and culture. And other documents from this period only allude to the presence of Aboriginal groups or to their "dispersal."[16] For example, colonial surveyors in the Anson Bay area report seeing Aborigines but do not state who they were or what happened afterward (see Goyder 1971).

In 1914, Baldwin Spencer, a well-know ethnologist, naturalist, and collaborator with Gillen and later chief protectorate of the Aborigines in north Australia, published a map showing the "approximate localities of the various native tribes" (6). It shows the "Larakia" in the Darwin area, the "Worgait" on the Cox Peninsula, and the "Brinken" on the southern side of the Daly River. In *Wanderings in Wild Australia,* Spencer recalls the quality of the camps and the relevance of the countries of the "Larakia" and "Worgait."[17]

In the afternoon I went with Inspector Beckett to examine the native camps in Darwin. There are two of these, one on the top of the cliffs, called the King Camp, and one immediately below it on the shore. The first is really the camp of the Larakia, which is the native name of the original tribe inhabiting the Darwin district. . . . The second camp is mainly occupied by Worgait people whose country lies on the opposite side of the harbour. Nowadays the different tribes have become very mixed up and "civilised." (1928, 610)

Herbert Basedow, an ethnographer who also conducted research in the Darwin–Cox Peninsula–Daly River areas in the early 1900s, presents a somewhat different account of the "traditional" localities of the "Larrekiya," "Wogait," and "Berringen." First he distinguishes between coastal and inland Laragiya groups, the "Binnimiginda" and "Gumajerrumba," respectively. The Laragiya, in Basedow's account, have a large "domain" extending "southwards between the Howard River on the east and the Finniss on the west . . . and forming the southern boundary at about twenty-five miles inland" (1906, 1). Between the Wagaitj and the Laragiya are the "Sherait" or "paperbark natives" who disappear from the anthropological record a short time later.[18] Wagaitj country is said to extend "across the Daly River to about Cape Ford" (1906, 2). Finally, the Beringgen's "domain extends from Cape Ford to a point about 18 1/2 miles north of Point Pearce, known to them as *Allaitperra* [Allait creek] (1906, 2). Based on the word lists he provides, Basedow's Wagaitj are the Wadjigiyn (and perhaps the Kiyuk as well) and his Beringgen are the Emiyenggal and Menthayenggal. If Basedow was right about the location of language groups' paternal and maternal countries, they were, at the time, considerably more southward than now thought.[19]

Although Basedow divides the countryside into discrete language group "nations," he reestablishes the links between these countries by describing the ritual connections that existed among the Aboriginal groups. It is significant that he notes ritual connection, not joint economic activities, although he describes a mixed Wagaitj and Laragiya camp at Point Charles. One ritual link Basedow describes is the sending of bamboo message sticks between the Daly River and Cox Peninsula people as a means of "summons and invitations to initiation ceremonies" (1906, 46). Where the various groups received these messages is unclear; that is, few people discussed actual Aboriginal practices, focusing instead on formal models of landownership.[20] We do know that the Wagaitj living with Laragiya on the Cox Peninsula returned south for an initiation ceremony after receiving a summons.

After Spencer and Basedow, few ethnographic reports were published about the Wagaitj or Laragiya for a generation. In the 1930s, A. P. Elkin traveled to Delissaville (Belyuen) where he befriended the superintendent, Bill Harney. Elkin wrote in 1950 that most of the "Wagaitj" lived at the Delissaville settlement. He states, "This tribe formerly occupied the coastal country from the mouth of the Daly River north to Pt. Charles, Northern Territory of Australia" (1950, 67; Pt. Charles is located on the northern coast of the Cox Peninsula). He is one of the few ethnographers who subdivided the Wagaitj and Beringgen groups. In his field notes,[21] he distinguishes between the "Rakragerle" (presently known as the Kiyuk; *rak* is a Batjemal modifier for estate), whose country included the Peron Islands and the coastal region up to the Finniss River, the "Wadjigiyn," whose territory was the northern coast of the Daly River, the "Amiyangal," whose country was the southern coastal side of the Daly River, and the "Mendayangal" whose country was the Cape Ford region. Also living at Delissaville were the "Marriamu Wagaitj" or "Brinken" from the *Nadidi* area near Cape Dombey.

As Basedow, Elkin highlights both the sociocultural connections and cultural differences between Laragiya, Wagaitji, and Beringgen. For instance, he notes that Laragiya and Wagaitj performed mixed ceremonies, had a high incidence of intermarriage,[22] and had conception Dreamings (*maroi*, B) from the Cox Peninsula region. In an article about name sharing (*ngirrwat*), he interrelates the two groups further by stating that, while name sharing is a Wagaitj "custom," it establishes connections between a number of Laragiya, Wagaitj, and Beringgen families and countries. According to Elkin, other cultural systems mitigated against a complete merging of the various groups. The *durlg* of Wagaitj and Beringgen families were found in the southern Anson Bay region, while the *durlg* of Laragiya families were found on the Cox Peninsula and Darwin region. This remains the case today. Most Wagaitj and Beringgen continue to have separate paternal and maternal *durlg,* whose mythic focus for them is located south of the Cox Peninsula. Basedow's descriptions of Wagaitj returning south for ceremonies is significant in this light.

Today, most Beringgen, Wagaitj, and Laragiya Aborigines and non-Aboriginal ethnographers say that the Cox Peninsula is Laragiya country, that one should address the land in the Laragiya language if one can speak it, and that Laragiya ceremonies and mythic creatures organized the countryside in the Dreamtime Past. My own extensive research, as well as that conducted by Michael Walsh, Maria Brandl, and others, has consistently confirmed the same combination of precolonial "facts" that summarize and canonize certain parts of the disagreements, inconsistencies, and contradictions of the historical record: that the Laragiya are the "traditional Aboriginal owners" of the Cox Peninsula and Bynoe Harbour areas, that over the last hundred years the Laragiya and Kiyuk-Wadjigiyn have had a high incidence of intermarriage and ceremonial exchange, and that there have been far fewer marriages and ceremonial activities between the Laragiya and, as a group, the Southern Wagaitj (Emi and Mentha) and the Beringgen (Marriamu and Marritjaben). Perhaps ironically, it is the perspective of Paul Foelsche, the police inspector of the early Port Darwin settlement, that is most clearly represented in current portraits of Aboriginal tenure.

Present ethnography cannot and historical documents do not tell us how different Aboriginal groups used the Cox Peninsula, Port Patterson, and Anson Bay regions before colonists arrived, nor do they tell us how Aborigines dwelling in the area understood the economic potential and cultural meanings of their labor-action. Nor, finally, do they tell us when the Wagaitj and Beringgen moved to the Cox Peninsula. From surmises based on genealogical work, the Wadjigiyn-Kiyuk could have arrived one to two hundred years ago; that is, before or after Europeans arrived on the northern shores. Ancestors of the Emiyenggal and Menthayenggal families *now living* at Belyuen probably arrived fifty-odd years ago. A smaller set of Marriamu and Marritjaben siblings migrated to the Cox Peninsula with them. We have few good clues to indicate whether other Emi, Mentha, Marriamu, or Marritjaben families lived and traveled across the Finniss River and Cox Peninsula regions before this. The oldest person now living at Belyuen, a Marritjaben woman, was about ten years old in 1930, roughly fifty years after the *Northern Territory Times and Gazette* reported the Wagaitj and Laragiya holding joint corroborees. It is not surprising, then, that today Wagaitj and Beringgen living at Belyuen say the Laragiya and Belyuen groups have "always been mixed" (see App. 1, part B, 3–7, below).

The authentic and the corrupt

Writers not only placed local Aboriginal groups in a geographical landscape, they also placed them in a comparative social landscale. In the Top End of the Northern Territory of Australia, authors usually described the Laragiya as suffering the worse effects of European colonization. This might not have been the case if the Port Essington settlement, established north of Darwin on the Cobourg Peninsula in 1824, had not been abandoned just less than five years after its founding (Spillett 1972). But traders did not grace the port of Essington, and so colonists moved the epicenter of their settlement to the middle of what is now considered to be Laragiya territory. By 1881, Foelsche was already noting the dramatic effects of white incursion on the Laragiya. He writes that their knowledge, customs, and society were already "dying out" (1881–82, 6). As evidence, he reports instances of smallpox, influenza, syphilis, and venereal disease among Laragiya families. Corporeal disease synedochically evokes cultural decay. Local newspapers also represented Laragiya social life as becoming increasingly degenerate, often mocking the Aborigines' speech and behavior in the local courts.[23]

Ethnologists and many settlers regretted the loss and supposed corruption of Aboriginal society during the first years of northern development. Many attempted to record and to understand what local and regional Aborigines did and how they conceptualized their world before the corrupting process of civilization was complete or, in a more gross formulation, before there were no Aborigines left to observe. Researchers did not, however, record everything. Research instead focused on material and social practices thought to be more traditional and so more likely to be disturbed by contact with Anglo and Asian culture.

Most researchers had dual roles. As government officials they provided goods to Aborigines and advised government economic plenary councils on Aboriginal welfare, often emphasizing the value of Aboriginal labor in an attempt to garner some government protection and services for their wards.[24] The information Aborigines provided was also valuable to the emerging field of anthropology, which, reciprocally, saw the potential of administrators for the collection of cultural knowledge and artifacts. In 1930, the British Association for the Advancement of Science passed a resolution "directing attention to Australian aborigines as being among the most valuable living people for the scientific study of the early history of mankind and urging that the Commonwealth Government should provide for the proper anthropological training of officials entrusted with the administration of aboriginal affairs" (*NTT&G*, 30 December 1930). This resolution was published in the Darwin daily newspaper and provided its readers with an academic counterdiscourse to earlier settlers' views that there was little or nothing of economic or cultural value in Aboriginal society.

The exchange of Aboriginal knowledge for Western goods and protection and the effect of that exchange on the "purity" of the information thus obtained—the resultant tensions between ethnological practice and its goals—was addressed directly and indirectly. Many early researchers observed that Aboriginal cultural knowledge and material had been "up for sale" in the Northern Territory since the turn of the century. Some writers highlighted the contradictions of ethnological work in the Darwin region: even as the exotic Aboriginal subject was being recorded for Western readers, he or she was participating in European trade. To record was to engage in a cultural and economic exchange that undermined the recording project. "Close by, a Larrakeyah man, a fine specimen of humanity, anatomically, is attending to some spears. He wears nothing but a hair belt and an apron made of twine. He is quite willing to be photographed for the usual bribe—tobacco" (W. R. Smith 1924, 137).

Herbert Basedow, though not directly commenting on the contradictory roles of government dispensary and independent ethnographer, recorded similar cultural and economic entanglements. He wrote that around 1905 a number of "Wogaits" followed him from their camp at Charles Lighthouse to the Daly River and "arranged all sorts of festivities in our honor in return for our *benevolence*" (Basedow 1935, 38; my emphasis). One of the "festivities" Wagaitj men showed Basedow was a women's ceremony considered so dangerous as to warrant revenge slayings if the secret-sacred element of it were witnessed or revealed. Perhaps someone did die. We have no way of knowing. But as elsewhere in the colonial world, male anthropologists' recording of Australia secret-sacred rituals tied into existing gender and economic relations (Hercus 1989). A precolonial aspect of Aboriginal ceremony may have been a competitive and interdependent relationship between men and women.[25] Colonial ethnologists introduced a new dimension: the uneven access that Aborigines and non-Aborigines had to goods and supplies. Aboriginal men and their knowledge mediated between male goods-laden Anglo officials and the Aboriginal group who desired them.[26]

Because of these political-economic entanglements, whether or not they explicitly acknowledged it, all Western observers faced a nagging problem: How could they know when they were observing a precontact Aboriginal practice and when they were observing cultural or material objects produced for exchange? Distinguishing between a "pristine" and "contacted" (understood as corrupted) native was an exasperating task.[27] Competing philosophical positions surfaced in the early northern newsprint as well as in academic discussions about what people would see if they were looking at a genuine native. Stanner wrote of the Daly River area that "in places where no European had ever set foot, or was to do so for many years, a demand had grown up for iron goods, tobacco, tea, sugar, and clothes. There was also a hankering for a sight of such marvels as houses, machines, vehicles, firearms, and bells, one of the most alluring things of all" (1979, 81).

One of the pressing local debates about Aboriginal society was whether Aborigines had, by nature, a genial disposition and were forced to act atrociously only in response to acts of violence, or whether missionaries and others confused a naturally savage disposition with the civilizing effects of a Christian colonization (see, e.g., Attwood 1989; Reynolds 1982; Gribble 1932). Because word of the violent and goods-laden white man spread more rapidly than did the whites themselves, an untouched Aborigine was hard to locate; the debate of who such a person would be continued.

The clearest sign of an Aborigine's traditional outlook was his or her ability to perform a ceremony or to recite a mythic text, although government officials and ethnographers believed that "at any moment" Aborigines would lose this ability. There was, on one hand, a real immediacy to the quest of recording the supposedly timeless myths and ceremonies of northwest Aborigines. The attacks of some settlers on north Australian groups did imperil people and their knowledge. However, the anxiety to collect Aboriginal mythic texts is itself more timeless than the society itself—for no matter in what year the researcher stands, the stance of recording the past is an anxious one. In the Western understanding of oral societies, the past is always being lost and falling into confusion; the present ɿ always falling away to the stonelike silence of the unrecoverable past (Williams 1973; Roseberry and O'Brien 1991). More important, an anthropology focused on acquisition and display as a sign of cultural purchase (see Clifford 1988, 215–52, "On Collecting Art and Culture") frames its lack as evidence of cultural disintegration. As an aside, in contemporary Australia, the struggle is to shift these meanings. Aborigines are reacquiring the power to hide knowledge and artifact, proof of their increasing cultural and political power (Gelder 1991).

Paul Foelsche was a key interpreter for the European settlers of the status of local Aboriginal groups' traditional outlook. Although he is noted as having been on the accommodating side of the law's attitude toward Aborigines, Foelsche's complex position is reflected in how he balanced his roles as a student of Aboriginal practices, a member of the small European community, and the dispenser of European justice against the very Aborigines he studied.[28] Foelsche describes the anxiety he felt searching for Laragiya mythic texts.

> The subject of conversation was *the origin of their race*. . . . *I felt anxious* to obtain what information I could from the Port Darwin native on the same subject, and on questioning him he stated that he knew very little about it, but that "Lirrawah," of the Southport branch of the Larrakeah tribe, could give me the whole history. . . . This native is a *doctor,* and held in great esteem by the whole tribe as a learned man, who, as they term it, "knows plenty all about." (Foelsche 1881–82, 15; my emphasis)

When Foelsche asked his questions to Lirrawah, he was told:

> "Nangánburrah," who lives in the ground, is designated "all same Government." He can read and write, and when blackfellows growl write it down in a book. When blackfellows die they go down into the ground to "Nangánburrah," and if they have been good, which is ascertained by referring to the book, "Nangánburrah" gives them a letter to give to "Mangárarrah," with whom they then live among the stars. If they have been bad and growled they are sent to a place deep down in the ground called "Ohmar," where there is plenty of fire; and long way under this place is a large water called "Búrcoot," where one blackfellow named "Mádjuit Mádjuit" sits down. He regulates the tides according to the changes of the moon. He,

like "Mangárarrah" and "Nangánburrah," never dies. (Foelsche 1881–82, 16–17)

What a man in Foelsche's position received and presented as traditional Aboriginal viewpoints would have had to negotiate his social roles and others' expectations. Aboriginal informants would have known Foelsche as the police inspector.[29] Foelsche's readers would have known his other social positions in the European community as well. All of which is to say that the process of communication across social planes itself creates cultural narratives of the Other that seem, on any one side, strange and incoherent, a synergistic mix of Aboriginal and Christian narratives of life and death. But the incoherences of text and context that result when the "orientation" of cultural messages go awry were evaluated in emerging power hierarchies between Europeans and Aborigines. European writers and government officials were increasingly in the position to evaluate Aboriginal cultural coherence and to write social legislation based on their assessment.

Soon after Foelsche's work, most Laragiya failed to pass the test of coherent ritual performance. Most reports about the Laragiya, as reports about and descriptions of other city-dwelling Aborigines, would refer to this failure as evidence of the "engulfing" nature of the colonization process.[30] By the 1910s Spencer considers the Laragiya tribe "which once inhabited the country round about Darwin . . . much too decadent to retain anything more than mere vestiges of its old customs" (1914, 152). In *Wanderings,* he describes the supposed breakdown of Laragiya attachment to their traditional country. This cultural disintegration is provided as a reason why Laragiya can be moved away from their traditional camps. Referring to, among others, the Laragiya, he writes,

> *Genuine* wild natives would be miserable away from their own country, but in the case of a heterogeneous crowd, such as is now gathered together in Darwin, there was no need to pay heed to this aspect of the matter. They have all long since got beyond any traditional feeling and will only object to being removed from their old quarters because it will interfere with their freedom to do exactly what they like in regard to intercourse with Chinese, Malays and a certain class of Europeans. (Spencer 1928, 612; my emphasis)

The negative evaluation of Laragiya social heterogeneity was extended to the mixed nature of their ritual activity. Rather than seeing heterogeneity and mixture as methods of cultural continuity through succession (Stanton 1983; Sutton 1980), it was viewed as evidence of cultural disintegration. In his textual juxtapositions of various Aboriginal ritual and economic practices, Spencer creates a cultural geography of the Darwin–Daly River coast in which Aboriginal cultural identity and practices become more coherent as one moves down the coast away from Darwin. Laragiya culture and society are in shambles, Wagaitj less so, and Beringgen even less so. For example, Spencer observed segments of Laragiya and Wagaitj male initiation, noting for the reader the type of initiation, the age of the initiate, and the ritual roles of various male and female kin. In Wagaitj initiations, the young initiate is seized and taken through the bush to the "country of another tribe, such as the Larakia, amongst whom they will spend two or three months" (1914, 157). During this time, the young man is taken to a series of "Larakia camps," including sites in Darwin *and* on the Cox Peninsula, which Spencer has earlier described as Wagaitj country. He finally describes a circumcision rite at one site, emphasizing the joint participation of Laragiya and Wagaitj. While the "mixed" Laragiya ceremonies,[31] Spencer tells us, are a result of colonial dislocation and evidence of ceremonial corruption, the mixed nature of Wagaitj ceremonies are described as relatively traditional and socially complex. In 1906, Basedow also reported that Wagaitj and Laragiya had "mixed" male ceremonies, but unlike Spencer he does not describe this as a corruption of former practices.[32]

This portrait of Laragiya cultural incoherence continues to this day. And, as did previous portraits, newer ones are used to justify dispossession of land where Laragiya live or hope to live. In the Aboriginal Land Rights (NT) Act, 1976, land claimants must be a local descent *group* with a coherent set of traditions, beliefs, and practices. In the legal and political climate of Australia, if the Laragiya are an incoherent and "dead" remnant of a previously strong culture, then, "unfortunately," no rights devolve to them. This is the position intimated in the attorney-general for the Northern Territory's submission to the land commissioner reviewing the Kenbi Land Claim.

> The geographical barrier of Darwin Harbour has insulated the Wadjigiyn/Kiyuk against some of the more destructive consequences of white settlement. Concomitant with this relative insulation is relatively little intermarriage with non-Aboriginal people. While they have resided in the claim area for 100 years, their original lifestyle has not been disrupted nearly so much as the Larrakia. (Attorney General for the Northern Territory, 1990, 32)

This general theme was developed much earlier. A south Australian Parliamentary report noted of an excursion to the Adelaide River, "We had four blackfellows on board—Wilwongas, whose *habitat* is on the banks of the Adelaide. They are intellectually far in advance of the wretched Larrakeeyahs, but it is after all as the intelligence of a mule to that of a donkey" (Sowden 1882, 110). Land Commissioner Mr. Justice Olney recently rejected the Laragiya's traditional land claim to the Cox Peninsula, an action which suggests his partial acceptance of these positions. He writes, "The impact of European and Asian migration had a devastating effect upon the Larrakia, the worst effects of which were compounded by factors such as the Second World War and the development of Darwin as a modern, urban area. In the result, the Larrakia all but disappeared as a *readily identifiable and coherent group of people*" (Olney 1991, iii; my emphasis).

In their assessments, both the attorney general and the land commissioner utilize older and available, if transformed, "tribal types,"—in this case, oppositions between the friendly Laragiya and the savage Wagaitj.[33] Below I examine how colonial representations, which deemed certain Aboriginal groups as having savage dispositions, had a devastating effect that has influenced where those groups are found and what they are doing today. Important to the creation of an Aboriginal group's identity were travel journals and newspaper reports. Journal writers assumed, as did many ethnologists of the time, that the country an Aboriginal group owned was the place where it would be encountered. There were violent implications of this belief.

Savages and native sons

Paul Carter has recently proposed that "in the place of the fictional characters of the novelist, the explorer-writer introduced the character of the country" (1987, 73). For settlers, the character of the country included the character of local Aborigines, who were part of the natural flora and fauna. Those intending to settle in a new part of the country usually read the accounts—in journals or regional newspapers—of travelers who had been there before. In contrast to ethnologists, most settlers wanted to know what Aborigines were likely to do when contacted, not what they had done before the arrival of Europeans. Knowing the character of the country included knowing the character of its indigenous people who might, more or less violently, oppose white pastoralists' and miners' appropriation of their lands. The journals themselves provide narrative traces of their intended use ("for the information of future explorers" and "[so that] anyone intending to travel or settle in this locality may know what to expect and be prepared").

Since Stokes first introduced a difference between the Port Darwin natives who "presented themselves without spears" and the southern "tribes" who crawled "along the ground" with a mind to attack his ship, this difference in temperament has become an established theme of writings by Northern Territory journalists, settlers, and explorers. *The Northern Territory Times and Gazette* featured the antics of "our natives" (the Laragiya) throughout the 1870s and 1880s. While articles were by no means unwaveringly sympathetic, they paternalistically portray the Laragiya as the poor victim of more hostile, aggressive groups such as the Wagaitj and Wulna.³⁴

> The recent disturbances amongst the blacks, and the evident discomfort the Larrakeeyah tribe was put to, leads me to enquire whether the Woolners should be allowed to molest them, and why they should not be protected as *in the early days of the settlement*, which protection the Larrakeeyahs *now naturally look for* when other tribes make a raid on their otherwise peaceable existence. (*NTT&G*, 22 May 1875; my emphasis)

Harriet (Mrs. Dominick D.) Daly, the daughter of the second government resident, Bloomfield Douglas, arrived in Palmerston in 1870, and eventually married the surveyor Dan Daly.³⁵ She states that the Laragiya were unusually friendly; "though they were inclined to pilfer and steal where they could," the only "serious mischief they did" was to spear "one of the horses that was turned out near Fannie Bay" (quoted in Daly 1887, 72–73).

On the contrary, the Wagaitj very quickly obtained a reputation for being deceptive and brutal "bush blacks" who "haunted" the Daly River. The same Parliamentary party that traveled to the Adelaide River ominously noted of Aboriginal people working on a Daly River plantation, "The blackfellows give very little trouble now. They did at first—they stole all the stores, but they were punished for it. They have not forgotten the lesson taught them" (Sowden 1882, 107). Local Port Darwin news reporters also traveled frequently to the Cox Peninsula and Daly River and recorded northern perceptions of the Daly River Aborigines: "Very few natives were met with, and those seen showed altogether a friendly disposition; we are glad to learn this, for previously all the tales we have heard of them would lead one to believe them a very bloodthirsty lot. All that were seen belonged to the Wargite tribe (in "Trip to the Daly," *NTT&G*, 17 May 1879).

An extract of Gilbert McMinn's travel journal of November 1877 published in the *Northern Territory Times and Gazette* reports an incident that may have paved the way for future violence between Aborigines and non-Aborigines in the Anson Bay area.

> We are on a very large lagoon, about 20 miles west of the Daly River, which appears to be the head quarters of a large number of natives.... About eleven o'clock in the evening, while engaged in taking an observation, the man on watch gave the alarm of natives, they having succeeded in the darkness of the night in reaching to within twenty feet of the camp: but on the alarm being given and a shot fired at them they dropped what weapons they had and made for the lagoon, 100 yards distant, jumping in and swimming to the other side. After this when we discovered where they were

> hiding we fired a few rifle shots which kept them quiet for the remainder of the night. . . . Two days later at about ten o'clock in the morning a large number of natives were discovered following the party evincing that they had anything but friendly intentions towards us, and not wishing to have any bother with them, they were quietly given to understand that we did not wish them to follow us. This, however, they paid no attention to, for in about half an hour they appeared in increased numbers, and owing to their conduct it became absolutely necessary to rid ourselves of them; this was accomplished after some difficulty. All the natives I saw about here were fine stalwart fellows, who showed evidence of being well nourished. *I write this fully regarding the natives so that anyone intending to travel or settle in this locality may know what to expect and be prepared.*[36]

From McMinn's directions, I assume he was in Menthayenggal country at Nganthawudi, an important estate of many Mentha families now living at Belyuen. To the south it joins Tjungarak, another Mentha estate, and to the north Mabaluk, an important Emi estate. As did Stokes, so McMinn describes southern Daly River Wagaitj as a treacherous lot.

Another incident in the Daly River further exaggerated settlers' view of the brutality of the Wagaitj. On 3 September 1884, three miners, Noltenius, Landors, and Houschildt, were killed near the Daly River. Harriet Daly wrote the following of the "Daly River outrage" in her book *Digging, Squatting, and Pioneering Life in the Northern Territory of South Australia*.

> It is difficult for men who have worked shoulder to shoulder in mines and on cattle stations in a new country, to stand with any degree of patience seeing their friends cut down before their eyes by a cowardly gang of natives; and if more of the "Woggites," the tribe who haunt the Daly River, lost their lives than the few who actually murdered the men, it would be nothing to wonder at. These aboriginals were of the finest physical development of Australian natives, many of them being over six feet in height. The police were sent off at once, and every endeavor was made on the part of the Government to bring the murderers to justice, but a civilised penal code does not meet the necessities of a case like this. Imagine a policeman in uniform, with a warrant in his pocket duly signed and sealed by a magistrate, riding through miles and miles of uninhabited country, trying to find a certain native whose appearance is unknown to him, who may possibly have throw the fatal spear unperceived by his victim, and unobserved by any witness. (1887, 261)

Four weeks later, in light of the "murders" of the miners on the Daly River, the *Northern Territory Times and Gazette* reflected on the rightfulness of Queenslanders' "hav[ing] been roundly abused for the manner in which their aborigines have been *dispersed*" and concludes that "some of the right class men are now on the tracks of the Daly River natives, but we do not expect to hear many particulars of their chase; the less the better, in such cases as the present, it is far more sensible to avoid complications by the exercise of a judicious reticence" (*NTT&G*, 4 October 1884). The "policeman in uniform" was George Montagu, who led an "investigatory" party to the area and is thought to have killed scores of Aborigines without regard to their involvement in the deaths.[37] Montague was exonerated of "undue severity," but many southern newspapers regarded the official inquiry as a judicial cover-up. One of the few insights we have to what went on at the Daly is a chilling comment Montague made about the usefulness of the repeating rifle for his "investigation."

> What the other parties have done I do not know, but I believe the natives have received such a lesson this time as will exercise a salutary effect over *the survivors* in the time to come. One result of this expedition has been to convince me of the superiority of the Martini-Henry rifle, both for accuracy of aim and quickness of action. (*NTT&G*, 26 December 1885; my emphasis. See also *NTT&G* 11 July 1885)[38]

One must remember that most of the colonial world was experimenting with methods of controlling indigenous populations and, in the process, was discussing how notions of civil society and barbaric behavior could be reconciled in colonial settings. Were men like Montague more barbaric in their actions than Aborigines were portrayed to be? Southern Australian papers said so. But northern writers claimed that in remote areas civilized notions such as dispassionate and discriminate justice had to be modified if economic development was to commence: "sickly sentiment and Exeter Hall humanitarianism should be valued at their true worth; our European settlers must be allowed to till the soil and extract the wealth from the land which they have made their home, free from the murdering raids of these savages" (*NTT&G* 4 October 1884). All settlers, moreover, were well acquainted with what Robert Hughes (1986) describes as the "sadistic excesses" of the southern penal system. Some writers stressed the isolation of the Northern Territory and the unsettled quality of the landscape as the reason that "normal" justice could not always occur. Other writers justified local action by locating it within the global political economy; colonial European governments, under siege worldwide, were using similar tactics to control indigenous populations.[39] In the northern papers local incidents of slaughter and revenge were reported alongside other articles about Maori trouble in New Zealand, Northern American Indian Wars, and African insurrections on the "Dark Continent."

Whatever their reasonings, settler attitudes and actions toward Aborigines, often based on journals and news reports, established patterns between colonizers and colonized that set in motion years of violent or friendly, but always persistent, land appropriation. We do not know if the Wagaitj had always used the Cox Peninsula as a hunting and ceremonial ground, but we do know that because of the violence of this period and the settlers' belief that Wagaitj could be found near Anson Bay, the area that was all but depopulated by the mid-1900s. This is a large part of the reason that in 1930 Elkin found most of the Wagaitj and coastal Beringgen living at Delissaville. Much earlier, a south Australian paper referred to the Wagaitj and Laragiya at the Charles Point Lighthouse. The *Weekly News* reported as early as 1906 that the European lighthouse keeper "who had been formally adopted a member of the Wogite tribe took Larrakia with him on a trip to the Daly River the Wogite blacks being all away."[40] Of course, violence in the Daly River was not the only reason Wagaitj and Beringgen are now found on the Cox Peninsula. Certainly the proximity to Darwin goods and services was an important motivations for staying in an area through which they might have always seasonally traveled.

Although colonial reports emphasized the fixity of an Aboriginal group's native country (even as their own notes showed that Aboriginal groups and countries were interconnected by ceremony and social and economic practices), most regional Laragiya, Wagaitj, and Beringgen families were moving in and out of the Anglo economy and up and down the coastal region. And while this discussion has emphasized the early colonial representations of the traditional aspect of Darwin–Coastal Daly River Aboriginal groups, I now turn to these groups' economic interaction with Europeans, concentrating on the years 1930–50. In general terms, the travels of the Beringgen-Wagaitj up and down the Cox Peninsula to the Daly River coast accomplished two things: groups established long-standing cultural and economic ties to the Cox Peninsula while maintaining similar ties to southern countries and they gained information about Euro-Australian "customs." An examination of the historical economic practices of Aborigines now living on the Cox Peninsula provides a framework for later discussions of how Belyuen Aborigines assess their historical action and cultural identity.

"SWEET POTATO . . . HN EVERYTHING"

Making Aboriginal Farmers

Today Belyuen women and men describe both a long-standing, intimate, and culturally appropriate connection to the Cox Peninsula and a long-standing participation in Anglo economic practices such as unpaid agricultural work and paid service-industrial labor.[41] Belyuen women interpret and present their historical involvement in the Anglo economy as a clever manipulation of white people and a deft use and evasion of white resources and controls. Oral histories emphasize both Aborigines' involvement in and disengagement from white economic activity; they describe their ancestors and contemporary relatives continually moving across a mythically informed colonial landscape. But if history is read from the Euro-Australians' regulations and records, Aboriginal history is one of increasing curtailment and control. Here I examine how Euro-Australian government and private enterprise attempted to control the social and economic activities and products of Laragiya, Wagaitj, and Beringgen, from 1870 to 1945. Most governmental policies were oriented toward containing the movement of these "former foragers" by turning them into wage laborers or agriculturalists. Indeed, Aborigines were supposed to be transformed by their entrance into civil society.[42] By teaching them the art of agriculture, European colonists thought European culture would sprout forth from them. The political-economic theory of the day had predicted that "the mark of successful settlement was the transformation of natural landscapes [and indigenous peoples] into simulacra of those of Europe" (Hamilton 1984, 366).

The garden confines of colonial plantations on the Cox Peninsula, including the De Lissa sugarcane plantation at the present site of the Belyuen community, are examples of the two "arms" of colonial and postcolonial land appropriation. In the outer reaches of colonial Australia, European administrators attempted to sever Aboriginal groups' ties to their country by containing them on settlements, "out of harm's way." Although settlement is often represented as providing protection to those settled, "harm's way" is both the extended arm of capitalist development, wherein entrepreneurial explorers open up trading routes by massacre and extortion, and, schizophrenically, the illusory arm that colonial administrators project in order to present something from which they can protect their indigenous "subjects."[43] For instance, in 1916 John Gilruth, professor of veterinarian science and administrator of the Northern Territory, declared a large swath of land in and around the Port Patterson and Port Darwin region to be "prohibited" to Aborigines.[44] He justified this action based upon the need to protect Aborigines from the corruptive influence of town life and the developmental needs of settlers, never elaborating that the former was caused by the latter. Likewise, the geography of productive gardens—fenced in, even rows of agricultural produce—symbolically represented what European administrators wished to do with Aborigines: transform their economy, instill in them a capitalist work ethic, and restrict their movements. The gardens failed to produce either commodities or wage laborers. Indeed, even the countryside, "opened" by the supposed confinement of Aborigines onto the Delissaville settlement, failed to produce any measurable value and instead exemplified European economic failure in the region.[45]

Although people's oral narratives are about the economic conditions they experienced between the 1930s and the 1960s, they reflect a much longer history of European and Aboriginal economic interdependence. Aborigines in the Daly River and Cox Peninsula regions engaged in three distinct forms of labor. Women dug and tended gardens, worked as domestics, and, later during the war, trained as nurses' aides. Men worked in gardens, built roads and houses, and were scouts during World War II. All groups continued to hunt, fish, and collect foods and materials, although this activity is not well recorded. Aboriginal hunting practices are described either in very general, reified, and often romantic terms or as asides in administrative records—such as how Aborigines were kept from "going bush" during enforced labor periods or how they were compelled to "go bush" after a season of work.[46]

While we know that Euro-Australian-run gardens, plantations, and pastoral projects were started on the Cox Peninsula and near the Bynoe Harbour very soon after the founding of Palmerston (Port Darwin)—the "Douglas Peninsula" (now the Cox Peninsula) itself was renamed in honor of Dillen Cox, who had a large plantation there in the 1870s—the use of Aboriginal labor on these projects is hard to piece together. In the 1800s, few records were kept. Even in the early 1900s, records are scant, and Aboriginal men's and women's names and country affiliations are variously spelled and interpreted. Medical records kept for Aborigines living at Talc Head and Charles Point record several seemingly contradictory linguistic and totemic affiliations for the same individuals. Therefore, while the presence of Laragiya, Wagaitj, and Beringgen Aborigines on the Cox Peninsula during the early colonial period is rather easy to demonstrate in the primary literature, documenting their use as a labor force on local plantations is more difficult. There is some evidence. After reporting a trip to the Douglas Peninsula, a *Northern Territory Times and Gazette* reporter writes of Clopenburg and Erickson's plantation at West Point:

> About three years ago these enterprising pioneers, with little more than two pairs of willing hands and a few spades, axes, and picks, &c., entered upon the arduous task of making a bit of a clearance near the beach for the purpose of rearing pigs and poultry . . . Whatever was made outside went into the "clearance and plantation fund," and so happily has the plan been carried out that at this day these two working men have, without any hired

labour beyond the assistance of a few natives, cleared and fenced in 105 out of their section of 320 acres. (15 April 1882)

Who were these "few" Aborigines; what group were they from? Reporters for the *Northern Territory Times and Gazette* traveled to and from the Cox Peninsula, Bynoe Harbour, and Port Patterson Islands reporting the progress of economic projects in the area, but rarely do the Aborigines they casually mention have any social identity beyond "native." Clopenburg and Erickson were not the only ones who used Aboriginal labor in the early settlement of the Cox Peninsula. We know, for instance, that Aboriginal women ("lubras") were working on Harris and Head's plantation at Kunggul Beach, also on the northeast coast of the Cox Peninsula, but we do not know what group they were from. The newspaper reports of Harris and Head's plantation that

> Between 40 and 50 acres of the jungle have been cleared, and the stumps remaining in the ground having well rotted they expect to be able to put in the plough next year. The soil has almost the same characteristics, except that it does not carry to such a depth before joining the bed-rock, as that at West Point Plantation. I may mention here a peculiarity which may be interesting to geologists and ethnologists. A thin white chalky-kind of layer, not more than a third of an inch in thickness runs between the soil and the bed-rock, and this the lubras eat in large quantities, and evidently relish.[47]

Sometimes an Aboriginal presence at a site appears and disappears like a phantom depending on what paper one is reading. A few months before the article on Clopenburg and Erickson's plantation appeared, the same newspaper reported: "On Wednesday morning Mr. Peter Erickson took over to the Peninsula about fifty natives, who, we hear, are to work on his plantation near West Point" (*NTT&G,* 9 January 1882). Perhaps Erickson brought Darwin-dwelling Laragiya to the peninsula, but he might have brought other groups as well. De Lissa used a "gang of natives" from the East Alligator River to work on his sugar plantation, and he banned any contact between them and the "tribes round Palmerston."[48]

While agricultural labor was supposed to move Aborigines from the Stone Age to a modern political economy, no such transformation occurred. Aborigines refused to break their backs trying to plant the outback soil and Euro-Australians were forced to come to uneasy terms with Aborigines' dislike of the drudgery of menial wage work. If Aborigines were supposed to be transformed by the civilizing effects of an Anglo presence, they were also expected to die off. But although there was a very high death rate among them, Aboriginal people remained a presence in towns, failing to disappear into the background. Northern Aborigines' failure to die off and their failure to signify the mark of civilization in which raw materials are transformed into useful, profitable objects presented government officials with the problem of how to manage the population. By the late 1930s, most legislation about Aborigines was characterized by containment.

As Darwin emerged from a rustic settlement into a city-town, government policy on Aborigines was oriented around the containment of their movement and practice, and Aborigines became like store supplies, to be listed, counted, moved to places of need, or stored until further required. For example, laws were passed that were supposed to keep Darwin Aborigines on the Bagot and Kahlin reserves unless otherwise employed.

G.N. 140/39
EMPLOYMENT OF ABORIGINALS WITHIN THE TOWN AREA OF DARWIN

The attention of employers of aboriginals is directed to Regulation 33 under the Aboriginals Ordinance 1918–1937 which enacts:

(1) An employer, who employs any aboriginal within the town district of Darwin Centre shall not, without the written authority of a Protector, suffer or permit that aboriginal to be or remain upon any premises which are owned, occupied, inhabited, used or controlled by that employer and which are situated within the town district of Darwin Centre at any time between the hours of seven o'clock in the evening of any day and six o'clock in the morning of any day following.

(2) If any employer referred to in the last proceeding sub-regulation contravenes the provisions of that sub-regulation, any licence to employ aboriginals held by him may be canceled by any Protector.

Employers who do not possess the required authority are requested to instruct their aboriginal employees to return to the Bagot Compound every evening.

CE COOK

Chief Protector of Aboriginals
(*Northern Standard*, 31 March 1939)

Most Laragiya families were "barracked" in these reserves, where their indigenous language, ceremonies, and economy were harshly discouraged (Bartells 1988a). C. E. Cook was chief protector and medical officer of Aborigines in the Northern Territory from 1927 to 1939 when Aborigines were issued steel-disk name tags (called dog tags by Aborigines and Europeans alike), were hired out as a cheap domestic labor force, and had their films censored (see Brandl et al. 1979, 215).[49] "They were not to see any film which tended to lower their respect for the white man; an odd provision indeed, when white men were daily trying to prostitute their women" (Powell 1988, 185).

Like older ones, new laws that barred Aborigines from the center of Palmerston-Darwin were often justified on the need to protect white moral sensibilities. Earlier letters and reports in the *Northern Territory Times and Gazette* and the *Northern Standard* argued for a separation of the two groups for the good of both. Moral outrage was a sensibility in great supply.

> About eleven o'clock, on Tuesday night, a charge of dynamite was thrown over the cliff into the black's camp. We cannot bring ourselves to believe we have any among us who would be so diabolically inclined as to wantonly injure them, but some care should be taken by thoughtless youths for the future, or they may bring themselves into trouble. (*NTT&G*, 9 November 1878)

> Sir—With others of your readers I was pleased to read your animadversionary [*sic*] remarks upon the above subject [the "Black Nuisance"], in your last issue but one; and I for one think that some steps should at once be adopted to abate if not remove the same. Several of the principal streets of Palmerston are periodically infested by gangs of unkempt, jabbering niggers—loathsome in aspect, scab-ridden in body—and caricaturing [*sic*] the decencies of civilized citizens by an ostentatieus [*sic*] display of semicinctures almost as repulsive as nudity itself. For reasons of decency and morality such exhibitions should, I think, be restricted. (*NTT&G*, 25 December 1880)

Earlier attempts to control Aboriginal movement were intensified in the mid-1930s, with officials creating regional camps for local Aboriginal groups. While Laragiya and other Darwin-dwelling Aborigines were barracked inland behind Port Darwin, the old Delissaville camp—which had been used in the years after De Lissa's sugarcane failure as a small garden interest and as a general store—was chosen as the site where the "Wargite" would be settled. This geography of settlement reflected current views of where various groups customarily resided.

During daily expeditions and midnight raids, Aborigines living throughout the Cox Peninsula and Bynoe Harbour areas were removed by force from the beaches and jungles and interned in the settlement. Or so Bill Harney wrote. Harney is well known throughout Australia as a bush poet and a radio personality; with A. P. Elkin's encouragement he became the author of a dozen books on Aboriginal life in the Northern Territory.[50] Harney presents a picture of the settlement of the Aboriginal "Wargites" on the Cox Peninsula in terms that reflect his own bush prowess and that position Aborigines within a naturalized social domain and in a racialized natural domain.[51] "We headed the nose of the *Pirate* towards a group of natives on Foster's Beach, and as we neared I could detect a restlessness in them similar to that of a flock of magpie-geese when the hunter creeps upon them, and the numbers on the shore became less and less" (Harney 1961, 52).

Harney continues his pragmatics of bush morality by describing how he and Jack Murray, the future superintendent of Delissaville, tried to sneak up on the "unseen horde of Wargite in the green jungle," but only succeeded in finding one "half-blind woman."

> Realising that this method of approach was useless, I returned to the beach and stacked all their rags and personal gear into a large heap. I spotted a large pet pig they kept, and pointing to this and the heap of rags, I delivered my ultimatum. They must come down to the beach and hear my story, otherwise I would burn the rags and kill the pig. This was final.
>
> After this oration I dressed; then boiling the billy we had a cup of tea and awaited results.
>
> My idea of burning the rags and killing the pig was really a bluff, but I knew that aborigines have a great horror of having any of their clothes burnt—for such a thing would bring on a sickness and cause them to die—and, having a real affection for pets, they cannot suffer them to be killed. I was simply using a law of the tribal elders—magic versus force! (Harney 1961, 54)

Older women and men now living at Belyuen and quoted throughout this book were no more than eight years old when Bill Harney and Jack Murray "rounded up the Wargite." While to the reader the following list might seem a bewildering array of personal and place names, its diversity demonstrates the broad history of people living at the Belyuen community today. Mary Eladi was living at a northeast coastal site which is presently the private non-Aboriginal Mandorah Pub and Hotel. With her were her parents, her sister, her half-sister, and other Emi, Mentha, Wadjigiyn, and Kiyuk families. Her Emi kin included Emily Nela, Nela's parents, brothers, and paternal uncles—one of whom was named after a nearby site where he was initiated. Jean Ziya was a small child living in the Doctor's Gully Aboriginal camp at Darwin close to where Spencer had removed the "heterogeneous mix" of Laragiya and Wagaitj and where residential and commercial buildings now stand. Grace Ziyesta's parents took her to and from Cox Peninsula sites on the northwest and east coasts where they maintained fish traps for subsistence and trade. Joan Ela was born in Katherine at the "Donkey Camp" during World War II. Catherine Burga, now in her seventies, was living near the Finniss River with her husband and sister-in-law. When one of her party was involved in the murder of a "cheeky" white miner, they fled south to the Daly River and then north to Darwin. Catherine Burga avoided Bill Harney's net (as did a group of Emi, Mentha, and Laragiya who remained at Euro-Australian stations in the Talc Head and Charles Point regions) because private Euro-Australian pastoralists and miners refused to release "their Aboriginal help" to Harney and the Department of Native Welfare. Other Aboriginal camps were located at Madjalaba, Bendjigoin, Milik, Binbinya, Bemandjeli, and Belurriya—sites located throughout the coastal region of the Cox Peninsula.

The Department of Native Welfare consciously attempted to control and to rationalize these bewildering movements by interning Aborigines onto the Delissaville settlement. Bill Harney removed children from their parents if the parents refused to come into the settlement. He rated and ranked people's abilities ("A+1 *works* 'Good Native as Control'") and personalities ("sulky"). If Harney thought persons were quiet, sullen, or in need of discipline they were punished by exile from the settlement and kin. This was thought to have a "quietening" effect on troublemakers because it severed the power people drew from local kin and countryside. Delissaville women were often sent to the Catholic mission at Port Keats, while men were sent to Garden Point, an Aboriginal compound on Melville Island (Bartells 1988b).

While Harney's views of Aborigines seem paternalistic at this point, his writings are a good example of how Euro-Australians' self-identity was intimately tied to and constructed by their views of Aboriginal culture and economy. Throughout his work, Harney emphasized the links between the white Australian character and national identity and the character of "real bush" Aborigines. He and Ion Idriess, another popular writer in the 1930s, developed portraits of outback Aborigines that allowed middle Australia to embrace them as part of their own national character.[52] These men were attempting not so much to record the sociological facts of Aboriginal life, as to explore the links and discontinuities between the identity of Australian Aborigines and Euro-Australian bushmen, quintessential Euro-Australian national heroes—the equivalent of American cowboys. But to substantiate their claim that a link existed between black and white men, popular writers such as Harney had to participate firsthand in local economic and cultural practices. And writers had to distinguish between what most Australians witnessed of Aboriginal life and what Aboriginal life was "really like" (Healy 1989).[53]

Popular writers' sorting of Aboriginal action into "real" and "corrupt" sides has, as I have shown, an older history in ethnological and exploration texts. And rooting their advocacy in a strategy of cultural apartheid again called into question the life-style of one Aboriginal group as it defended another. Of importance to this book, Harney's writings have left a narrative account that calls into question the life-style of urban and settlement Aborigines, including "Delissaville natives."

> Now and then some Aborigines on "walkabout" from their settlement at Delissaville, about fifteen miles to the southeast, go strolling by. Some call in, others do not, and we prefer it that way, for a lot of them are hangovers from Darwin and know more about the modern method of hunting their "game" in the town areas than in the bush. Over here one sees that slow decadence of tribesmen more than anywhere else, for town and settlement life has divorced them away from the tribal pattern and it does not take long for contact to turn a good family of Aborigines into a horde that only thinks of the white persons, foodstores, and their unhampered sex drives. (1965, 14–15)

Although European records describe an increasing containment of Aboriginal movement and restriction of customary social practice, Beringgen-Wagaitj living on the Cox Peninsula remained in many ways outside the full control of European government. While official policy in the 1930s was based on assimilation, "full-blooded" Aborigines living in remote areas away from European population centers were able to elude policies implemented for their "benefit" (Rowley 1970b; Collman 1988). This was especially true for nonmissionary-run settlements. Although older Belyuen women distinguish between the "mitjenry" (run by missionaries) and "not mitjenry" white members of the early community, the Delissaville settlement itself was never "mitjenry"; it was always "government." And so, while subject to European social welfare imbued with a Christian cultural ethic, Delissaville Laragiya, Wagaitj, and Beringgen were not subject to the full regulatory practices and symbols of Christianity as were other missionary settlements in the region. The elusion and manipulation of white policy is an important theme of Belyuen women's informal narratives of the past. In them they portray life in the mid-1930s as a clever series of movements in and out of Euro-Australian spheres of control as they and their parents traveled to and from the Daly River and Cox Peninsula.

Their movements crisscrossed several world historical events. Jack Murray took over as superintendent of Delissaville in 1942 on what turned out to be the eve of the Japanese bombing of Darwin.

BOMBING DARWIN (6 February 1989)

Speakers in order of appearance
me: Mary Eladi (father Wadjigiyn, mother Emi) born circa 1930
dz: Deborah Zirita (father Emi, mother Marriamu) born circa 1950
je: Joan Ela (father Marritjaben, mother Marriamu) born 1943

me: *laik pip>l fr>m DarwIn dæt Jæpani ben start kaming dIswei
      naw   yeh   yeh*
   like people from Darwin, the Japanese were starting to come this way
      now,   yeh   yeh

dz: *reidiyow caling war hn den ben kam*
                                  the radio was saying "war"
                                  and then they came

me: *yeh n wi dIdent now enithing hahaha wi lök dæt irplein naw. BIG MOB!*
   yeh and we didn't know anything hahaha we saw the airplanes now, BIG MOB!

je: *dæt en wer akras*
   that and where across

me: *yeh dei ben baming dæt DarwIn eriya naw!*
   yeh they were bombing, that Darwin area now!

dz: *plein la darwIn*
   planes were at Darwin

me: *yeh   wi ben onli ben stend>p lök laik dæt gæmen*
   yeh   we were only, were standing and looking like this [mocks looking at sky] like

je: *yu mab lang wei*
   you mob were a long way away

me: *wen ala plein ai ben ai ben ownli lIt>l gerl der b>t wi dident now dæt waz jæpani dæt*
   when all the planes came, I was just a little girl here, we didn't know they were Japanese. That
   DarwIn eriya waz a lIt>l blek, smowking
   Darwin area was a little, black, smoking place.

Whereas Harney's writings reflect the ease with which he and Murray were able to coerce Aborigines onto the settlement, Jack Murray's (1942) diaries and letters reveal the difficulties he had controlling the movements of the local Aboriginal population. Murray is constantly attempting to centralize the "Wagidj" so that he can distribute them to various economic concerns: to the army at West Point, to Tom Waite from the Department of Native Affairs in Darwin, and along the various projects on the settlement itself. Murray addresses several letters to Euro-Australians living on and around the Cox Peninsula who were "harbouring natives." He continually cajoles those in charge to collect any "natives" nearby and either keep them off the beach or send them to the settlement.[55] Few Europeans complied.

94   Chapter 2

   The repetitive labor of the Delissaville settlement shows up in present-day narratives of older Belyuen women. Perhaps there is no topic that dominates women's recollections of their childhood and young adult lives more than their descriptions of the early Delissaville settlement and Katherine war camps and of their attempts to leave the settlements and to return to family sites on the Cox Peninsula. The Delissaville settlement is described in terms of the produce women planted in the garden and the fights that erupted between distantly related Aboriginal groups interned there. In "That Old Garden," Mary Eladi describes life on the old Delissaville settlement. Although Mary tells most of the story, it is not "her story." In local discursive notions, she is not the only one who owns the rights to recount it. Instead, her description of the Delissaville, Katherine, and Daly River camps is a community text told by many people in a similar form.

   The description of the Delissaville settlement reads like a litany of foods, a list broken only by Mary's description of the bombing of Darwin and of her trip to Katherine. She describes what was grown in the garden and by the water pool, what was carted from the old boat landing, and what seeing the bombing of Darwin was like. Then she describes how the trucks came and the dogs went, and finally, how more food was moved. The story ends as the Delissaville families leave for Katherine. I present three segments of the conversation.

THAT OLD GARDEN (6 February 1989)

Speakers in order of appearance
me: Mary Eladi (father Wadjigiyn, mother Emi) born circa 1930
je: Joan Ela (father Marritjaben, mother Marriamu) born 1943
cb: Catherine Burga (father Marritjaben, mother Marriamu) born circa 1920
dz: Deborah Ziya (father Emi, mother Marriamu) born circa 1950
cm: Claire Mamaka (father Marritjaben, mother Marriamu) born circa 1935.

me: yeh wi yuz tu grow >p owld garden der pawpaw painep>l,
      watermelan, swit
      yeh we used to grow a garden behind Belyuen, pawpaw, pineapple, watermelon, sweet

      powteitow, benene, pinut der hn kasava
      potato, banana, peanut were there and cassava

je: wat kasava laik a powteitow?
      what is a cassava, like a potato?

me: kasava naw, en dæt bin yu now bin lang wan ya sneik bin.
      that is a cassava now, and that bean you know that bean, long one, yeh, snake bean

cb: *lang wan kasava Im grow ala lang said av the fenz*
long one cassava, it grows all along the side of the fence

me: *dæt eriya naw*
in that area now
[noise]

me: *watermelan p>mpkIn sneik bin ahm painep>l benene wat-Im dja painep>l benene*
watermelon, pumpkin, snake bean and pineapple, banana, what is this, goodness, pineapple, banana

je: [faint]

me: *wi yuzd tu grow-Im >p der der en denatherwan bihaind dærr>n dawn bilow*
we used to grow them up there there and the other place behind, that place down below,

athersaid
on the other side

dz: *der w>zent der a bar der In thowz owld deiz eh dei hed*
there wasn't, there was a bore there in those days, eh? they had

cm: *water erye*
water here

je: *dem water*
dam water

dj: *dem water*
dam water

me: *yeh dem water*
yeh dam water

dz: *hn dei uzd tu kari water far garden end iven drinking water dætz rait he?*
and they used to carry water for the garden and even drinking water that's right, huh?

me: *<hn dawn bat>m der agen wi vzd tv grow-Im garden der agen*
yeh and down below there again we used to grow a garden there also

dz: *dawn de bat>m?*
down at the bottom [of the community]?

me: *yeh yu ken si lemanz der k>p>l a triz der lemanz orwendjez*
yeh you can see lemons, there are a couple of trees there, lemons, oranges

dz: *hn end wen yu hed am ownli meibi bred end an bek b>t wi hed tu*
and and when you had am [noise] only maybe [noise] bread and on the back, but we had to

me: *yeh bik>z wi dIdent hev ani vihek>l sow pip>l yuztu wak dawn fr>m her tu der*
yeh, because we didn't have any vehicle, so people used to walk down from here to there

lending karIm >p naw keis kam bek evri pip>l yuz tu
to the boat landing, carry them up now, case of things, come back, every person used to

karIm >p wan kart>n id bif
carry up one carton each of beef

je: *beit*
bait

me: *bred beit tIn kap bikuz wi never hed vihak>l her si? dætz wai wi yuztu gu*
bread, bait, tin cup, because we never had vehicle here see? that's why we used to go

dawn hn pIkIm >p wak >p wak >p en dawn
down and pick it up walk up, walk up and down.
[noise]

. . . .

je: *meik mi lef tellm aliya dæt aliya dæt mab pIkInIniz yubela si dæt lending dei*
make me laugh, tell them, all this group of kids, you kids see that boat landing, they

ala taim wak >p wak >p bifar
used to walk up from there all the time in the past

cm: *dei al ben slip sambela*
they all have fallen asleep, some of the kids

jz: *dei al slip dIs mab pIkInIniz*
they are all asleep, this group of kids

dz: *yu mab kId yu ben lIsening?*
have you group of kids been listening?

je: *yu tellm aliya lern Abi*
you tell them, all of them will learn Abi [me]

me: *yeh, wel yu mab mather naw dei yuzta wak >p en dawn getImbet bredi*
yeh, well your mothers now they used to walk constantly up and down to get bread

. . . .

dz: *Katherrain naw*
Katherine now

me: *"teik wan dag idj"*
"take one dog each" [said the Army officers]

dz: *hn dæt bIg*
and that big [faint]

me: *yeh wi ben kam bek fram Katherrain naw. wi ben gow fr>m er geta trein der hef*
yeh, we came back from Katherine now, we went from here, got a train there half way

wei. Yu now wer dæt reilwei dæt trein ben der weiting far the pip>l naw fr>m er
you know where that railway is? The train was there waiting for the people from here

wi ben teik everithing fr>m er ala vegetab>lz fr>m eriya
We took everything from here, all the vegetables from here

je: *dæt redwan*
that red one

me: *swit powteitow, pamkin, watermelan, pawpaw, hanyoin, kebedj, hn evrithing wi*
sweet potato, pumpkin, watermelon, pawpaw, onion, cabbage, and everything we

ben growIm >p erye. wi ben teik al dæt st>f yu now ala vegetab>lz.
were always growing here, we took all that stuff, you know all the vegetables.

Some Belyuen persons worked for the army at the Katherine war camps where Delissaville Aborigines were interned after 1942. Ronald Berndt describes the positive effect of the war camps on the self-esteem of Northern Territory groups (1987). C. D. Rowley (1970a, 1970b) likewise argues that World War II began a new phase of Anglo-Aboriginal relations. Indigenous groups, for the first time, understood the value their labor held for Euro-Australian government and business. It is a value that has been, subsequently, reevaluated. In retrospect, Aboriginal women drily comment on the "big money" they made working long hours at the Katherine camps.

AT KATHERINE (17 May 1989)

Speakers in order of appearance
me: Mary Eladi (father Wadjigiyn, mother Emi) born circa 1930
en: Emily Nela (father and mother Emi) born circa 1925

bp: Beth Povinelli (Italian American) born 1962
jz: Jean Ziya (father and mother Emi) born circa 1935

me: *shap ben der*
shop was there [at Donkey Camp in the Katherine War Camp]

en: *big mab m>ni*
lots of money

bp: *wer fram m>ni?*
where from money?

en: *m>ni fram pip>l mama*
money from people momma

bp: *ow yu werk le kemp?*
oh, you worked at the camp?

me: *yeh dei werk nat big mab mait bi wan dala fIfti ai think hahaha*
yeh they worked, not for a lot of money, maybe one dollar fifty I think, hahahaha.

For many older Belyuen men and women, the most significant part of being taken to the Katherine war camps was leaving. The long walk from Katherine through the Tipperary Plains to the Anson Bay and then up to the Cox Peninsula from which they had been taken, narratively encapsulates Wagaitj-Beringgen longing ("wanting," "being hungry for," and "Dreaming") for the country surrounding the Belyuen community. The following conversation is a fairly standard version of the path some families took and the motivations they had for leaving Katherine and returning to "country" and "home," here described as different, but elsewhere as the same place.

LEAVE KATHERINE (17 May 1989)

en: *dæt dæt thinkabet naw ai ben teIembet dæt stari main ai ben wak rait bek*
that that I always think about it now, I tell that story of mine, I walked right back [from Katherine]

streit >p le mai bainagula kuntri
straight up to my country, Bainagula country

bp: *dæt rait rait naw rait bek yu ben waak >p Bainagula*
that's right, right, now, right back you walked up to Bainagula

me: *fram der naw*
from there [Katherine] now

en: *mibela ben haid der*
my group hid there [at the Daly River]

me: *dei ben dei ben gowei fram der naw dIs mab pip>l ben sei "ai think*
they, they went away, went away from there [Katherine] now, this mob, [noise] people said "I

dæt pleis klows >p naw" dei ben drimbet naw dei ben think—
think that place is closed up now," they kept dreaming now, they thought

bp: *—yeh sow sam—*
yeh so some

me: *—hardbela sambela. b>t dei now mar wana stap der tu lang*
hard way some of them, but they didn't want to stay there too long

bp: *wai*
why

me: *bikuz dei ben howmsIk bla dIsh>n le bitj*
because they were homesick for this one, the beach

bp: *far the bitj ident it*
for the beach, isn't it

en: *yeh*
yeh [noise]

me: *thIs>n ben In It*
this person [pointing out jz] was involved in it

jz: *wibela ben wak >p naw*
our group walked up too

bp: *hmm ben In It tu?*
mmm you were involved too?

jz: *yeh mai mather wak >p gata sweg egen en dei ben splIt >p den*
yeh, my mother walked up with a swag also, and they split up then

me: *dei ben wak >p Adeleid RIver yu now wer adeleid rIver Iz*
they walked to Adelaide River, you know where Adelaide River is

bp: *yeh ai now thæt*
yeh I know that

me: [noise]

en: *fram TIperari bIg mab djaina men bIg mab pip>l ben lIving der*
from Tipperary [name of a pastoral station] [noise] lots of Chinese men, lots of people were living there

jz: *Abi mipela ben kam bek dIswei*
Abi [me] we came back this way

bp: *yeh djainamen naw. widj wei*
yeh chinese men now, which way

jz: *deili rIver wei*
     Daly River way
bp: *sam ben gow Adeleid sam ben gow Deili rIver?*
     some went to Adelaide, some went to the Daly River?
me: *now mar haiwei dei ben gow b>sh rowd*
     not on the highway, they went bush road
bp: *yeh Deili rIver wei b>sh rowd*
     yeh, Daly River way, bush road
jz: *kam dIs wei hef wei kip an wak wak*
     come this way, half way there, keep on walking, walking [noise]
     hernaw kam awt BInbInya naw.
     finally they arrived at Binbinya [on west coast of the Cox Peninsula] now.

In the midst of these migrations brought on by the pressures of war, the dangerous powers of foreign country, and the personal and cultural attachments the Wagaitj and Beringgen had to the Daly River and Cox Peninsula countrysides, Delissaville Superintendent Jack Murray understands Aboriginal flight from the Delissaville and Katherine camps (where he also worked) only as attempts "to make contact with the soldiers" or to be too "independent."[56] He is constantly at his wits' end trying to motivate women to pull weeds and men to dig postholes rather than to go "walkabout." For almost two years, the dull repetition of his entries about women's activities on the Delissaville settlement deviate from their daily routine of cleaning up the garden and camp only when he notes the issuing of a rare food-gathering permit, overhearing or supervising a fight over men, and discovering a woman's escape from the settlement. In one attempt to motivate women to come to work, Murray ceases all rations except to the aged and infirm and to those who work.

Murray never acknowledges that the goods women received from the soldiers at Talc Head were in any way a justifiable motivation for their trips, although he uses the same material, if not sexual, motivations to induce the women to stay at his camp. Perhaps Murray would have been surprised to find himself part of a larger genre in Belyuen women's historical narratives about Anglo's men's attempts to control their economic and sexual activity.[57]

Murray's attempts to control women's sexual practices were consistent with a general view of the time: control had to be assumed by the state because the Aboriginal male, the real owners of these women, had degenerated into drug-addicted pimps. Douglas Lockwood, a friend of Harney and a longtime resident in the Daly River area, notes in *The Front Door*:

> The union newspaper, *Northern Standard,* suggested they [newspapers in the south] should not interfere in matters that did not concern them. People

in Sydney Domain could have no conception of Aborigines as they were. They were allowed to wander the streets of Darwin while drinking methylated spirits and hawking their women. The newspaper asserted that there had to be adequate means at hand to protect white women from black men (though it said nothing about protecting white women from white men or black women from white men). (1977, 117)

Though racially progressive for his time, Lockwood gives little thought to what rights Aboriginal women had over their own and their children's marriage and sexual practices. Harney and Lockwood wrote that when "eternal triangles among the native people" arose, as "the women herself had no say in the matter, and wouldn't be consulted, the men often went to an independent arbitrator—generally the policeman or a patrol officer—to make a decision" (1963, 65). But in the conversations undertaken in the course of my fieldwork, Belyuen women state that mothers *and* fathers decided to whom to give their children. Their stories portray women as actors in their own right. They tell of women in the past who ran away, fought, and appealed to other female and male relations when they were in marriage situations they did not like. But women's independent sexual and marriage practices, including women's long walks across the Top End's landscape, only reinforced European men's sense that Aboriginal women had to be controlled, if not by their own men, then by the state.

Thus, irrespective of how Aborigines viewed their own marriage practices, in the 1900s the Euro-Australian welfare system was established to control Aboriginal women's sexuality and its "products." Section 45 of the Aboriginal Ordinance of 1918 outlawed the marriage "between female aborigines with persons other than aboriginals."[58] This was a change of heart from the early colonial days when marriages between white men and Aboriginal women were portrayed as a method of "cleansing" the Aboriginal race (Reece 1974).[59] But by 1928, J. W. Bleakley, chief protector of Aborigines in Queensland, wrote, "Perhaps the most difficult problem of all to deal with is that of the half-caste—how to check the breeding of them and how to best deal with those now with us." (quoted in Powell 1988, 187). In the mid-1900s, children of "mixed blood" were hunted down, separated from their parents, and sent to barracks in Darwin and on Crocker Island. A Wadjigiyn man and woman with mixed parentage "escaped" (their words) with Emily Nela from the internment camps at Katherine and walked to the Daly River and then to the Cox Peninsula only to flee south to the Daly again—hiding their young, light-skinned children in sugar and rice sacks along the way—in order to avoid the Department of Native Welfare. Laragiya women who had their children removed from them often wrote to government officials asking for their return. Their requests were granted only after they proved that they had abandoned their former "immoral" lives, lives that might include stable productive partnerships with men of the wrong color.[60]

What started as an informal policy to assimilate and advance "half-caste natives," through their protection as government wards, was formally extended in the Welfare Ordinance of 1953, to include any person

> who, by reason of—
> (a) his manner of living;
> (b) his inability, without assistance, adequately to manage his own affairs;
> (c) his standard of social habit and behavior; and
> (d) his personal associations, stands in need of such special care or assistance as is provided by this Ordinance.

As Alan Powell notes, "this Ordinance applied equally to all Territorians; in practice, almost solely to Aborigines and all but about eighty of those in the Northern Territory ended up on the Register of Wards" (Powell 1988, 233).[61]

For Aboriginal men living on the Cox Peninsula during the early days of the Delissaville settlement, life may have been, at times, less tedious than for their female kin. Their sexuality was not seen to be a risk or a threat to anyone because seldom were white women (who were seen to be the group most at risk) on the Cox Peninsula. Because the Cox Peninsula had never been a site of serious interethnic violence, the country itself was seen as a safe ground for whites, and so the specter of Aboriginal men's (not to mention women's) organized resistance to white authority was minimized. Although young men were regularly planting in the garden, digging postholes, and making roads to the various camping sites around the peninsula, they were also more regularly allowed to go hunting than women, and they acted as scouts for Murray and the army based at West Point during the war, which allowed them some freedom in their movements.[62]

The use of Aboriginal men as "trackers" for the army, an old racially motivated profession of dark-skinned men for white men, was, in fact, Murray's best justification for the funding of Delissaville, other than its use as a human storage bin. Murray was able to present Delissaville Aborigines as valuable to the army because he could represent them as retaining "traditional skills" due to their isolation on the Cox Peninsula. They proved their worth. In January 1942, two pilots were found by Murray and "five boys" (including Jean Ziya's now-deceased husband and Grace Ziyesta's now-deceased father). The *Northern Standard* (23 January 1942) reported this incident, noting with feigned aplomb that a thousand Euro-Australian soldiers were involved in a three-day search, but "it is believed that the men may have been found by party including a number of aboriginals which went around the coast in a lugger."

But even a patrol of Aboriginal scouts was seen as dangerously outside the government's control. On 19 June 1942, Fortress Command Headquarters wrote Murray that in order "to bring the Black Watch under proper Military Control the following instructions have been laid down."[63] Murray was to enlist in the Darwin Volunteer Defense Corps so that he would be under the "control of Fortress Command," "to organise and carry out" patrols to search for crashed Allied and enemy aircraft, and to serve West Point Battery in any capacity they deemed necessary. Murray was paid Australian Imperial Force rates and received "normal Military Rations." The "personnel of the Black Watch" were not paid and received a smaller ration: it was thought that they could supplement their rations with bush foods.

YOU GANA TALK

The Cultural Politics of the Past

Belyuen women's memories of the past include moments of violence, pleasure, freedom, and constraint as well as experiences of the legal and political-economic assessments of those moments and memories. Garden work, domestic drudgery, foraging escapades, and the interethnic violence that often accompanied these actions are all facts about older Belyuen women's lives. But they also provide these women narrative frames for asserting and controlling their identity and the illegitimate nature of Western practices and histories. They also present women with a number of discursive pitfalls.

Belyuen women's assessments of the "olden days" before whites and the "rubbish times" after their arrival present considerably more ambivalence and negotiation over the boundaries between Euro-Australian and Aboriginal dominated space and time (see also McGrath 1987; Attwood 1990) than do early Euro-Australian descriptions.[64] But as are Europeans, Belyuen women are presented with a problem of knowability: How can they describe a time and a way of life they never experienced? And how do they tell a history that will not trap them in the various disempowering Western narratives I sketched above? When women tell stories about the precolonial period they negotiate rather than select what will constitute the outlines of a history they have or have not experienced. They have several motivations for describing these pasts. These include constructing and maintaining various local social identities through the narration of shared histories and cultural backgrounds (Sansom 1982, 1988b) and presenting a countervoice to Western histories of their "place" in the northern landscape. Western descriptions have changed through time; the supposed savage opposition of Beringgen-Wagaitj to European incursions has come to explain their traditional bent, while the friendly accommodation of Laragiya to Western colonization has come to explain their cultural disintegration. Such a historical narrative is found in the attorney general for the Northern Territory's submission on traditional Aboriginal land ownership in the Cox Peninsula.

> The establishment of Darwin attracted Aboriginal groups from the immediate area, as well as the Larrakia from both sides of the Darwin Harbour. These people became the Northern Territory's first fringe dwellers and by the 1870's Europeans had already started to inter-marry with the local Aboriginal people. To the west of Darwin Harbour a territorial vacuum was being created: Larrakia people who had lived in the Kenbi land claim area since time immemorial were now spending more and more time on the eastern side of the Harbour. The coastal neighbours of the Larrakia to the south—the Wadjigiyn and Kiyuk—started to move into the Kenbi land claim area around 100 years ago. They were attracted by the fine hunting and foraging country of their northern neighbours and by the new goods and services available in Darwin. These southern neighbours of the Larrakia came to occupy a pivotal role in the Kenbi land claim area (Attorney General for the Northern Territory 1990, 32).

Therefore, alongside the freedom Belyuen women have in describing their views of the past is the force and unequal power inherent in exchanges between Aborigines and Euro-Australians. Force is found in the form of history, in the legal needs for various kinds of histories, and in the social relations between storytellers and audience—that is, in the subject of history, in the purpose of history, and in the social relations that constitute and form the object of history. Because popular writers, researchers, or land claim lawyers typically have the final say in what worth Aboriginal history holds for non-Aboriginal Australian consumers (the voters, the nation-state, industry), enormous pressure exists on women to "tell all" and hope that some part of their story will strike a chord in those listeners' ears who have access to goods and materials, much as, in the early colonial past, enormous pressure existed on Aboriginal men to show their protectorates ceremonial practices in order to obtain goods or protection. Today, women find themselves asked to "tell all" even when it violates local rules for speaking and behaving and even if it is a past they cannot know or about times they would rather not discuss.

Thus there are several interlocking loci of power in women's narrative accounts of the past. First, local narrative rules present guidelines for how and when to disclose various levels of meaning in various social contexts, larly listed as precolonial: the absence of clothes and sickness, the daily presence of dance, music, and, especially, bush foods, medicines, and materials. In women's conversation the bush is a space that discursively and symbolically opposes the settlement, although many foods—mangoes, cashews, possum, pig, and wild honey—are obtained within the Belyuen reserve. Topics that concentrate on this nonsettlement space reflect one of the women's stated motivations for describing the precolonial past; they want to teach their children and grandchildren Aboriginal heritage. In the following segment, Belyuen women describe the past as the repository of the cultural.

NO CLOTHES, STRONG CULTURE (6 February 1989)

Speakers in order of appearance
me: Mary Eladi (father Wadjigiyn, mother Emi) born circa 1928
en: Emily Nela (father and mother Emi) born circa 1926
cb: Catherine Burga (father Marritjaben, mother Marriamu) born circa 1920
bp: Beth Povinelli (Italian-American) born 1962
dz: Deborah Zirita (father Emi, mother Marriamu) born circa 1950
je: Joan Ela (father Marritjaben, mother Marriamu) born 1942

me: *wen ai w>z bawn ai ben hev klowz fr>m erye*
when I was born I got clothes from here [Belyuen]

en: *ai ben stend >p n>ting*
I walked around with nothing on

cb: *wi ben laikdawt, yu, dei ben laikadjet na dIs>n merukak (E) n>ting dIs>n*
we were like that, you, they were like that now, this bottom nothing covered this

meru (E) n>ting dIsaid
bottom nothing on this backside.

en: *eeh yeh dætz al naw ownli dIs>n*
eeh yeh   that's all now. We only had a front covering.

cb: *now bleingket dærr>n n>ting peiperbark getImbek kaverIm >p meru (E)*
no blanket in that time, nothing, get paperbark cover up the backside.

en: *ai remember dæt*
I remember that

bp: *>hh> far naitaim wen Im kowld*
ahha for night time when it's cold

en: *mmmm   kowld n>thing*
mmmm   cold nothing

dz: *far rein far sheid*
for rain, for shade

cb: *ya*
    ya

en: *edja narra meru kainyi (E) sIster bliInmi yutubela laik*
<u>another of my sister's backsides was lying outside</u>, our sister, you two were like

dæt na <u>meru</u> (E) aniting
that now <u>backside</u> was outside with no covering

bp: *yu   mami   yu tu*
you   mom   you too

en: *ya   mi tu*
    yes   me too

ai neve ben hev dIsting
I never had these things [clothes]
[noise]

tItI awtsaid
breasts were outside

cb: *ownli dIs ding j>s tai Im >p*
only this thing [breast harness] to tie them up

je: *mait tai kuz j>mp >p en dawn plopplopplop meibi dei lök*
might tie breasts because they fly up and down "plopplopplop" maybe they see

demselvz on vIdiyow
themselves on video

dz: *dei didnt weri* [noise]
they didn't worry

cb: *dædan <u>ngarron</u> <u>yIngi</u> (E/Mar) b>mbai yInmi <u>wula</u> (E/Mar) toptoptop b>mberrai*
like that <u>goanna's breast,</u> when you and I dance,

dIsan <u>yeingi</u> (E/Mar)
the <u>breasts</u> go up and down up and down.

. . . .

dz: *now sIknes spesh>l b>sh medIsIn*
there was no sickness, they had special bush medicine

je: *dei w>z far pip>l er der wer far Rowzi h>zbend, Belerridj, trai trai*
there were four people here, there were four: Rosie's husband, Beleritj, they kept

*dei ben hev tu get b>sh medIsIn. [personal name] f>t sow ai gat
b>sh medIsIn, yu*
trying; they had to get bush medicine for [personal name]'s foot. So I got bush medicine, you

smellm strang laika bIks
smell it, it's strong like Vicks [mentholated rub]

. . . .

bp: *ownli dei lIsen end raitIm dawn efta putIm langa bök*
[referring to taped ethnoclassification sessions] only they listen and write it down later in a book

dz: *ye get awldæt infameish>n, dowz dei dei hed strang kultje dei hev seremoni*
you get all that information, those days they had a strong culture, they had ceremony

evri dei karabari en dens; tudei wi strag>l naw.
everyday, corroborree and dance; today we struggle now.

Even when the motivations for describing a precontact past are clearly stated—to record Aboriginal heritage for oneself and one's children—the meanings of that past are polyvalent and ambiguously oriented. Sensitive to the various social constituencies in their audience (or the various social roles of a single member of that audience), women layer their stories with multiple meanings; they themselves often have not decided what the meaning of a practice should be—traditional, nontraditional, shameful, or empowering for the group. Whether Australian Aborigines think that a practice should have one meaning any more than a mythic site have only one story associated with it is itself not clear (see Berndt 1970, 16). Belyuen women see local knowledge, in fact all human knowledge, as partial insofar as it can be supplemented by further revelation (through dreams, topological discovery, or the performance by an outside group of a new story for a site) and as emergent insofar as the future can shed light on the meaning of past events (see Povinelli 1993a). At the same time, power for the group and the individual is derived from the control of local knowledge; an individual derives power for the self by knowing something even if no one else recognizes or knows of that knowledge—"no matter, I know myself." Aboriginal people's descriptions of what they know, including what they know of the past, have, therefore, exclusive and inclusive elements: guarding what one knows protects its accompanying power, while it keeps open the possibility of supplementing one's own knowledge with newly discovered meanings.

The orientation of women's conversations about the past, especially those that concentrate on "family history" or "Aboriginal culture," can therefore be understood in two senses. First, women orient their talk to their audience. We must be careful, however, not to restrict artificially that audience to those few people who have gathered in the classroom. Although the women's audience does include the diverse sets of Aboriginal and non-Aboriginal groups gathered together for the day, it also includes the women's Aboriginal kin living on the Belyuen community and on other Aboriginal communities up and down the Daly River–Darwin coastal region. The women would consider their audience to include all those who have told them about family history, have participated in it, or have interests in lands discussed in relationship to that history. The women's audience—the social group that is *interior* to the conversation I examine here—also includes non-Aboriginal persons who, over the years, have influenced how they think about Aboriginal (and non-Aboriginal) action in relationship to land use. The audience, then, even includes those Euro-Australian allies and enemies discussed above. Second, women orient their conversation to several time periods: the olden days before the arrival of the white man, the early days of their arrival, and the contemporary period. In both aspects of conversational orientation, women are not only reacting to the social constitution of their audiences, but also to their cultural notions of time and community.

Tell Im "All Dead": Orientation and the Audience

How women orient their talk to their diverse audiences, physically present and absent, can be seen in the classroom history lesson. The cultural domination and resistance described in women's historical narratives is mirrored in the power relations that define the social organization and narration of that history. In both the classroom family history lesson and in legal testimony, Aboriginal women find themselves faced with the possible transgression of their conversational praxis. In Aboriginal Australian speakers should not directly refer to others, especially the recently deceased, by their personal names (Stanner 1936–37; Sansom 1988a, 1988b). They should also avoid confrontational talk—speech that includes direct disagreement with or refusal of another person's request. During the schoolroom session, in order for women not to discuss the dead, which is the topic of the history lesson, women have to use "hard talk" (cf. Liberman 1985; Brenneis 1988; Watson-Gegeo and White 1990). Either way (to discuss or not to discuss the dead) they engage in antisocial and, therefore, potentially dangerous behavior. Yet because women can gain access to needed resources, here a school bus ride to a local grocery (part of the day's history lesson includes going fifteen kilometers down the track to the Mandorah Pub), they try to balance the school's expectations and rules of behavior with their own.

The following exchange shows how women balanced these rules and expectations. The first part of the women's conversation is about who is going to talk, why, and what people are going to say. The discussion begins with Emily Nela telling the schoolchildren where to sit. As is usual when adults visit the school, children are running around asking their mothers and grandmothers for money to buy snacks. After Emily organizes the children, she asks Catherine Burga where they are going to tell their stories, because it is still not clear whether all the histories will be given at the school or some at the Mandorah Pub. Catherine replies that they will have to wait to see. Deborah Zirita, the young Aboriginal schoolteacher, asks the schoolmaster what he wants the old women to talk about. While all this is going on, Joan Ela tells Mary Eladi and Emily what she and the schoolmaster have already decided would be a good topic, simply, how their families used to live at Madpil and how in the olden times "we all the time been there." She then tells them to speak in a "straightforward way to the white woman" (one of the local schoolteachers).

YOU GANA TALK (6 February 1989)

Speakers in order of appearance
en: Emily Nela (father and mother Emi) born circa 1925
cb: Catherine Burga (father Marritjaben, mother Marriamu) born circa 1920
je: Joan Ela (father Marritjaben, mother Marriamu) born 1943
dz: Deborah Zirita (father Emi, mother Marriamu) born circa 1950
bp: Beth Povinelli (Italian-American) born 1962
me: Mary Eladi (father Wadjigiyn, mother Emi) born circa 1930
jz: Jean Ziya (father and mother Emi) born circa 1935
sm: Schoolmaster (Anglo-Australian) born circa 1950
(Present but not speaking is Claire Mamaka [father Marritjaben, mother Marriamu] born circa 1930.)

en: sIdawn her nathe mab <u>kaw</u> wulgamen <u>themamal:yuwa kana</u> (E)
 [to school children] sit down here, you other mob <u>keep going</u>. Old lady where are we telling stories. is he going there (to Mandorah)?

cb: <u>kumanyrredi kug>k</u> (E)
 they're still standing, wait yet

je: [Noise]

dz: [to principal] *yu wana takbet dæt ah ting or Mændara*
 you want to talk about that ah thing or about Mandorah

bp: [to kids] *yu lIsen dIswei nat mi*
 you listen to them not to me

je: *Im wana tellIm wi Imben tellIm mi dæt "stap st>ri"*
he wants us to tell them [the children] we, he told me to talk about that "stop story"

sæbi ai ben sæbi dæt yu sæbi
you know, I knew that you knew it:

"M>dpil hnn wulden taim wi ben ala taim der"
"In the olden times we stayed at Madpil all the time."

streitfarwed wei le mitjitj
talk in a straightforward way to the whitewoman

?: *. . . lending . . .*
. . . [boat] landing . . .

je: *le lending le lending?*
at the landing, at the landing?

Emily Nela uses a common Belyuen speech strategy for withdrawing from the conversation. She disclaims the whole activity by stating, "Do not look at me I was not there," a position she will take later in the conversation ("No I can't tell it . . . because I was not there," in "You Can Run," chap. 1). So confronted, Mary Eladi attempts to cajole Emily into the conversation by describing its purpose, but immediately backs away when Emily confronts her.

en: *now mar löking et mi ai neve ben der*
don't look at me, I was never there

me: *nu mar, laik djidge <u>yera maka</u> nada <u>yera maka piya</u> (E)*
no more, like the teacher, <u>for the children</u>, another, <u>for the children's heads</u>.

en: *now mar sIdawn erye ala taim*
no, I sat down here all the time

After Emily and Mary discuss the reasons for speaking and how to speak to the non-Aboriginal participants, both tell part of a short story. They describe stealing bananas from the old Delissaville garden for an old Wadjigiyn-Kiyuk woman, Ngalgin, who lived in the old camp (Delissaville was first located on the opposite side of the Belyuen creek).

jz: *mænd>ra*
Mandorah?

en: <u>*kamaga*</u> *(B)*
<u>nothing</u>

cb: [to kids] *hu toidjIm dærr>n*
who touched that [tape recorder]

me: *yu gana sei laik* [noise] *far dæt men*
   you are going to say . . . for that man

en: *yuwaingow? (E) that waitmen?*
   him there? that whiteman?

jz: *yeda kanarri kana yena Mænd>ra yena* [noise] wakai yentha
   [noise] *(E)*
   look he is going he is going, to Mandorah [noise] nothing now.

me: *wakaiyenthayuwaigow? (E)*
   nothing, long gone now?

je: *n>ting Im now mar duIm yet*
   no no, he hasn't gone yet

me: *mibet gIda nana benenez wulkembet yuzta bi owld pip>l yu*
   I used to get grandmother bananas from the old camp, use to be, old people you

   now yuwa kunyin ngaingye (E)
   know, they stayed there.

jz: *wel wiben* [faint]
   well we used to

en: *ngapa kanan yena kumanye ngalgin (E)*
   we carried them [bananas] standing back there for Ngalgin [personal name].

me: *wel ngalgin naw* [noise]
   well Ngalgin now

en: *yu tellm al dai*
   you tell him [schoolteacher] all die

This story prompts Emily to comment on the direction the conversation is going, a common intervention when women are asked about the olden days. Mary asks Emily to tell a story about Ngalgin, and Emily responds that Mary should tell the white schoolmaster that the people he wants to hear about are all dead. Emily's statement that the old people have all died is a hard response (as was Mary Eladi's earlier response, "I don't like to keep telling this kind of story all the time," in "You Can Run," chap. 1). There are good reasons for its harshness. Although women talk about deceased relations among themselves and their children, they do so only when some event calls to mind a particular person. In this way, women are not talking about the past as a time now gone, but the present, that is, about the deceased peoples' place in the present. For example, if a woman finds a very large yam or collects an unusually large number of crabs, she might say that a deceased relative, who was known for his or her ability to collect that food, helped her "see" (find) the food. When brought up in this way, deceased people (and *durlg* for that matter) like to be remembered and talked about because they are included as part of the present group: they are a living memory. Non-Aborigines are more likely to ask about the past rather than to remember it, simply because they do not know it and usually do not stay in the community long enough to hear stories as they arise in a casual manner during fights, corroborees, hunting trips, and so on. In short, when they speak, women take into account not only the social relations of the audience but also local cultural notions of the efficacious power of words (*mal,* also "stories") and of the sentimental relationship that exists between contemporary persons, deceased relatives, and Dreaming beings.

After Emily's comments, the conversation slows until the women decide on a new topic, "the story of those two." At this point, Mary Eladi says, "Tell the story, tell the story," and the conversation refocuses once again on events in the past.

je: *ye g>na tak In lenggwedj*
      you're going to talk in language

cb: [faint to agnes]

me: *yeh*
      yeh

cb: <u>*poi*</u> *(E)*
      <u>go on then</u>

me: *weit naw mama <u>kanan</u> (E)*
      wait now momma [to cb] <u>he's still sitting</u>

      yu sæbi wulamen <u>manggin kumangita marrdja</u> (E)
      you know old man <u>cousin Morrdja</u> [personal name]

en: *hahaha*
      hahaha

me: *merrdje, einIt It mama <u>themowwa</u> (E) yu now mar sæbi dæt wulman?*
      Merrdje ain't it momma <u>where now?</u> You don't know that old man?

cb: [faint]

me: *ye Im sæbi <u>merrrdjenga</u> (B)*
      yeh she knows <u>that Merrdje</u>

bp: [to children] *aim gana ternIm Imaf If yu mab downt stap*
          I'm going to turn the tape recorder off if you kids don't stop

cb: <u>yuwai yena</u> *(E)* [children noise]
<u>there at</u>

me: *edja now edjatoi kama kana manggin (E)*
sister knows, sister came and took cousin.

ei? <u>mal:ga</u> *(E)* <u>mal:baka</u> *(B)* [loud children noises]
eh? <u>tell the story, tell the story</u>

<u>karrabedj karra edja medanye</u> *(E)*
<u>about how he grabbed sister, those two</u>

bp: *Im fain, ye gowhan*
it's fine, go on

Those Two: women's orientation to the past

After the interruption of the story about stealing bananas from the old camp, the conversation turns to another story about the past that seems, on the surface, every bit as sensitive as the last. However, the focus of this part of the conversation is on something other than the characters discussed. Examining the course the conversation takes allows us to understand the second orientation of women's talk about the past; that is, how they use narratives about the past to talk about the continuing coercion and violence they face in the present and to negotiate the dangerous shoals of Western discourses on the authentic and corrupt Aboriginal subject. This part of the conversation shows, in particular, how the *setting* of the past in the countryside frames "the old Aboriginal way."

The story Mary Eladi tells describes a period when she was living with her parents at Madpil and Bitbinbiyirrk (a topic suggested by Joan, the adult education assistant) and an event that occurred at Kunggul, a beach not far away (Mary's innovation). Mary starts her story by describing the practice of "wife stealing" as the old Aboriginal way of obtaining a mate. In the old Aboriginal way, if a man wanted a wife he stole a person's daughter by grabbing her from behind some bushes. Women describe this practice as *ngapa* (carrying away on the shoulders).

IN THE WANGGIGI SHADE (6 February 1989)

Speakers in order of appearance
me: Mary Eladi (father Wadjigiyn, mother Emi) born circa 1930
dz: Deborah Zirita (father Emi, mother Marriamu) born circa 1950
sm: Schoolmaster (Euro-Australian) born circa 1950

me: *wel In the wulden deiz naw laik yunow In de wul eberIgIn>l wei naw wi ben der*
Well in the olden days now, like you know in the old aboriginal way now, we were there

wen wi w>z ownli lit>l gerlz dæt dei wi yuzd tu llv æt M>dpil en BItbInbiyirrk
when we were only little girls; that day we used to live at Madpil and Bitbinbiyirrk on

hn bitj dæt Wangglgi bitj naw Mænd>ra. ai w>z n>ther rawnd K>ngg>l krik wel,
the beach, that Wanggigi beach, called Mandorah. I was at another beach, Kunggul creek.

biK>z nowwan, wan wulmen, mai father, stil samb>di di—wan y>ng gerl fr>m dirye. In
Well, one old man, my father, stole somebody—a young girl from there [Kunggul creek]. In

the eberIgIn>l wei, dei get, If dei wana waif dei gow, dei gata snik >p bihaind
the Aboriginal way, if they want a wife they have to sneak up behind the

b>shez hn dei g>nha stil dat gerl awei, si, fr>m mather hn father
bushes and then steal the girl away, see? They steal her from her mother and father;

hn wel wi went der far h>nting tu get s>m kreb, sep dæt wulmen keim dawen hn
and well, we went to Kunggul to get some crab, but that old man came down and was

w>z trai tu stil wan y>ng gerl, mai c>zIn dærr>n, dæt mai c>zIn, hn wi w>z kraiying
trying to steal one young girl. She was my cousin, that was my cousin. We were crying

dæt dei bik>z ai w>z ownli lIt>l gerl ai waz kraiying far help mai mather'n mai
that day because I was only a little girl. I was crying for help. My mother and my

father ræn æn græbIm mai k>zin awei fr>m dæt mæn; iz ownli owld men
father ran and grabbed my cousin away from that man; he was only an old man

dz: *nowb>di kempIn an the bitj then dIdent now this eriya yet dæt dæt pleisez then*
no one was camping on the beach then, they [white people] didn't know this area yet, those places then

ownli j>s bösh rowd [noise]
there was only a bush road

me:	*bösh rowd*
	bush road

mmm traid tu teik dæt gerl awei fr>m mai mather and father dæt dei b>t dæt
mmm he tried to take that girl away from my mother and father that day, but that

wulmen b>t Im ben hert Im leig erye lök erye fr>m mai mather
old man, but my mother hurt his leg here [on the shin bone]

lata pip>l w>z der dringkin emiyanggel
A lot of Emiyenggal people were drinking there.

dz:	*this w>z bifar the war ar efta the war*
	this was before the war or after the war
me:	*bifar the war bifar the war*
	before the war, before the war
dz:	*bifar the war, ei, yu awl ben muv arawnd, ei, bifar war ben erye*
	before the war huh? you all moved around, huh? before the war started?
me:	*den wi ben end >p erye naw*
	then we ended up here now
dz:	*end >p erye*
	ended up here
me:	*dæt jæpani war ye wi ben erye mIsh>niri skul ala skul kId wi ben*
	that Japanese war yeh, we were here yeh, missionary school, all the school kid, we went

mish>niri skul
to missionary school

There are two time frames evoked in this short narrative: the time before and the time after Europeans came. Deborah Zirita comments that there were no non-Aboriginal Australian dwellings at Kunggul beach (the Wagait Residential Development is now located adjacent to Kunggul beach) and Mary states that wife stealing is the old Aboriginal way. However, this story occurred after the arrival of alcohol on the Cox Peninsula. Mary describes the Emiyenggal drinking camp at Kunggul. What do we make of this old way of getting a wife and the motivations that Mary might have for telling about it in a school setting?

The schoolmaster, who has taught in other "more traditional communities," asks a question that is helpful to us. This question seems to assume that women are only referring to the first time frame, that is, the precolonial period and a precolonial practice, and thereby to suggest that the relations between these Aboriginal men and women were wholly understandable within kinship and affinal structures. He asks about the traditional marriage practices of the Belyuen groups: "in old days, did people have promised husbands and wives here?" Mary tells the schoolmaster, "If mother and father promised you that man, you have to take that man," but the young woman who was being "grabbed" was not promised to anyone. Then the schoolmaster comments, "So he wasn't stealing someone else's wife?" Mary agrees that the man was not stealing someone else's wife, but was about to have sex with a young girl to whom he was too closely related.

sm: *hmm unaited. In owld deiz pramIst, did pip>l hev pramIst h>zbendz end waivs her*
hmm United. In old days, promised, did people have promised husbands and wives here

me: *yeh In owlden deiz If mather en father pramIst yu dæt men yu hæv tu teik dæt men*
yeh in old days, if your mother and father promise you to that man then you had to take that man

sm: *thæt gerl yer thæt k>zin av yerz w>z shi pramIst tu s>mwan els*
that girl, that cousin of yours, was she promised to someone else?

me: *now*
no

sm: *shi w>zent*
she wasn't

me: *now thæt owld men wanted tuuu, tu a, meika waif h-*
no that old man wanted tooo, to a, make wife h-

sm: *rait*
right

me: *k>z shi w>z y>ng, shi w>z mai k>zln*
because she was young, she was my cousin

en: *wulman* [faint] *kalIm*
old man   call his relationship.

me: *wi kal Im grendfather b>t In eberIgIn>l wei wi kal Im laik föl meit*
we call him grandfather but in Aboriginal way we call him like full mate

sm: *yeh sow hi w>zent stiling samwan elsez waif*
yeh so he wasn't stealing someone else's wife

me: *now hi ben gow far y>ng gerl hahaha*
no he went for young girl hahaha

en: *hahaha*
hahaha.

Placing this conversation in a community context, it is clear how and why women's historical narratives tack between precolonial and postcolonial references. In the classroom situation where young and old, white and Aboriginal people sit, women must negotiate various moral traditions and gender narratives. History as a moral narrative includes the women's own ambivalence about certain precolonial practices, here the "old Aboriginal way" of getting a wife, and their views of the present sexual practices of their children. The point of the story is not, or not wholly, the "exchange of women" as part of a traditional economy,[66] but rather how the use of narcotics upsets one's ability to act in a correct manner and how the problems of the olden days are the problems (or not, depending to whom one is talking) of the present. This is an important educational story for the Belyuen schoolchildren. The alcoholism of their sons and daughters is of great interest to older Belyuen women. In other conversations, referring to male-female interaction and drug abuse, women say, "It was like that in the old days, and it still is."[67] Old men go for young girls, as old women go for young men; people sleep with their wrong kin relations. But these old ways are now spliced with new social stresses. Aboriginal revenge killings and sicknesses continue, heightened, it is argued, by the "silliness" of men and women who drink and then are not able to protect themselves from *munggul* men (E, sorcerers). Other drugs increase the causes and results of violence.[68]

Along with their own views of Aboriginal men and women's changing marriage and sexual mores, women must also negotiate Euro-Australian views of their marriage and sexual practices. We saw above that all of these women confronted, directly or indirectly, the Australian government's attempts to control their sexual practice and children even as many Euro-Australian men were sexually involved with or were sexually harassing and abusing Aboriginal women. Good and violent encounters between European men and Aboriginal women continue; some Euro-Aboriginal men harass Aboriginal women when they travel to Darwin. Rapes by members of the white community around the Cox Peninsula happen just often enough to prejudice most women's views of white male strangers. Other forms of interethnic social and physical intimidation link the present to the past. Olden time European killings and threats of killings are today mirrored by Ku Klux Klan shootings at Aboriginal organizations and residences in and around Darwin. Old government policies of taking children, country, and ritual paraphernalia from responsible senior Aborigines are compared to new welfare and land tenure laws that attempt to regulate peoples' practices.

All of these interethnic interactions reinforce the oppositional framework of the settlement/bush practices that underlie Mary Eladi's story. While the socially destructive settlement practices are located in the bush drinking camp, nevertheless, Mary Eladi's story juxtaposes the resistive and ultimately successful strategies of food collectors (the bush foods are metonymically associated with precontact Aborigines) to the morally confused and ultimately unsuccessful practices of the drinkers (the drink is metonymically associated with Euro-Australians). In their historical narratives, older women continually anchor the present in the form of the foraging past or evoke this past when talking about the present much in the way Sansom describes Darwin fringe dwellers (many of whom are relatives of Belyuen men and women) as conceptualizing "persons . . . [as] particularised into existence and . . . in themselves, the past emergent in the present" (1988b, 158). Because these conversational practices link the present to the past women can move quickly, without being challenged, between their experiences and "the" Aboriginal experience, an experience connecting urban and rural Aborigines.

> Widely appreciated ways for getting things in train, for dealing with the problems that whitefellas pose, for bringing the dispersed people of a region together for celebrations, for coping with financial difficulties in family life, make Aborigines of town and country continentally "all same." (Sansom 1982, 118)

Before discussing a final aspect of women's historical narratives, I want to outline briefly a part of another conversation I had with some Belyuen women in order to show the *internal* aspect of social relations in women's talk. In particular, I want to stress that no discussion about the past is ever limited to the past. As part of its form, function, and meaning (its social performative), conversation is always about the present social situation.

An example of the way in which the multiple layers of the social present are embedded in narratives of the past is seen in the following story. It describes how the "black watch" found a World War II pilot trapped in a local mangrove. The pilot is said to have kept one bullet in his gun in order to kill himself if captured by the enemy. In these, as in other stories about the customs of whites, Belyuen women emphasize how Aborigines must constantly intervene in European action lest their ineptness and hysteria in the bush prove fatal. Note also how the ethnic identity of the parachutist switches between two sets of enemies: the Japanese who were at war with the Australians and the "English" who, as the second segment makes clear, were, if not enemies, then not friends of the local Aborigines.

POSITIONING ABORIGINES 121

ARMY SCOUTS (17 May 1989)

Speakers in order of appearance
jz: Jean Ziya (father and mother Emi) born circa 1935
en: Emily Nela (father and mother Emi) born circa 1925
me: Mary Eladi (father Wadjigiyn, mother Emi) born circa 1930
bp: Beth Povinelli (Italian-American) born 1962

jz: *Abi thei ben faind jæpani alrait tubela dæt pleis*
Abi [me] they found a Japanese man alright, two men at that place

en: *Abi dei ben ingglesh alrait dei ben sei Im sei mama dæt men*
Abi [me] they were English alright, they said, he said, momma, that man

jz: *ingglesh dei ben getIm*
English they found

me: *dei ben get Im parashut kut Im put Im le grawnd armi pip>l yu now armi mab*
they got him, cut his parachute and put him on the ground, army people, you know, army mob

bp: *yeh*
yeh

me: *yuzd tu wakarawnd her everiwer sIgnal naw gata smowk sIgnal*
use to walk around here, everywhere, signalling now, smoke signaling

bp: *>s mab naw sIgnal?*
our group, now signaled?

me: *fram blekbela gat dæt men naw kam >p end pIk Im >p dæt men naw*
from Aborigines, "got that man now," "come and pick him up," that man now

bp: *wat dæt, ai ben lIsen Im ben hev wan b>let*
what's that, I heard he had one bullet

me: *hmm Im ben hev wan b>let trai tu shut Im Imself*
hmm, he had one bullet to try to shoot himself

bp: *yeh*
yeh

me: *b>t blekbela ben kedjIm >p tu kwIk*
but Aborigines found him too quickly

bp: *l>ki l>ki*
lucky lucky

me: *faindIm*
find him

122 Chapter 2

en: <u>yukai</u> *(E)*
you're right

me: *Im w>z gana shut Im Imself Im wan b>let*
he was going to shoot himself with one bullet

en: *ow now*
oh no!

. . . .

jz: *armi*
army

en: *dIs>n Im shutImbet mibela gata erplein mama watz rang wIth Im*
this one, he kept shooting at us with an airplane momma, what's wrong with him?

bp: *ai d>now*
I don't know

en: *hInggIIsh alrait b>t shutImbet mibela kIti*
English alright, but they kept shooting at us, goodness!

bp: *ingglIsh naw ben shutImbet yu?*
English now always shot at you?

en: *hinggIIsh, yeh*
English, yeh.

bp: *f>k dæt sow dæt de thing naw?*
fuck that, so that's the thing now?

me: *kam >p erye naw efta the war*
came here now after the war

bp: *yeh*
yeh

me: *kam bek erye*
came back here

bp: *sIdawn naw, fInIsht?*
lived here now, finished?

jz: *sIdawn her*
lived here

me: *sIdawn erye dei ben ribIlt this set>lment agen*
lived here, they rebuilt this settlement again

jz: *fInIsht wi ben meik Im set>lment*
finished, we made this settlement

bp: *thIs, wat Im ben lev>l*
this, what, was it demolished

me: *yeh, meiklm garden evrithing wer naw pleis fr>m benene, swit powteitow,*
yeh, made the garden, everything, where now place, banana, sweet potato,

painep>l, orwendje
pineapple, orange

en: *kasava kasava*
cassava, cassava

me: *kasava*
cassava

Mary's first statement in the second segment of the conversation is a common way in which violent and ambivalently understood topics are mended and returned to a more sanctioned course. Using repetitive patterns common in local discourse strategies (see Povinelli 1993b; see also App. 1, pt. A, below), she directs the conversation to a less stressful topic, in this instance to the Delissaville gardens: "came up here now . . . rebuilt . . . the garden." This effectively ends the "hard story" that Emily has been telling and silences a troublesome part of the past that cannot be easily reconciled with the present group of people, one of whom is a white American woman. The prowess with which Mary Eladi is able to manipulate subtly this conversation is probably the surest evidence of her necessary, unavoidable, and long involvement with European culture and economy irrespective of the isolation the region afforded the Wagaitj and Beringgen. Moreover, it is this type of deft conversational practice that characterizes Belyuen women's handling of the cultural politics of the past.

Whether the past is used as a repository of Aboriginal cultural heritage or as a commentary on the evolving or devolving nature of current intra- and interethnic social relations, one of the motivations for entering that past is political: it positions Aboriginal groups vis-à-vis each other and non-Aboriginal groups in social and physical landscapes. And the political agenda of historical narrative cannot be cleanly separated into opposing Aboriginal and non-Aboriginal sides. Precolonial practices are ambivalently understood and portrayed by European and Aboriginal Australians alike and have been used to serve both Aboriginal and non-Aboriginal political purposes (Harris 1990; Harker and McConnochie 1985). For example, the conversation labeled "No Clothes, Strong Culture" valorizes certain precolonial practices—no sugar, no tea, strong teeth, strong bodies—as it thrusts these practices and social and physical states into an irrecoverable past. Women are not arguing for the return of these practices—any more than they argue in "In the Wanggigi Shade" for the return of the old way of obtaining a wife. Rather, they are locating a site of cultural difference and historical divergence that defines the encounter between Europeans and Aborigines. Not mentioned in these short oral histories, but often cited in conversations about the contours of the precolonial past, is the precolonial lack of tea, sugar, and flour in the Aboriginal diet.[69] Foods are an especially useful boundary because they link the present action of women to the olden days. But the meaning of any practice located between Aboriginal and European spheres remains open to contextual manipulation by listeners and speakers. Take for example Joan Ela's description of the precontact past. Of the three items considered to be characteristic of the precolonial past, memories of nakedness provoke the most laughter. Joan states a reason why "they" presently tie up their breasts: "Might tie breasts because they fly up and down 'plopplopplop,' maybe they see themselves on video."

The reference to video underscores the women's sensitivity about the evaluation of their practice by viewers. Historically, the ethnologist, ethnographer, and the government official have viewed and evaluated Aboriginal practice. While past Aboriginal informants set the conditions for non-Aboriginal knowledge of indigenous practice, Aboriginal informants have been portrayed negatively within this economy. W. Ramsey Smith wrote curtly of his work in Port Darwin in the early 1910s.

> We pass into the scrub or bush just outside the township, where we find here and there a small day camp of perhaps half a dozen natives. The first thing to do is to pass the usual compliments, the next to ask the ever needless question, "Do you smoke?" and then exhibit a stick of tobacco. The natives hereabouts do not chew. Then we ask, "What name your country?" i.e., What is your tribe? Every separate handful of blacks we came across is composed of members of one tribe. Afterwards conversation becomes general, and we can ask about property, or custom, or dress, or inspect their body markings or their teeth, and finish up by taking a picture and departing, leaving behind more tobacco. (Smith 1924, 126–27)

Smith left behind more than tobacco. He and the other colonial actors I discussed above established a radically unequal economy of inspection and representation, which at Belyuen now has a distinct gender component.[70] As the countries of the Laragiya, Wagaitj, Beringgen, and other Aboriginal people were slowly appropriated, mythic stories, whose meaning and power derived from a living relationship to that country, became objects of purchase across stratified economies based on ethnicity and gender. This political economy of cultural exchange continues. Blurring the lines between private economic publishing ventures and governmental land claim practices, Mary Eladi commented on how cultural texts are also political-economic instruments. During an afternoon at the adult education center in 1989 she stated, "You're going to keep telling mythic stories, you're going to keep telling stories in the true form, and maybe they will give you and me this country."[71] Mary Eladi has had two Dreamtime stories published; she and the women I discuss throughout this ethnography have contributed to over a dozen other books on Aboriginal economic and cultural practices in the north. Moreover she, Grace Ziyesta, Annie Ziya, and others are also central witnesses in the Kenbi Land Claim.

However, it would be misleading to define evaluation and the surveillance of practice as a wholly Euro-Australian initiated moment. While teaching self-censuring to indigenous people was an important colonial strategy for cultural and economic domination (Asad 1986; Ranger 1983) and indigenous articulation of the self and group through colonial discourse is a good sign that this strategy is working (such as women's unease with nudity; see also Fanon 1967; JanMohamed 1983), Aboriginal evaluation of cultural practice and performance is an indigenous part of conversational practice (the constant monitoring of the form and content of persons' knowledges previously discussed) and of the ceremonial relationship between owners and managers (Maddock 1983).

Thus embarrassment over nudity marks only one side of the cultural hegemony of the Christian colonization process and the customary relationship between Aboriginal performers and audience. On one hand, attitudes about nudity signal a change in Aboriginal outlook since the contact period. For example, Joan's discussion of bare breasts and the laughter it provokes signal the ambivalent meaning of nudity in contemporary settlements and, therefore, its availability for social manipulation across ethnic and gender stratifications. But, on the other hand, these new attitudes are reabsorbed into customary positions. Baring one's breast is both a moment of embarrassment and sanction in the contemporary community (which although not "missionary" certainly resides well within a Christian perception of proper clothing) and a performative moment of cultural power. For instance, women dance for corroborees at various ceremonies and tourist events in Darwin, on the Cox Peninsula, and in the Daly River area. The question typically asked is whether performers will have to dance with or without a shirt, a useful index for gauging the importance of an event. The "shame" of going without one's top is counterbalanced by the pride that Belyuen women have of being able to perform their cultural heritage. Whether or not a woman is "strong for her culture" in front of Aborigines and non-Aborigines is an issue that affects young and old alike.[72] A similar issue arises among young men who wear body paint and "diapers" when they dance at ceremonies and tourist corroborees. Presenting oneself without standard attire becomes the mark of a traditional outlook at the moment that it is noticeably other, and, in the Enlightenment paradigm, measurably better or worse. No matter how white men stare, say Belyuen men and women, Aboriginal people should have pride in their culture. *It is a thing* that they do not want to lose. They argue that women must be willing to go *yingipalat* (E, breasts outside) when the occasion warrants such as for ceremonies and land claims. However, the performance of "nakedness" does not bridge the distance between the precontact past and postcontact present. Belyuen men and women are aware of this saying, "use to be people never thought about it"; before white people came "no one worried about their breast hanging outside."[73]

The Cultural Politics of the Past

I want to close this section and chapter by returning to a question that dogs researchers' and women's attempts to apprehend the "traditional" precolonial past. We saw above that when women use the past as an index to traditional practice, they cannot avoid the links between their own present social practices and the narrative coherence of the past. How then do they avoid decreasing their status in the process of evoking positive images of past indigenous practice and identity? In other words, how do women evoke a past without presenting themselves as a corrupt part of the present?

Belyuen women do so, first, by a process of cultural editing that cuts out obvious nontraditional elements from current practices and, second, by blurring the distinction between what they experienced as children and what the precolonial olden days were like. One can see evidence for this in how women treat non-Aboriginal researchers, for example, ethnobotanists and ethnozoologists. Because of long experience with the academic and culture industry, when a researcher contacts the community, Belyuen women find out what the person is interested in recording (bush foods, bush medicines, language, culture), then what will satisfy this desire and, at the same time, satisfy some desires of their own. Belyuen women then begin deciding what will count as, for instance, a traditional medicine and food: What is the difference between a medicine and a food? To answer this type of question, women choose between the various goods that they now use and those that can be recorded as traditional. They say things like, "Not that one, that came from white men" or "I don't know about showing this plant to him; it might be a white man's plant; this researcher wants traditional Aboriginal plant medicines."[74] Before researchers have crossed the Darwin Harbour, then, what will be shown to them, where it will be revealed, and who will talk has all been decided. Usually all this organization goes for a small price: a ride in the countryside, a few soft drinks, and a quick day of gathering dyes or seafoods for some women, as others entertain the researchers and exchange information among themselves. The "feedback" that results between researcher and older women affects how Belyuen women understand their food collection practices and what they tell the next researcher who drives down the road (cf. Giddens 1986).

Belyuen women's ability to perform ceremonies and to recite cultural texts or ethnoclassification principles distinguish them as people who know their cultural history and who know the importance of its presentation. In the current political economy of "performative difference," both Aborigines and their Euro-Australian legal and ethnographic representatives are encouraged by governmental and political-economic structures to exoticize Aboriginal knowledge and practices in order to regain economic and political rights to land. In contemporary Australia, cultural difference, whether marked by women dancing without a shirt or pointing out bush foods, is politically advantageous to some communities because social legislation supports Aboriginal traditions and because current economic structures provide Aboriginal and non-Aboriginal communities alike with profits in an increasingly tourist-oriented regional, national, and international economy. While Belyuen women know a great deal about the local countryside (see App. 2), the use of their knowledge (of history, customary stories or law, language, or hunting and gathering skills) as a "canary in the coal mine" for cultural authenticity is, ultimately at this point, to their disadvantage. As much as women know, visiting researchers can present other facts either sifted from the ethnographic record—that Aborigines can read only at the risk of losing their traditional status—or learned from other Aboriginal communities.

Pressures on Belyuen women to create, emphasize, and exoticize the cultural gap between Aborigines and non-Aborigines come from a variety of local, regional, and national sources. Locally, for instance, the schoolmaster's interest in old Belyuen marriage practices directs some of the conversation. The school topic, Aboriginal family history, itself organizes the focus of history: stories should be about Aborigines, not about whites or Aborigines and whites. My interest in matters of productivity skew other conversations. The West's historical interest in the boundaries and personality traits of Aboriginal nations has guided most discussions of precolonial Aboriginal history. Nationally, in the last ten years, the publishing industry in Australia has marketed the Aboriginal culture of the north; this market is rooted in and dependent upon the notion of cultural difference. Glossy coffee-table editions that highlight the foods and products that northern Aborigines collect and the uses they make of them have been especially profitable. High-quality pictures show colorful and exotic animals, plants, and sea products held in the hands of smiling Aboriginal children, sage Aboriginal men and women, and a younger set of healthy, happy-looking people. These "bush foods books" provide a counterpoint to a Euro-Australian view that northern Aborigines have sunk into an inescapable mire of welfare programs and alcoholism; they instead present a smart and resourceful people whose culture is interesting and full. How do popular writers reconstruct the hunting-gathering scene and make it appear pristine? How do Belyuen women create a "traditional" precolonial practice from their modern hunting and gathering activities? Like the cultural editing that Belyuen women are encouraged to do, popular writers also achieve images of traditionality by asking women and men to show them their "traditional" foods, medicines, and products and then editing from the written and photographic record the modern implements that litter the scene—expensive four-by-four vehicles, soda and junk foods eaten alongside the bush foods, plastic grocery bags in which the foods are collected, and so on.

The difference between how women act, what they show, and how and what researchers present to the public creates a good deal of amusement and frustration among Belyuen women. Some older women, tired of the seemingly endless parade of researchers, shake their heads and say, "All of these bush foods are Aboriginal, mangoes and everything, animals too, cows; let the researchers photograph anything now."[75] Women express a similar sentiment about the creolization of local Aboriginal languages. Words like *pudan* or *pudawen* (Port Darwin) and *butjigat* (pussy cat) are part of the "real" Emiyenggal language now. Other women who believe it is important to record what older women still remember of 'precolonial' food collection practices, bush lore, and language become frustrated themselves when researchers ask the same questions over and over: "We do the same thing all the time. Why can't that mob of researchers get together and talk to one another? You should tell them."[76]

Even if non-Aborigines were to begin talking to one another, the need for researchers to gather their own material, and disagreements about how to interpret data, would drive them back to the field. For Belyuen women who enjoy doing some aspects of this work and who can find a researcher who will pay them for their time, doing "language-language" or doing "culture business" can be personally satisfying and profitable. It also serves to increase older women's status on the community: they know their culture and make a good name for the community within the region. Belyuen women take advantage of this and turn what *was* it like to what *is* it like to be an Aboriginal person in Australia?

By blurring the gap between their present practices and the practices of their ancestors, Belyuen women postpone the question of whether their histories refer simply to their own past or to a past conversant with the Aboriginal Dreaming. Women elide their years of interaction with Euro-Australians, an elision mandated by new economic and political demands, by organizing what they will tell: stories about the olden days, stories about cultural and ethnic difference, and especially stories about exploits that occur on food collection trips. These food collection stories can be easily linked to the current practices of most Belyuen women.

Blurring the gap between their own practices and precolonial practices does not mean that women believe the past has been bridged. At times, for Belyuen women, it seems far easier to touch the mythic force of the Dreaming—the bridging of the present with the Dreamtime—than it is to bridge the social and economic conditions of the contemporary world with those of the precontact world. For example, Belyuen men and women stress the importance both of knowing their traditional foods and of being able to do without European foods periodically (see chaps. 4 and 5 below). On outstations, people pride themselves for being able to live off the land and not needing to dip into *bedagut* (European) foods stored in camp boxes. Everyone uses these commercial foods, but everyone also counts the rate at which they use them. Families that live off *lour* (flour damper) when staying at their outstations are considered shameful. However, the daily collection of foods, while providing cultural "training" to younger Belyuen adults and children, does not provide them access to their precolonial past. Rather, the outstation context and the predominance of hunting and gathering activities often prompt people to think about the great difference between their own lives and the lives of their ancestors. At night, after a long day hunting, fishing, or sitting about, people describe their ancestors' lives as "same but different": people in the past did not "shortwind" (have asthma or ill health) when they hunted. They went out every day and did not have flour, rice, canned beef, and sweet tea waiting at camp if the fish did not bite. Belyuen women remind me that life without these European foods is a life they "can't imagine," although people often speculate on what it might have been like, "just a little bit of sugarbag mix it up with water." It is the gap between what people need and want and what they perceive their ancestors needing and desiring that causes them to comment caustically when whites expect them to tell stories about times and peoples they never met and do not and cannot know.

part two

ASSESSING LABOR-ACTION: DREAMING, DEVELOPMENT, KNOWLEDGE/POWER

3 Labor's Lot

The Construction of Human Bodies and the Countryside

> In our modern understanding, we tend to see "mind" and "body," "body" and "spirit," "spirit" and "personality," "personality" and "name" as in some sense separate, even opposed, entities though we manage to connect them up in some fashion into the unity or oneness of "person" or "individual." The blackfellow does not seem to think this way. The distinctiveness we give to "mind," "spirit" and "body," and our contrast of "body" *versus* "spirit" are not there, and the whole notion of "the person" is enlarged. To a blackfellow, a man's name, spirit, and shadow are "him" in a sense which to us may seem passing strange.
>
> —W. E. H. Stanner, *White Man Got No Dreaming*

LABOR-ACTION AND CULTURAL LINKS TO LAND

The cultural meanings and products Belyuen Aborigines draw from their everyday economic practices—how their actions produce their cultural relationship to and their political authority over the Cox Peninsula region despite the fact that they do not claim to own these lands—are oriented inward toward the local group and outward to other Aboriginal and non-Aboriginal groups, mediating and responding to the entangled two-sidedness of Aboriginal life (Bakhtin 1986). The everydayness of their labor-action is swept within the suprahuman realm of a sentient landscape populated with ancestors and totemic beings (Munn 1970) and into the supralocal landscape populated with competing social groups and political-economic agendas (Peterson 1991; Merlan 1991). All economic action is a potential moment of political and cultural interpenetration and interpretation: What are the meanings of this labor process, product, and performance in relation to the Dreaming, historical and contemporary totemic and social landscapes?

It might surprise a newcomer to the Belyuen community to learn that local Aborigines do not consider themselves to be the "owners" of the Cox Peninsula region. Their actions within and attitudes toward this land are consistent with the authority and confidence a Westerner expects of an owner. Belyuen Aborigines consult with one another for economic and cultural information about the surrounding countryside. When problems arise or unexpected incidents occur (a site acting in an unusual way, such as being over or underproductive or being suddenly hit by a wind- or rainstorm), young people consult older Wagaitj and Beringgen, and older Wagaitj and Beringgen consult their memories for an answer: Why did the site act in that way? Wagaitj and Beringgen rely on their own knowledge, history, and practice to understand the signs of the country. Nevertheless, Belyuen men and women leave no doubt that the Cox Peninsula is Laragiya country in the sense that Laragiya mythic beings created and now maintain the shape of the countryside. The totemic origins and the present occupation and knowledge of the Cox Peninsula seem, then, to be split among several Aboriginal groups.

Because of where they say their parents' countries lie ("Daly River but they always been here"), their often contradictory statements about the location of their country, and the way they relate to and use the Cox Peninsula, Belyuen Wagaitj and Beringgen are often described as an Aboriginal group interrupted in the process of land succession. In this scenario, Belyuen families were forced to confront their origins and remember whence they came because the traditional process by which secondary rights—derived from land use and prompted by colonial disruptions to regional Aboriginal life—are transformed into primary rights was interrupted prematurely in large part by the Kenbi Land Claim.[1] In successful transitions "the historic past . . . is usually quickly forgotten and often actually suppressed" by the older generation in order to expedite the process of succession (Sutton 1988, 261).

Some processes described as cultural succession seem to have been occurring on the Cox Peninsula. Brandl and Walsh (1983) report, for instance, that due to their prolonged use of and residence on the Cox Peninsula, many Belyuen men and women have conception totems (*maroi*), and, for the same reason, Wagaitj men received responsibility for Laragiya ceremony in the region (for the latter, see Brandl, et al. [1979]). Moreover, through their prolonged residence, Belyuen Wagaitj and Beringgen have come to know the region's totemic and ecological landscape more thoroughly than any other living Aboriginal or non-Aboriginal group: knowledge (Berndt 1982; Hiatt 1982) and experience (Myers 1982a; Peterson 1972) being key means by which claims to land are converted into rights in it. Belyuen individuals and families have other "secondary rights" to the Cox Peninsula region, including matrilineal totems in the area, personal names and nicknames from Cox Peninsula sites, and affiliations to totemic tracks connecting the Cox Peninsula and the Daly River regions.

Irrespective of their multiple totemic connections to the region, Belyuen families are sensitive to Anglo and other Aboriginal perceptions of their historical origins. No matter the historical conundrums outlined in the previous chapter, they take these perceptions into consideration when discussing land ownership. For while "boundaries are to cross" and may be downplayed in any given instance in Aboriginal Australia, they are not ignored (Williams 1982, 1986). Because "land grabs" deny the accepted cultural mandate of the totemic order, they are grounds for serious conflict between Aboriginal groups. Belyuen men and women carefully and repeatedly note they are not "hungry" for someone else's country; instead they claim that they are "stuck" on the Cox Peninsula because of the long-term effects of their land-use practices on the cultural disposition of the sentient countryside. Rather than a choice, they frame their residency and cultural economic practices as a duty; implicit in this formulation are the political benefits, from an Aboriginal perspective, of "working for country."

Faced with historical changes in Aborigines' totemic and land affiliations—often a result of violent colonial dislocations—and with the primacy that the Aboriginal Land Rights (NT) Act, 1976 gave land-owning versus land-using groups, anthropologists began to discuss the long-term effects of land use and residency on Aboriginal land tenure.[2] When Aboriginal labor is discussed in relationship to land succession or to cultural ascendancy, however, it is often portrayed as an enabling device; the foraging mode of production allows various groups to develop rights to the same stretch of land, and these rights can, given the right historic conditions, be converted to a higher or lower order. The flexibility and choice Aborigines have in identifying with places (Sutton and Rigsby 1982; Myers 1982b) is linked to the multiple bases on which land tenure is built (Barker 1976; Williams 1982, 138–41; Peterson 1983). These multiple bases are, in turn, directly connected to the moving and flexibile nature of the hunting "band" (see Turnbull 1965; Lee 1979; and, for a critique, Morris [1982]).

One basis on which the flexible nature of land tenure is built is the complex sign relationship between Aborigines and mythic countryside. The sign function of totems have been discussed at length (Stanner 1965b; Munn 1973; Williams 1986). In short, the marks left by the action of mythic beings provide the conditions and the opportunity for an interpretation or reinterpretation of the relationship between an individual or social group and a stretch of land; that is, they are both sinsigns and legisigns insofar as they point to a relationship and are the grounds by which the indexical relationship can be interpreted (Shapiro 1983). Mythic marks are the product of meaningful events (totemic sites are a product of a Dreamtime being's action in the past while other topological and bodily marks are signs of mythic action in the present, although not all mythic events leave physical traces) and the means by which that event and further events occurring among persons and that place can be interpreted. Whether mythic marks are the products of meaningful action or the means of interpreting that action depends where they are located in the action-interpretive process.

A problem with portraying economic activity as a motor that drives cultural action is that motors break down. Hunting practices might not occasion new totemic affiliations like conception Dreamings or the transfer of ceremonial knowledge. Where no totemic or ceremonial transfer occurs, economic action's effect on a group's cultural relation to land is usually ignored, reintrenching the opposition between Aboriginal land users and landowners. Economic practices remain just that, economic moments of physical subsistence rather than central cultural and political moments in the development of human-human and human-land relations. Even where totemic transfer occurs, the politicization of "traditional ownership" is such in contemporary north Australia (see Smith 1984) that to claim primary responsibility for a totemic site outside one's patrilineal "estate" (see Stanner 1965a; Barker 1976) is to risk being accused of a land grab and socially or physically reprimanded. However, even without the rediscovery or reinterpretation of a group's relationship to a mythic site, events that occur while people are hunting or otherwise moving across the countryside contribute in large part to the cultural "process by which space becomes 'country'" (Myers 1986, 67; Stanner 1965b).

Given the political climate in which Belyuen families live and the current representations of their origins, it is not surprising that they turn away from ownership and succession as key discourses for land affiliation and toward a cultural understanding of labor as the means by which they have become "straight" (also "right") for the Cox Peninsula region. A focus on the multiple lots and transformative powers of their labor is receptive both to the historical features of their residence on the Cox Peninsula and to the mythic conditions under which they reside there. Rather than engaging in a head-to-head fight over the ownership of particular sites, Belyuen Aborigines make a much broader claim about the importance of their labor practice to the life of the entire totemic landscape. To understand these claims we must examine, first, how Belyuen women and men portray the Aboriginal body and its economic labor as a product of mythic action and how they highlight the use and value of the human hunting body to the mythic countryside—the latter being especially important for understanding why landed action is seen as a duty. Second, we must reexamine, as against the products of mythic labor, the products of Aboriginal historical and contemporary economic action and discuss how hunting contributes to a transformation of Aboriginal bodies and landscapes into depositories of social value. Consider a paradox: If human labor is an object of the mythic countryside's intentionality, how can the human object produce the landed subject during hunting activity? Throughout this discussion I leave open the origins of Belyuen representations of their labor. By doing so, however, I do not mean to suggest that these meanings and representations are "traditional" in the sense that they predate contemporary social and political conditions. I think they are interesting insofar as they do show the dialogical nature of contemporary Aboriginal society and the Australian nation-state. Nor by leaving open the origins of these representations do I intend to present these women's views as the Belyuen view. Rather these representations are women's positions in the sense that women are the main source of them and the community's in the sense that they are one of the options that the community has found for articulating the often contradictory needs of satisfying mythic country, making sense of their histories, and living in contemporary north Australia. Therefore, this chapter should be read against the last two, especially my previous discussion of the land claim.

Myers (1982b, 1986), Munn (1970, 1973), Merlan (1981, 1986), and Ingold (1987), in their different ways, have worked on many aspects of the problems I discuss below. All have pushed our understanding of Australian Aboriginal action (and, in the case of Ingold, hunter-gatherer action more generally) to include how Aborigines articulate human and landed subjectivity and intentionality and what the implications of these articulations are for how we understand Aboriginal practice. In addition, Peterson (1972, 1991) and Hamilton (1982, 1984), while not making the cultural construction and social implications of intentional mythic and human action central to their writings, have set the theoretical conditions for understanding the role totemic systems play in the "politics of locality."

LABOR'S INTENT: THE ACTION OF THE MYTHIC COUNTRYSIDE ON THE HUMAN HUNTER

From an Aboriginal perspective, all matter is the congealed labor of mythic action. While some mythic actions were concentrated in the Dreamtime past at certain, now sacred, sites, the land is more generally permeated by signs of present-day mythic intentionality and agency (see also Stanner 1965b). The Dreaming is the "given condition of 'what there is'" (Myers 1986, 47) both in the phenomenal and noumenal sense: what one finds here in the world and what establishes the parameters of that world.[3] Even here, however, the "world" is uneasily articulated. The world Belyuen Aborigines describe as possibly encompassed by the

Dreaming includes indigenous landscapes in Africa and the Americas; but they quietly wonder over the foundational order of white European lands given their own experience with white European actions and beliefs about how to value land.

It is the present-day physical features and intentional nature of the world that Dreamtime beings founded. The movements and adventures of Dreamtime beings such as Dingo and Dugong laid the physical features of the world in which Belyuen Aborigines now act. Moreover, these beings remain critically present, touching and commenting on the actions of the living and acting as ancestors, successors, consociates, and contemporaries to Aboriginal families. Along with the geographic order, references to Dreamtime beings provide narrative shape and meaning to human practice. Aborigines say, for instance, that these beings cause events both in their responsibility for general conditions and for their triggering specific incidents. Everyday action's meaning emerges from the general narrative frame of Dreaming intentionality. It is not true that every event touches, in an immediate way, the Dreamtime. Belyuen women will laugh pointedly when a person attributes an event to Dreaming intervention when it is really due to her own stupidity, such as getting drenched in a sudden rainstorm, or to her own dumb luck, such as stumbling upon a huge goanna. "Not Dreaming that," they say. Deciding what is Dreaming and what is not in a landscape filled with unusual occurrences ("im different this one")[4]—note not extraordinary events that can be fairly easily attributed to Dreaming action—involves making political and ontological decisions.

Decisions about what events touch and are directly in contact with the Dreamtime are inherently political because moments of contact establish a relationship between the person, Dreamtime being, and the place where the event happened. The relationship so established can be of more or less significance to the person and the social group, but each event lays down a sediment of relatedness (Myers 1979, 1986) between the human group and the country in which it occurred. Humans, born into a body already shaped by the mythic intentions of its patrilineal and matrilineal ancestry, are subject to new rounds of mythic action throughout their lives.[5] These rounds of mythic encounter articulate more subtly the place of persons within that mythic order, including their place within the landscape. Although the way that ritual and the various totemic systems (descent, birth, and name totems) common in the Daly River position and orient individuals and persons in the countryside have been well discussed, exactly how hunting-gathering activity and historical events are subjected to and contained by mythic ancestral action has yet to be fully theorized, even though economic activity interacts and is daily refracted by mythic ancestral intentionality. This theorization is critical in the present case because, for Belyuen Aborigines, everyday hunting is the mode by which they ascertain the intentions and meanings of self and group.

The relationship between hunting action and cultural expression is as rich as it is multifaceted. First, all hunting trips interact with the sentient landscape, and the sentient landscape most commonly encounters humans engaged in economic, not ritual, activity. No hunting or camping trip is wise to ignore possible manifestations of mythic action, since such manifestations can signal where foods may be found in abundance or where dangerous Dreamings may emerge. Second, the temporal, spatial, and dietary patterns of people's economic labor (economic activity itself) are understood to be the embodiment of human and mythic ancestral desire. Third, hunting and gathering anchors local discourses of power and land tenure, providing critical knowledge that is used to discern the "real" meaning of an event's lineage to a mythic source from possible meaning; that is, in local idiom, a true story from a claim ("Im just say" or "Im been just put that story there"). But perhaps most important, attention to the intersection of cultural and economic spheres shows us how Belyuen Aborigines are able to negotiate the shoals of the various social histories in which they are politically and legally enmeshed and through which their local identity emerges.

How mythic ancestors body forth human hunting activities and interact with social history can first be seen in the work of *maroi* (conception Dreamings) and *durlg* (descent totems). *Maroi* and *durlg* are two important "themes and overarching principles" that Belyuen Aborigines use to "maintain, discover, and create particular relationships" to places and to each other (Williams 1986, 5).

The work of maroi (conception) Dreamings

The action of *maroi* or "conception Dreamings" demonstrates most clearly how mythic labor produces human economic activity; and, therefore, how cultural and economic spheres interact and how social history is embedded in totemic processes that occur during the day-to-day use of land. Elkin (1950) notes the link between conception Dreamings and country affiliation in the Daly River region. He writes that *maroi* are "connected with the natural species in or through which the child to be born reveals itself to its father." This spirit is found in the "father's part of the tribal territory and so the child's 'Dreaming' will be the same as the father's, unless there be more than one 'Dreaming' in the latter's clan country which is sometimes the case" (Elkin 1950, 68). Elkin assumes here that Aborigines are living and hunting in their father's country a significant amount of the time. As a review of their social history showed, this was not the case for the Wagaitj and Beringgen living at Delissaville when Elkin did his fieldwork. Moreover, it is unusual for a patrilineal connection to an estate (clan country) to be a necessary condition for a personal Dreaming (Barker 1976; Merlan 1986). Although in some Aboriginal groups conception and birth totems "come out of" an estate totem or Dreaming nearby—one of the permanent marks that mythic ancestral creatures left in the landscape—Belyuen Aborigines do not always associate a conception totem with a known, nearby Dreaming. In fact, it seems that only a generalized conception association with the Belyuen water hole ("All a kid been come from that Belyuen") and a specific connection to turtle and dugong sites for the children of a *danggalaba* woman are specifically linked to a totemic site.[6] However, other conception Dreamings may later be revealed to come from a nearby mythic site.

Aborigines depict how *maroi* (child spirits) act in many ways. Francesca Merlan (1986) has reviewed some of the ways child spirits are described (they are playful beings "looking" for parents) and the ways people themselves describe encountering them (they find, dream, or accidentally eat them; see also Kaberry 1935–36). At Belyuen *maroi* are said to "catch" people hunting, camping, and traveling through the countryside (*mirrkamenaiyi,* "the *mirr* [or *maroi*] hid,"E). As people go along, a *maroi* hears them or smells their sweat, then manifests itself as a food. Sometimes men are said to catch the food and give it to their wives; other times women are said to come upon the *maroi,* hidden in the food, themselves. Either way a woman unintentionally eats the *maroi.* It then creates a child, in the process marking the fetus with a birth anomaly, an index pointing back onto itself, such as a cleft lip for a snake or thick hair on the back for the seaweed caught on the shell of a sea turtle. A metonymic association is established between the child and the species, but it is a metonymic relationship that, as in the case of metaphorical relationships, combines two previously unrelated domains. As Terry Turner argues, "outside, *a priori* to the metonymy itself, they may well be seen as belonging to separate wholes" (1991; 134).

As others have noted, the Aboriginal body is like the physical landscape in that both are the result of mythic action; like the bush they move through, Aborigines' bodies are made and marked by the travels of Dreamtime beings. The Aboriginal agent is, however, a critical component to the mythic process insofar as he or she provides the act of interpretation necessary to understand the associations of sites in the landscape with sites on the body. Through naming practices and narrative associations, speakers link and interpret bodily and mythic sites. All names, other than most Anglo names, are metonymies that establish social and political relations between present and past, persons and sites.

The following description of how Belyuen Aborigines gain *maroi* was given during the Kenbi Land Claim.

Mr. Parsons: Yes. Well, before I ask any questions, can you explain to us—just you explain in your own way, what is the maruy? What does it mean? Is it important? Why is it important? You explain in your own way.

Agnes Lippo: Say like you by ———, go hunting and mother and father say—father and mother and my father go and get a fish or crab or snake like that you know—water snake and bring that fish back home and then my mother cook that fish or something like that. And when we say like we have dinner, or something like that, so we eat that fish. But there is another thing is that he probably maybe special fish like a baby fish. So my mother eat that fish and couple of days come and I vomit.[7] So we knew what that was that fish he ate she ate and we know that was baby. Couple of weeks time come, you know, baby in every generation, baby come, you know. Everybody got to have baby here. (Kenbi Transcripts: 1989–90, 2009)

Agnes's reference to vomiting as a sign of *maroi* action is common in north Australia, although any "unusual occurrence or natural phenomenon" is a potential indication of it (Merlan 1986; 475). Belyuen Aborigines note the strange actions of any plant and animal as possibly indicating a *maroi* event. Indeed numerous ethnographers have noted that "almost any phenomenon can be thought of as an ancestor" given the right circumstances surrounding its occurrence (Munn 1973, 24; see also Myers 1986; Stanner 1979b, Elkin 1936–37). Bodily functions and appearances such as birthmarks, however, are the typical way in which Belyuen Aborigines tell when an encounter with a *maroi* has occurred and what *maroi* it was. Although she does not do so above, at other times Agnes Lippo describes how *maroi* leave marks on the fetus's body. Moreover, from a political perspective, resultant transformations of the child's body by the *maroi* are the best way to establish a relationship among the child, the species, and the place where the child was conceived (Merlan 1986) and, more significantly, was *preconceived*; that is, where the child was formed as an idea in advance of its being.

Because the *maroi* preconceives an image of the child before making it, the relationship between persons and their *maroi* (once established; see Falkenberg 1962) is considered an essential, constitutive part of persons' characters. To cut off or sew up a "deformity" is seen as a grotesque Western practice that severs a person's self and social identity and his or her relation to places and mythic life. Here, then, intentionality is central to an Aboriginal notion of human production (Ingold 1987), but intentionality is relegated to the action of mythic ancestors. *Maroi* intentionally hide in foods and create children. Men and women unintentionally capture and ingest them. Country intentionally provides marks on the body for people to find, Anglo-Australian doctors and nurses, without being aware of what they are doing, cut them away.

Even from this brief description, one can see how the actions of *maroi* Dreamings are embedded in human economic practices and social history. Human hunting activity "triggers" *maroi* action: Aborigines must be passing through the countryside for the spirits of animals and plants to react to them. Therefore, while I agree with Merlan's insightful claim that "a child 'conceived' (in the Aboriginal sense) in a certain place, given its specific totemic associations, is not the *same* child as it would be were it to be conceived in a different place" I disagree that there is "no idea of a methodical relation between human activity and the emergence of children from the Dreaming" (1986; 479). It is just that the human activity necessary for the emergent child is neither sufficiently sexual nor intentional; but a present, acting human is needed for the full expression of the potential totemic and ecological world—a necessity with political ramifications in interethnic struggles over land in which one solution to the protection of Aboriginal sacred sites is to put up fences and develop around them. Perhaps we as researchers can only see the significance of hunting action to the mythic order when hunting is no longer the inevitability of Aboriginal labor-action.

The connections between child spirits and human actions continue after their first encounter. Once triggered, *maroi* rely on hunting processes to be embodied in the fetus—they must be chased, captured, and ingested. Once embodied, *maroi* bear on the economic practices of their hosts, influencing what foods people hunt and eat and the places they visit. They do so by creating powerful wants and repulsions; indeed, *maroi* are part of a complex local theory of economic compulsion. Aborigines *must* visit and hunt in places because of the siren-like pull of their Dreamings and because of the human ancestors who are embedded in their body and the place. Of course, not everyone visits or hunts in the region where they received a conception Dreaming. Irrespective of actual action, Belyuen Aborigines tend to hold to the stronger form of "must" rather than the weaker form of "should." The difference between what must happen and what does happen is noted ("Must got to go there, but nothing") but does not lessen the prescriptive nature of the relationship. Instead, the prescriptive relation is kept as an available explanation for why the Belyuen must continue to use regional lands. For similar reasons people are said to be able or unable to consume certain foods. Swallowing and regurgitating are noted to be mythic themes in many north Australian texts (see Hiatt 1975). But at Belyuen the ability to swallow and keep down foods can be an everyday expression of the link between Aboriginal action and its mythic ancestry and, thereby, Belyuen hunting action and land use. For instance, a Belyuen man's inability to eat or to hunt sea turtles skillfully is attributed to the action of his mythic ancestry (here his descent totem, *durlg*). His Dreaming creates a powerful repulsion in him; it does not simply effect but produces his abilities and disabilities, in this case, to hunt turtles and eat them without regurgitating their flesh. But his inability is also an explanation for why he does not hunt turtles as do many of his Kiyuk brothers.

According to Belyuen Aborigines although *maroi* will "catch" anyone who wanders by, to be caught by a *maroi* is a sign that the countryside has claimed the person—and kin often then associate themselves with him or her—as its own. This claim is understood in several ways. Viewed from the land's perspective, humans satisfy *maroi*'s desire to express itself "outside" (here, "in a human body") and to embody itself in matter. An Aboriginal theory of mythic labor's production of the human hunting subject sees this production as constitutive and permanent. But such a theory is at once radically ontological and deeply political, not only in the way that conception totems are usually described as contributing to the Aboriginal polity. As is widely discussed elsewhere in Aboriginal Australia, birth and conception affiliation are types of association, along with descent and initiation, that a person can stress to claim rights over ritual parphenalia and the land associated with it (Hamilton 1982; Falkenberg 1962; Merlan 1981). In other words, conception provides persons with one "orientation" in space, relating people to places (Peterson 1972, 24); descent, initiation, and historical experiences provide persons with others. Aboriginal individuals, for political and social reasons, choose among the "constellation of parameters" that define their "possible avenues" to land affiliation (Barker 1976, 232; Meggitt 1971; Strehlow 1971).

While Belyuen Aborigines point to birth and conception affiliation as one reason they are "straight" for the Cox Peninsula, it is not birth or conception itself that they see as decisive. Rather, it is the process by which people and land interactively bind themselves together, using the human body as a depository of cultural value—of which *maroi* is an example and a part—that defines their rights over the countryside. Conception Dreamings, increase ceremonies (Kaberry 1939), and such are part of a more general process by which the social and historical interactions of humans and mythic creatures are embedded in and marked on the environment and human body. It is, however, only when people have the choice to hunt or not to hunt that putting one's body into the countryside to be acted upon becomes a powerful discourse of cultural work. At this moment, different "modes of production" can be distinguished and culturally valorized, although at an earlier time different types of labor (men's and women's) were also symbolically invested. Labor-action, like the *maroi*-marked body, becomes a form that is associated with the traditional countryside and traditional practice. Not surprisingly, then, whenever records portray their ancestors using the land, Belyuen men and women see this as evidence of their long-standing willingness to uphold the Dreaming processes inherent in land use. Interacting with the sentient country, daily expressed in their conversational orientation toward it and physical exploits in it, is the "work" Belyuen Aborigines describe themselves doing "for country." It is important to note that this type of work is compatible with the very social history (discussed in chap. 2) that calls into question the identity of the "traditional owner" of the Cox Peninsula.

Sutton (1988) and Myers (1986, 68) rightfully caution, however, that a central question remains about what part of social history "endures" and what is erased in Aboriginal narratives. The brief social history below shows to some extent the narrowing or editing involved in the plotting of social history into the totemic landscape: that is, how social history is selectively narrated as a series of geographical and corporal marks associating persons and places. Marjorie Bilbil's description of her and her daughter's *maroi* demonstrates how, as Wagaitj and Beringgen groups moved across the countryside, they collected mythic attachments to different sets of countries. Ordinary hunting trips are transformed into signature events of mythic want; traveling in mixed social groups remixed totemic and land affiliations in that group (see App. 1, part B).

In the early 1900s, Marjorie Bilbil's father, a Marritjaben (Beringgen) man, camped and traveled with an Emi group throughout the Daly River and Cox Peninsula region. As this group moved up the coast they learned about the ceremonial and ecological landscape. During the period after Delissaville Aborigines escaped from the Katherine war camps and were camping in the Daly River, Marjorie "caught" her *maroi*.

> MARJORIE BILBIL: They found this wild cat under the hollow log and they found this wild cat, and my father the other step-brother of his, they were poking that wild cat under the hollow log, and my father always get under that log. He could not touch that cat, but the other one usually say to him I can feel him right here on the end of the hole, so they decided to put fire and burn it to chase it away. So they burn that hollow log and the cat—the wild cat came out from that hollow log. So my father told me that was your maruy from Red Cliff, and he got—I got a little black mark around my ears, because the cat got burns on his ears. That is why. My father told me the story. (Kenbi Transcripts 1989–90, 2074).

After the 1950s Delissaville (later Belyuen) was reestablished and Daly River groups moved or were moved onto camps there, at Wadeye (Port Keats), and at other Aboriginal settlements in northwest Australia. Marjorie grew up at Delissaville and married an Emiyenggal man. They lived at Delissaville but camped, hunted, and traveled throughout the Cox Peninsula region. Her daughter, Kathleen, received a *maroi* from a site on the Cox Peninsula. Marjorie's husband is one of the "two brothers" described below.

> MARJORIE BILBIL: Two brothers went out with that old man, and they went to look for turtle, and it was not far away deep water. They went around those reef and they found this turtle sitting on the reef and it was covered with sea week [*sic,* weed] and they killed that turtle and it took them long way down near deep water to float up to pick that turtle up so that old man said, "Oh," he was a bit tired, "when this turtle going to float [so] we can pick it up," and that old man said, it is probably one of your going to have a kid.
> MR. PARSONS: Yes.
> MARJORIE BILBIL: So, he said to them, "You two blokes going to have one of the kids, I think." That was Kathleen maruy at Gamarrng-gamarrng. (Kenbi Transcripts 1989–90, 2076)

In the above examples *maroi* encode social history, thrust it out onto the landscape;[8] but *maroi* are also embodied, absorbed, or forced within the human hunter: into her body and into a particular economic practice that influences and creates her desires and spatial orientations. Particular and unusual features on the human body and the surface of the land are read against mythic intention and everyday human action. Other features are left out, for example, all reference to the character's descent affiliation. While left out, the problem of descent is not side stepped. As I discuss in the concluding chapter, the critical role genealogical descent plays in land politics is resupplied by the legislative process. And, I should reiterate, a discourse of descent does not benefit male or female Wagaitj and Beringgen in the context of traditional land claims. Descent from patrilineal and matrilineal totemic sites for both groups most often leads them back to the Daly River.

While *maroi* are one example of how social history and economic action are embedded into the landscape there are other nontotemic methods. Early descriptions of the Wagaitj and Laragiya noted the environmental effects of their economic practices on the shape of the surrounding countryside. Herbert Spencer, for instance, described the effects of Wagaitj and Beringgen practices as short-lived. Likewise Stanner argued that within weeks of being abandoned, an Aboriginal camp showed no signs of past occupation; it was swept clean by the wind and rain and tide (Stanner 1979a, 32). More recently, Nicolas Peterson has distinguished between accidental and deliberate effects produced by Aboriginal labor based on the intentionality of the producers themselves.[9] One type of mark occurs as a "side product" of foraging activity, another as a deliberately produced "reminder of particular events" (Peterson 1972, 16). The latter intentional marks are images of "other marks of a larger scale left on the landscape . . . the results of the activities of ancestral heroes" (1972, 16).

Belyuen Aborigines see social and cultural history in both the side products of their economic labor and the deliberate marks they make. Deliberate marks include acts to lodge memory in the landscape, for example, hanging up a can to remember where a truck bogged or leaving unfilled the hole left by the bog for the same reason. Side products include the "leftovers" of previous actions: the lonely flapping of bright nylon strings left tied to poles once used to secure a mosquito net, the husked shells of various seasnails and crustacea left half-buried in the sands of a seasonal camp. While the flapping of strings is often the only obvious remainder of an outstation after it has been abandoned for some time, it is invested with sentiment and occasions stories about the place. And a shell-midden, created from numerous trips to the same spot, is a moment for expressing social memory—expressions that serve to establish and support the social group (Gumperz 1982, 6–7). As a Belyuen woman told me: "Just chuck shell here. Im go more and more [bigger and bigger]. All a old people from before sit down eat im finished now. Chuck im. Im go now finished. Make all a shells, this place now. We keep going [with it] now" Even without the string or the shells, a place holds memory insofar as its use is remembered. Further, memories are seen as a product of work like other products of economic and mythic Dreaming action.

The terms "side product" and "leftover" are unfortunate, however, because they obscure how the remains of a previous action are themselves reinterpreted as a sign of the Aboriginal group's active productive relationship with the countryside. Things or events that are products of meaning and action may be the means of interpretation in another. It is not enough to see land use as depositing social and historical debris to be gathered up and remembered, a kind of local archaeology of the self and social group. According to Belyuen Aborigines land use also creates and refashions the preexisting features of the countryside that are then put to use. Places begin to body forth the likenesses of people living by them; people note them doing so and use this mirroring to establish or reentrench their political rights to the place. For instance, in 1989, on an access road to an outstation on the northern coast of the Cox Peninsula stood a pandanus tree whose fire-browned leaf pattern resembled the hair of the senior woman whose family camped nearby. Its spindly trunk also resembled her body, creating, overall, a quite striking portrait of her as it and it as her. Passing the tree usually provoked laughter from her grandchildren and calls to it, such as, "Look there's *tjemila*" and "Hello *tjem-*

ila." This woman's daughter and niece referred to the tree as an example of the funny tendency of land ("Im funny like that, place") to mimic the people who live on it. It is in this landscape that people leave and find marks of their relatedness that, in their turn, rearticulate the relationship between humans and places.

Of note, the above stories are not only about the geographical embodiment of social history, but also illustrate the two-way process of meaning construal. Marjorie's *maroi* narratives and the daughter and niece's comments about the pandanus tree overlay the landscape with an interwoven plot ("path") of human and ancestral interaction—a plot that is contested and negotiated in the formative moments of storytelling on the community—firmly rooted in everyday land action. Moreover, stories (*mal*) are themselves locally understood forms of work; they "pull" the Dreaming into view. The persuasiveness of stories emerges from the traditional framing of events and from the placement of the mythic in everyday experiences. This placement allows women to speak from the powerful position of having been there. Marjorie's stories, for instance, follow mythic narratives in tense (*always, usually*), and in framing devices (two brothers, old man) and plot (how mythic ancestors and modern humans moved, hunted, and interacted with other mythic beings, creating the signs and marks of the present-day topography). Her stories are instances of what Basil Sansom notes of south Australian narratives: "The contents of the stories [for taking country into ownership] are distinctly 'modern' for legend has replaced myth and human identities walk the Dreaming tracks of collectively evoked adventure where men . . . have usurped the mythical figures of the Dreaming" (Sansom 1982, 121). Thus people reanimate *maroi* and influence the form of the environment by simply being (human physicality allows *maroi* expression) and by narrative emplotment wherein present action is embedded in mythic plots.

The work of durlg (descent) Dreamings

The action of *maroi* are most sharply distinguished from that of *durlg* (descent totems) in the former's close association with hunting action. But, while descent totems (*durlg*), are less directly tied to economic behavior, they do interact with and critically structure the vicissitudes of history that play a significant role in where Aborigines hunt and camp. And, over time, Aboriginal hunting helps produce *durlg*.

Durlg (and its synonyms) refers both to localized mythic creatures with permanent sites (each having a sex, age, and language affiliation) and to a sea creature—the Rainbow Serpent, an aquatic equivalent to the Australian Aboriginal desert culture's Rainbow Snake. The Rainbow Serpent roams the deep blue sea lanes between the Daly River and Port Darwin and beyond. Elkin quotes his Delissaville Wagaitj informants that the cult hero Wariyn, a *durlg* Dreaming site on the Cox Peninsula, made all other *durlg*, and that the Rainbow Serpent was second to Wariyn in being and power. "The 'Dreamings' or 'dorlks' were brought or 'made' by a cult hero, Waran. Second to him in Wagaitj thought is the Rainbow Serpent, which is the 'shade' of all water 'Dreamings'" (1950, 68).

Tentatively, then, today *durlg* are those permanent marks associated with the Dreamtime ancestor Wariyn. Individuals acquire rights and duties to the sites of *durlg* through their parentage and assume responsibility for them as they mature and learn the appropriate stories and practices for places. Descent totems are seen to conceive and to preconceive humans like conception Dreamings do: they preconceive the descent of themselves in the form of humans before they are actually born into a new generation. Rather than humans passing down sites from generation to generation, the interior mythic power of sites passes itself down through the human body (see also Barker 1976; Munn 1970).

My tentativeness is defining *durlg* as those permanent sites created or associated with Wariyn lies in the processual nature of Belyuen Aborigines' knowledge about sites. There are many ways that sites are referred to and known. They may have a formal Aboriginal place-name (which is sometimes substituted with an Aboriginal English version) or a nickname like "old camp" or "donkey yard." Place-names can refer to a mythic creature or event, to a natural species, and to nothing other than the place itself (it is "just a name"); that is, not all named sites are *durlg* sites. The main difference between a nickname and a place-name depends on to whom its origination is attributed. Wariyn gave some sites their place-names in the mythic past; humans provide others with nicknames. Examples of each type of place-name are found on the Cox Peninsula. *Bulpulnyini*, for instance, is a site on one of the Port Patterson Islands named for the species *bulpul*, "passion fruit," with the addition of the locative *nyini*. Another site on the Cox Peninsula named after a plant species is *winganyinidurlg*. This site is a mythic site of the Red Apple Dreaming and so is modified by *durlg* and the locative *nyini*. Buwambi is the name of a site on the west coast of the Cox Peninsula. Although no one remembers the meaning of the word, in the past, some Belyuen people say that, "something" was at Buwambi. This past can be rediscovered if, in the future, an Aboriginal person rediscovers its name and meaning through physical or Dreaming interaction with the site; in a common metaphor of value, this person may find "diamonds" (or, in the case of the Pintupi, "gold" [Myers 1986, 67]). Therefore, which place is *durlg* and which is not, like which human action touches the Dreaming and which does not, is part of a body of knowledge and practice mediated and expressed by individuals who see their knowledge as partial and predicated upon continued ritual and economic interaction with the countryside. It is this predication that most clearly ties *durlg* expression to human economic action.

Not only are *durlg* sites embedded in the processual nature of human knowledge, they are also part of a totemic transformation more generally. The difference between *maroi*'s compatibility with social change and *durlg*'s emphasis on social stasis is resolved by the eventual transformation of *maroi* (conception) sites into *durlg* (descent) sites. Elkin's informants stated that one's personal Dreaming was sometimes the same as and sometimes different from one's patrifilial Dreaming (*durlg*, B; *therrawin*, E). Today Belyuen women's descriptions of "cult totemism," "conception totems," and name sharing are similar to those of Elkin's informants; sometimes they collapse and sometimes they separate conception (*maroi*) and patrilineal (*durlg*) identities. Some are said to have both a "conception Dreaming" and their father's paternal Dreaming; others "get" their father's paternal Dreaming at birth (often at a different place than he received his) and no distinction is made between the two categories. But, in either case, in order for a *maroi* to pass through people into new life, these people must come into contact with the spirits who live within the animals and plants that men and women encounter when hunting, camping, and traveling in the country. Without the country left open for *maroi* to congregate, without people free of work commitments to camp in the country, an integral part of the natural productive order itself is unraveled.

Maroi can come from some unknown site and become, over time, a *durlg* site proper for that place; in other words, a place can assume the *maroi* of a person as one of is *durlg* Dreamings. For example, some twenty years ago, in the Daly River area, a wallaby "conception" Dreaming disappeared into a nearby water hole while an Emi man was hunting in the area (his Emiyenggal family had lived in the Wadjigiyn-Kiyuk country for many years). Soon after his wife became pregnant. The wallaby was the child's *maroi*. But the Emi man also Dreamed (discovered) that there was a wallaby *durlg* in the water hole of special significance to his entire family. It was from this discovered *durlg* site that the *maroi* had come. This "Dreaming for wallaby" is Emiyenggal within what is otherwise called Wadjigiyn-Kiyuk country. Through this Dreaming, the Emiyenggal family established residential rights for the area. Here we can see that historical changes in residence influence spiritual affiliations which, in turn, affect the rights of residents. As a group lives in a place, their personal Dreamings become increasingly clustered and revealed to be (or to be confused with, depending with whom one is talking) *durlg*. In this way, the land's symbolic self shifts to accommodate new human groups and their spiritual selves. Brandl et al., writing in the Kenbi claim book, make a similar observation.

> As we collected information from informants on their *durlg* and *maruy* and associated natural species and features, we noticed that what was a *maruy* for a man, could become a *durlg* for that man's children. Thus among the *durlg* belonging to Olga Singh (nee Lyons) associated with the claim area, is *djalawa,* or, kingbrown snake. This was a *maruy* for her father. Similarly *wilar,* the cheeky yam Dreaming near Rankin Point, was her father's father's *maruy* and is now one of her *durlg*. (Brandl et al. 1979, 162)

Nowadays older women also state that *durlg* are always represented by a physical object, whereas *maroi* need not be. Belyuen men and women say that, although they can be physically destroyed, *durlg* never change; they do not suddenly become "just a rock" or become a snake when before they had been a crab (although a snake Dreaming can join a crab Dreaming at a site).

Aborigines encounter these *durlg* physically and verbally during their economic practices. Perhaps no other aspect of the Belyuen description of the natural world is as startling as the way that mythic *durlg* creatures emerge from the seemingly impenetrable surface of the ground to reward or to punish people. The terrible aspect of this can only cautiously be compared to Western reactions to earthquakes, fault lines, volcanoes, and—perhaps more pertinent as of the late twentieth century—the radioactive and chemical waste dumps that bubble up cancer-causing sludge. What we take to be stable suddenly and quite uncomfortably gives way under our feet. However, the analogy between a sentient, mythic site's reaction to a social group and the so-called ecological and climatic upset of the natural environment quickly breaks down. Because the country is sentient, the ground, for Belyuen Aborigines, is always potentially liable to act for its own reasons. They attribute catastrophes such as oil spills, skin cancer, the ozone hole, and pollution to country acting as an agent and punishing Aborigines and non-Aborigines alike for their transgressions of mythic and ceremonial areas. Some people may plead ignorance—they did not know that they had upset a site. But ignorance and arrogance are no excuse, Belyuen men and women say. The country exacts its revenge on "big-eyed" (arrogant) Europeans worldwide, though it is often the indigenous people who suffer first. (Belyuen women speculate that the North American and African continents originally had spiritual centers that processes of colonization and industrialization disturbed or destroyed.) The country comments on what is happening around it by emerging from or submerging into the sea or ground and by sending out disease or other natural objects.

Country can be placated if treated in the right way. When Belyuen Aborigines walk or drive across bumpy Cox Peninsula and Daly River roads, they pass by sites where mythic creators "sit" or "sleep." When they do so, a senior woman or man calls out to the site in one of a ranked series of languages to let it know who is passing and why. People also "chuck sweat" at the site;[10] they figuratively throw their body smells toward it so that they will not disturb the mythic being. Belyuen women and men "approach" Dreamings in their conversations with the same caution as they approach them in the countryside. Good speakers avoid the names of a *durlg* during parts of the day and year, and they switch to an appropriate language to talk about the antics of a Dreaming. Moreover, speakers mark themselves as knowledgeable by these code switches and by the canon of mythic and everyday stories they know. Whether or not listeners hear these verbal strategies depends in good part on what they know of local practice and how they view the position of senior Belyuen women and men. A listener might not know that code switching "means" the speaker is paying respect to a site, or a listener might not "follow" senior persons' practices as a guide to the traditional. Most younger people, however, watch senior women in particular for guidance in how to act and think about the mythic countryside.

Aborigines do not just encounter *durlg*, they also carry *durlg* within themselves; namely, they are themselves instantiations of the mythic being. A person can have several *durlg* ancestors. For Belyuen residents the reasons for this are several. In the violent conditions of the colonial past, as a group lost its members, the surviving males or females transferred the rights and responsibilities for a *durlg* to another patrilineal group. In an opposite move, many different patrilineal and matrilineal groups associated with different *durlg* merged and became associated with one "totemic" group when *durlg*s were "lost" (forgotten) because of forced relocations. The several descent totems individuals have provide them with a choice (locally described as people being more strongly influenced by one or another of their mythic and human ancestors) of which to follow, as do the various kinds of totems they have: descent, conception, and name. But while most Belyuen individuals have a number of *durlg*, only three young people are descended from *durlg* on the Cox Peninsula, other than in the sense of conception from the Belyuen *durlg*. In other words, all Belyuen families have a choice of which *durlg* they will emphasize, but few people have a choice of emphasizing a *durlg* relation to a site on the Cox Peninsula.

In summary, descent (*durlg*) and conception (*maroi*) Dreamings draw differently on spatial and temporal dimensions of human action and geography. Conception *maroi* embody themselves in each new Aboriginal generation that lives and hunts on land, while descent *durlg* embody the sons and daughters of its previous self no matter where they are living. Both types of mythic ancestry, however, are perceived to orient hunters in space and to their prey. The difference between *maroi*'s compatibility with social change and *durlg*'s emphasis on social stasis is resolved by the eventual transformation of *maroi* sites into *durlg* sites. This transformation of Dreamings further elaborates the critical dimension of social history to the production of the Aboriginal cosmology. The cause and consequences of this transformation necessitate a turn away from a discussion of the action of Dreamings on the human hunter to a discussion of the effects of human actors on the sentient countryside.

LABOR'S LOT: THE ACTION OF THE HUMAN HUNTER ON THE MYTHIC COUNTRYSIDE

There are two broad ways in which the hunter produces the cultural countryside. In the short term, the two immediate products of human hunting action, speech (*mal*) and sweat (*wenterre*), or more specifically, the marks and by-products of human action, "work over" (causing "it to think about us" or providing the conditions by which "we entered its ears") the mythic countryside's identity, disposition, and desire. Aborigines diverge from some Western analysts in their understanding of work's effect on objects and countrysides. Rather than congealing in the objects made or gotten, in the short run Aboriginal labor is seen to penetrate them, in a way analogous to how sound passes through the ears and air and sweat penetrates the body. Evidence for this comes from several areas. In local medicinal practice, underarm sweat, applied to a painful region of the body, "digs into" the area and helps heal by applying warmth to the hot area of the sickness where the sickness is seen to be lodged. Likewise, sweat penetrates (*kanamutpirr,* you chuck sweat) its surroundings and is noticed (*kingmenayi m>rrimin,* "it smelled different sweat"). Words also pass into the body and lodge there (inside the belly, *mari*) like sicknesses; indeed they cause sickness and social disturbance if they are improperly used, as in the wrong use of words, the wrong place for certain words, or the wrong story for a person or a place. Social health is restored when words and stories no longer lodge in the belly, but instead pass easily through (*piyamal kanabritj mari*).[11] Human labor does, however, congeal in the countryside in a positive way in the long run. People who live and labor in an area (and who are thereby seen to be "stuck" to it) permeate the region with their words and sweat. When they die, they are embodied at the site; their spirit/self resides there. They visit relatives who happen by and humbug strangers. Thus hunting's cultural production unfolds through time in a process that includes human hunting action, mythic reaction, and eventual mythic transformation. In the following I look at each of these processes more closely.

The transformative power of language and sweat

At Belyuen language and sweat are used and are seen to affect the actions of country and people. Country and people listen to the sounds around them. Both are angered to hear "wrong words" (the wrong language or the wrong use of language) and to be around the "wrong sweat"; they are comforted to hear the sounds and to be in the physical presence of their relatives. Francesca Merlan (1981) has noted that mythic sites "hear" the language of their people. And Aboriginal groups represent the ability of a site to understand their speech as a sign of their custodial rights and duties. Country that recognizes a people's languages and sweat provides abundant foods, offers safety from mythic danger, and accepts the spirits of the deceased. This process is related to others David Biernoff has described elsewhere in Aboriginal Australia. Places can become safe or dangerous by virtue of the events that transpire in them because events sink into a place and affect the character of a site (Biernoff 1978). John Bianamu, a senior Belyuen Wadjigiyn man, describes the dynamic between human language and sweat and mythic reaction. David Parsons and John Bianamu are discussing the Cheeky Yam Dreaming that travels up and down the Bynoe Harbour.

> MR. PARSONS: Can you talk other language to him?
> JOHN BIANAMU: Oh, well, I do not know. You have got to wash the sweat, you know, with the salt water.
> MR. PARSONS: Wash the sweat with the salt water.
> JOHN BIANAMU: Wash his sweat and drink cold water and take it and you can smell the way it is different people.
> MR. PARSONS: Yes.
> JOHN BIANAMU: And you turn back then.
> MR. PARSONS: Yes.
> JOHN BIANAMU: If you do not talk or if you do not do that, he might drown you.
> (Kenbi Transcripts 1989–90, 1674)

Because speech and sweat communicate to and penetrate the county, rites exist for formally introducing a young Belyuen member's sweat and sounds to the country. In one practice, humans don protective "garments" of smoke and clays when passing by mythic sites so that Dreamings will not be traumatized (made deaf, or *tjeingithut*, "block the ears").

Lenny Singh, a senior Kiyuk man at Belyuen, describes another common practice. Note how he discursively interrelates the action of the human hunter with initiation and totemic activity.

> LENNY SINGH: Well, what you do is, when you go down Bakamanadjing, well, you got dreaming site there. You got Wutwut there and Wariyn. Now, the younger people that pass through initiation ceremony, they have got to be painted up and then sprayed with salt water or dip them in the water, you know, and they can go across, and whoever person that can talk Larrakia, you know, other people, they will be travelling along, you know, talking at the same time saying that we are going hunting, you know, and otherwise the dreaming site will not give you anything, you know, fish or turtle, anything like that. (Kenbi Transcripts 1989–90, 2030)

Belyuen Aborgines state that their parents and their parent's parents were dipped into briny seacoast sites and inland freshwater holes before going hunting and that, now, they dip their sons and daughters into these same mythic conduits. Through the historical mingling of human sweat and watery sites during hunting trips and initiations, Wagaitj's and Beringgen's language and sweat sank into country, allowing it to recognize Belyuen men and women. Like John Bianamu, Lenny Singh states that Laragiya should be used to speak with mythic sites on the Cox Peninsula, but he and other senior Belyuen men and women say that, because of the historical mingling of Belyuen languages into the landscape, if there is not a person in the group who knows the Laragiya language then other Daly River languages can be spoken.

How human language and activity, mythic disposition, and hunting behavior interact can be seen in three short stories, each commenting on how a "foreign" presence affected hunting sites. They describe "foreignness" based on linguistic skill and sweat, sex and age, and ethnicity. The stories also point to the role interpretation plays in negotiating the space between event and meaning. The first story describes a visit a group of Belyuen women and I made to an inland Daly River settlement.

During the dry season in 1989, a group of Belyuen women and I traveled to the Daly River to visit relatives and to drop off a collection of ceremonial bamboo. While there, our Maranunggu kinswomen invited us to hunt longneck turtle in a nearby creek. To catch the turtles, one walks down the creek in waist-high water probing its sides with long poles for turtle holes. In any hole one can find up to a dozen turtles or a small, freshwater crocodile, which are dangerous little creatures. Although we traveled to the hunting site, Belyuen women demurred entering the creek for several reasons. First, women hunt turtles in a far safer way on the Cox Peninsula: with long thin metal poles, they poke along the dried surface of a freshwater swamp until hitting a turtle's back. But women had better reasons for declining than personal safety. The most important of them was their linguistic inadequacy. They did not have the language to talk to the crocodiles, telling them not to pester us as we hunted, an ability the local Maranunggu women had and used during the trip. Lacking these language skills, Belyuen women said they would jeopardize not only their own health but the health of others. For, they said, their foreign speech and sweat would permeate the water, causing not only the turtles to "disappear" but summoning a crocodile plague as well. Among other things, this would ruin everyone's chance for a turtle feast. Far better, Belyuen women said, to let the local women hunt and for them "to act like Queen Elizabeth": to sit on the bank and to wait for the food to be brought back.

Human labor's negative effect on the mythic countryside is also seen in the second example. South of the Cox Peninsula is a vast wetland plains once filled with longneck turtles. In past dry seasons, Belyuen families traveled south for day and weekend tips. They burnt the towering grasses, then fanned out across the hardened wetland region, poking along with metal rods until they heard the resonant thump of a turtle's back. On one edge of the wetland was a Dreaming. Whenever there, people called out to it in Emiyenggal and Batjemal, two Daly River languages, and "chucked" their sweat toward the site. They also, more casually, remarked on other trips families had made to the site and pointed to various marks left in the environment, for instance, old holes where men and women had earlier dug large turtles out of the ground.

In 1987, razor grass began covering the plains making it difficult to hunt in them. Many possible explanations for this "plague" circulated, some involving the devious intentions of Anglos, but most theorizing that the nearby Dreaming had "sent out" the razor grass. The consensus was that a family from the inland region, unfamiliar with the totemic topography and with foreign language and sweat, had upset the Dreaming. When one member of this family sickened soon after, this view was further reinforced. The Dreaming had "sent" the plants and then "gone underground." Because it had submerged into the countryside, it was no longer able to recognize even its own kin: the Belyuen hunters.

Countryside's differing reactions to local and nonlocal groups is a common theme of everyday stories about the land. Some of the most gruesome stories about a Dreaming's angry reactions to persons are, however, reserved for non-Aborigines. The violent details of these stories are indirect comments on the foreignness of Euro-Australians and on their great disbelief in a mythic, sentient country.[12] Country must go to extreme lengths to prove its sentient nature to them; it is only then that Euro-Australians *sebi* (understand or "know for themselves") the truth of what Aborigines describe. A particularly horrific story told about an

Euro-Australian man who transgressed a site in the Daly River area serves as a useful example.

During World War II, a group of Wagaitj Aborigines stayed in the Anson Bay area to make sure that the Australian Army stationed there did not inadvertently "rubbish" a particularly dangerous site. After the war, other Euro-Australians moved back into the area. They would not listen to the advice of local Aborigines (as the army is said to have done). One white man in particular continued to camp in a certain area after being told repeatedly not to. One day an Aboriginal man walking down the beach found the white man's body which had been eaten alive by white ants (*pengainme*, E). The ants are said both to have emerged from the ground (*kamani*, E) around the site in order to devour the transgressing white man and to have emerged from the man's body when he was found (*yena yin yenayi manthayena kanayi*, E; "it came from his nose, from his neck").

An inability to understand the meaning of an event or to listen to others who can understand is the "tragic flaw" of many mythic women and men as well as whites; for instance, in one story, a set of mythic women are described as too intent on a project (weaving a dillybag) to hear the rapes of their daughters. The women, and in other stories men, are also described as *tjeingithut* (E, or, *thuttjeingi*), as having blocked ears.[13] They both cannot hear what is happening around them and will not listen to the advice of others. If humans suffer from *tjeingithut*, they are said to mimic the country; country and people are said to become "deaf" when they have experienced a traumatic event, such as was the case described above in which the wetland plains' Dreaming sent out a plague of razor grass and then submerged underground. A clever man or women can also produce a traumatic seizure of the ears in order to keep a person from remembering an attack or to make a person unable to hear the warnings of others (see also Elkin 1980). *Tjeingithut* is critical alienation; it is to be cut off from outside influence. You cannot be influenced by another's words or actions. This is a very unhealthy state, for speaking and acting with country and one's kin is, normally, a way of keeping both "loose," "sweet," and productive (see Myers 1979, 365). The difference, however, between Aborigines who suffer from *tjeingithut* and Europeans who suffer from the same is that the latter seem to be constitutionally deaf. Whereas Aborigines are born into the world listening and must be made deaf, Europeans are born into the world *tjeingithtu* and, if they are lucky, can be made to hear by Aboriginal people.

These last two stories are especially interesting because they touch on a major theme in this ethnography: Belyuen informants couple a person's inability to recognize the signs that the country sends with a person's refusal to listen to those people who can understand the meaning of the countryside's shape and action. Many stories are told of Euro-Australian men's and women's *tjeingithut* activities in the countryside. Euro-Australians are commonly described as unwilling and unable to listen to words intended for their benefit. When the inevitable happens, so say Belyuen men and women, it is no fault to local Aborigines. As we see in due course, the bankruptcy of grocery stores and the death of tourists in the jaws of crocodiles are linked to white people's seized-up ears; they do not or cannot listen to good advice. Through such narrative associations, Belyuen women link insensitivity to a wider socioeconomic practice of land use. Euro-Australians should not be allowed to gain control of a rich and productive area such as the Cox Peninsula because they obviously are not able to hear and understand its needs or warnings.

Others have discussed the importance of knowledge in inter-Aboriginal ritual and land disputes. For example, Ronald Berndt noted,

> Ownership, therefore, is not ratified simply by making a claim to land, even though substantiating genealogical information may be available. A major issue is *knowing* that particular land—knowing about the sites, their songs and rituals.... The land is a living thing, the source of all life, and the mythic deities who symbolize that land and its inherent life-giving properties need to be nurtured. The implications of this view are far-reaching in the present-day situation, where cultural knowledge has been considerably modified. (1982, 7)

In the Belyuen case, however, knowledge is not simply a list of objective facts about a site. For Belyuen men and women, knowing the meaning of the countryside includes but is not bounded by these facts. It goes beyond them in understanding that people must have an empathy, created by daily interaction, with the mythic countryside. It is this empathy that foreigners (here non-Aborigines) generally lack.

Foreignness to a place is also discussed in terms of age and sex. A *durlg* site, which itself has an age, sex, and language affiliation, responds to each of these qualities in the human hunter. An Emi women's site, for instance, reacts differently to older, female, Emi than to persons who differ by any one of these social identities. In mythic stories, social conflict results not from any simple social opposition embodied in two Dreamtime beings, say, the timeless opposition of men and women signified in the mythic opposition between Old Man and Old Woman; it results instead from the complex intersections and contrasts of a number of social identities. Old Man and Old Woman are also related by age, kinship, and language affiliation. Everyday stories about mythic sites and, more generally the country, also comment upon the complex nature of social identity. In most everyday stories *durlg* react to a combination of men and women, young and old, Belyuen and non-Belyuen Aborigines, Aborigines and non-Aborigines.

The following story, describing how a Kookaburra Dreaming (banyon trees) reacted to a party of women passing it, provides a good example of how the sex, age, and local status of hunters have a powerful effect on the mythic countryside. The Kookaburra women are dangerous, cheeky (*malarritj*) personalities. In order to avoid angering this Cox Peninsula site by their strong sweat as they pass, young Laragiya, Wagaitj, and Beringgen men and women should walk in silence, have white clay smeared on their bodies, and surround themselves with smoke. Just to be sure, most men and women avoid going too near the Dreaming altogether. However, one day, on a mapping exercise, I was with a group of Belyuen women and a young woman and her mother from another Aboriginal community as they walked to the Kookaburra site and then beyond it to another mythic site on the coast. The Daly River woman and her daughter broke off from the main party because the mother had been drinking that morning and was too tired to walk all the way down the beach. Unknown to the rest of the party and quite unintentionally, they both went near one of the banyan trees as everyone else went on to the next site. Angered at the hung-over condition of the older woman and the youth of the younger woman, the Dreaming "sent out" a devildevil (*pederra*). The devildevil attempted to "sing" (mesmerize) the older woman into the dense vine entangled bush. When the other women and I returned and found out what was going on, we helped, with much force and persuasion, the daughter drag her mother back to the truck. A plan to collect oysters was abandoned and we returned to the Belyuen Community. Several versions of the day's events unraveled as time went on; most, however, centered on the Kookaburra tree's ability to "come out" in response to the strong, foreign sweat of the women.

Belyuen men and women agreed that the Kookaburra reacted violently to the young foreign woman's sweat. In other instances, Belyuen men and women disagree over what caused the mythic creature to react. They, like the Western Arnhem Land Gunwinggu, bear in mind several considerations when assessing a story, including the participants' relationship to the land concerned, their age, and their sex (see Berndt 1970). But while Belyuen Aborigines have these considerations in mind, the sex and age politics of interpreting everyday events in the countryside make each social fact more of a starting point for a group's position than a simple index that provides a method for accessing the truth. For example, men, who control most of the boats and vehicles in the community, argue that the presence of women of menstruating age endangers sea-hunting parties because the women's sweat provokes mythic deep-sea creatures such as the Rainbow Serpent and the Cheeky Yam Dreaming. Women emphasize the connections between age and gender and the effect that both have on the emotions of the country. They do not deny that young women imperil sea trips, but they argue instead that both young men and women are dangerous to sea-based or seaside Dreamings.

All of these examples show the effect that hunter's foreign and familiar languages and bodies have on the mythic countryside and on the productivity of the hunt. Familiar language and sweat make the countryside "sweet" and willing to give its produce; foreign language and sweat cause the countryside to "dry up" and to send out human and ecological sicknesses. How then do Belyuen Wagaitj and Beringgen understand the effects of their own language and sweat on the Cox Peninsula? For, if the country is listening, it hears a different combination of languages today than it did in the past. Today, as in most north Australian Aboriginal communities, Belyuen Aborigines speak and understand a number of languages. Aboriginal English is the lingua franca of the community.[14] Older women and men also speak several Daly River languages: Batjemal, Emi, Mentha, Marriamu, and Marritjaben.

In D. T. Tryon's (1974) taxonomy, all of these Aboriginal languages, except Laragiya and Belyuen English, fall within the "Brinken-Wogaity" group.[15] Batjemal is in the Wogaity subgroup, Emi and Mentha in the Maranunggu subgroup, and Marriamu and Marritjeban in the Brinken subgroup. Belyuen Aborigines cluster their languages and social identities somewhat differently. Michael Walsh (1989) writes that, in the past, Belyuen Aborigines used the term "Wagaitj" to refer exclusively to the Wadjigiyn and Kiyuk people. Now it is used to refer to the Emi and Mentha as well. Belyuen people usually use the term "Beringgen" to refer to the Marriamu and Marritjaben language groups at Belyuen, although it can refer to a wider group of southern coastal and inland Daly River groups. They also distinguish the "easy" (familiar) sounds of Wagaitj and Beringgen languages from the "hard" (unfamiliar, foreign) sounds of the Laragiya language; the former group of languages is said to be easy to master, the latter language quite hard. If Laragiya and Daly River groups experienced each other's languages as foreign, must not Laragiya mythic sites, at one point, have experienced the Daly River languages as foreign, strange, and annoying?

For reasons outlined in the Chapter 2, we must be cautious in estimating how different the current social geography of the Cox Peninsula is from the precolonial or colonial period. It is difficult to know whether, in the immediate precolonial period, Aborigines on the Cox Peninsula spoke Laragiya with its several dialect forms, or whether, because of existing ceremonial and economic ties, a number of a Daly River languages were spoken there as well. We can safely assume that the linguistic diversity of the Beringgen, Wagaitj, and Laragiya camps around the Cox Peninsula region in the late 1800s and 1900s was greater than that of the Belyuen community today. First, there were more speakers of each Aboriginal language. Second, there were a greater number of languages spoken: Kiyuk, other dialects of Batjemal and Laragiya, and, presumably a Djerait language or dialect.

People now say that, other than Laragiya, which all mythic sites can understand and which no one can speak fluently, Batjemal is the best language with which to speak to the Cox Peninsula and its sites. This in some ways reflects the linguistic code of site names. While the sounds of many languages filled the Cox Peninsula countryside, the names of sites are exclusively in Laragiya and Batjemal.[16] Emiyenggal and Menthayenggal are the next-best languages to speak to Cox Peninsula sites, and Marriamu and Marritjeban are understood "a little bit" depending upon who is speaking to which site. It is reasonable to assume that preferences reflect the historic waves of Wagaitj and Beringgen migration, the varying degrees of mythic (*durlg*) and ceremonial relatedness of the various Wagaitj-Beringgen groups to the Laragiya, and real political divisions between competing Wagaitj and Beringgen groups for preeminent status on the Cox Peninsula.

Questions remain: How is Wagaitj and Beringgen action in the landscape understood to be something other than foreign? What role does time play in this understanding (see Fabian 1983)? To find answers, I return to Basedow's (1906) and Elkin's (1950, 1955–56) earlier evidence of the mythic connections between the Daly River and Cox Peninsula regions, in particular how *durlg* tracks may act as a bridge or a barrier between sociogeographically distinct regions. I also discuss how violence among competing groups can become, over time, the condition under which groups are incorporated into regions.

Conflict and Commitment

In the land-human equation, what looks like a human choice of Dreaming affiliation can look like, from the totemic side, a safe way of hedging one's bet. If people seemed to each other to be scarce in the precolonial landscape,[17] a situation that prompted the well-known hunter-gatherer social strategies of sharing and group inclusion (Sahlins 1972; Gould 1982) then so must they have seemed scarce to the totemic landscape. Providing people with multiple totems is one way of safeguarding the cultural value lodged within the human social and physical body. Another safeguard can be found in the tracks that link totemic groups across wide stretches of an area. "Tracks" that connect similar *durlg* (e.g., the path of a Sea Turtle Dreaming) in the Anson Bay and in the Cox Peninsula regions played an important role in creating and mediating social conflicts on the Cox Peninsula in the nineteenth and twentieth centuries and, thereby, in influencing the present-day hunting activities of local groups.

Tracks can entice and provide a boundary. They constitute a path that can be followed or blocked depending upon social and ecological conditions. The social history of Delissaville (Belyuen) is a good example of how *durlg* tracks provide the means by which travel can be distributed (from a totemic perspective) and the means by which travel can be restricted. Elkin (1955–56) describes the Delissaville settlement of the 1950s as spatially organized by social divisions loosely based on language group affiliation. In an aside to his description of a *wangga* (a type of Daly River trade dance) sound recording, Elkin notes that the Delissaville settlement was divided into a Laragiya-Wadjigiyn camp and "across the road" an Emiyenggal-Mentha camp. However, the language group affiliations Elkin described reflected underlying totemic connections between *durlg* and their human manifestations. The Wagaitj Kiyuk and Wadjigiyn living with the Laragiya had existing affiliations to *durlg* sites on the Cox Peninsula. In the 1950s, the Laragiya remaining on the Cox Peninsula were mainly from the *danggalaba* (crocodile) and *ingyarainy* (green sea turtle) *durlg* groups. The Kiyuk were from the *ingyarainy* (green sea turtle) and *memoradjamul* (sea cow) *durlg* groups. The Wadjigiyn were from the *moiyin* (wild dog) and *boiya* (rays and sharks) *durlg* groups. Other than the shark groups, Wadjigiyn and Kiyuk groups had representative *durlg* sites in their own country and on the Cox Peninsula. A series of *ingyarainy* (green sea turtle) and *moiyin* (dog) *durlg* sites, for example, extend from the Daly River to the Cox Peninsula–Darwin area.

According to oral and written histories, Emiyenggal and Menthayenggal (who locate their language group's country on the southern side of the Daly River) had fewer marriage, ceremonial, or *durlg* connections to the Laragiya and Laragiya country, although they had many to Wadjigiyn people and country. Among their important paternal and maternal *durlg* are *kugon* (sugarbag), *kurraguk* (dove), *merrumerru* (long yam), and *ngarron* (plain goanna). None of these *durlg* traveled to or left a mark on the Cox Peninsula. The mythic connections are even more tenuous for the Marriamu and Marritjeban Beringgen. Elkin does not say where the Marriamu and the Marritjeban sibling set, who traveled with their Emi and Mentha classificatory brothers (see App. 1, part B, no. 6), camped on the Delissaville settlement, but one can assume from their affinal ties and from oral histories that they lived with the southern Emi and Mentha Wagaitj. Other Beringgen without the marriage, sentimental, or totemic links to the northern and southern Wagaitj traveled south to Port Keats (Wadeye) or inland to the Daly River mission.

Whether or not the land reacted negatively to non-Laragiya Aborigines, the various Aboriginal groups living on the Cox Peninsula often reacted violently to one another. But rather than prohibiting the incorporation of any one group into the surrounding land, the often-violent conflicts between the Laragiya, Wagaitj, and Beringgen living on the Delissaville settlement actually and, we can assume quite unintentionally, promoted it: violent conflict created the spirits of the dead that tied a new generation of Aborigines to the region. The spirits of human ancestors lodged in a place are called *nyoitj,* they are the self embodied at a site. When the identity of the spirit has been forgotten, *nyoitj* become "devil-devils" (*pederra*). The social lives of *nyoitj* are interesting because they show how initially hostile everyday relations among peoples and places are transformed over time into sites of sentiment and affection.

During the 1930s, when the Northern Territory government created a series of concentrated Aboriginal camps at sites in the Darwin township and along the Cox Peninsula to the Daly River regions, the resultant concentration of disparate groups onto small areas increased social distress and intergroup violence. In their oral histories, Belyuen women and men say that *munggul* (sorcerers) from each group attacked the opposing groups in retaliation for the "mistakes" that young men and women made during brawls. Older men and women describe the southern Wagaitj and coastal Beringgen as being under "siege" (see Sansom 1980, 133–134). During this time, many Laragiya men and women were still living on the Cox Peninsula, and many Wagaitj and Beringgen were still living south along the Daly River.[18] Mistakes made anywhere along this chain could (and still can) result in a *munggul*'s punitive response. Beringgen-Wagaitj Aborigines, unable to draw magical and spiritual power from the immediate countryside, suffered tremendously in these "wars."[19] On several occasions Wagaitj men were brought into Laragiya higher ceremony (see Elkin 1955–56). While Elkin states that the ceremony was conducted in order to discipline the men, present-day Wagaitj say that it provided the Wagaitj group as a whole with some share of the country's power and it ceremonially linked the disparate Aboriginal groups living on the Cox Peninsula.

Although Laragiya, Wagaitj, and Beringgen men and women in the past may not have planned it, the ceremonial links they made among themselves may have had, at least in the short run, less of an effect on human-human sentiment than the wars had on human-land attachment and the day-to-day process of human-land interaction. Attacks can occur in a variety of ways. Clever men and women can *getimim* (attack) a person directly or indirectly. A clever man can sneak up on his victim and remove his kidney fat, which will eventually cause his death, without the victim ever being aware of the assault. This is a practice widely reported in the Daly River and beyond (cf. Elkin 1950). A clever person can also *tjukpiya* (throw spit) at one person causing them to kill unintentionally another person, the clever man's real victim. Ironically, these direct and indirect attacks (or wars) have filled the countryside with historical markers that have become the informal spiritual centers (alongside formal Dreaming sites) for a new Belyuen generation. These *nyoitj* sites are very active, appearing and disappearing quite regularly. Their appearance signals that some event, troublesome or otherwise, has happened or is about to happen. The following provides an example of *nyoitj* action and human interpretation.

On a road to and from the Belyuen community is a spot where a particularly horrific car collision occurred in the late sixties. When driving by, people typically wave and "remember" the story of what happened there, although everyone knows the incidents already: how a long-standing intergroup dispute prompted a sorcerer-initiated car wreck, who died, what relationship the deceased had with the passersby. Depending upon the speaker's linguistic abilities, people call out to the site in Batjemal, Emi, or Belyuen English. One day in 1989, I was driving with five older and a few younger women and children down this road. As we passed the site, an older woman saw the young man who had died in the accident sitting, and then disappearing, next to the tree where it had happened. We stopped and looked at the tracks that this *nyoitj* made in the dirt and then returned to the community to see why this *nyoitj* had "come out."

Rather than focusing on the immediate purpose of these *nyoitj* appearances—a warning or a welcoming—Belyuen residents often look at what such appearances signify for group attachment to the country. Belyuen Aborigines state that appearances of *nyoitj* demonstrate that the country responds to local Aboriginal language and sweat and show that their ancestors' bodies and spirits are literally and metaphorically residing in the land. Spirits act as migration officials, as it were, protecting residents and humbugging strangers. Apparitions (*walakantha*) in the Daly River serve a similar function. In the southern Daly River country, if you are a foreigner with alien sweat, dwarf-like spirits with faces that look like your relatives "sing you" (mesmerize you) into the bush from which you never return. In the Cox Peninsula region, the country responds to the nearness of strangers or kin by sending out *nyoitj* to bedevil or to protect them, in a manner similar to the *durlg*'s response to the presence of different social groups. *Nyoitj* on the Cox Peninsula do not seem bothered that they are considered by many to be strangers (migrants) themselves.

The links I have discussed so far between totemic action and social groups are always endowed with some kind of prefiguring will, an endowment consistent with Belyuen Aborigines' view that the country is filled with mythic beings who are themselves agents cognizant of what people are doing. The distinction between the actions of particular mythic agents and those of the countryside more generally is often not drawn.[20] By blurring the lines between "the country" and "that ancestor" Belyuen Aborigines draw attention away from the political entanglements of particular localities and toward their more generalized responsibility for the entire Cox Peninsula.[21] What they do is what "mythic persons" and, more generally, "the country" does. Disputes over the meanings of Belyuen actions are referred to a generalized mandate from "the country." In short, like mythic creators linked places across the countryside as they traveled, so clever Belyuen men and women, through Dreaming insight (apperception) and hunting interaction with particular mythic sties, link up various countries or social groups. The clever person acts as the mythic countryside, seeing behind (rather than beyond) what is immediately present and showing how present social events were mythically preconceived and organized. Seeing behind things or "underneath" them weaves back to the past to get into the present—from the mythic Dreamtime to the contemporary period and back again.

An example of how the prefiguring will of the country is harnessed to human purposes is seen in a discussion that occurred on a dry-season day following an afternoon of hunting in nearby mangroves. Several women and children and I were sitting at a beach waiting for some sea snails (*Nerita lineata*) to cook. We were talking about a grey-hair crocodile Dreaming (*danggalaba*, L; *berlu*, B, E) at Bagadjet and a grey-hair Dreaming at Djibung, an estaurine creek connected to an inland swamp. Gracie Ziyesta, a senior Marriamu Belyuen woman explained, "The *berlu*, grey-hair Dreaming, links up the Bagadjet and Djibung sites;"[22] Gracie Ziyesta emphasized that the will of the *berlu* is the connection between the two sites: it wants to get from one place to the other; its desire created the track ("He wanted to go there, he made a track and joined those two places").[23] When describing how their various paternal and maternal ancestors became associated with each other and the Cox Peninsula region, she says that they likewise "joined up places" and "families," solidifying links between themselves and the region by their desire to move up and down the coast. Perhaps more critically, Belyuen women narratively frame their own social history and economic action as joining the various countries from the Daly River to the Cox Peninsula. By traveling in mixed groups up and down the coast, families joined themselves together through marriage and experience, and they reenacted the "straight line" (also "path" and "track") that Dreaming ancestors created between Laragiya and Beringgen-Wagaitj countries. Further still, by their narrative practices, Belyuen women mix the diverse social identities found at Belyuen and "track" their own practices back to a Laragiya mandate (see App. 1, Pt. B): the practice of their human ancestors mirrored the prefiguring will of their mythic ancestors. Today, Belyuen men and women similarly see themselves as revealing the preexisting connection between countries when they "line up" and "join" sites by listing them during ceremonial and more modern legal performances.

Before concluding, it is important to note that hunting-gathering activity per se is not essential to the action of ancestral beings. Human action in general allows mythic beings to appear in new generations: giving birth allows descent totems to body forth, and any action involving sweating and speaking allows *maroi* to find new wombs. Nevertheless, juxtaposing it to other types of productive labor, Aborigines now understand the spatial component of hunting and gathering to be critical to the range of mythic acquisition and, therefore, to the countryside's full mythic expression.

For example, one of the most important Cox Peninsula sites that combines both *durlg* and *maroi* is the Belyuen water hole. As the Northern Territory government began forcibly interning them onto the Delissaville settlement, Laragiya, Wagaitj, and Beringgen Aborigines' actions were increasingly restricted to the confines of the community, and their children were increasingly "caught" by *maroi* from the water hole. Although a score of Belyuen residents have *maroi* from sites around the Cox Peninsula, older Belyuen men and women state that most local Aboriginal children now "come from Belyuen" itself. Belyuen is the name of the mythic hero who sank into the ground at the water hole behind the main camp. The Belyuen water hole is also where the *durlg* (Rainbow Serpent) and other dangerous Dreamings in the Bynoe Harbour first smell the sweat of young Belyuen people. And it is the site of the regionally important *kenbi nyini durlg* (Didjeridoo Dreaming). The *kenbi nyini durlg* (Didjeridoo Dreaming) is an elaborate, mythic underground hollow tube, like a didjeridoo, or "bamboo," that extends throughout the region. By bathing in the Belyuen water hole, then, young men and women "give" their sweat to other sites around the Cox Peninsula. Women sometimes describe the water hole, Belyuen, as acting like a "telephone"; it rings up other Dreamings around the Cox Peninsula and tells them not to harm the Beringgen-Wagaitj people who are hunting nearby ("Like im boss man for all of them"). "These my kids," Belyuen is said to say.[74] Because the body is able to exude sweat and the country is able to absorb it through such "pores" as the Belyuen water hole, and because the country is able to penetrate bodies through *maroi* and bodies are able to absorb them, the Beringgen-Wagaitj on the Cox Peninsula see themselves as producing a coherent and rich cultural environment, as well as their own community, from the disparate groups that once inhabited it. So although colonial processes progressively narrowed the flexibility of the hunting group to the domestic settlement and reciprocally narrowed what *maroi* creatures and sites were able to body forth into people, Aborigines were able to find a culturally appropriate way of reestablishing severed ties with the broader countryside. Belyuen residents, introducing these processes in their conversations, articulate their connections to the Cox Peninsula and to the southern Daly River regions through ritual body metaphors and hunting discourse.

However, although Wagaitj and Beringgen are able to mitigate the constriction of *maroi* action to the Belyuen water hole, gaining *maroi* from only one site is a potentially dangerous restriction given the current reading of the Aboriginal Land Rights (NT) Act, 1976. The act stipulates that, on its enactment, all Aboriginal reserves convert into Aboriginal land.[25] Thus the seventeen square miles of the Delissaville settlement was converted into the Belyuen Community, Incorporated, in 1976. Because of this, the Belyuen reserve need not be claimed—it is already unalienable Aboriginal freehold. Thus, having a concentration of totemic connections on community land does not necessarily help in the claim for the surrounding region.[26] The restriction of knowledge and human-mythic interaction to the Belyuen community can, therefore, have cultural and political implications. From a cultural perspective, for *maroi* to pass into new life, people must encounter the plants and animals in which they hide. Moreover, for humans to know what plants and animals are acting "strangely," and so which are likely candidates for *maroi*, they must have a grasp of their "normal" behaviors. This knowledge is acquired by regular use of the land. From a political perspective, Aborigines lose rights and claims over countrysides where they do not have *maroi*, although they may have other cultural attachments that mitigate this loss—in this case, using the extension of the water hole to reestablish ties throughout the region. Older government policies, then, that restricted Laragiya, Wagaitj, and Beringgen to settlements on the Cox Peninsula and in Darwin have subsequently curtailed the means by which they can reclaim that land. I talk more fully about the politics of spatiality and development in chapter 5.

In summary, Belyuen Wagaitj an Beringgen ground their authority over Cox Peninsula lands in the various ways their hunting, camping, and traveling produce and were produced by the mythic landscape. Belyuen Aborigines see a deep interplay between economic and informal and formal mythic action. Various Dreamings "produce" the human body and its various hunting dispositions, but human hunting activity "triggers" Dreaming action and exploits Dreaming connections (tracks). More informally, the by-products of human labor—sweat and speech—are seen to influence directly the productivity of the countryside by effecting the disposition of mythic ancestors found there. Over the short run, the familiar sounds and smells of laborers calm the countryside and create within it an abiding sentiment and compassion for the people that is marked by the country's provision of foods, goods, and conception

Dreamings. Confronted by foreign bodies, the landscape sends out climatic changes or mental and physical disease. But over the long run, even foreign bodies sink into the countryside, and in doing so rearticulate both the formal totemic sites (*maroi* transform over time into *durlg*) and informal sentimental/spiritual sites (sites of death become sites of affection and memory).

Perhaps it is overly cautions to remember that the "grounding" of social groups in landscapes is achieved through the formal and informal speech acts I discussed above. As it is through language use and labor that countrysides are lost or won, so it is through the work of speech that persons may be convinced of the meanings of events that occur (see App. 1, pt. A). Moreover, Belyuen cultural understandings of economic action, no matter how they are negotiated in conversation, are the products and grounds of regional, national, and international conversations about the meanings and importance of indigenous hunter-gatherer economies. In the next two chapters I discuss the temporal and spatial implications of these conversations on Belyuen economic practice.

4 "Today We Struggle"
Contemporary Hunting, Fishing, and Collecting and the Market

> At dusk we packed people and food into my car and drove to a new homeland centre on the coast a few kilometres from Nhulunbuy which I had never seen. The homeland centre consisted of a cluster of large two room tents in a hollow behind a long white beach and beside a large grove of casuarina trees. As the goanna was being carved up and partitioned into paper-bark for the various family groups a new Range Rover drove in, dwarfing my car. The clan leader to whom it belonged and who had just finished the day's work at Yirrkala, welcomed me and then went to a small shelter and started a generator. The spotlights on top of the aerial belonging to the two-way radio came on, flooding the area in light. Hearing the generator the children rushed up from the beach and pulled the covers off a colour television set! . . . As we ate our goanna meat we watched the evening's ABC programmes, beamed since 1980 by satellite from Sydney. . . . I finally went to sleep to the shrieks of delight from the children at the antics of Jacques Tati in a replay of "Mon Oncle."
>
> —Janice Reid *Sorcerers and Healing Spirits*

A POLITICAL ECOLOGY

In the next two chapters I examine the material productivity of Belyuen food collection trips from the cultural vantages I discussed above; in particular, I draw attention to interethnic land conflict in contemporary north Australia. After a brief portrait of the economic conditions of the community and the ecological character of the countryside, this chapter concentrates on the dietary contribution and temporal organization of hunting-gathering activity and its relationship to local cash markets. Chapter 5 concentrates on conflicts that arise between the Northern Territory government and the Belyuen community over the spatial use of the Cox Peninsula.

The cultural meanings of Belyuen Aboriginal labor-action—its effect on the country and on the social group—articulate with local and regional political and economic assessments of that action. What type of action is productive? Who decides? These old questions in the classic political-economic literature are here inserted into new cultural contexts. At its most stark, the conflict is over what leisure produces: How is "just sitting" productive in terms of the various social and political landscapes that now make up north Australia? In addition, disagreements center on interpretations of Aborigines' everyday landed practices (Certeau 1973), their spatial and temporal organization, and their economic contributions to Aboriginal physical life.

What surprises many field-workers in Australia, including me, is not simply that culture and economy meet, but that they meet in ways that disturb our sense both of the boundedness of cultures and of the compatibility of different kinds of cultures and political economies. The Australian literature gears us to expect sociocultural and political phenomena to occur in a time separate from the day-to-day "grubbing and chasing for subsistence foods." If cultural and political phenomena do "intrude" when we are hunting, fishing, or collecting, we expect intrusions to be of a local sort. This is not the case. On fishing trips Dreamings surge from beneath motor-powered dinghies; over a campfire meal heavy-metal music roars. On the dirt tracks that lead to isolated outstations, the Northern Territory government stretches car-count meters to monitor "public access" on and around Aboriginal lands. The meaning of an event that occurs while Belyuen women and men are hunting, fishing, and collecting, though interpreted locally, seems at times to be incompatible with Aboriginal economic forms and to be drawn from a bricolage of regional and national political-economic and symbolic systems.

Settlement Economies

Between 1989 and 1990, Belyuen's population fluctuated around 210 persons, increasing at times to 225 or more. Of the usual population, there were ninety-two children under eighteen years of age (45 percent) and approximately fifteen persons over fifty. Belyuen women often remark on how the composition of the community is bottom heavy. "More and more" children are said to be born "all the time." While a birth is always celebrated, people compare the high number of children to the scarcity of old people. The community is said to be "falling away" because "all the old people gone now, only babies, this Belyuen." Yet, according to records, the relative youth of the Belyuen population was sightly more pronounced in 1973 with 45.9 percent of the community under the age of fifteen (Altman and Nieuwenhuysen 1979). Although the group was smaller at that time (196), there has been a slight aging of the population. Far from being unusually young, the Belyuen community is near the top of the age curve for Aboriginal communities. Sixty percent of the population of many groups is composed of children under the age of fifteen.

While these records present an image of the Belyuen community aging slightly over the last seventeen years, the elders' perceptions and rhetoric of community composition is based on the relative *number* of older and younger people. Senior Belyuen Aborigines say that the large number of young people is an important reason why they fight for country and why they continue to hunt, fish, and gather. They must do both in order to maintain the life of their families by meeting the needs of their households with the bush foods they gather and to maintain the life of the country by providing the necessary regular human presence. Balancing these two productive spheres can be very stressful.

The middle-aged women, who will take the place of the old people passing away, increasingly ask, Who is going to pay for all the Belyuen children? They attempt through this rhetoric to negotiate the receipt, distribution, and use of moneys coming into the community. Will people buy beer, cars for outstations, fishing lines, or steaks? In the past, senior Belyuen women controlled access to most of the community's welfare economy, although this varied according to a person's kin networks, luck in redistribution schemes such as card games, and problems with social security paperwork (Povinelli 1991 see also Berndt and Berndt 1947; Peterson 1991 for discussion of other settlements). However, the use of government benefits on the community has increased significantly over the last six years. In 1989, over a third of the community (seventy-seven people) received some form of social security payment. This included fifty-three individuals receiving unemployment benefits, nine receiving family allowances, and fifteen receiving pensions. My records show that in 1984 less than half this number received unemployment benefits—and they were receiving them more sporadically. A similar number received family allowances and pensions.

Between 1984 and 1989, then, welfare income in the community doubled. But in the previous five years there had been little increase in welfare income. Fisk notes that, at Belyuen (Delissaville) in 1978, ten people received unemployment benefits, eighteen received pensions, and five received family allowances. In 1981, he shows a similar number obtaining benefits: Seven people were receiving unemployment, and there were fifteen pensions and seven family allowances. The unemployment benefits that had increased over the past ten years were paid mainly to young and middle-aged men, a changing income pattern that shifted the concentration of money from older women to younger men.

Although the majority of people at Belyuen receive government benefits, the community and the local government employ a number of people.

The Northern Territory government, in an effort to lower unemployment in outback towns by providing skills to young people, initiated community-based employment schemes (Community Employment Program or CEP; see Baker, Nicoll, and Yik 1985) whereby, for short stretches, women and men on the unemployment rolls are hired to learn skills such as carpentry, first aid, and cooking. While the program lasts, communities can choose to cut the social security and welfare benefits of those who refuse to work or are fired from the job. By working, participants can double their incomes. But the loss of income from the large number of people who lose their unemployment compensation (through refusing to participate or being fired) cancels out any increase in funds flowing into the community.

In addition to direct government aid, the Belyuen Community Council employs about eighteen people in various administrative, janitorial, construction, and maintenance jobs. The Northern Territory Education Department employs another six people as teaching assistants for the otherwise Euro-Australian run school. Finally, a small crafts industry accounts for some community income. About eight women periodically make and sell crafts, while about ten men are employed by a hotel to dance corroborees for tourists during the dry season. These markets are subject to international fluctuations in tourism and to local limits on cultural trade (see also Peterson 1991; Myers 1989). In 1992, for instance, both a regional slowdown in tourism and the death of a senior Wagaitj singing man contributed to the cancellation of the tourist corroboree (the latter had a much greater effect on the cancellation than the former).

At Belyuen, various employment patterns emerge according to one's perspective. If one views employment based on family connections, council jobs are dominated by one sibling set. Of the eighteen positions, eleven are held by one family and their affines. However, looked at from a difference in sex, the jobs are distributed almost equally between men (twelve) and women (thirteen). Yet the types of jobs that women and men hold reflect what Gayle Rubin (1975) has called a "sex-gender system." Six women work in the school, two in the community office, one in the community grocery store, and two work as janitors. These jobs are paid less than the jobs men hold. Two men work in the council office and the rest are mechanics or hold grounds jobs.[1]

Although more persons within the Belyuen community are receiving benefits and salaries, the monetary solvency of Belyuen households has not changed much since the early 1980s. Several factors have intervened. Belyuen, like other communities, has had to accommodate itself to the shifting tides of the Australian economy. As government subsidies lessen and there is a corresponding policy shift away from assimilation to self-determination, communities must find ways to increase their revenue.

One controversial way is through the payment of rent. In order to collect rent from those who use a house, the Belyuen Community Council retreats to the notion of a residential unit: What group lives in a house, which is the primary kin unit there, and who is its senior head? When these persons are confronted for payment, they use extended kinship and the valorized notion of the traveling Aborigine to disassociate themselves from any particular building to which they are assigned: "I got big family here. . . . I just leave this stinking house anyways, I shift [move camp] for a change."

The notion of "household head," so necessary for rental relations, problematically intersects with Aboriginal notions of autonomy and custodial relations. In a capital sense, the Belyuen Community Council is the owner of the community houses. Occupants rent from them; in the past the rental fee was nominal. But on the community, capital relations are translated into the local cultural economy. People ask not who owns a house, but "Who is the boss of this house?" based on who lives there. Belyuen Aborigines describe the occupant (the custodian in a land sense) as a person who dwells in a place, thereby keeping it open, warm, and productive, inundating it with their language and sweat. Because of the importance of this work, "owners" (traditional land owners or owners in a capitalist sense) are beholden to occupants, not occupants to owners. It is, therefore, total nonsense for owners to demand rent from a family who is doing them a favor. Owners who act in such a manner find their houses or country unoccupied and therefore subject to harm. The custodians "shift" to another place, either to their own country or to another where they have residential rights. The abandoned house, like abandoned land, "dries up." However, the long-term effectiveness of a strategy of abandonment and return is doubtful. In a community or settlement where everyone has to pay rent no matter to which house they go, the rent will eventually find them. Also, when people move to outstations or camps on the Cox Peninsula during extended rent crises, attachment to the community, and often to a particular house, brings them back. They "worry" for Belyuen and the places where their parents and parent's parents have lived and died—*nyoitj* sometimes residing in a house—just as their parents "worried" for the Cox Peninsula, pulling their families back to regional camps after the Second World War. In the present context, often by the time a family returns to the community, the rent crisis has passed.

The economic policies of the city of Darwin also affect the economic solvency of the Belyuen community. For example, in 1987, the city stretched electrical lines across the harbor to the small Wagait Residential Development, a non-Aboriginal residential block on the northeast coast of the Cox Peninsula. At the time, the Belyuen community acted on an option to link up to Darwin power. Whereas electricity was formerly supplied free of charge to Belyuen residents from a community power plant, electrical charges are now tacked onto the rent bill. It is hard to tell how severely these new bills cut into the real earning power of households because households only pay them sporadically, avoiding them as they avoid rent payments. But even if the cost continues to be absorbed periodically by the council, Belyuen women see the talk of bills as fitting into a dangerous pattern:[2] "Getting harder, we used to get things free, now we have to pay for everything. Might as well go to my own country now. Getting more and more like a Bagot here."[3] This is a surprising statement when one considers the past hardships that women describe in their oral histories: enforced labor, sexual abuse, internment camps, periodic and random incidents of violent racism and war. But it does have a strong resonance with other aspects of the conversations women have about the past: "You get all that information. Those, they, they had strong culture. They have ceremony every day, corroboree and dance. Today we struggle now."

It is important to contextualize Belyuen's position in the Australian economy. Economic conditions on Aboriginal communities are generally poor when viewed from a perspective of income and commodity wealth. Figures from the 1986 government census showed that 90 percent of territory Aborigines earned less than the average wage, and that more than 60 percent earned less than half the average wage. The situation elsewhere in Australia is similar.[4] Belyuen falls solidly within an economic context of structurally impoverished Aboriginal communities.

Ecological Environments

Over the last hundred years, a number of ecological, demographic, and technological changes have affected the hunting, fishing, and gathering practices of local Aborigines. Most Belyuen families use cars, trucks and dinghies to get to hunting grounds.[5] They use nets, fishing lines, shotguns, and axes to hunt there, and use buckets, bags, ice chests, and cloth sacks to carry the products back. Colonial and postcolonial efforts to develop the land commercially through mining, agricultural, and pastoral industries, and residential and commercial schemes have altered the countryside. Colonial planters cleared large sections of the northern and central open forests, drained wetlands, and introduced new species, the most ecologically and economically significant being cattle, pigs, and fruit trees, especially the mango.

Beginning in 1870, as local Aborigines were being forced off the beaches, European settlers were slowly moving into the area. Since the 1960s, a newer patchwork of small European residential clusters, tourist enterprises, commercial fisheries, mines, legal leaseholders, and illegal squatters have alienated sections of land on the Cox Peninsula. The resultant multiplication of well bores has significantly lowered the water table (Whitling 1990), which in turn has caused freshwater swamps to dry more rapidly after the monsoonal rains. As local Aboriginal hunting grounds are being restricted, sea-hunting Belyuen men view the ever-expanding nets and buoys of non-Aboriginal pearl shell gardens that stretch across the path of the mythic Cheeky Yam (*gulida*, L; *wila*, B; *minthene*, E) and obstruct their own hunting routes. Similarly, when Belyuen women go longneck turtle hunting, they see enormous earth-moving trucks gutting the turtle plains in order to collect gravel for roads. Laragiya living in Darwin have witnessed a more radical transformation and appropriation of their traditional ceremonial and foraging grounds in and around the city.

Along with a restriction of available land, then, Belyuen families have to contend with a decrease in the ecological quality of the land they are able to use. Belyuen men and women give a number of interlocking demographic and cultural pressures on the landscape as reasons for these environmental changes. Belyuen Aborigines attribute some changes in the ecological landscape to the foreign sweat and language of non-Aborigines and other changes to the overuse of areas. For instance, Belyuen women and men say that animals smell Anglos and go somewhere else, which results in a decrease in the amount of fish, crustacea, and shellfish available to Aboriginal hunters. But they also say that Darwin's proximity and its reliance on port trade and commercial fishing has affected the migratory patterns of fish, sea turtles, and sea mammals. Whether due to business practices or body odors, photographs taken in the late 1800s indicate that the density of vegetation has decreased since European contact on the northern coast. Lighthouse keepers photographed in a small boat along one of the northern estuarine creeks are surrounded by thick vegetation no longer present. While some environmental changes have occurred over a long period of time, other changes have been noticeably abrupt. Belyuen women note that in their lifetimes creeks have dried up, swamps have turned into open forest plains or paperbark forests (or have simply disappeared because of gravel mining), and dense vine tangles, once the gathering grounds for long yams (*Dioscorea transversa*), small mammals, and reptiles, have given way to beachfront houses.

In addition to the effect of too many people competing over too few resources, Belyuen men and women say that the land is affected by the lack of Aboriginal users. The absence of Aboriginal people hunting, camping and, more generally, talking about a place causes many sites to "feel sorry" and "go underground" or "go inside." An elder Wagaitj woman, whose deceased husband had been a senior *danggalaba* Laragiya man, described an instance of such withdrawal at a site on the west coast of the Cox Peninsula. I had gone with a large group of Laragiya, Wagaitj, and Beringgen women to hunt during a recess in the Kenbi land claim hearings. It was evening and we were eating the various bush foods we had collected (yams, mangrove worms [*Teledo species*], fish, shellfish, and wild honey or sugarbag), waiting for a barge to come and take us back to where we were camping. The elder Wagaitj woman pointed out to the other women and myself an indentation in the beach down a ways from where we were relaxing. "Use to be creek there," she said. "Nobody visited it, camped there. It's sorry now, it dried up, it went inside now." In part the comment was oriented to the Laragiya women, most of whom live in Darwin, reestablishing the moral tenor of Belyuen women's practices: "We do the best we can, you should help" (which, as Wagaitj and Beringgen recognize, many Laragiya men and women do). But the comment was also oriented toward the absent group of lawyers and government officials I synecdochically represented: "If you do not allow us to properly mind country, it will dry up like this place."

Today, the region is typical of the Top End monsoonal environment. There are three pronounced seasons: a humid, hot "buildup," a period of four to five months of heavy rain, and a cool, dry season. Pietsche and Simons (1986) report that the mean annual rainfall is 1,600 mm with the lowest rainfall at 1,025 mm. Temperatures range from an average daily high of 34 degrees centigrade to an average daily low of 27 degrees centigrade from November to December; the coldest month is July when the average daily high is 30 degrees centigrade and the mean minimum is 19 degrees centigrade.[6] The Cox Peninsula and Port Patterson Islands consist of small monsoon forests, coastal dense vine tangles, tropical savanna and eucalyptus open forests, and coastal and estuarine mangroves.[7] There are also freshwater creeks that spill into large wetland swamps.[8] The general ecological pattern of the Cox Peninsula is a mangrove belt around the seaward coast, a sandy boundary between mangrove and dense vine tangle, scattered bands of dense vine tangle, and an inland of varying open forests, monsoon forests, grasslands, black soil plains, and swamplands.

While many aspects of Belyuen hunting-gathering practices have changed—many items have been dropped from the diet and many technological innovations incorporated into the practice—what has not changed is the stated desire of all Belyuen family groups to visit and to live near the sea. We can see reasons for this and evidence of it at many levels. Peoples' past and present 'subsistence economies' center around the exploitation of sea products.[9] Today, in the dry season, Belyuen families move off the community and onto outstations located on the beaches of the Cox Peninsula. (All but one outstation is located there.) Also, roughly 80 percent of all hunting-gathering trips stop at the seashore, although inland sites are utilized along the way. Moreover, their cultural and, for older Belyuen Aborigines, social historical identity inheres in this environment. Creation narratives center on the relationship between saltwater and freshwater creatures—in particular Wariyn (Old Man), Kenbi (Didjeridoo), Rainbow Serpent, and Cheeky Yam—and link who the Belyuen Aborigines are with the landscape these Dreamtime beings traverse. In addition, older Belyuen Aborigines' narratives of their journeys up and down the Anson Bay to the Cox Peninsula shorelines further root local identity in the coastal regions. The paths they followed are marked by a series of coastal place-names and by the winds that indicate the seasonal flux of tides. In the past, when the wind picked up, so supposedly did the people.

CALORIES: THE BUSH AND GROCERY STORES

Belyuen men and women and Western economists look to similar phenomena when assessing the importance of bush foods to the health of the Belyuen community: How much food (or how many calories) is obtained from the surrounding bush, how much time is spent getting it, and what places are used most frequently? To what profit? While drawing on similar phenomena, Belyuen Aborigines and Western economists reach different conclusions about the significance of bush food collection practices because they weigh differently the importance of productive and, so-called, nonproductive and underproductive labor.

Belyuen Aborigines have two main sources of foods and goods: the grocery store and the bush.[10] People draw out the metaphorical similarities between the two "stores" in their ordinary conversations. People say that young men go "hunting the green cans" (a particular brand of beer) when they walk single-file through the bush to the local grocery store some fifteen kilometers away. As they walk, men collect what foods they find along the way and when they get to the store they "hunt around" for credit and cash. Deciding who is to be asked for money to buy food, tobacco, and alcohol is seen as a form of hunting and fishing: What should be the bait and who is likely to take the hook today? Alternatively, when women walk down the beach looking for turtle eggs or return from a hunt in the mangrove they "shop" for items that the tide brings or that non-Aboriginal campers have left behind: large fishing nets, utensils, water bottles. The two "shopping markets" are very different in some respects. Whereas in a grocery store, money intervenes between a person's examination of an item and his or her ability to obtain it, on common land, sight itself intervenes between a bush "shopper's" discovery of a desirable object and his or her ability to get it. Seeing the object first is the Belyuen hunter's capital; sight is what purchases, so to speak, the article for the hunter. The person who sees the food first, no matter who actually digs or catches its, is the "owner" (see Myers's discussion of "private property" 1988a).

Most of the foods Belyuen Aborigines obtain from the countryside come from the sea or seashore (8.2 million kilocalories vs. 6 million kilocalories derived from inland sites).[11] I summarize the contribution of various bush foods to the Belyuen diet in table 2. If one uses Betty Meehan's estimate that the regular caloric intake of an Aboriginal woman is, on

TABLE 2

THE CONTRIBUTION OF BUSH FOODS TO THE BELYUEN DIET, JANUARY 1989–JANUARY 1990

A. *An Overview of the Contribution of Bush Foods*

	Gross Weight (kg)	Kilocalories
Shellfish	64.66	51,727
Crustacea	597.9	305,835.6
Inland "meat"	2,455	5,468,657.4
Fish-stingray	2,518.1	2,414,858
Sea mammals	2,462	5,287,275
Eggs	1,613	161,300
Vegetables	353.2	400,255
Total	10,063.86	14,089,908

B. *The Collection of Vegetable Products*

	Gross Weight (kg)	Flesh (kg)	Kilocalories
Dioscorea transversa	279.75	279.75	363,675
Potatoes and bush palms	15.05055	15.05055	19,565.72
Fruits/sugar grass	50	25	15,000
Nuts	8.3925	.3357	2,014.2
Total		353.19305	400,254.9

C. *The Collection of Shellfish*

	Gross Weight from Nine Sites	Gross Weight from Other Sites	Total
Hermit crab	68.72525	3.73	72.46
Nerita lineata	20.2539	5.0355	25.29
Nerita didymus	10.12695	1.119	11.25
Telescopium telescopium	113.67175	2.238	115.9
Batissa violacea	2.89075		2.891
Mactra obesa	30.6/925	.373	31.05
Mangrove "worm"	30.0265	7.087	37.11
Chiton	7.6465		7.647
Crassostrea amasa	.746		.746
Terebralia palustris	3.5435		3.544

Note: Rather than provide an exhaustive list of all the foods that Belyuen men and women collect, sec. A groups these foods into appropriate categories for my discussion. "Vegetables" include any plant products: grasses, fruits, tubers, bulbs. "Inland 'meats'" include honey, reptiles, mammals, and fowl as the local ethnoclassification system stipulates (cf. Povinelli 1990).

average, 2,000 kilocalories per day and men a bit higher, then the contribution of these high protein bush foods to the diet of this study's core hunting group (some thirty adults) would be 62 percent of their yearly caloric intake.[12] If one divided these bush foods' caloric value by the total number of people living at Belyuen, these calories represent 10 percent of the intake of all Belyuen persons. A more moderate view indicates that these foods are distributed along a network of about one-third to one-half of the Belyuen community. Again, these results represent a large segment of the total bush food contribution to the community diet; they do not represent it entirely, and another one-fourth of the total number of calories could easily be added. Extra calories come mainly from fishing and offshore hunting. In this new total, the contribution of bush foods to the Belyuen community's diet would be, roughly, 12 percent.

Grocery stores provide the majority of foods that most Belyuen persons consume, approximately 80 percent of their total caloric needs. An outline of foods Belyuen Aborigines purchase from local stores and their caloric contribution to the diet is given in table 3. A significant proportion of the calories that Belyuen Aborigines obtain from groceries are in the form of refined sugars and wheats, alcohol, and fats. The poor nutritional quality and periodic scarcity of Western foods are augmented by a steady collection of bush foods. Coombs, Brandl, and Snowdon (1983) describe the Belyuen diet during the late 1970s and early 1980s as one of periodic malnutrition and hunger.[13] Many researchers have blamed Aborigines' boom and bust spending habits for these periodic food crises.

The notion that Aborigines spend their income without consideration of their long-term budgetary needs has begun to give way to an understanding of the saving strategies they employ. Altman notes the ways Gunwinggu fluctuations in expenditure are linked to methods of saving. He argues that a common way for Gunwinggu outstations to "save" their money is to stock certain supplies that are easily stored and preserved, such as drums of floor, tea, sugar, and rice. Money left over from the purchase of cheap bulk items is used to buy or maintain equipment for the camps. In the Belyuen community, this "banking system" is typically used only at the beginning of the dry season before a family moves to its outstation camp.[14] Drums of food are then bought and transferred to the camp and left there even if the family moves back to the community for a short period of time. Buying large, cheap drums of food while living at Belyuen has the unintended result of attracting large numbers of extended kin to one's table. Households that have a large supply of food staples or tea find it very difficult to refuse to share them without incurring serious social isolation: one may be labeled as too "greedy," a person who "cares too much" for items such as rice and not enough for enduring ties for kin

TABLE 3
Monetary and Caloric Values of Foods Purchased from Grocery Markets

A: *Percentage of Expenditure for major consumption items*

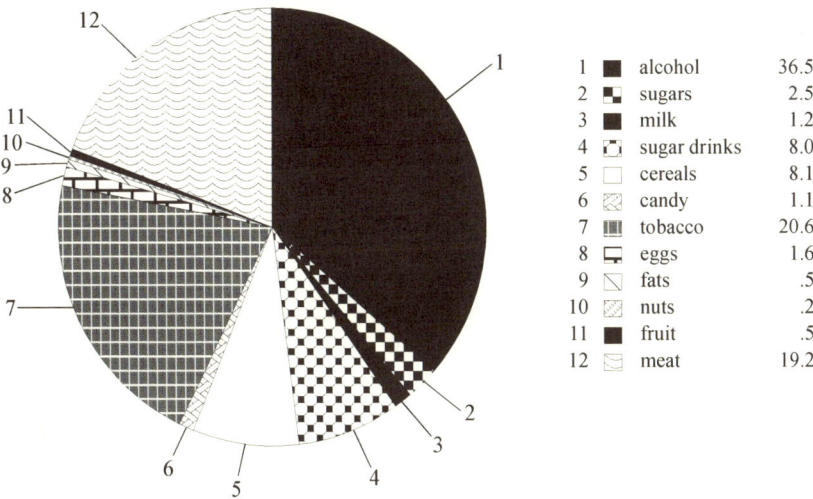

1	alcohol	36.5
2	sugars	2.5
3	milk	1.2
4	sugar drinks	8.0
5	cereals	8.1
6	candy	1.1
7	tobacco	20.6
8	eggs	1.6
9	fats	.5
10	nuts	.2
11	fruit	.5
12	meat	19.2

B: *The Monetary and Caloric Values of Foods Purchased from Local Groceries*

Foods	Weight	Kilocalories	Expenditure (A$)
Sugars (kg)	5,330	2,145,325	8,658
Sugars (l)	9,366.6	3,812,202	27,185.60
Milk (kg)	452.4	24,401,820	3,689.40
Milk (l)	364	2,629,900	364
Cereals (kg)	8,211.8	30,794,250	18,176.60
Roots/legumes (kg)	1,341.6	1,577,000	4,596.80
Vegetables (canned and fresh) (kg)	1,585.5	586,635	2,077.40
Tobacco	33.85	—	70,296.20
Fats (kg)	486	4,252,500	1,768
Nuts (kg)	26	6,000	832
Fruit (kg)	697.58	523,125	1,638
Meat (kg)	9,807.07	29,421,300	216,923.20
Eggs (kg)	38.9	64,947.5	5,460

and country, traits associated most strongly with white men and women. In fact, people are liable to label another person greedy not only for storing bulk items, but for keeping any item that can be segmented, be it a wallaby, a hamburger, or a stick of gum. Those who eat "straight through" neither looking to the right or left are "too fucking greedy."

Camps and houses, like foods, are seen to be infinitely divisible. One can always find a "bit of room" or give a "teeny piece" for kin. Responsibility for kin can be dissipated only if everyone has nothing and nowhere to go. The more one accumulates, the less one needs all of what one has and the greater pressure on the saver to share. Belyuen women and men respond to these pressures by buying little, relying on small fluctuations in the cash supply, and collecting bush foods to make ends meet.

However, it is not altogether clear what contribution bush foods make to the Belyuen Aborigines' diet. Janette Brand and Vic Cherikoff write that Australian native plants are richer sources of some nutrients than one might expect on the basis of comparison with similar cultivated plants (1985; also see Brand et al. 1983). But Belyuen men and women do not collect a large amount of plant food products; they collect 3.5 times more kilocalories from animal products than from plant products (see table 2). While they do not get a large number of minerals and vitamins from plant sources, Belyuen women and men gain important fresh salt-water proteins from animal products. The fresh seafood in the Belyuen diet makes up for the otherwise general "lack of fresh food at the local store" and, even when available, for its cost (Coombs et al. 1983, 356).

From these figures, one can begin to see the relevance of the food preference model that Hawkes et al. have described (1986). Some aspects of the Belyuen diet, such as their preference for marine foods over terrestrial foods, would be difficult to measure by an optimal foraging model (Yesner 1987, 287). Some shellfish, like plant seeds, are abundant, easy to collect, and extremely low in calories—800 kilocalories per kilogram of flesh (table 2, part C). However, the time and energy required to process and to convert these products into foods is significantly lower than for plant products. For instance, the cycad nut requires extensive processing; after collecting it, one must soak, pound, and cook it. Sea snails simply require cooking on top of coals. The energy expended in collecting other seafood, such as large mud crabs (*Sesarmi smithi*), varies across the Northern Territory. Near eastern Arnhem Land, crabs are found lying in the sand. Near the Daly River, crabs burrow long tunnels into hard, thick clays that lie exposed during low tides. On the Cox Peninsula, women travel across dense mangrove jungles and through thigh-high soft mud. Here, the crabs often burrow meter-long holes in the soft, silty soil and are difficult to drag or dig out. For all this work, the return per kilogram of crab flesh is only slightly higher than sea snails—some 930 kilocalories—although the fat content is eight to twelve times higher. Other marine products provide much larger returns. Many sea turtles and sea cows have the bulk and caloric value of small bovines and large kangaroos. However, the relative density of land versus sea cows would need to be predicted in order to make claims about the comparative returns of hunts from the two environments.

Other aspects of the Belyuen bush food diet fit Hawke and O'Connell's core claim that abundant plant foods that require intensive processing will drop from the diet before less abundant high caloric items. Most notable is the absence of the cycad nut (*Cycad media*), the "pumpkin yam" (*Amorphophallus galbra*), and various water lilly species from the diet of Belyuen families (table 2, part B). All of these were important to the precolonial diet and are abundant and easy to collect. But all require intensive preparation to process or to remove their toxins, and they have a lower caloric return per gram than mammals and fish.

An even more accurate picture of the decreasing importance of plant foods as dietary items to Belyuen women and men is reflected in their knowledge of the names and uses of plants and animals versus their actual use of them. Provisionally, it appears that of the 125 plant taxa that senior women can name, 54 are still said to be *miya* (E; *meidjem*, B, plant foods), but only 27 are considered safe to eat because techniques for removing toxins are not needed or are still known, and only eleven are regularly collected.[15] Further research can demonstrate if the number of known plants is significantly higher, but even these figures indicate that there has been a drastic reduction in the consumption of plant foods. This, however, tells us little about the importance of these foods in other aspects of Belyuen socioeconomic life, especially how women's knowledge of foods is used to construct an Aboriginal identity that reverberates into other political and economic spheres.

LOCAL ORGANIZATION OF TIME

Temporal Patterns

Hunting trips change over the course of the year in two ways: there is an increase in the number of trips made and in the amount of time people spend in a particular environment from the wet season to the dry season. In table 4, I present several ways of viewing Belyuen food collection practices over time. I look separately at temporal patterns that arise from the duration of the trips and from the "person hours" that Belyuen men and women spend outside the Belyuen community. Person hours are the combined time that an entire party spends on a hunt: the total number of people times the duration of the trip. The duration of a trip is simply the length of time beginning when a group leaves the community and ending when it returns. So, if a group left at noon and returned at 8 P.M., the lapsed time was eight hours. If seven people were on the trip, then the person hours equal fifty-six.

TABLE 4
TEMPORAL ASPECTS OF BELYUEN ABORIGINES' HUNTER-GATHERING ACTIVITY

A. *Total and Average Lapsed Time (Duration) Spent on Hunting and Gathering**

	Total Hours	Total Hours with Author	Average Hours	Average Hours with Author
January	93	80	4.89	5.33
February	131.75	114.75	4.38	4.41
March	159.5	155.5	4.83	5.02
April	182.5	120.5	6.08	5.74
May	104	77	4.52	4.05
June	125.25	93.75	3.8	3.9
July	281.5	257	9.08	10.28
August	393.75	198.75	8.75	8.61
September	473.25	292.75	8.76	8.71
October	296.35	178.35	7.41	7.43
November	80.25	49.25	4.01	4.91
December	146	127	4.42	5.3

B. *Total and Average Person Hours Spent on Trips into the Countryside Compared to Time Spent Hunting and Gathering*

	Time in Bush	Average Time in Bush	Time Hunting	Average Time Hunting	Average no. of Adults per Trip	Data/ Participation Trips†
January	743.75	43.32	369	19.92	6.8	19/33
February	1,123.5	40.13	706.75	26.39	8	28/42
March	1,099.75	39.28	523.15	17.37	7.6	30/45
April	1,299	55.79	404.5	18.39	7.9	22/40
May	536.5	31.39	371.25	19.36	7.6	19/33
June	659.75	46.58	340.5	24.32	9.2	15/41
July	1,658	100.59	446	28.09	9.1	16/42
August	1,524.75	64.96	368.65	12.86	6.7	24/51
September	1,408.5	59.7	335.45	14.63	7.1	23/64
October	1,176.4	66.1	344.8	14.62	9.3	18/48
November	550	50	214.7	21.47	8.6	11/47
December	1,441.7	66.72	678.95	30.04	11.5	22/46

*Average here equals mean hours per day in each month listed.
†This column represents the number of trips used in data compared with the number of trips in which author participated.

Viewed in this way, several patterns emerge from the data. Most trips lasted about six hours with or without my presence. Also, both the total and average number of hours people spent hunting rose, as would be expected, from a low in the hot, rainy season (December–February) to a high in the cool, dry season (June–August). In some months the average number of hours people spent outside Belyuen almost doubled.

Parts of this data are best explained by sociopolitical aspects of community life. The significant drop in the hours spent in the bush in May, June, and November is an artifact of my absence from the community (and subsequently the absence of a truck and a reliable driver). I was absent for a week and a half in May while working on aspects of the Kenbi land claim in Darwin; in June there was a "dry run" of the land claim hearing in which most of the adult Belyuen community participated; and in November the claim was heard in full. Generally, because school has recessed in the dry season, many people spend from late morning to late evening away from the community, or they camp day and night at their outstations for a few months or more. Three families spend the majority of the year on outstations, using the Belyuen community as a base camp.

In table 4, part B, I summarize what people are doing during their time away from the community. The data come from time allocation charts for hunting trips in which I participated. The last column of table 4, part B shows what part of the total number of trips per month the data represent. Instead of figuring small children into the total time, I counted the person who minded these children as contributing to the work of the hunt.[16]

Figured in this way, the amount of time spent away from the community over the course of the year still shows an increase from the wet to the dry season, except for lows in May, June, and November. People go on longer trips during the dry season, but they do not spend more time hunting on those trips. Instead, the time people actually spend hunting increases and decreases in a wave-like manner. The average number of persons going on a hunting trip also shows no direct link to seasonal shifts. This is explained by the local mode of transportation: flatbed utility vehicles that I and most other truck owners on the community use carry comfortably about eight to ten adults, plus children and equipment. What are people doing while they are away from the community? Table 4 clearly shows that they are spending only about one-third of their hunting trips hunting, in the normally understood meaning of this term. This time allocation squares with field trips I made in 1984–85, 1987, and 1992. Belyuen Aborigines spend a significant amount of their time in the bush engaged in what economists call unproductive labor. And women spend far more time being unproductive than do men.

In table 5, I explore differences between food collection practices of men and women. Three women's activities (fishing in the sea and estuarine creeks, collecting crustacea and snails in mangroves, and digging for freshwater turtles in black soil plains) are compared to men's dominant foraging practice in 1989, sea hunting. Women's and men's practices are assessed according to the average number of persons participating, the

TABLE 5

A Comparison of the Difficulty of Hunting-Gathering Activities versus the Returns from Those Activities

Type	Average no. of People	Average Time per Person	Average Caloric Output per Person	Total Time per Year (Hours)	Total Caloric return	Output per Year (kg)
F: S/E	8	2.6	150 (390)	635	8*=762,000	2,318,629
F: M	3	1.5	357 (535.5)	188	3*=201,348	334,596
F: B	5	1.5	200 (300)	112.4	5*=112,400	90,223
Me: S	5	3	200 (600)	234	5*=234,000	5,287,275

Note: F = female, Me = male; F: S/E (seashore and estuarine creeks) returns are for fish, rays, and prawns; F: M (mangrove) returns are for crab and sea snails; F: B (black soil plains) returns are for longneck turtles; Me: S (sea) returns are for sea mammals and turtles.

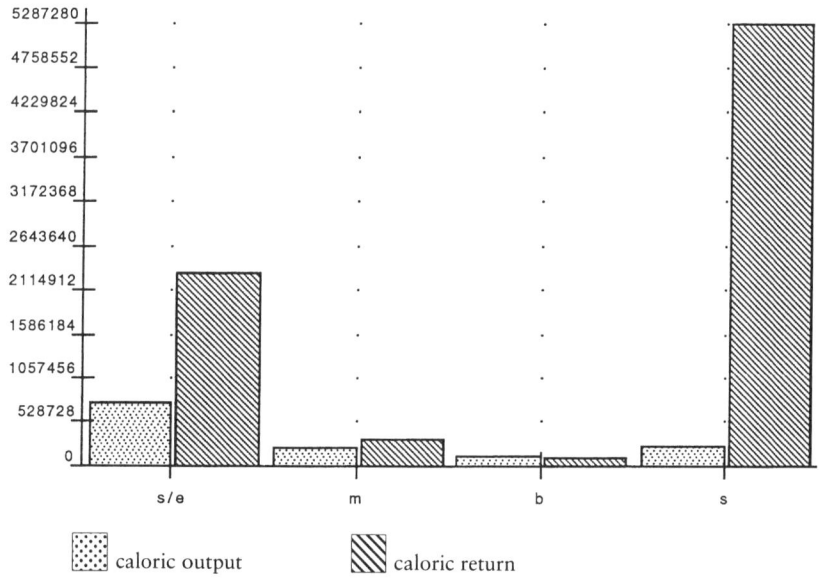

average time people spend on an activity, the total duration of the trip, and the total caloric return. The accompanying graph shows the caloric gains and debits for each activity. As the table shows, women spend about 635 hours per year fishing, 188 hours hunting in the mangrove, and 112 hours hunting for turtle in black soil plains. Clearly one reason women spend four times the number of hours fishing as they do crabbing is because the return from the former is much greater than from the latter—it is even greater still when compared to the return from longneck turtle hunting. However, men are able to spend a third of this time to produce twice as much as the women do in all their activities. Moreover, fewer men have to be engaged in the practice.

Two additional points must be made about gendered differences in productivity. First, other than when they are collecting longneck turtles, women get a good return for their effort. And women typically look for turtles before or after a day spent fishing or crabbing. If I analyzed separately the time women devote solely to turtle hunting, the time would fall to about thirty hours per year. Finding a turtle is a bonus to the bush basket, but it is not profitable enough to devote much time to the activity. Second, men's sea hunting practice is so productive that one wonders why they do not do it more often. A partial explanation is based on market issues. The amount of money people spend on foods, alcohol, and small commodities leaves little left for the purchase of dinghies or for the petrol to run them. Also, most of the men who are responsible for the maintenance of Belyuen vehicles and who are reliable drivers work full-time on the community. This leaves them with little time to hunt, unless they go after a day's work. These after-work hours are usually devoted to fishing, not sea hunting; most sea hunting occurs on weekends. This tells us why men do not hunt more. But why do women collect crabs at all? (Note that the return on foods like yams, fruits, and bush potatoes is even less than on crabs and longneck turtles.)

The productivity of leisure and the purpose of underproductive work

At this point a question plagues the analysis. How should we understand and assess the large amounts of "leisure" and underproductive time spent during Belyuen hunting trips? In the literature on hunter-gatherer societies, the ratio between work and leisure time has been widely discussed. Marshall Sahlins's (1968) path-breaking claim that the amount of leisure time hunter-gatherers "spent" was a strong indication of their *original affluence* has been critiqued and defended on a number of grounds including the factual (see Wilmsen [1983] and Hawkes [1987] for two very different critiques) and the conceptual (Bird-David 1992; Povinelli 1993a). Other researchers have differently assessed work itself, looking both at work density and at work-leisure ratios to determine relative affluence (Altman 1987b). From a sociobiological perspective, leisure and underproduction (as well as "food, comfort, security, health power, affection") is little other than a means toward the end of the "highest fitness payoff" (Hawkes 1987; 349–50; cf. Martin [1983] for a critique of this approach).

The best explanation derived from a materialist perspective, I think, demonstrates the interconnections of hunter-gatherers' "low production targets," their little difficulty in "meeting their nutritional needs and [the] strong pressures [on them] for immediate use of food and artefacts" (Barnard and Woodburn 1991, 12). In addition, in the contemporary world hunter-gatherer activities are "effectively subsidized" by a market that allows food collection to be "undertaken at an energetic loss if that proves necessary to bring in adequate supplies of other essential nutrients" (Ross 1987, 11). These studies, however, purport to explain only "immediate-return societies" not with the "delayed-return societies" of Australia (Woodburn 1982, 1988; Altman and Peterson 1988). Moreover, Wilmsen's much broader critique of ecological and structural-functional arguments as applied to contemporary hunter, fishers, and collectors is pertinent here; their simplification "of production relations has nurtured a parallel simplification of social relations" (Wilmsen 1989b, 4). Myers has similarly noted in an Australian case that to understand fully "the regulation of resources among the Pintupi [Aborigines] we have to consider the internal structure of relations within the society, a structure which does not merely reify 'ecological necessity' but which has taken on its own emergent values" (1982b, 192).

Few studies critically examine the "cultural ordering of action" (Sahlins 1968) or the political ordering of assessment; that is, How are conflicting assessments of productive labor resolved? In the Belyuen region, the productivity of leisure time resists neoclassical economic or ecological analyses and, while better served by political-economic and cultural analyses, are not completely comprehended by them. Given local notions of the power and mythic purposes of their labor action, the leisure and underproductive time Belyuen Aborigines spend is productive in areas usually considered peripheral to economic analyses, including the production of their own and others' cultural and social identity and authority. These other ends of production, explored below, are critical to disputes over land use and land management inside and outside the community.

During unproductive time spent on hunts, people sit, talk, weave, travel from place to place, and play. But Belyuen Aborigines say that this "leisure time" is producing economic well-being by providing the conditions for country and people to "find" the historical and mythic relationship that exists between them. Being in a place jogs the memory; women often say, "Sitting down here makes me remember all the old stories." But being in a place also provides the conditions for people to remember the historical and mythic narratives that they subsequently use to claim rights to a place. For example, an Emi sibling set established an outstation at a site on a north coast of the Cox Peninsula during the 1960s and 1970s. When the senior male sibling died, as did his younger brother soon after, the camp was abandoned for a while along with the dinghy that they used. This is a common practice in Aboriginal Australia. "Places where people have died or been seriously ill must be avoided. The spirit of the dead man may still be in the vicinity, as may be the powers which caused the death (or illness)" (Biernoff 1978, 97).

The children, widows, and the brother and sister of the Emi men began returning to the northern outstation in the 1980s, not only to collect foods, but also to collect the stories that demonstrate their relationship to the area. The deceased men appear regularly to the family. Belyuen Aborigines from all language groups discuss the brothers' appearances as a sign that their kin must look after that section of the country. This is not just political talk. Those Emi who can meet and interact with their deceased loved ones have reasons for wanting to live in that section of country that are quite compelling and deeply ontological.

In their leisure time people are also creating the sociality that is the Belyuen community. People remaining on the Belyuen community during the dry season call the place a "ghost town" and indeed it has that abandoned feeling: eerily quiet and hot. The disquieting feeling of abandonment results not only from people's absence, but also from the knowledge that stories and events are happening elsewhere. People who stay at Belyuen during the dry season are "missing out." People collect foods and narratives of self when they hunt, camp, and travel through the region. The resulting shared knowledge of and economic reliance on the Cox Peninsula binds together the Belyuen community, clearly evidenced in volumes of testimony collected during the Kenbi land claim hearings.

A third activity women, in particular, undertake with all their leisure time is the gathering of political and personal authority. Much of their leisure time is spent discussing the cultural and ecological landscape. For instance, women look at what flora and fauna are in the different regions of the Cox Peninsula and how these plants and animals relate to other places they have lived or visited. Foods have a social element not only in what they mean symbolically (Douglas 1966; Ortner 1970), but how knowledge of them can bring a speaker political gains. Women's ecological knowledge frames their mythic knowledge in the present tense—women discursively refer their mythic knowledge to their shared experiences on hunting trips with similes ("like when we," "like how we") and mnemonic tags ("remember when we/you?" "like before *sebi* [remember]?"). It is by these everyday conversational means that women position themselves as living within tradition rather than commenting on it. And it is through these means that women have become the narrators of Belyuen history (discussed in detail in chap. 2).

Older women use their knowledge of plant taxa and their experience in local lands, along with their knowledge of mythic sites and texts, to position themselves at the forefront of legal forums. When anthropologists and legal aides come from the Aboriginal Areas Protection Authority or from the Northern Land Council to collect mythic information about sites and country borders, they are directed to senior Wagaitj and Beringgen women. Likewise, when linguists and popular writers arrive at the community to conduct research, they are directed to older Belyuen women. Within a local context, Belyuen individuals claim authority based on their knowledge of bush foods: What is what? How do things act and how can they be used? When are things registering a sign of mythic intentionality? Trustworthy knowledge can be gotten from simply being on a trip, not necessarily by hunting during it.

Individuals also use their hunting knowledge to claim authority during ordinary face-to-face conversations about where and what to hunt on any particular day. This is shown in the following short exchange between a group of women in late April 1989. I was among the group deciding where to go to hunt later in the afternoon. Jean Zirita claimed, "This time now find two crabs in a hole and *rweri* (fat)!" Her statement is interesting because it is quite direct for a people who, usually, value indirect discourse. Similar statements are sometimes tempered by "might be, we just try and look" or framed indirectly, "one old lady said . . ." Jean's statement makes a claim both for what is true "out there" (an environmental fact) and for what is true "in here" (in her head); that is, she is making a knowledge claim: I know how the country works (Povinelli 1993a). Claims such as Jean's can be challenged directly or indirectly. In this case, Emily Nela, who is significantly older than Jean Zirita, tempers her rebuttal by the conditional "maybe not" (*mait be nuthing*). While this is a direct face-to-face challenge to Jean's knowledge and authority, she, and the Belyuen social group more generally, benefits from it. Jean leaves the conversation knowing, or remembering, that the white flower signals the fattening of stingray and that Emily Nela is someone to whom to defer. "The community" leaves the conversation with knowledge that has been further integrated; it is able to present a "coherent" body of knowledge to the numerous government officials and researchers who visit the community. It is in the context of the political significance of cultural coherence that Emily Nela's face-to-face correction should be appreciated (see also App. 1, part A).

Some challenges to a person's claim to be knowledgeable occur behind the scenes. When decisions of where to go and what to hunt must be made, people align and realign themselves for or against another's suggestion based on their own preference for a place, social group, and type of hunting-gathering practice, and their own evaluation of a speaker's ability to predict the spot where a type of food will be found. Such challenges are not age- or gender-specific and occur in contexts other than hunting trips. If a person is having a bad run of luck, the driver for the day hears behind the scenes: "Don't listen to her, you know what happened last time—*no meat.*"[17] People follow those who are on a lucky roll. The analogy to dice games is pertinent because of the analogy women and men make between luck in hunting and luck with cards (see Povinelli 1991). Personal authority is linked to an ability to pick a winner, whether it is cash in hand or a handful of geese. And the political and cultural authority that women achieve by acting in the countryside reverberates into the economic sphere: grounded in their cultural authority, older Belyuen women have significant, albeit not always decisive, influence in the day-to-day allocation of resources such as what items are bought with younger people's welfare checks.

The multivocality of women's productive use of leisure and underproductive work time can be fully appreciated when their organization of hunting trips is compared to that of men's. The gendered differences that emerge from hunting-gathering today lie not so much in which sex does what type of activity but in which sex does anything most often.

The social relations between Aboriginal men and women have been framed in two ways in the Australian literature. First, what were the historic dependencies and autonomies of age and gender classes within the foraging group? Phylis Kaberry described women's economic, social, and ceremonial practices in the 1930s. However, ever since Fay Gale edited a small volume titled *Women's Role in Aboriginal Society,* anthropologists have debated whether women's position in traditional society can best be described as a "junior partner" to men (C. Berndt 1954, 1965, 1980; Goodale 1980) or as a separate but interdependent equal to men (Bell 1983; Hamilton 1981, 1980–81).[18] All of these anthropologists agree that in precolonial Aboriginal society women had a great deal of autonomy and authority based upon their economic interdependence with and ceremonial independence from men. Gone are the days when anthropologists like Bronislaw Malinowski understood and portrayed the Aboriginal family and society as dominated by a brutal husband-father dragging wife and children in train.

More recently, Francesca Merlan has called for a change in the research perspective on Australian Aboriginal gender systems. She argues that because questions about "the comparative situation of the sexes in Aboriginal society" are "stimulated by European concerns about the nature of women's involvement in society," the focus has been on traditional sociocultural systems rather than on current negotiations of power and authority (1988, 63; see also Merlan 1992). The valorization of economic knowledge and prowess and the importance of visiting and using a sentient countryside is certainly critical in the current negotiations of power and authority between men and women in the Belyuen community.[19] Examining this can help us understand why women collect foods that do not have a high caloric return for the time spent getting them.

Just as handy men and women may be better at carpentry than at plumbing, so some Belyuen women are better at some food collecting practices than at others. Some women can find honey in a rainstorm when no bees are flying, and other can find the underground root "hairs" of yams long after a fire has passed through an area and pigs have tramped the ground. However, most women do a little bit of all forms of hunting, even those typically male activities of spear fishing and shooting. Belyuen women and men alike differentiate some food collection activities from others based on their perceived cultural authenticity. People say that what makes one activity "more" Aboriginal than another is both the activity's likeness to past practices and the degree to which non-Aborigines can perform it. Because most food collection practices bear some kinship to the past, practically everything is an authentic Aboriginal practice, even line and dragnet fishing.[20] However, if they wish to garner full authority, Belyuen men and women must demonstrate a competence and prowess in a hunting activity other than line and dragnet fishing because "any *bedagut*" (white person) can catch a fish that way. A truly impressive person is she or he who spends a large amount of time in the bush and who "sebiz [knows] hunting straight through."

One example of the social use and construction of hunting practice is how people assess women and men who can or cannot go into the thick mangrove mud and return with a large bag of crabs. The ability to hunt in the mangrove establishes an authentic Belyuen identity for both sexes that is pervasive and persuasive. To *sebi mud* (to be able to deal with it) is to establish an authoritative identity and presence that carries through to other more overtly political practices. In the past, it is said, knowledgeable clever women and men were expert crab collectors. Clever women, for example, could sense where in the mangrove the crabs would be clustered. They could go in any mangrove, fill one or several bags, and be finished before other people could find one crab. "Maybe by the time that lazy person found one periwinkle [thumb-sized sea snail], that old woman would have already found one full bag of crabs."[21] In these same olden days, senior people dug large "cages" (deep holes) into the hard, inland ground and filled them with saltwater to store the crabs they collected until they were needed.

The ability to catch a surplus of crabs and store them now signals a person's authentic Aboriginal identity. But this practice of "surplus production" and storage may or may not have been a precolonial practice. One of the uses of the earthen cages was to keep the crabs fresh until they could be taken to Delissaville or Darwin to be sold. It is not clear, therefore, whether the old clever persons that people describe today were taking advantage of precolonial storage techniques for new purposes or whether the entire project was developed as the need for money and goods progressed. Either way, crab prowess is yet another of the ways that the difference between past and present action is highlighted and blurred. What is more important than whether past people collected crabs for cash or energy is that present women and men articulate these practices as real traditions which distinguish between those who know and are able to practice their economic and cultural identity and those who do not and cannot.

Not only do Belyuen women garner foods and authority in this way, they also are able to mitigate rhetorically the importance of men's hunting, which although less frequent is very significant to the overall bush food contribution. One way they mitigate men's contribution to the economic well-being of the community is by involving themselves in men's hunting practices. Women spot game as their husbands, sons, or nephews drive along; the animal or plant food belongs to the person who spots it first. Even when women are not physically along on a shooting trip, or themselves shooting, they make sure they are "in on it." They do this by buying the cartridges, by lending the family gun, or by buying the petrol for the car or boat. In this way they ensure that part of the catch is returned to them.

Women also mitigate men's contribution to the Belyuen economy through discursive frames. By constantly claiming that men always drink and never hunt, always fight and never contribute to the grocery bill, Belyuen women, with the help of men's own self-description, push to the background male contributions to the diet. As more young men receive unemployment benefits and use them to buy alcohol, the women's discursive claims ring truer. The small amount of time it takes men to collect their foods and the small number of men who participate is here used against them. Rather than understanding men's productive contributions as coherent practices, women present them as incoherent and erratic. They present their own activities as constant. Their portrait carries weight in the community in large part because most people believe the sentient, porous countryside is beneficially affected by an Aboriginal presence.

The political climate of the year can be made the starting point for a broader discussion of how Belyuen men and women distinguish between groups, here ethnic groups, based on their activities over time in the countryside. The lower total and average time spent in the bush during late May, early June, and November occurred during different segments of the Kenbi land claim hearing. During the month of November, Belyuen Aborigines daily emphasized, in and out of court, how hunting keeps the countryside productive, open (sweet), and alive. As the hearing sputtered on, its endless grind and use of time became a source of irony for older Belyuen women. They said that they were asked to show how the peninsula was a living productive country, yet they were not able to go out "hunting and minding" country in order to make it so: "Maybe this country think we *nuku* le him" (AE, lie to him/her) was the apt way one older woman put the often-contradictory needs of acting politically and productively for country. However, even in November, when the hearing ran daily for three and a half weeks, people averaged nearly five hours in the bush per day, and their actual hunting hours increased. The tenacity people displayed in "going bush" after eight hours in court and in increasing their relative hours of hunting can be read both as an index of their commitment and "strength of attachment" to country and the hunting-gathering practice and as a palpable measure of the importance of the subsistence economy to the local diet.

The importance that Belyuen men and women place upon the amount of time people spend in the bush lies in opposition to the importance Western analysis places on productive and nonproductive activities: How much can a person produce in a certain amount of time? In short, Aborigines and non-Australians are engaged in a political struggle over the interpretation of their labor and over the use and development of regional lands based upon what they produce. Each emphasizes a different productive benefit. Euro-Australians produce commodities and thereby the wealth of nations and peoples; Aborigines produce the cultural and economic well-being of country and people. This pointed struggle over economic practice and meaning and its subsequent effect on the economic salience of the community can be extended to Belyuen families' use of two Cox Peninsula grocery stores in 1989.

AUTONOMY AND ADDICTION: BUYING INTO A MARKET ECONOMY

In 1984 and 1985, there were two grocery stores on the Cox Peninsula, one on the Belyuen community and one on the northeast coast some fifteen kilometers from the community. The Belyuen store was originally financed by a company that specializes in outback groceries, but it is presently run by the Belyuen community. Under the managing agreement, profits exceeding a certain dividend and loan repayment schedule are returned to the community, where they are used to finance community projects. For example, in 1987, the Belyuen Community Council bought a barge for the people to travel to and from the Port Patterson Islands. The other store is attached to the Mandorah Pub, a small tourist hotel and bar that sells a limited variety of canned and packaged foods. During 1985, most of the revenue that the pub derived from the Belyuen community was from the sale of alcohol, tobacco, and the fast foods that accompanied the purchase of the first two items. Because the pub had a virtual monopoly on alcohol sales on the peninsula, income from these sales was significant. While no figures are available that give a precise picture of how much was spent, one can estimate by comparing the figures that E. K. Fisk (1985) presents of Delissaville's welfare income by sex to the drinking profile of the community (see table 6).

In the past, Belyuen men and women used each store for a different set of consumer items. Most moneys spent on nonalcoholic goods went to the Belyuen grocery store and most money spent on alcohol went to the Mandorah Pub. Unlike other Aboriginal communities in the north, no "social club" exists at Belyuen where alcohol is sold to members at a lower rate. The purpose of social clubs is to keep money and people within the community during drinking sprees; a club's presence does not necessarily lessen the amount of drinking that occurs. The *Report to the Standing Committee on Aboriginal Affairs* noted that, in 1977, on Palm Island 25 percent of the community income was spent at the beer canteen, while another 25 percent was spent at nearby Townsville and Ingham. In the same year, at Bamiyili, a small community near Katherine where many relatives of Belyuen families live, 27 percent of the total income of the community was spent at the canteen (House of Representatives Standing Committee on Aboriginal Affairs, 1977). Aboriginal activists point out that while alcoholism is a problem on Aboriginal communities, it is also a problem in the wider Australian community. But the Aboriginal alcoholic enters into a racist discourse in which Euro-Australians

TABLE 6
Average Fortnightly Expenses, 1978 and 1981

Source of Income	Expenditure ($A)
A. *Amount spent on alcohol*	
Unemployment	738.58
Pensions	778.62
Total fortnight	1519.21
B. *Amount spent on nonalcohol items*	
Unemployment	738.59
Pensions	1305.35
Family allowance	168.11
Total fortnight	2212.05

view drinking as a sign of the loss of traditional Aboriginal social control and the continuing inability of Aborigines to adapt to a market economy (cf. Beckett 1964). The destruction of health and the depletion of funds caused by alcoholism are considered different from that caused by tobacco because the rhetoric of addiction does not as easily attach to the latter drug.

In 1988, the established pattern in which money for alcohol went to Mandorah and money for food to the Belyuen store was suddenly upset. The increased number of non-Aboriginal residents on the Cox Peninsula and the increased Aboriginal and tourist population were factors that led to the opening of a new grocery store in the center of the Anglo residential block, the Wagait Residential Development. The Alewa Grocery Store had a greater range of groceries and higher grade of consumer items, initially at lower prices.[22] It also sold alcohol. Within three months, most income from Belyuen was being spent at this store, threatening the continued solvency of the Belyuen grocery and the Mandorah Pub. The Alewa store owners explained these results as the inevitability of free market forces. Without romanticizing the plight of any one of these stores or of the Belyuen consumers, let us look more closely at the "freedom" of the market on the Cox Peninsula and how it relates to Belyuen notions of labor.

Belyuen Aborigines have a common market strategy of getting credit or delaying the payment of debts by making a store owner "sweet" in much the same way that one makes a place sweet by visiting and using it. The place, in this instance the store, gradually becomes familiar with the visitors and begins to give abundantly without requiring as much effort (here, money up front). Kin support each other's petition for credit: one person uses his or her own reputation for timely payment and long-term residency as "collateral." The practice of using someone else's familiarity with a place in order to establish a relationship with it can be compared to the way that women, when in a "foreign" place (such as in the Daly River, hunting turtles), allow local persons to hunt for them or how the Wagaitj and Beringgen dip nonlocal people into the briny saltwater to introduce them to the countryside. In a market economy extending the number of persons with debts also lessens, for a while, the debt burden of each person in a family. While obtaining a network of debts can only temporarily extend one's finances, Belyuen women and men know local markets often quickly open and close, ironically because of credit problems. In the past, they could expect to be able to charge a large amount of foods and goods without having to pay for them because the store would eventually close. They would then "move on" to the next store like they move from hunting site to hunting site.

The Alewa store owners also "sweeten" their customers by providing rides to and from the store at a fair rate and giving large portions of foods and free knickknacks. The store owners' motivations for extending credit are also straightforward. With several markets in the area, people have a choice of where to shop. Belyuen men's and women's income is distributed along a very wide system of kin, cards, and domestic and ceremonial obligations. A credit, or "bookdown," system helps mitigate the free flow of cash by tying the owner and customer at numerous points before the money enters the system. By inducing people to spend their money in the form of credit, store owners attempt to control the direction money will flow. While the Alewa store owners initially allowed Belyuen Aborigines to bookdown only a small percentage of their income, this official system was soon exceeded dramatically, and entire checks were handed over to the owners on payday. From an economic viewpoint, the possible individual greed of the owners is not an issue. In fact, Belyuen men and women pressed the owners to extend credit past their reasonable ability to pay. This is a good strategy insofar as a bill not settled is a free basket of foods and goods. The example is interesting because it demonstrates how capitalist demands for increased profit necessitate the contravention of the rhetorical freedom of the market and the economic logic of buyers and sellers. This is a microcosm of a larger global system of enforced debt (pressures of debt in Third World countries ravage aid plans, transform moderate governments into extreme ones, and corrupt a nation for hard currency, all ensuring that money flows back to the First World; see Enloe 1989). Unlike Third World states, however, the income and expenditures of Belyuen residents are relatively stable and basic breadbasket items remain fairly constant (see table 3). While women and men engage informally in the tourism economy (selling crafts) and a small bush food trade (collecting and selling fish and crab), this added income is no more than an extra two hundred dollars a year for about eight people and five hundred dollars a year for another fifteen people. In such a restricted monetary system, businesses must continually look for new ways to increase their share of the market. One way to increase one's share of the market is to extend credit, as was done first by the Alewa store and then, as a competitive measure, by the Belyuen store as well.

Because both stores were allowing bookdowns and people were taking advantage of the credit, Belyuen men and women did not have the income to meet their bills. Most nondrinking men and women began to pay one bill every other fortnight, or to pay "half and half" (half their check to one store and half to the other). Many drinking men and women charged bills at both stores but only paid back the Alewa grocery to ensure that their alcohol supply was not cut off. Because of the sudden strain on their cash flow and after repeated warnings, the owners of the Alewa store sent out legal notices advising Belyuen people to pay their bills or face court fines and jail time. However, because the financial solvency of the Alewa store depended upon Belyuen individuals' continuing to patronize it during and after the financial crisis, this "hard talk" (or "conflict talk"; see Brenneis 1988; Grimshaw 1990; Watson-Gegeo and White 1990) was supplemented by friendly explanations of why the Belyuen people had a responsibility to pay their bills on time. The owners pointed out that they had bills to pay as well and that the store was a business, not a free dispensary of foods.

In examining the historical emergence of capitalism, Weber's focus was on the "origin of the bourgeois class," especially its famous "Protestant ethic" (1958, 24); my focus here is on multiple and competing notions of work and monetary ethics. During the money spat, Belyuen women and men agreed as a group that nothing is free and that payment always accompanies a service. This view reverberates with their understanding of the necessity for ceremonial and ritual exchanges and their deep-felt responsibility for the correct management of country. However, when discussing the matter, they returned again and again to several issues. First, the owners "liked bookdown bookdown": no one forced them to allow people to bookdown, rather the owners themselves sweetened up people and then persuaded them to charge "more and more." The owners were portrayed as never satisfied until a person had charged to their limit or had surpassed it. Women and men portrayed themselves as coerced into a practice they did not like, but with which they had no choice but to comply. The conversational item "no more like" is a strategy speakers use to position themselves as unwilling laborers: if one does not like what they are being asked to do, then those who are asking should reward the labor in some way, with money, credit, transportation to somewhere, and so on. It is similarly used when they state a desire to leave the Cox Peninsula ("I been want to go my country, but nothing") but their inability to go because of the country's will ("Nothing now we stuck this Cox Peninsula," "Im want us this country") and when they discuss rent payment. Belyuen women also often say that they "do not like the business [work]" of telling stories, histories, or providing ethnoscientific data. For instance, Mary Eladi said, "I don't like to keep telling this kind of story all the time" (in chap. 1). Indeed, they do not always enjoy the work; it can be boring and tedious. The point is if they nevertheless work they should be compensated. People use this same conversational item to suggest that because the store owners liked what they were doing—they benefited from the practice—they had no right to demand immediate payment. To claim not to like the business of bookingdown, as Belyuen men and women did, is an attempt to realign the power structure and throw responsibility for its results onto someone else.

Another issue that Belyuen people raised in order to explain their position in the dispute was their permanent residence on the Cox Peninsula. People claimed that the country, sites in it, and local Aboriginal people were tied to each other's well-being for the long run and that this was the basis of proper land management. Because people and places are dependent upon one another for their physical and social life, each must necessarily look after the other—the one by visiting and the other by providing foods and the basis for self and group identity. But Belyuen women noted that no one has to go to every named site every day or even every week. Rather, a person should go hunting and camping at a place when it is the "right time." People must decide what is the best place for a food or activity on a certain day and who are the right people for a particular type of hunt in a particular place. The right time can be a matter of season, group consensus, available transportation, and whim. Likewise, deciding the right time to pay a bill can be a very complicated business. The right combination of personal sentiment, available funds, transportation, and an otherwise clean slate of debts is needed; that is, country custodianship and store management must be considered in a number of social, ceremonial, and economic contexts. The unswerving schedule of charging and paying off an entire bill every fortnight seems overly greedy and slightly perverse to local Aborigines. Namely it is to be unsatisfiable and hysterical (harried for no reason), therefore, dangerous and unthinking. No one can be responsible for such an excessive situation and so Belyuen men and women say that they should not be "punished" for the demise of the Alewa Grocery Store.

The issues of personal autonomy and proper social behavior that continually arose in conversations marked the seriousness of the conflict in many people's eyes. While there is some debate in the Australian literature about whether Aborigines have real "enduring" and "hierarchical" political structures (Sutton and Rigsby 1982; Hiatt 1986), there is general agreement that Aboriginal societies share a pronounced "ideology" of autonomy and egalitarianism (see Myers 1986). Such an emphasis is important in this case, for, even before the owners could discuss particular person's bills, they had to convince Belyuen families that they had a right to demand payment from them at all.

At Belyuen, senior men and women state unequivocally that there are "no bosses." This unequivocalness has as much to do with real emerging family-based class structures on the community as with the verity of the statement itself.[23] Even so, Athol Chases' description of boss-like behavior as excessive and loud seems to fit the Belyuen viewpoint very well.

There can be a "big man" for ceremonies, and a "boss" for sites and country, but rarely a "boss" for people. . . . The ethos is that to set oneself up as a spokesperson or a leader of people against others is an act of foolhardiness, and one which will lead to public humiliation. . . . Leadership, if it occurs, is covert. (In Hiatt 1986, 15)

People passionately feel that, outside of prescribed ritual exchanges, they have a right to decide to whom and at what time they will give and who can demand things from them. The asking itself should be done as a suggestion rather than a demand. One must "think about" the other person, must "feel for them" when giving, just as one visits a place because of deep sentimental attachments to it. Whether money, honey, or attention, people insist that neither sentiment nor goods can be demanded from them. Although "demand-sharing" happens, clever people know how to manipulate sentiments of relatedness, how to get what they want without asking.

Belyuen persons claim that actions, here debt repayment, cannot be coerced from them because of their ability "to walk away." Drawing on the social histories sketched out in chapter 2, Belyuen men and women foreground their selective engagement with non-Aboriginal economy and society. But, also drawing on the social histories discussed in chapter 2, skeptical, conservative whites living at the Wagait Development say that Belyuen Aborigines are soft and spoiled and that they would starve if left to themselves in the bush. They read or knew Bill Harney and other welfare officials who portrayed Wagaitj and Beringgen history on the Cox Peninsula as bounded by the fifteen miles of the Delissaville reserve and as increasingly controlled and contained by European practice and values. Conversely, Wagaitj and Beringgen Aborigines say that they can always go back and live off the bush. They emphasize their long walks to and from the Daly River and point to their regular camps and outstations on the Peninsula as evidence of their cultural and economic flexibility. As I demonstrated above, Aborigines have historically walked into and out of direct involvement in the regional and national economy. But the different responses of the drinking and nondrinking groups to the Alewa market crisis highlighted to local Aborigines and non-Aborigines how the production of needs intervenes between the Aboriginal rhetoric of the commodity-free unburdened, autonomous Aborigine and the non-Aboriginal rhetoric of the "spoiled black."

At the height of the market controversy, nondrinking men and women could quit most of their business at the Alewa store. No longer productive or sweet, the Alewa store was ignored by them; they slowed down their payments or did not pay at all. These people, especially older nondrinking women, remarked on how they were able to be satisfied with "just a little bit" and compared this with old bush practices: "Like in the bush, maybe you get little tea, sugar, smoke, that's enough. You gana be satisfied." The owners, faced with a group of people who could do without goods other than such basic foods items as rice, flour, tea, and sugar,[24] which could be purchased at the Belyuen store, decided they had been too hasty in their approach. They asked Belyuen individuals for smaller repayments and promised new items for sale as a way of reobtaining people's business. However, drinkers could not quit their business because they could not quit drinking. During this time, Belyuen families discussed the notion of the alcoholic as a person with a disease, an addiction. These two groups then faced each other. Older nondrinking women often facing younger drinking men associated their social misbehavior with Euro-Australian identity.

As a noteworthy aside, women achieve a traditional context for their practices, such as sobriety, by discursively framing them as exemplifying "limited need" and by the selective and innovative telling of mythic narratives that rhetorically root their practices in the Beringgen-Wagaitj cosmology. I noted earlier that mythic stories can be told to emphasize any of a number of a totemic site's social identities: the speaker can highlight that crab man is a crab, a man, or a father to someone else. When they tell stories to their daughters, older women typically highlight the serious consequences of insatiability in all social realms; e.g., stories might highlight the sexual trickery that exists between members of the family, especially between fathers, mothers, and daughters. Mythic stories that emphasize the sexual trickery and treachery between the sexes within a family teach and legitimate a certain stance that widows take: finding a good husband (or wife) is part skill and part luck but not something to be tested twice. To have had a bad husband (or wife) and to go "more and more" (to have unlimited desire, remarrying again and again) is to be silly and unable to learn from one's past; it is to have blocked ears (*tjeingithut*) like Anglo-Australians. To have had a good husband and to tempt fate by acquiring another is to exhibit the same deafness. Thus, at the roots of their age politics, older women rely on and manipulate stereotypes of gender and ethnic difference to achieve certain social ends.

In this case, older women argued that young people were acting like greedy non-Aborigines in their desire for "more and more" alcohol, and in their inability "to be satisfied" with what they had. Nondrinkers pointed to Euro-Australian appropriation of the countryside: this is what being white was like, having inordinate greed and disregard for one's country and kin. Drinkers, while staying within the cultural frames of the argument, argued that they were just getting "enough," which, because of the addictive quality of drinking, is more and more. They also pointed out repeatedly that nondrinkers were as "itchy" for tea, tobacco, and hamburgers as drinkers were for alcohol.

No matter who needed what more, after the major debts were repaid, only people on unemployment and a selection of other reliable debtors were allowed to charge their bills at the Alewa grocery. The owners decided that they had learned their lesson and were not going to be caught in such a tight bind again. However, by selecting young drinking men as suitable debtors, they got a reputation for "liking drunken people." Senior Belyuen women symbolically likened the owners and drunken people in their concern for money and grog, and in their need for more and more of whatever they desired. Older women and several nondrinking older men juxtaposed themselves to the store owners and the drinkers by saying that they were not able to think about one thing only. They were torn between refusing and satisfying the people for whom they cared. They look at their kin's starving bodies, "feel sorry" for them and feed them, or they look at the addictive shakes of their sons and daughters and buy alcohol to "cool them down." Moreover, older women say that they must bear alone the burden of support, that they have to stretch continually beyond the widening demand on funds to find food and clothing for an increasing number of younger people. From these women's perspective, the owners (and the law to which they have recourse) both support irresponsible behavior and addiction and punish attempts to restrict it.

So far, a person's refusal to pay a bill on time has not resulted in anything more serious than a loss of ready credit. However, the store's threatened recourse to the law changed the field in which Belyuen families played with stores. The conspiracy of the law and the economy was pointedly developed. Yet one reason why the Alewa owners never actually called in the police is that in the racial politics of the Northern Territory Aborigines are "bad risks." Those who extend credit to Aborigines lack sense, and the police suggest that all involved attempt to work things out. Not surprisingly, appeals by whites to blacks to be "fair" to them and pay their bills usually get nowhere, mediated as the requests are by a long history of white threat, intimidation, and sanction, especially in the historically violent context of European and Wagaitj interaction.

Although Belyuen Aborigines say that they cannot starve, one of the consequences of their losing credit is that they have to think of ways to extend their money through fortnightly payments. I discussed some of these strategies above, such as buying bulk food items and moving to outstations where they can be stored.

Men and women also receive several kinds of cash surpluses that can be used as savings: tax, research, and royalty payments and money from tourists. In the Northern Territory, through the Aboriginal Land Rights (NT) Act, 1976, businesses that extract goods from Aboriginal lands must contract with the relevant group. In the rich uranium fields of Arnhem Land and in the copper-rich country of the south, significant returns from mining flow into community coffers and into the Aboriginal political arms of the Northern, Central, and Tiwi Land Councils. In the rich tourist centers of Kakadu National Park, Katherine Gorge, and Uluru National Park, some money flows into Aboriginal communities from crafts and management schemes (see Altman 1987a).[25] The Daly River lands, from which Belyuen language groups receive royalties, have so far produced little of capital value. Yearly royalties have come from a small pet-meat industry that processes feral pigs and bullock and from a small bush safari outfit that guides tourists through the area. Indeed, Wagaitj and Beringgen men and women complain that their country "got no money," and younger Belyuen people joke that the money they do receive from it is worth no more than toilet paper when compared to Arnhem Land mining royalties. The relatively small amount of royalties the Wagaitj and Beringgen receive can be increased for some individuals and family groups in several ways: outright addition ("boxing up" money, i.e., everyone chipping in their allotment)—for items such as a car, gifts and debt repayment—and gambling.[26] Although small, the relative certainty of these royalty payments give women and men a bank against insolvency. They plan purchases or bookdown alcohol with these proceeds offered as collateral. The same use is made of tax rebates, except that this income is usually larger than royalty income, although the number of recipients is smaller.

Belyuen Aborigines treat money from researchers and tourism as money in the bank by postponing full payment for services and items. Many women and men who sell crafts and dance in tourist corroborees tell the buyer not to give them the entire payment, instead they gradually "draw out" (take) the money as they need it. Because they do not have the money in hand, kin cannot ask for it. When monies have been completely depleted, people ask for credit based on the seasonal return of crafts and dance and the ceaselessness of cultural knowledge. The response from merchants and researchers is mixed, and the outcome of this strategy often depends on the personal relations between the parties.

This kind of work, dancing and describing culture, opens up more than just a bank of funds. Through it, Belyuen women and men continually reexamine the open-ended cultural economy that now exists between Aborigines and Euro-Australians. Belyuen Aborigines constantly experiment with the efficacy and effectiveness of their demands for rightful payment and the form that these payments can take. They experiment as well with the needs of others: How much does this lawyer, anthropologist, welfare worker, or store owner need me and what I know?

I should note that no critical moment in the history of the Belyuen interaction with the market economy or culture industry has been reached since I have been visiting the community. Belyuen women and men have been engaged in complicated market interactions for quite a long time, which was precisely the point of earlier sections of this book. "Ideology" and "discourse" on neither the Belyuen nor the non-Belyuen side is wholly its own or wholly the other's. Instead, each begs, borrows, and coerces identity from the other in real power hierarchies. Moreover, the grocery debate is part of Belyuen women's broader production of their cultural identities through the grounding of their cultural histories in difference. It highlights and produces cultural and economic contrasts between themselves and the Anglos that are based on economic practices and encouraged by current national political-economic policies.

5 "Being There"

Dreaming and Development as Political Frames for Land Use

> MR PARSONS: And what kind of things you have said going out there and looking after, how do—how do you look after dreaming places?
> HARRY SINGH: Seeing it is not destroyed by just visiting those places, by just being there; being present helps protect it.
> —Kenbi Transcripts, 13 February 1990

INTRODUCTION

In chapter 4, social conflict pivoted on differing Western and Aboriginal assessments of leisure, work, and compensation. This chapter examines conflict centered on the meaning of social geographical space, in particular the meaning of "open lands." Aborigines and non-Aboriginal developers, both government and private, represent the meanings of space differently. When is space "empty"? Is empty land wasted land? What should be done with "empty" space? Does labor-action change a space into a place of human occupation? Whereas Belyuen Aborigines describe open country as productive country, the Northern Territory government describes open country as that which is unused, wild, and therefore potentially available for development. By claiming that large portions of the Cox Peninsula are unoccupied and un- or underdeveloped, Northern Territory administrators avoid engaging in a debate about what kind of development is best for the Cox Peninsula region: there is no other use plan than their own. They portray Aboriginal use of the Cox Peninsula as unplanned and haphazard and their own use and schemes as rational, future oriented, and productive.

The Northern Territory government's representations of its land use and land needs are contrasted, however, not only to Belyuen Aborigines' use and production of the Cox Peninsula region, but also to its own historic use and development of the Top End. They and Aborigines are faced with the same problem—both groups must present their productive prowess in a way that is receptive to their social histories and to a complexly composed audience that acts as interpreter and judge. The Aborigines' audience includes members of its own community, regional and national governments, and the non-Aboriginal community whose support was critical to the initial passage of the land rights act and other land claim legislation. The Northern Territory's audience includes its own local constituency and the national government that retains authority over Aboriginal affairs in the territory (see Powell 1988). Non-Aboriginal constituents (voters and national government) ask, How do Aboriginal and non-Aboriginal groups contribute to the future productivity of the region? When the Northern Territory government makes claims that its projects have been "blocked" by Aboriginal policy implemented by a southern know-nothing bureaucracy, how are those claims linked to their own historic use of the region?

To represent interethnic conflict over space on the Cox Peninsula in too stark of terms—the non-Australian government's attempt to restrict Belyuen Aborigines to the Belyuen community and the people's attempt to establish outstations and day camps away from it—is to miss the subtleties sketched in chapter 2. Historically and intermittently, government and private businesses have coerced Aborigines onto settlements for security, economic, and political reasons and have forced them off for the same. Pastoral policy that forced Aborigines to work in the dry season for little more than a meal ticket and then forced them away from the stations during the wet season (Rowley 1970b; Doolan 1977; Lyon and Parsons 1989) was similar to the government's restriction of Aboriginal groups to settlements when resources were available and its refusal to provide adequate food and housing when they were not (Attwood 1989). Both economic policies relied on Aborigines as a cheap source of labor and Aboriginal foraging as a supplemental economy. However, as recent historians and Aboriginal oral histories have shown, frontier life did not only consist of European acts of aggression and Aboriginal acts of resistance, but also of the accommodation and inclusion of various labor forms into Aborigines' customary life and European economic initiatives (Attwood 1990, 125; see McGrath 1987). As we saw above, Belyuen women's historical narratives describe their periodic, coerced and voluntary engagements with the Anglo economy and their periodic successes in transforming Western economic practices and social relations into forms consistent with their own beliefs.

THE SOCIAL GEOGRAPHY OF THE COX PENINSULA

From a policy perspective, the ultimate power to interpret and assess geographic dimensions of land use, like the power to assess temporal aspects of the same, rests with government. Policymakers often rely on or justify their proposals through scientific studies—the "fifth branch" of government (Jasanoff 1990)—that describe the socioeconomic and environmental effects of proposed uses of land regions.[1] In virtually all the reports commissioned by the Northern Territory government, Aboriginal reserves and land claims are represented as obstacles to development and causes of regional economic stagnation. For example, in a land-use proposal for the Cox Peninsula region, completed during the final stages of traditional evidence in the Kenbi land claim, the government writes,

> The land tenure on Cox Peninsula constitutes a virtually unique situation. The peninsula comprises predominantly vacant Crown land, the exceptions being the Belyuen Aboriginal Reserve and areas of freehold to the north at Mandorah and Mica Beach. This vacant Crown land has been subject to the Kenbi Land Claim, made under the *Aboriginal Land Rights (Northern Territory) Act*, 1976, since 1979. This claim is still under consideration and, while it remains unresolved, it would be extremely difficult for any legal development or subdivision to take place. (*Cox Peninsula*, 1990)

Northern Territory administrators have used the possible development of the Cox Peninsula region as the reason for restricting Aboriginal tenure on it for much longer than 1976.

The Belyuen community resides on land allocated to the Department of Native Welfare in the middle part of this century. In May 1941, the Commonwealth government acquired approximately 351 acres in the center of the peninsula as a reserve for Laragiya and Wagaitj living on the peninsula (Brandl et al. 1979, 121). The government was able to establish the settlement at low costs because De Lissa's earlier, failed sugarcane plantation had left a rude infrastructure at the site. The contrasting symbolic nature of the location is interesting. From a European perspective the site had been produced by and was overlain with Euro-Australian activity (see map 2); from an Aboriginal perspective, as we saw above it had been created by at least three Dreaming beings who met at the site.

After World War II, the government once again interned Aborigines at Delissaville but could not agree what area of land was sufficient to satisfy both local Aboriginal economic and social needs and non-Aboriginal commercial and residential needs. From 1946 to 1962, the government rejected several proposals for an Aboriginal reserve on the peninsula, including proposals of one hundred square miles and twenty-eight square miles. Both of these proposals specifically took into consideration the economic needs of the Delissaville community. But the government was reluctant to commit beachfront regions or potential agricultural land for Aboriginal groups: "The amount of land at present unleased in the Northern Territory in areas in which climatic conditions are favourable

Map Three: Trips Made from the Belyuen Community to Regions of the Cox Peninsula

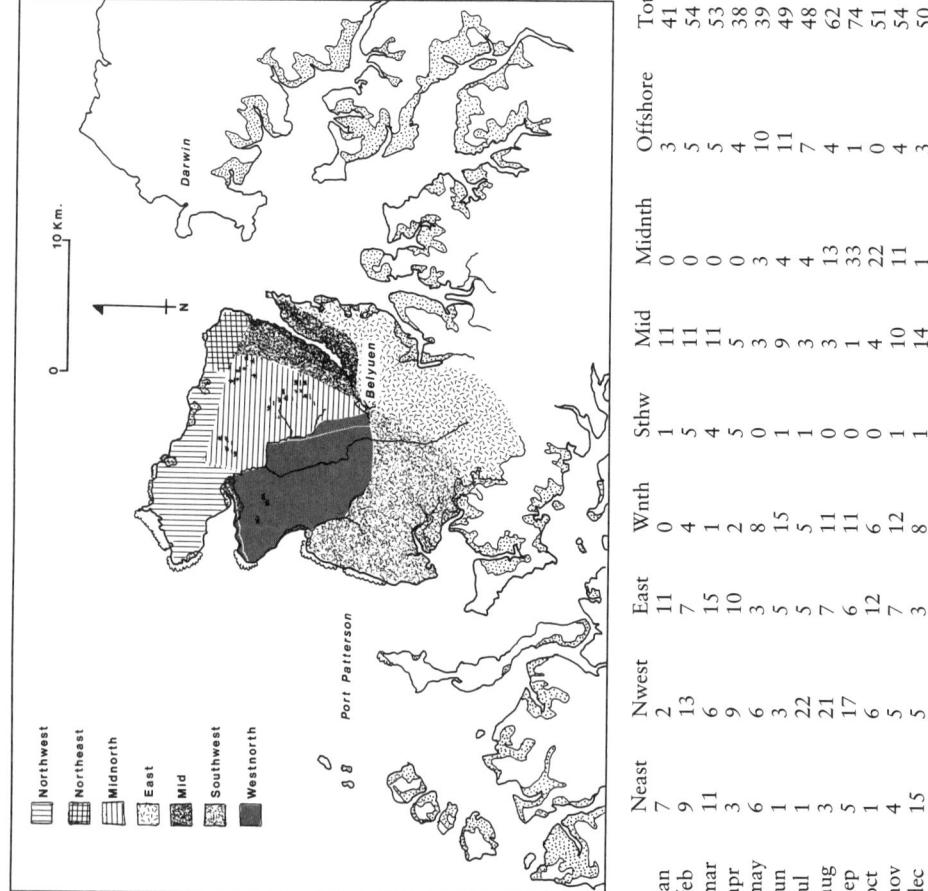

	Neast	Nwest	East	Wnth	Sthw	Mid	Midnth	Offshore	Total
jan	7	2	11	0	1	11	0	3	41
feb	9	13	7	4	5	11	0	5	54
mar	11	6	15	1	4	11	0	5	53
apr	3	9	10	2	5	5	0	4	38
may	6	6	3	8	0	3	3	10	39
jun	1	3	5	15	1	9	4	11	49
jul	1	22	5	5	1	3	4	7	48
aug	3	21	7	11	0	3	13	4	62
sep	5	17	6	11	0	1	33	1	74
oct	1	6	12	6	0	4	22	0	51
nov	4	5	7	12	1	10	11	4	54
dec	15	5	3	8	1	14	1	3	50

to close settlement are extremely limited and that they [the Delissaville Aborigines] have an enormous area already reserved for wards which is entirely undeveloped."[2]

In September 1962, the Department of Lands dedicated sixteen square miles near the original settlement to the Aboriginal Welfare Branch as a permanent reserve for Laragiya and Wagaitj (Brandl et al. 1979, 130). Several years later the director of welfare, E. C. Evans, noted the effect that the long delay between the first establishment of the Delissaville settlement and the final creation of an Aboriginal reserve had on the social conditions of the people living there.

> We should highlight our growing concern with the air of fatalistic depression that appears to be overwhelming the adults of the Delissaville community.... I am not over dramatising the situation at Delissaville—it is serious to the point of near-tragedy, and each delay in plans to halt the decline will only serve to ensure the ultimate decimation of these people into oblivion. (E. C. Evans to the Director of Welfare, memo dated 10 March 1970; quoted in Brandl et al. 1979, 132)

At Belyuen, housing, transportation, and living conditions have measurably improved since the 1970s (personal communication with Maria Brandl) when many people had no place to live, no money to buy food, and little transportation to camping and hunting grounds. With the passage of the Aboriginal Land Rights (NT) Act, 1976, Belyuen Aborigines began moving off the centralized community onto small outstations, part of what is called "the outstation movement" (Coombs, Dexter, and Hiatt 1982). There are various conjectures about why Aborigines moved off government and missionary settlements. Altman and Nieuwenhuysen believe Aboriginal communities are becoming less centralized because "life for Aboriginal people on government and mission-sponsored settlements is deteriorating in quality" and the "'comforts' of the material advantages of more available and European-style goods and services in centralised communities seem increasingly to be outweighed by the many social costs for Aboriginal groups of settlement life" (1979, 78). Belyuen woman agree that life is "getting harder" for local Aborigines. In what way?

As I have previously shown, since the 1970s welfare benefits have increased, although many children and young adult men and women continue to suffer periodic undernourishment. In addition, Aboriginal organizations like the Aboriginals Benefit Trust Account have grants available so that Aboriginal communities and social groups may purchase large equipment such as trucks, generators, and boats. Social stress caused by alcohol and overcrowding would be hard to measure as having increased or decreased significantly; it is high and constant. Deaths attributable to alcohol and fighting have occurred intermittently since the 1950s. But they have also contributed to the sentimental attachment that the Belyuen Wagaitj and Beringgen feel toward particular sites and the Cox Peninsula region more generally.

Altman and Nieuwenhuysen (1979) note that another cost of settlement life is the hardship some groups suffer when they reside on another group's traditional land. Virtually all people living at Belyuen are perceived by some people as "foreigners" (migrants) in the sense that their patrilineal countries purportedly lie to the south. However, the day-to-day process of living on the Cox Peninsula is not immediately affected by this perception because most Laragiya, considered by most to be the traditional owners of the region, live across the harbor in the Darwin region. So, while personal economy and autonomy are factors, it is not just the level of one's own life-style that is at issue when women describe their lives as "getting harder." The statements refer as well to the relative benefits and losses that Belyuen Aborigines have seen accrue to different ethnic and social groups; that is, to the social geography in which they live. They have seen Darwin grow from a small rural center to a medium sized tourist-oriented city where the local government highlights the affluence of the non-Aboriginal population's standard of living and the cultural resilience of the Aboriginal population as a means of attracting more tourists and tourist-related industries. These industries and people then require larger segments of land. Juxtaposed to these developmental projects and pipe dreams, the poverty of their own community seems to have become more entrenched, while economic conditions stay stable or even improve in some areas; meanwhile, the land that they have title over (the sixteen square miles of the Cox Peninsula interior) seems to be shrinking even though it remains the same.

Belyuen Aborigines' shifting perceptions of how much land is available to them comes not only from observing Darwin's changing demography, but also from watching the changing composition of the white population on the Cox Peninsula. Non-Aboriginal appropriation of the peninsula has not occurred in a simple, unswerving direction. Rather, Euro-Australians follow old Aboriginal paths, set up commercial or residential outfits, and then abandon them, leaving behind residues of infrastructure (e.g., roads and cleared land) which pave the way for future developments—the starting point, in fact, of the establishment of the Belyuen community itself. If land tenure were based on Aboriginal ideology, we might understand non-Australian development patterns to operate along the lines that Biernoff outlined—that is, non-Aborigines would feel that certain places were historically safe and others dangerous (map 2). In any case the non-Aboriginal presence on the Cox Peninsula has a clear social geography. In the late nineteenth and early twentieth centuries, the European population on the Cox Peninsula consisted of small plantation owners, miners, and lighthouse keepers. In the mid-1900s, the presence of non-Aborigines increased: army facilities were located on the north coast and on an east coast armlet. Bill Harney and Jack Murray, the two superintendents of the Delissaville settlement in the 1940s and 1950s, began running tours near both of these sites. The number of non-Aboriginal squatters also increased at this time. By the 1970s, non-Aboriginal squatting had further increased and building had begun on a section of alienated land on the northeast coast of the peninsula. This residential area, the Wagait Residential Development, blocked or bulldozed many Aboriginal ceremonial and food collecting grounds, in particular, a site where male initiation was held and a women's ceremonial business ground.

The building of the Wagaitj Residential Development on the northwest corner of the Cox Peninsula is an especially useful example of the slow and uneven development of the Cox Peninsula. In 1989, the population of mainly Euro-Australians living on the Wagait Development had reached about one hundred. Most residents are middle or upper class and are politically conservative. At no other time have Belyuen Aborigines had to live so close to Euro-Australians from this socioeconomic group. Although the sale of residential blocks was rapid, the occupation of them was far slower. This delay resulted in large part from a lack of infrastructure on the Cox Peninsula in the late 1970s and early 1980s. The relatively short distance across the Darwin Harbour was a prohibitive economic and social distance for those non-Aboriginal Australians who had to commute to work every day by ferry or by road. During the monsoonal wet season, the ferry ride was slow and tumultuous, while the road was severely gutted by the rains. As infrastructures increasingly link the conveniences of the Darwin urban landscape to the more isolated settings of the outback, more families are taking up residence in rural areas. The very environment that is seen as unsuitable for agricultural and pastoral industries may be potentially idyllic for residential blocks because they can be sold as places where people can experience the "outback life" while enjoying the cultural, artistic, and economic benefits of urban living (see Northern Territory Department of Lands and Housing 1990). The appropriation of the Daly River word *wagaitj* (sandy beach) for the non-Aboriginal Wagait Residential Development is also a further example of the way the Australian nation-state draws upon the signs of its Aboriginal heritage at the very moment it is appropriating Aboriginal country (see, more generally, Gold 1984). In an example of balder disregard and symbolic appropriation, the Northern Territory government has tentatively named the Point Margaret inland—where they have plans for an oil refinery—after the European surname of an old Kiyuk woman who fought for eleven years, before her death in 1989, against the government's plan to develop this area.

In a nationwide broadcast on 5 May 1980 soon after the lodging of the Kenbi land claim, an ABC television program documented the competing interests of Cox Peninsula non-Aborigines and Aborigines and framed the conflict as a clash between modern development and Stone Age traditions. Who had superior rights to this property? Euro-Australian developers who were increasing the value of the land by building houses and infrastructures or local Aborigines who were attempting to maintain a "timeless" undeveloped countryside? While supposedly neutral or even somewhat sympathetic to the Aboriginal point of view, the ABC program remained solidly within a Western framework for assessing labor-action, a framework that Territory government argues is best able to determine the real needs of various social groups. Local government officials contrast their development plans to Aborigines' supposed slight commitment to and effect on the Cox Peninsula, as demonstrated by its "wild," "empty," and undeveloped condition. More pointedly, government functionaries ask, How much land do Aborigines need to continue a traditional way of life that is no longer based on a traditional subsistence economy? My data on hunting, gathering, and fishing might surprise regional officials both in that it shows a frequent Aboriginal use of regional lands and a steady contribution of foraging to the local diet, but it would not significantly alter their argument. Within Marxian, structural-functionalist, and economic frameworks, hunters and gatherers do not develop the country or significantly increase its value even when they are wholly engaged in hunter-gatherer activities (see Wilmsen 1989b). It is not surprising, then, that Northern Territory government officials claim that the bush food practices of "settlement blacks" might as well be described as "recreational," so small is their impact on the transformation of regional landscapes.

It is worthwhile to examine briefly the history of non-Aboriginal economic activity in the Top End of the Northern Territory in order to contextualize the claims of the Northern Territory government and the reception those claims receive in regional and national politics. Several authors have described at greater length and complexity the history I review below. In particular, Philip McMichael (1984) has discussed the subordination, between 1788 and 1901, of the Australian agrarian economy to an urban-based commercial economy. This struggle between a conservative, oligarchical landed class and a liberal commercial bourgeoisie had an important effect on squatter rights in the Northern Territory which, in turn, undermined northern settlers political-economic relationship with southern states.

"HUNTING WILD CATTLE": DEVELOPMENT AND THE DREAMING

As the discussion above begins to make clear, conflicts over space occur in "real time" and in a discursively formulated past and future time—the time of Dreaming and of Development. When Belyuen Aborigines use the countryside or when they unite with Laragiya to claim authority over regional lands, they conflict directly with commercial businesses (tourist ventures, fisheries, groceries) and residential developments that have been established there. But when and how Aboriginal and non-Aboriginal groups use the land is discursively wrapped in and assessed by a future-oriented social history rooted in, on the one hand, the Dreaming and, on the other hand, Development. In most instances, government development plans outweigh the religious or economic value land has for indigenous groups. Certainly in the United States, economic considerations, including the construction of highways, dams, and ski resorts, have outweighed the religious concerns of Native Americans.[3] In the Northern Territory of Australia, however, because of non-Aborigines' historical failure to develop regional lands, Dreaming and Development run a good race.

Although Britain was slow to develop its Australian colonies, by the mid-nineteenth century a south Australian manufacturing and industrial base had been established.[4] In this time south Australia moved from a pastoral economy based on conscription convict labor to an industrialized capitalist economy based on free wage labor (O'Malley 1983; McMichael 1984). Although no little effort has been expended to accomplish the same transformation in the Northern Territory of Australia, this region historically has had limited success in moving its economy from an agrarian to an urban-industrial base (Allen 1980; MacKenzie 1980; Davidson 1980; Powell 1988). The history of the Euro-Australian economy in the Northern Territory and its relationship to Western political-economic notions of productive and acquisitive labor are critical to understanding the contested nature of Aboriginal claims to and use of northern lands.

White interests in Northern Territory lands were first acted upon by the annexation of the Territory by South Australia in the 1860s. Since the 1860s, local administrators have decried southern management of northern lands, but have been dependent on the southern states for economic support. During the initial period of settlement (1788–1830) in New South Wales, Victoria, and Tasmania, an elite resident group of Marine Corps officers owned and developed land in the area through the savage exploitation of convict labor (Hughes 1986). Squeezed out of local lands, squatters from a variety of social backgrounds moved their livestock into the frontier. Crawford quotes Gideon Scott Lang's description of the colonial squatter in his 1845 volume, *Land and Labour in Australia*.

> To become a perfect specimen of the Australian squatter . . . an emigrant must be a pushing determined fellow, who can dispense with all the comforts of civilized life, from wine and windows to carpets and crockery, and will look to nothing but making the most of his Capital regardless of risk and hardship, so long as they lead to increased profit. ([1952] 1961, 90)

No matter this glowing description of their profit orientation, "bush harpies" have had a mixed reception in Australia.[5] On one hand, squatters exemplified the natural initiative of the maximizing individual who turns the savage wilderness to productive enterprise. On the other hand, the conservative nature of the squatter plantations during the mid-1800s—their reliance, for example, on conscripted convict labor—restricted the establishment of a full-fledged liberal capitalist economy. When conflict ensued between an emerging urban commercial class and the pastoral industry, a license system was established to provide squatters with renewable leases for the use of crown lands; "The license system fulfilled the imperial desire to reserve the land for 'respectable occupation' against occupation by a potential working class . . . and it restrained colonial [pastoral] oligarchy" (McMichael 1984: 92). Later, police action would eventually eliminate most squatting altogether (Crawford 1961).

In the Northern Territory during the first half of the colonial period, absentee speculators controlled large swathes of prime land around the Port Darwin area. They acquired these lands in March 1864, when the sale of northern land opened simultaneously in London and Adelaide. There were 455 applicants for 118,880 acres of country land and 743 town allotments of half an acre for a rough total of £44,719. Proceeds of the sale went to the cost of surveying and settling the country (Hodder 1893, 377–78). Surveyors, including Finniss and Goyder, gridded the boundaries of large properties in the Darwin and Daly River regions for South Australian investors who might never live in or visit the area but who hoped to capitalize on the materials produced from it. What William Cronon noted of American exploration and survey journals, one could also say of Australian travel journals: they listed the commodities found on parcels of land and, in some sense, turned a patchwork of ecological spaces into a regular grid of commodity value and private ownership (1990; see map 5). Geographic space was given a number of productive ratings: good for fishing, ideal residential living, potential mining country, and so on. What was missing from these early survey maps were the Aboriginal groups already occupying the land. This is not surprising given the common view among colonial administrators and missionaries of the time that Aborigines added no value to the countryside; they produced

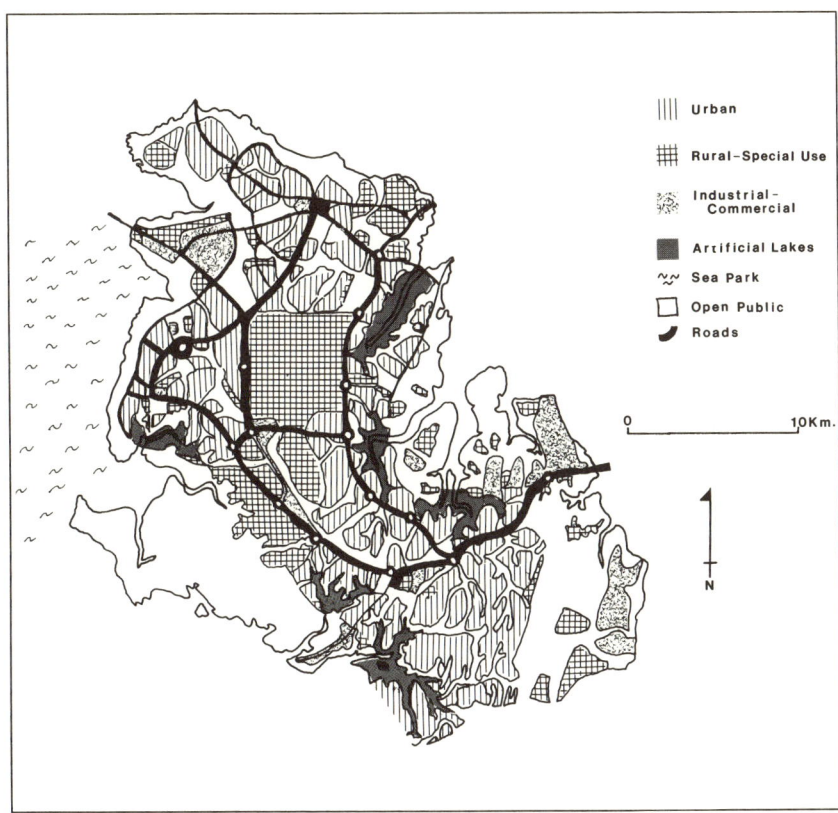

Map Four: Northern Territory Land Use Plan, 1990

no commodities; and even if one counted their "rude" weapons of war and hunting, they had no known large-scale exchange networks. Dismissing the effect of indigenous work on the productivity of the countryside, settlers turned their attention to arguing with south Australians about who had the right to administer the north.

Land sales, like the earliest ones in 1864, established an uneasy relationship between southern bourgeoisie investors and "the working settlers" who actually moved north. As Alan Powell, a historian of the Northern Territory, writes, private speculators had no intention of pioneering the north. "It was most unlikely that any of the eminent citizens who backed these companies had any intention of pioneering in the Northern Territory. Neither, it seems, had most of the smaller buyers whose background has been traced. They were far too comfortable in Adelaide" (1988, 78).

Because few investors ever dreamed of pioneering, the settlement period that followed the surveying expeditions was marked by debates about the right of southern absentee owners to preside over large tracts of valuable property in the Northern Territory (see Hodder 1893; Powell 1988). As they had earlier in the southern colonies, these arguments pitted the hard work and pioneering efforts of the squatter class against the urban commercialist. Arguments filled northern newspapers and southern parliamentary sessions: What group had the more legitimate right to the vast lands of the north, those with the money to speculate in land or those with the willingness to pioneer it? Basing his opinion on such debates, the duke of Newcastle refused the South Australian request to annex the Northern Territory in the 1840s. He did so because "it was certain that, at no distant date, independent settlements, which could not be governed from a distance, would have to be established on the northern coast" (Hodder 1893, 374–75).

To say that government at a distance is unworkable makes little sense in the colonial context: Britain, Portugal, Spain, and France were all governing their colonies at great distances. However, it is consistent with the Lockean sense that property is created by the critical component of human labor and the subsequent transformation of the land and object. In fact, it was just this doctrine that allowed the British Crown to claim Australia as *terra nullius* no matter that it was originally occupied by another group (see also McMichael 1984, 41; Hocking 1988); and it was on the basis of this doctrine that northern settlers based their claims to land and "self-determination."

South Australia did end up exploring, establishing, and governing the Northern Territory from 1850 to 1910. And government from a distance did fuel varying degrees of resentment from northern settlers. Of importance to my purposes here is the rhetorical nature of this conflict. The *Northern Territory Times and Gazette*, the *Northern Standard,* and a Queensland paper, the *Northern Miner,* took different ideological positions but argued a similar point: settlers who produced goods from the countryside—created value—had a superior right to administer northern lands. The *Northern Territory Times and Gazette,* a conservative paper, ran columns that reflected the double bind of the Top End settlement; it needed southern economic support, but it was supposedly hampered by southern laws dictating how the north should be developed. At different times the paper would take different stances: South Australia and Queensland should invest capital for the building of a rail line so that "rich [northern] lands can be brought into profitable cultivation" (*NTT&G,* 2 March 1878); legislation should be passed making it easier for settlers to buy land close to town;[6] private settlers and miners who came to the Northern Territory to live and to work should be lauded, while speculators and owners who stayed away should be chastised.

> Now private settlers are bringing their wives and families to the country for the purpose of making it their home, and these, together with the miners attracted by the reputed richness of the gold reefs, must at length start the settlement of North Australia.... The offices of Government were sent round to reside here without any particular object in view, beyond giving some sort of protection to the persons who had bought land, and who might come to settle in the new country. But those purchasers of sections did not show any disposition to come here. They preferred waiting on Providence. It was never their intention apparently to occupy the land which they had bought. (*NTT&G*, 14 November 1873)

The *Northern Miner,* a Queensland paper, took a radical labor approach to southern administration. It lauded the productive work of miners with separatist slogans such as "Who form the voting power, the bones, muscles and sinews of the North, but the miners and working men of the towns?"[7] The *Miner* drew on then-common themes of political economy—first, the importance of labor in the colonial and industrial process and, second, the increasing alienation of the laborer from control over land and commodities. The *Northern Miner*'s anthropomorphic description of the northern economy highlighted the "common notion" that it was the worker's labor that fueled the economy and produced the value of the landscape. The paper was not Marxist or socialist; instead, its self-professed democratic stand was based upon the labor theory of value developed in works by Adam Smith and David Ricardo. Miners added to the value of the land and to the economy, whereas the southern gentlemen and legislators simply collected—note the parallel to hunter-gathering rhetoric—its bounty. As a result of separatist agitation and a healthy economy grounded in lucrative cane fields and copper mines based upon the labor of kidnapped Pacific Islanders, local Aborigines, and immigrant Chinese workers,[8] Queensland did secede from South Australia in 1859.

In the Northern Territory, squatters played a critical role in the early development of the pastoral industry and helped shape the image of the North as a rugged, "labored" environment. Local government encouraged pastoral squatting as a way of increasing the territory's meager European population. Harriet Daly, the daughter of the government resident of Darwin in the 1870s, wrote,

> By degrees the well-watered lands of the Northern Territory attracted the attention of the Queensland squatters. Each Resident's report showed that a vast area of grass country, suitable for carrying stock, was lying idle near

the magnificent rivers of which Arnheim's [sic] Land has such reason to boast. (1887, 218)

She quotes her father as writing:

> Nothing can exceed the inducements held out to squatters in this country. It is impossible to conceive a finer place for breeding and maturing cattle and horses. It needs no special report on the subject, as in most cases it is only necessary to make transient examination to prove the eligibility of the country for stock. . . . In my opinion, the settlement of this country will mainly depend upon its pastoral settlers. (1887, 218–19)

Pastoral squatting could not, however, solve the territory's recurrent problem with an anemic population. Since Port Darwin's establishment, government plenaries and other advocates of Northern Territory expansion have noted the lack of laborers, and more generally a low population, as the major impediment to the development of hypothetical northern resources. Along with squatting, many settlers proposed Asian immigration as a method of increasing the northern labor pool. Proponents of increased immigration argued that Queensland had successfully transformed itself from a southern annexation to an independent state through the use of immigrant labor.[9] However, the Queensland economy was differently structured. Queenlander holdings were based on large cane plantations and gold mines. And Queensland plantation owners used immigrants (often kidnapped Pacific islanders) as the Marine Corps officers had used convict labor in the earlier south Australian colonies, as virtually free labor. In spite of legislative setbacks for permanent immigration, there was soon a proportionally large resident Chinese population in Palmerston, Northern Territory (Port Darwin), because of the unwillingness of Euro-Australians to migrate north. The violent conflict between Chinese laborers and Aborigines was often described in the local newspapers. It presented a racial discourse in which Europeans could retain a magisterial aloofness and ponder the various characteristics of other races without the discomfort of critical self-reflection.

The Northern Territory has never achieved the economic independence of its Queensland neighbor. In the first years of settlement, gold mining was the primary industry; but gold productivity dropped sharply thereafter.[10] South Australia eventually lost millions in its northern investment and in 1910 negotiated a deal with the new Australian Federation that ceded responsibility for the territory to the national government (Northern Territory Acceptance Act, 1910). The economic prospects of the Northern Territory have not dramatically improved since then. By the 1920s, the politics of "white Australia" and the economic depression of the north forced or encouraged northern industries to fire their Asian workers;[11] this further entrenched the problems of the northern economy. Ihain MacKenzie notes that "the decision to replace Asian labour with Europeans robbed the north of its one efficient work-force and the reputation of the AWU [Australian Workers Union] did little to encourage investment" (1980, 61). Since the 1940s, the northern economy has remained grounded in a rural mining and pastoral base and has been plagued by a low population. Today, squatters are no longer "induced" to reside on or use crown lands. Instead, residential squatters are often portrayed as "bludgers," "blights on the landscape," and a class of shirkers who stand in the way of government initiatives in the mining and tourism industries. They are portrayed as people who live off welfare and the land without increasing the worth of the world around them. In political-economic terms, theirs is an unproductive labor that adds nothing to the worth of the land upon which they live.[12]

In the last decade, tourism has become an extremely important part of the Northern Territory economy. It also, from a government perspective, productively links Aboriginal and non-Aboriginal interests. Jon Altman, in a short study of Aboriginal participation in the tourism industry at Uluru National Park, wrote

> In the Northern Territory, tourism is regarded as a potentially leading, and extremely important, sector of the Territory's economy. For example the latest *NT Travel Monitor* for the year 1984/85 shows that 594,000 visitor trips were made to the NT, with 6.584 million visitor nights; it is estimated that overall tourism spending totalled $281 million in the last financial year. The aim of the NT Government and the NT Tourism Commission is to almost double this figure to one million visitor trips by the year 1990. The growth of the NT economy and the growth of tourism are regarded by policy-makers as being closely correlated. (1987b, 4).

The value tourism mines, so to speak, is not rooted in the land but in a particular form of the landscape: an adventurous river tour and an authentic Aboriginal presence. But the global tourism industry does not simply find autochthonous landscapes and peoples, it transforms economics and environmental contours so that local governments can produce a commercial, exotic scenery (Enloe 1989). "Bushmen" and other hunter-gatherers have been one of the more successful means of luring visitors looking for exotic ecological and social landscapes (Gordon 1989).

While in a Western political-economic tradition, the idea of a sentient landscape is preposterous, the starting point for the commoditization of the northern landscape and for the Northern Territory land rights act is the spiritual relationship between Aborigines and the "living landscape." With Aboriginal or non-Aboriginal guides to explain the contours of the sentient landscape to scores of national and international tourists, the very part of the country that economists refuse to acknowledge seriously as producing and being produced by Aboriginal labor (their speech and their sweat), becomes the starting place of a profitable tourism industry. Difference becomes the selling point, even as this difference is subsumed into a commodity system. By promoting difference as a commodity value—the startling difference between an objective and a spiritual view of the countryside—the actual difference in perspective is threatened to be subsumed into a common market system (Peterson 1991). And Aborigines must themselves maintain a particular form (the traditional man and woman) in order for them to remain commodities in the economy of difference.

The fit of "traditional Aborigines" into Disneylike playgrounds remarks on the suitability of the Aboriginal Land Rights (NT) Act, 1976, for the tourism industry. The act, in part in language and in part in practice, necessitates a traditional perspective on the part of Aboriginal claimants; that is, claimants must demonstrate a living knowledge of and a desire to use, even sporadically, the land under claim. Several of the largest and most contested claims have been for lands in which spectacular natural features exist: Katherine Gorge, Uluru (Ayers Rock), and the Olgas. In negotiated agreements, the land was handed back to Aboriginal owners after they agreed to joint management of it as a national park. Arguably, the land so owned is now more valuable to a tourist as an authentic frontier experience: "for many Australians the Ayers Rock region is being associated in indefinable ways with 'The Outback Experience'. Tourists commonly said that not only is the area worthy of a visit because it is spectacular and different, but also because one somehow becomes more 'Australian' having seen Ayers Rock" (Altman 1987b, 6; see also Hamilton 1984).

The sweetness of an Aboriginal-based tourism industry has not stopped the Northern Territory government from opposing land rights. Upon limited self-government in 1978 (Northern Territory [Self Government] Act, 1978), the federal government retained important rights and responsibilities for the territory, including heavy subsidies of its economy and, because of southern perceptions of the historical violence between northern settlers and Aborigines, responsibility for Aboriginal affairs. The Country Liberal party, a conservative Northern Territory political party in office since limited self-government, has steadfastly and polemically portrayed the "Canberra bill" (the land rights act) as but another example of southern interference in northern matters. The Northern Territory government's resistance to southern administration reflects a historical view that southern legislators are unable to administer the lands that white Northern Territorians develop. Again we have to ask, what has the Northern Territory non-Aboriginal economy developed?

Even the pastoral industry that remains a solid part of the territory's tripartite economy (along with mining and tourism) has failed to develop fully. Instead, as Bruce Davidson has argued, because of the specific demographics and environment of the north, "It is not surprising that the only economically viable agricultural industry in the Northern Territory and the Kimberleys is grazing cattle on large unimproved holdings using a system of husbandry *which might well be described as hunting wild cattle*" (1980, 75; my emphasis). Some northern economists have blamed a continued cultural, political, and economic dependence on the south (Canberra's "economic and political imperialism" [Allen 1980, 33]) for the historical failure of the Northern Territory economy.[13] Wherever the ultimate blame lies, the agricultural and pastoral projects that the Northern Territory government has depended upon to keep the economy going have been a series of highly publicized failures (MacKenzie 1980; see table 7). The history of the Cox Peninsula itself reads, in many ways, as a study in Northern Territory pastoral, agricultural, and industrial failure. Opposite the Darwin Harbour, the Cox Peninsula was named after Dillen Cox, an agriculturalist who had a plantation there in the 1880s. The

TABLE 7

NOTABLE EUROPEAN ECONOMIC ACTIVITIES IN TROPICAL NORTHERN TERRITORY

Year	Event
1858	South Australia annexes the Northern Territory (NT).
1863	Land act allows sale of 202,000 hectares of land prior to NT survey.
1867	North Australia Company is compensated by South Australia government for its inability to survey land.
1869	Goyder finally completes NT survey.
1871	Gold is discovered at Pine Creek.
1872	Overland telegraph completed. First gold rush begins.
1880	Speculators lease land for pastoral and plantation activity. Sugar cane eventually fails as crop.
1885	Darwin–Pine Creek railway line is completed.
1911	Commonwealth takes over the administration of the territory.
1920	Meat works is closed. Private and government farms fail to develop agriculture.
1940	Army Farm Unit is formed and begins farming at Adelaide River.
1942–45	Army Farm Unit expands and eventually supplies fresh food to 100,000 defense personnel. Killing works built near Katherine.
1954–59	Territory Rice, Limited, plans to cultivate 200,000 hectares of land at Humpty Doo. Rice cropping fails.
1967–70	Tipperary Land Corporation plans to cultivate 80,000 hectares under sorghum. Attempts fail.
1971–74	Northern Agricultural Development Corporation plans similar venture at Willeroo. Attempts fail.

Note: Adapted from I. MacKenzie (1980, 57).

plantation rapidly failed. Before Cox, the peninsula was named after W. Douglas, a failed land speculator. Delissaville itself is the site of a southern businessman's 1886 sugar cane plantation, defeated by the long months of the dry season.

The rhetorical soundness and persuasiveness of such an economy is questionable within the existing political-economic frameworks still haunting political pragmatists. Productive government and labor is that which increases the value of land or commodities (goods); labor which "might as well be described as hunting" is the basis of only the most primitive forms of economic development—it was on the basis of this type of rudimentary Aboriginal economy that Australia was claimed as *terra nullius* in the first place.[14] Moreover, the original rhetorical groundwork on which the territory was settled—squatting—is now viewed as a drag on the economy. It is not surprising, therefore, that while no majority of residents advocates land rights for Aborigines within their own state boundaries, a majority of Australian residents support land rights in the Northern Territory. From a national perspective, Northern Territory lands are grossly underpopulated and underdeveloped and are, therefore, expendable for socially liberal projects. If land rights can settle a history of violent appropriation of indigenous lands and establish the Australian nation-state at the forefront of human rights in southeast Asia and the Pacific, is anything really lost in granting land to a scattered band of Aboriginal hunter-gatherers rather than to a scattered band of pastoral EuroAustralians? As an aside, it should be noted that more recently, support for Aboriginal land rights in the north has tempered in the face of a persistent national recession and a mining-industry media campaign that represents northern lands as having critical commercial mineral value to the nation during its economic crisis.

The territory government has tried to overcome its negative economic history by focusing, once again, on the future of the region and by discursively framing development plans as the natural end of sound city and regional planning. What they have not yet made commercially productive is potentially productive, because they have the vision and resources to transform "nonproductive" places into "urban areas," "rural–special use areas," "artificial lakes," "sea parks," and other "use areas" (map 4). The Northern Territory government's "town plan" for the expansion of the Darwin region builds around structures created as "natural" to the country, including the region's natural trading alliance with southeast Asia (note the oil pipe on map 4 that would connect to the East Timor oil reserves). Geographical space is given a number of productive values: good fishing, ideal residential living, proximity to a recreation area. Contour maps with productive values etched in geographical space coax the countryside into being in a certain form: they are the Euro-Australian equivalent of Aboriginal "songlines," the *durlg* tracks that caused the countryside to have its present shape. Moreover, these maps suggest a timeless quality to the various proposed developments—as if "urban area," "recreation area," and "special use area" were natural parts of the landscape just as "good for mining," "pastoralism," and "squatting" were shown to be in the maps of the 1800s.

The government can speak of the natural resources that are waiting to be developed, exploited, and put to productive purpose only if they are not already being used. To claim the land is undeveloped and unoccupied, territorial government must refuse to recognize the productive use that resident and regional Aborigines make of it. The easiest way to deny that resources are being used is to deny Aborigines access to the equipment that would mark the landscape in a way that non-Aborigines can read—that is, with permanent shelters, water bores, and roads. But adversarial governments can also refuse to document or acknowledge local Aboriginal meanings of space and its use.

THE SPATIAL ORGANIZATION OF BELYUEN HUNTING-GATHERING

Closing Up the Land

In contemporary Australia, the social geography of Aboriginal occupation and the use of the Cox Peninsula is predicated on local cultural and regional political-economic motivations as well as on ecological patterns of resource availability. The regional political economy of land allocation significantly affects the spatial patterns that arise from a year's hunting, fishing, and gathering practices. The complex interaction of cultural, historical, and ecological motivations for how people choose a foraging and camping ground is seen, first, in how they organize to resist non-Aboriginal encroachment onto regional lands and, second, in their use of six mangrove and estuarine sites on the peninsula.

In the past, when Laragiya, Wagaitj, and Beringgen were confronted by the arrival of European settlers, they would attempt to draw off resources without being drawn permanently into the camp as forced labor. But, in time and when they could, Aborigines would move away from the European site. Belyuen women say, "Better they left that place before that *bedagut* (white man) shoot im." One way of measuring the effect of a non-Aboriginal presence on Belyuen Aborigines' use of the Cox Peninsula is to analyze the number of camping and hunting sites that people refuse to visit and how this number has changed in their lifetimes. Twenty-three named camping sites on the Cox Peninsula have closed since the 1930s (see also Povinelli 1989). These places are located mainly on the southwest and northeast sections of the peninsula where there are large Euro-Australian residential, squatting, and commercial interests.

The presence of non-Aborigines at a place and the corresponding Aboriginal abandonment of it feeds into a system of land and resource alienation in two major ways. In a direct manner, land claim legislation directs the commissioner to consider issues of "strength of attachment" when making a recommendation for land. In the back rooms of trials this is sometimes described as the "bums on sand" test. While historical factors are taken into consideration, the best and most likely way of being granted a section of land is to have Aborigines living or visiting that section for long periods of time. When Aborigines associate a place as "dangerous" because of the potential for racial confrontation and abandon it for this reason, it weakens any claim they have in court. Courts do not see themselves as deciding "political" issues of fairness; instead they test how forensic evidence conforms to the language of an act. Legal testability of forensic evidence is seen as a better criterion by which to measure acts than such subjective issues as fairness. This testable approach to the ravages of history and the resilience of social groups claims not to engage politically the contradictions outlined earlier; rather it supposedly assesses the relationship of evidence to the law in a neutral way. But the law does support the historical alienation of the countryside. By spatially confining the Laragiya, Wagaitj, and Beringgen on the Delissaville (Belyuen) settlement, the government can, in time, rely on the law to support its claims that only this restricted land should be granted to those groups.

But Belyuen Aborigines abandon a place primarily because time has shown that Europeans and other non-Aborigines will eventually move away from it. The historical failure of most commercial enterprises on the Cox Peninsula has reinforced this Aboriginal strategy of temporary abandonment and eventual return. However, this strategy has created long-term difficulties because of increasing population pressure on the Cox Peninsula. Aborigines can no longer expect to be able to return to a place they have left to white squatters and campers. That might have been done when land seemed plentiful or might have had to be done when the outrages of white violence seemed to go completely unpunished. But Belyuen family and community leaders have now learned through interaction with government representatives and ordinary squatters and residents that government and business want all the land, not only one beach or one section of the Cox Peninsula.

Increasingly, Belyuen Aborigines maintain outstations throughout the year in order to resist white encroachment. People without jobs stay and mind a camp, where they are supplied by those with cars and money. This is an effective way of using prejudice to one's advantage, for just as Wagaitj and Beringgen are loath to camp near non-Aborigines, so non-Aborigines are uncomfortable around black camps and rarely approach. This "blocking" strategy is increasingly being used for places near Dreaming sites, which suggests that the economics of land appropriation continues to be articulated through a sacred vernacular.

Attempts to block non-Aboriginal encroachment onto regional lands helps explain why no one Belyuen family group has monopolized the use of any one area. Perhaps we should be surprised that few Belyuen families have gained control of large segments of the peninsula for themselves. For, I have shown, one family holds many of the Belyuen Community Council jobs and, therefore, the vehicles and large equipment controlled by the council. This can make an enormous difference in a family's ability to build solid shelters at an outstation and to provide water and food to outstation members. Still, Belyuen people say that no matter the discrepancy in income and access to goods, there are no Belyuen bosses over the rich and productive hunting areas on the Cox Peninsula and Port Patterson Islands. Everyone must pay respect to the mythic and secular sites throughout the countryside. And everyone can use the land. This ideological position is backed by local economic realities. Because families that have council jobs and access to council vehicles must spend most of their time away from the outstation at jobs, they are left with the problem of how to block non-Aboriginal Australians from various sites in the country. David Yesner points out that "much of the real cost of marine hunting, however, involves not so much the technology as the social relations of production, ranging from the cost of maintaining family or clan territories in order to restrict access to areas where resources aggregate" (1987, 289). At Belyuen, the cost of maintaining Aboriginal territories and outstation infrastructures is shared by various families who work as a somewhat cohesive group to keep others off the best hunting grounds. No matter their access to money and materials, better-off families need other, unemployed people to maintain the outstations. But social relations on outstations can be seriously tested no matter the economic interdependence of family groups.

Often, visitors from Belyuen to an outstation create a significant volume of social disturbance by drinking and then fighting over boyfriends or girlfriends. Tempers flare, knives or pickets fly, and people scatter into the moonlit mangroves or down the glimmering beaches. Those who have set up the outstation and are seen as its permanent residents are unable to tell troublemakers to leave because they are usually kin who have come "to keep them company" (to make them "fat" by visiting). Instead, the residents themselves either move away from the main camp or return to the Belyuen community until everyone has sobered and returned to the community as well. This can make for a series of rather hysterical moments as sober people try to avoid troublemakers, and troublemakers keep following them out of affection. In one aspect, Yesner's remarks are quite fitting for the Belyuen situation: only those with a close personal or kin relationship to members of an outstation visit and so share in a camp's resources. However, the tangled web of Belyuen kinship is such that someone usually can be the front person for a polite "request" (see Myers 1982b) to use an area around someone else's outstation. Or a more distantly related group can establish a camp some five hundred meters down the beach. The rationale for such requests and camp spacings is consistent with ideas about how country is enlivened by living on it. Belyuen men and women argue that those doing the hard work of maintaining the life of a place should be able to benefit from its resources.

From an Aboriginal point of view, the problem with a strategy of permanent residence is clear. Over time, places become more or less dangerous as people are born, live, and die at them. If Belyuen Aborigines are to follow certain cultural traditions—such as letting a place "rest" if someone associated strongly with it has recently died—they must abandon a site periodically. But to abandon a site is to invite non-Aborigines to move into it. People are attempting to balance these pressures by moving to the far edge of a site when there has been a death. In this way they can monitor the area without having to camp on top of it.

Another method used to slow the advance of the white holiday camper and permanent squatter is to keep areas "closed up" by not maintaining the infrastructures that allow non-Aborigines easy access to a favorite camping ground. These include the construction of roads, the clearing of camping areas, and the storage of equipment at sites. The term *infrastructure* may sound very modern for the practice of hunter-gatherers. But Laragiya, Wagaitj, and Beringgen have kept areas clear, maintained paths, and left dugouts and chipping equipment at sites for a long time. Further, the paths noted in myth had enacted in ceremony or story demonstrate the existence of an integrated and functioning network that Aborigines use to increase their output by decreasing the time needed to reinvent the landscape upon every return to a camping ground. Whereas in the past, keeping a place "open" by regular visits meant decreasing one's overall labor, now it often means inviting the visits of unwanted strangers who then block the use of an area. Because of this, Belyuen Aborigines leave roads in disrepair and areas partially cleared. This is interpreted by non-Aborigines in an typical way: Aborigines do not develop or produce the countryside or, in an even grosser claim, they claim that because the countryside is not developed, Belyuen Aborigines must be settlement bound.

Economic practice and socio-cultural identity

Aboriginal people are not the only ones on the beach. The territory government encourages visitors to Darwin to explore "outback" regional lands by publishing maps and by supporting safari outfits. Belyuen Aborigines watch the tourists, along with local Euro-Australian residents, who descend on the Cox Peninsula during the dry season. From what they see of these people, Belyuen men and women make claims about the effects of European activity on the countryside, and they adjust the place of their own hunting activities. It is through hunting that women say they learn about the differences that exist among themselves and between themselves and other groups. Belyuen people watch where in the countryside various ethnic groups live, camp, and work and they monitor how these groups act. Doing so allows Belyuen Aborigines to judge a group's character and to construct a social identity for them. This identity becomes the ground of Aborigines' social and political stances. When they say that they oppose non-Aboriginal expansion onto the Cox Peninsula they say it is because they have seen what non-Aborigines are like (they know because *they have been there*).

Belyuen understandings of non-Aboriginal identity have a geographic bent. While Wagaitj and Beringgen at Belyuen prefer the open beach as a camping spot to the "hot" inland or mangrove-enclosed beaches, non-Aborigines are said not to prefer, but to be unable to use anything else but beaches and these only in a certain way. During the dry season in the Top End, the days are breezy and warm and the nights clear and brisk. The humidity that haunts the landscape throughout the wet and buildup seasons evaporates, taking with it mosquitoes and sand flies. During these months, tourists flock into northern towns on their annual migration to Katherine's famous gorge and Kakadu's cinematic, crocodile-infested wetlands. Stray tourists take a ferry across the Darwin Harbour or drive around to the Cox Peninsula. They usually aim for the Mandorah Pub because it is the only sign of inhabitation, other than the Belyuen community, on most maps. From Mandorah they explore sites on the north and east coasts nearby. Although Belyuen women and men take advantage of tourism to sell a few crafts and foods, women usually avoid any area that non-Aborigines are using (other than the Mandorah wharf, but even here use drops dramatically during the dry season). During the peak of the tourist season, the Belyuen use of the western region of the Cox Peninsula increases as tourists move into northern and eastern hunting grounds (map 3). Even when no whites seem to be around, a Belyuen group's day at the beach is often highlighted by the appearance of a group of Euro-Australians or foreign tourists who decide to take advantage of the "remote" area to strip off their swimsuits or who decide to drive up a

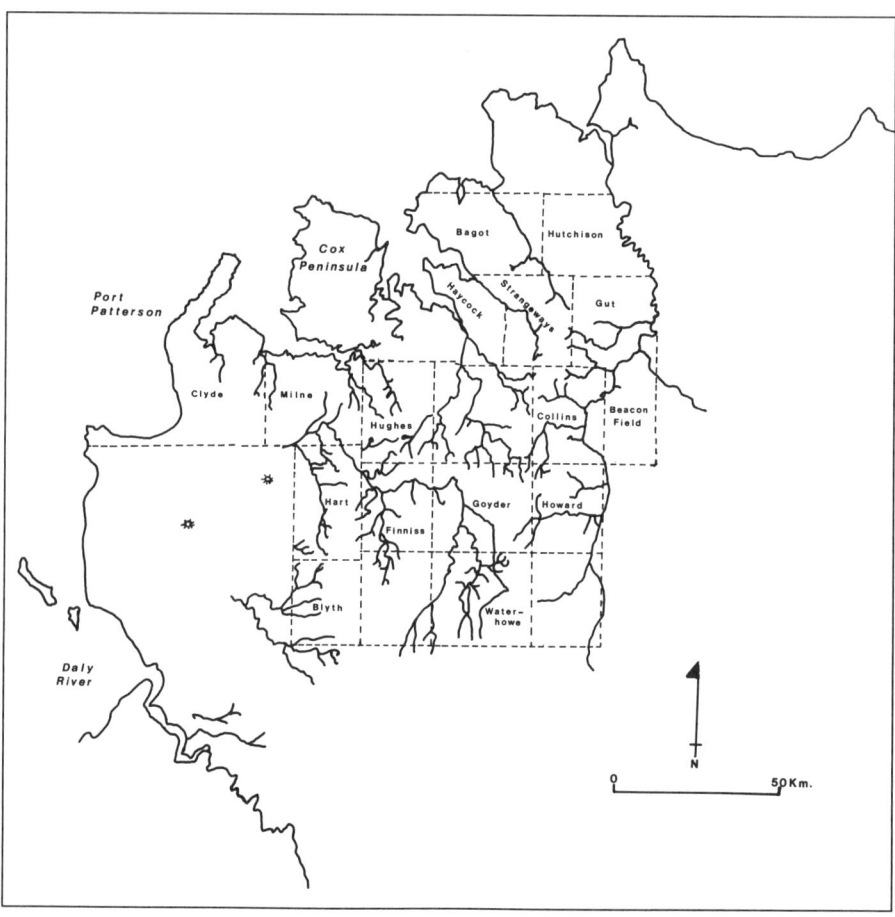

Map 5: Ownership of Land in the Darwin Region in the 1880s

crocodile-infested creek on ski jets. Both sights are topics of scathing commentary for those of our group quietly fishing inside a dense mangrove swamp.

While non-Aborigines perform such socially and personally dangerous acts, Belyuen women note that they "panic" when traveling in the inland forests or mangroves. The overenthusiasm ("They like themselves") of the bathers and the skiers is rearticulated in a different environment as excessive and out of control ("They got no *meru*").[15] The excessive, volatile character of non-Aborigines is seen as well in their historical violent and racist treatment of Aborigines. Euro-Australians in particular have shown themselves in the present and the past to be loud, disturbing, and generally, to have an inappropriate way of acting in the country. Belyuen women and men's lives are marred by incidents of Euro-Australian sexual and physical abuse and harassment, although women's evocations of the past veer between explicit descriptions and studied avoidance of white male violence. Because of the real and perceived character of white bushwhackers, Belyuen families will often change the place of a desired hunting trip to avoid non-Aboriginal campers.

Although non-Aboriginal activity can interfere with the placement of a hunting trip, it also makes possible the construction of identity based on differences between the activities and placement of non-Aborigines and Aborigines in the countryside. When Belyuen women note that life is getting harder and that Euro-Australians want all the best places, they are also noting that although Euro-Australians take the good places they do not enliven them or maintain their sweetness. Instead, by their "silliness" country is ruined; it returns into itself and refuses to produce. Smelling the sweat of foolhardy people, the country refuses to give its fatness and all people suffer. People from Belyuen have only to point across the harbor to Darwin to make the point that white inhabitation of an area usually spells environmental disaster. That the appropriation of an area is backed by intimidation and by structured, differential access to law and resources only cements the differences Belyuen women and men construct between white and black people, their countries, and their laws.

Six Mangroves and Their Uses

The complex engagement between local and regional cultural and political-economic histories and their effect on Belyuen Aborigines' spatial organization of hunting, fishing, and gathering trips can be seen in how and why people use different sections of the Cox Peninsula. In table 8 I provide a general overview of the kinds of environments people use throughout the year, and the amount of time they use them. The tables showing the use of different environments "spatialize" the time charts I discussed in the previous chapter; they break down the time women spend in the bush into the specific environments.

As shown in table 8, women and men make a high and steady use of the sea and of estuarine creeks throughout the year, but they fluctuate their use of the open forest regions: women seasonally collect craft objects and men seasonally hunt for feral pigs, bullock, and kangaroo. Women use the inland region around Belyuen during the wet season to collect stringy bark for bark paintings, small hollow eucalyptus trunks for didjeridoos, and bush palm fronds for dilly bags and baskets. These products are most pliable and easy to procure after the rains have slowed and the

TABLE 8

Time Spent Hunting and Gathering Foods and Materials

	OF	M	DVT	RC	SS	B	S	E	SW	SP
January	2.3	9.4	.5		2.7		20.5	33.3		
	(.56)	(1.18)	(.5)		(.88)		(2.93)	(3.33)		
February	17.5	9.8	.5		4.8		33.8	37		
	(1.75)	(1.22)	(.5)		(1.58)		(2.41)	(2.64)		
March	15.7	4.9	12	5.4	1.3		42	21.5		
	(1.57)	(.97)	(2.4)	(1.1)	(.42)		(2.63)	(2.69)		
April	5.4	17.6	9.5	3.3	9.1		26.1	16.1		
	(.68)	(1.6)	(2.38)	(1.32)	(1.31)		(2.17)	(2.17)		
May	18.8	9.2	2	1	1.3	.4	20.8	27.5		
	(2.35)	(1.31)	(1)	(1)	(1.25)	(.18)	(2.31)	(3.44)		
June	9.3	18.5	12.8	1	2.3	3.2	22	16.8	2	4.5
	(1.32)	(1.85)	(2.13)	(1)	(1.13)	(.81)	(2.75)	(3.35)	(1)	(.9)
July	20	21.3	7.5	6	4.8	4.8	27.3	61.5		2
	(1.82)	(1.63)	(1.25)	(1.2)	(2.38)	(2.38)	(2.73)	(3.84)		(.67)
August	5.3	25	1.75	2.25	5.6	19.9	44.8	24	6.3	9
	(.88)	(1.79)	(.58)	(.75)	(.69)	(1.65)	(2.48)	(2.67)	(1.56)	(4.5)
September	5.9	22.5	.5	2.5	13.5	14	55.4	18.5	31	.25
	(.66)	(1.6)	(.5)	(1.25)	(1.13)	(1.25)	(2.31)	(2.64)	(1.42)	(.25)
October	5.5	23.3	3.75	2.5	2	10.8	22.8	14.8	28.1	
	(.92)	(1.59)	(1.25)	(1.25)	(.67)	(2.15)	(2.28)	(2.11)	(1.52)	
November	8.5	16.7	2.75		2.5	.2	10.7	17.5	6.7	
	(.71)	(2.09)	(.69)		(.83)	(.15)	(2.14)	(2.5)	(1.33)	
December	19.3	9.8	1	4.85	1	59	18.8	1.8	.25	
	(1.53)	(1.63)	(.5)	(1.21)	(1)	(3.05)	(2.68)	(1.45)	(.25)	

Note: Numbers represent average number of hours spent in an environment during a single trip. Numbers in parentheses are averages over the same time period. OF = open forest; M = mangrove; DVT = dense vine tangle; RC = rocky coast; SS = offshore; B = black soil plains; S = seashore; E = estuarine creek; SW = Wetland swamp; and SP = freshwater spring.

ground has dried slightly. Their collection falls off dramatically during the dry season when the bark begins to stick to the tree and the bush fronds become brittle. Women also pace themselves, working hard late in the wet season and taking a break from craft work during the dry season when there are more enjoyable things to do such as sit on the beach and fish. Although women use the mangrove year round, they increase their use of it in the drier part of the year. Men and women use dense vine tangles, black soil plains, and wetland swamps only when foods associated with them become available in large quantities. What these tables do not show is the different amount of time they spend in, say, two different mangroves. There are, after all, many mangroves on the shores of the Cox Peninsula. How do people choose between mangroves, for instance, or black soil plains?

Belyuen men and women are presented with a number of choices about where they can go to collect an object. To which mangrove of the numerous named hunting camps should they go? Over the course of a year, roads dry out and increase the number of sites available. Belyuen Aborigines significantly increase the number of places they visit in the dry season. Hunting sites also provide women with a choice between different combinations of environments. For example, each of the estuarine creeks on the Cox Peninsula has a different surrounding countryside, and so a different selection of foods. Like people, places have certain personality traits, contours, and characters that make them appealing to some and not to others. Examining Belyuen families' use of six estuarine creek regions—two eastern sites, Madpil and Bitbinbiyirrk, two northern sites, Bemandjeli and Belurriya, and two northwestern sites, Bagadjet and Binbinya—highlights the complex sociocultural and political-economic motivations for contemporary indigenous use of the countryside.[16]

Table 1 presents an overview of Belyuen families' use of six estuarine creeks. It predicts the amount of foods they would have collected if they had used each place an equal number of times (assuming that productivity does not drop from increased usage). Seafood is not the only type of food collected at these sites, but they can be usefully compared from place to place. Nor did people only collect the foods listed in table 1. In particular, the two western sites, Bagadjet and Binbinya, were used significantly more in the dry season than this table indicates. Because I was camping at Bemandjeli on the north coast, I was not able to collect data on how western outstations used the surrounding region. In 1985 and 1987 I stayed at west coast outstations. At several points I refer to this earlier data.

Bagadjet is a hunting camp located behind a vast mangrove, part of a large estuarine creek on the northwest coast of the Cox Peninsula. A small wetlands swamp lies to its east, fertile yam beds lie on either side, and fruit trees (including green plums [*Buchanania obovata*], billy goat plums [*Terminalia ferdinandiana*], and milky plums [*Persoonia fulcata*]) are in the southern open forest. At different times of the year, this campground appeals to different sets of people. During the early buildup, when crabs are most abundant and heavy, women who like to collect them prefer Bagadjet because its size allows a number of people to hunt profitably there. Other women prefer Bagadjet during the dry season when days are less hot and geese and turtles can be found in its swamp. At this time men hunt pigs, cattle, and kangaroos in the surrounding jungle. Young children collect green plums in Bagadjet's open forest—one of the most productive green plum sites—during the late buildup. Bagadjet is not used unless these foods are in season; and, like most northwest coast sites, it is rarely used in the wet season. Moreover, people prefer places other than Bagadjet as a day camp. They often collect foods then move on to another place, complaining that Bagadjet is "closed up" and has "no breeze." The mangrove blocks the view of the sea and a dense vine tangle darkens the country immediately behind the camp. Women note that they cannot see dangers approaching such as hostile "kidney fat men" (*munggul*, E, sorcerers) and Euro-Australian "rebels."[17] In addition, a *pederra* (here described as a gorilla-like being) is thought to live in the swamp. Numerous people have seen its tracks or heard its loud wailings. As a consequence no permanent camp is presently maintained at Bagadjet. Thus although it is a rich crabbing site, the number of visits to it is relatively low (although it is higher than indicated by my data because of the unrecorded use made of the site by nearby outstation members).

Binbinya is southwest of Bagadjet and consists of a small beach lying between a long mangrove, an estuarine creek, and a wetlands swamp. The swamp is home to feral pigs, cattle, and freshwater turtles; however, access to the swamp is difficult. Most day trips stop at the site for crabbing or fishing. Fishing, as table 1 shows, is quite productive, particularly when salmon run up the creek. During my stay from September 1984 to June 1985, and again in 1987, I helped dig long yams in a nearby jungle. How those yams got there is a point of contention: some women claim they grew "themselves" (they were "wild" in local sense of able to move about themselves), others claim that a senior woman who camped in the area brought the yams from Bagadjet. It seems likely there is truth to both claims. The senior woman probably oversaw the use of the yam ground and made sure that people replanted yam heads (helping regrowth) and did not overexploit the region. The Belyuen are presently letting the area "rest" for a while until the number of yams increases. Lack of nearby foods other than fish and crab (yams, longneck turtles, sea turtle eggs) is one reason women often decide to go elsewhere for a day's foraging, which lowers the number of visits made to the site.

But Binbinya also suffers because of its historical and cultural habitat. Though a highly productive fish and crab site, Dreaming and burial grounds "humbug" people camping there, sending out apparitions during the night, taking away foods if distant relatives ("people with strange sweat") join the camp, and causing people to act in mysterious, inexplicable ways. Just up the coast, along a red cliff region, another set of families live "out of the way" of these mythic forces. The "Bagamanadjing mob," as they are commonly referred to, has several dinghies and four-by-four vehicles that allow them to hunt sea turtle and dugong. They can avoid Binbinya because they do not rely upon fish from its creek or crabs from its mangrove.

Bemandjeli and Belurriya are small estuarine creeks on the north coast. Unlike the northwestern and eastern coastal regions, with their short beaches and long mangroves, the north coast has long, white sand beaches and small estuarine creeks and mangroves. The long beaches are nesting grounds for sea turtles and, therefore, hunting grounds for Aborigines. Behind the beaches and further inland lie a series of freshwater swamps. The northern wetland swamps are one of the most productive hunting grounds for geese and pigs. Use of them increases dramatically during the dry season. Indigenous honeys, fruits, palms (*Livistonia humilis, Carpentaria acuminata*), and nuts (*Brachychiton parodoxum*) are found across the entire region. Drawn to the swamp lilies, the sugarbag bee (an indigenous honey bee) nests throughout the region. Outstation members or day collectors spread out across the open forest and collect the honey from antbeds, tree trunks, and, sometimes, old concrete building foundations. Drawn as well to the long white beaches of the north coast are non-Aboriginal weekend campers, a point to which shall I return.

Belurriya is at the western end of the north coast. During the 1920s and 1930s, a plantation was run nearby at Charles Lighthouse. Aboriginal women were often forcibly removed from their families to work in the peanut, coconut, and pawpaw fields. Social and economic conditions were harsh: the work was monotonous and grueling, little food was provided, and sexual abuse was common. Older women who worked there as children and young adults describe "escaping" from this plantation (and others like it) to hunt at Belurriya. The very shape of Belurriya (like all six sites) is a reminder to people of their history. Events of the colonial and postcolonial period have left tangible marks: deeply emotional marks, such as nearby burial sites, and ecological marks, such as trees that grandparents planted to provide shade for their foraging trips. Many women avoid the Charles Lighthouse region when they go to Belurriya because of the emotional stress it causes them. The name Belurriya itself has passed down through three generations of women linking them to the historical trauma of the colonial period.

Bemandjeli, located east of Belurriya, is also a small estuarine area. It is a good example of how local strategies for maintaining the mythic and emotional health of people and places interact with regional land development and use. I mentioned aspects of the following story throughout this book, but return to it here in more detail. Bemandjeli has long been an important campsite for Aborigines. Popular and ethnological writings from the 1880s onward report Aborigines staying there (see Harney 1965). Many reasons exist to think such was the case long before Europeans arrived, for nearby are several sacred sites and a young man's initiation ground. In the 1970s, an Emiyenggal sibling set established a permanent outstation at the site. The senior brother, a clever man and astute politician,[18] was the head of several important ceremonial and ritual complexes. When this man died in the early 1980s, his family abandoned the site following a local custom. During the time that families were letting the site "rest" so as not to aggravate his spirit, the outstation was stripped: Euro-Australian squatters carted away several thousand dollars worth of materials (mostly corrugated iron sidings). Gradually members of his family began returning to the beach, building outstations, and putting in applications for leasehold rights. Several extended families, most from the Emiyenggal and Menthayenggal language groups, now maintain a year-round outstation there. The deceased Emiyenggal clever man protects and "plays fun" with them: a clear example of how people's identity adheres in places motivating why and when they use them. As researchers we must understand that the ability to interact with a deceased relative—one's husband, mother, or child—by visiting a place provides a very compelling reason to go there no matter if one looses a fish or two. This is especially true in communities like Belyuen where grocery foods temper the vicissitudes of the hunt.

Bitbinbiyirrk and Madpil are located on the east coast of the peninsula. Each site is home to a short beach, mangroves, and a small estuarine creek. But they are also sites where global, regional, and local economies interact. In 1989, Bitbinbiyirrk was mainly used for the collection of sea snails and the central stalk of the Agave plant; the latter is collected for manufacturing dilly bags for sale and personal use. Women typically collected several liters of unhusked sea snails, then either returned to Belyuen or moved to another site for the day, often to Madpil. Sometimes they stayed, cooked, and husked the snails at the site, adding to a shell midden there. During 1985 and 1987, women used Bitbinbiyirrk quite differently. Then, as in 1989, women collected a large number of sea snails, but they also fished regularly in the nearby creek and collected sugarbag and long yams in the nearby vine jungle. With increased squatting in the region this pattern changed dramatically. While women were afraid that rebels might be hiding in the Bagadjet jungle, they know they are camping at Bitbinbiyirrk. According to local reports, a series of arrests were made of Anglo bushwhackers camping there.[19] To Belyuen women the burned-out remains of their camp (husks of cars, cooking instruments, and bedding) were a sign of the campers' haste to escape, proving their criminal nature. In 1992, at least one white man was murdered nearby, further marking this region as dangerous.

Madpil is south of Bitbinbiyirrk and can be reached by walking down the coast when the tide is out or by driving along an inland road. Its mangrove is larger and links to another southern site, Midjili. Women often travel south through the mangrove from Madpil to Midjili collecting crabs, then north through the open forest ("overline") as the tide comes in. Some fruit trees are found in the high ground above the site. At Midjili, a wetlands swamp is often used for pig hunting. Other motivations for using Madpil and Bitbinbiyirrk are the nearby Mandorah Pub (on the northeast tip of the Cox Peninsula) and the Alewa Grocery Store. Like more traditional campsites, these stores provide a place for social interaction and the acquisition of foods. People usually stop there for supplies and foods: the well-known bush stock of flour, sugar, and tea, and the more recent fast food innovations of hamburgers, meat pies, and cokes. During the dry season a tourist corroboree is held at the Mandorah Pub, drawing national and international visitors. Throughout the tourist season the Belyuen Kenbi Corroboree Crew maintains an outstation at Madpil, using it as a base camp for sea-hunting trips that provide foods for the tourist buffet and for crew members. The returns from these trips are not reckoned in my data.

When Belyuen families choose to use these various sites underscores the multiple historical, sociocultural and political-economic influences on land use. In some sense, the Belyuen Aborigines' use of the peninsula reflects a "seasonal round" of the type Altman (1987b, 22–26) described among the Gunwinggu of Arnhem Land (see also Meehan 1988). In 1989, from the wet to the dry season, groups shifted generally from using northeastern to using northwestern sites; although, for reasons I explain later, the north continued to be an important camping spot throughout the dry season (see map 3). (Notes from my field trips in 1984–85 show a clearer correlation between regional use and seasonality. In 1989, unusually late rains kept most hunting and camping sites accessible by vehicle late into December.) People themselves describe a northwest coast season—that time of the year when the west coast is usable. Because of the predominantly rock base of its road, Binbinya usually is available before more northern sites such as Bagadjet. The Belyuen "seasonal round" would, then, seem to support Stanner's well-known dictum that one "can almost plot a year of their life in terms of movement towards the places where honey, yams, grass-seeds, eggs, or some other food staple, is in bearing and ready for eating" (1979b, 33) and Jon Altman's more recent analysis of the "effects of the annual [seasonal] cycle on band movement" (1987b, 25).

Environmental signs tell Belyuen Aborigines when the west coast season has begun; these signs are like cues they followed for older Aboriginal travel practices. Old people describe their parents following the winds, moving up the coast from the Daly River to the Cox Peninsula with the dry season winds (*medawok*, E) and returning down the coast before the monsoonal winds (*kunaberruk* and *perrk*, E). They similarly frame their use of the west coast of the Cox Peninsula; they wait for the *medawok* winds before they use the region. But these discursive frames blur, or at least do not reveal, significant differences between why they and their parents followed winds to certain regions. Today's seasonal rounds are influenced by such social matters as people's sentimental attachment to places, such cultural issues as the enlivening of sites and the acquisition of Dreamings, such political-economic matters as interethnic conflicts over resource allocation and wage-labor's demands on people's time, and such logistical matters as the availability of water and vehicles. The *medawok* winds are anticipated because they dry the roads to the west coast and thus allow vehicles, the principal means by which people travel from place to place, to pass. But all of these factors interact. For instance, people with community jobs have access to community vehicles, land movers, and dinghies, but they have limited time to use them. And vehicles are the main means of travel not only because of their productive efficiency but also because of the historical relationship between Euro-Australian administrators and Aborigines camping on the coast. This point deserves to be developed in more detail here because it connects, most clearly, historical issues of control and containment discussed in chapter 2 with issues of land use discussed in this and the last chapter.

The primary reason people give for why they do not use the northwest coast in the wet season is that roads are impassable. So persuasive and accepted is the rhetoric of the "west coast season" that one must remember feet do not bog in black soil plains. Indeed, this region was regularly used during the rainy season as recently as 1950. However, the same welfare records that tell us of earlier rainy season travel show us why vehicles have become a virtual necessity for bush camps and, therefore, why the northwest coast is closed during the wet season. Operating an outstation or a day camp without a vehicle is now seen as too risky for a number of reasons: trucks are needed to supply water to outstations and to provide transportation to jobs in the community. But most important, a vehicle is needed to transport sick persons quickly back to the community clinic.

In their oral histories Belyuen women describe many scenes of interethnic violence, but perhaps none is more disturbing than Aboriginal deaths and their investigation by Euro-Australians. The grief caused by the death of a child or old person was, and still is, interrupted and mixed with fear that the death will incite an inquiry by local law enforcement officials. From the 1920s to the 1950s, at Aboriginal camps throughout the Cox Peninsula and Port Patterson Islands, tuberculosis, gonorrhea, alcoholism, and fighting resulted in a high death rate. Leaders of camps where deaths occurred, or parents whose children died, were rounded up, questioned, tested for diseases, and punished by internment on the Delissaville settlement. An older Belyuen woman sometimes describes the horror of sitting in a Darwin "jail" unable to speak English after her young son died. People often fled down the coast rather than submit to what they saw as harassment, especially by people who created the conditions for their ill health. While such traumatic events no longer occur, the personal and social costs surrounding a person's injury and death is an important reason why no camp is run for long without a vehicle. No one wants to be blamed for having let a sick person remain at a camp when help was nearby. In other words, one of the spatial dimensions of the Cox Peninsula relates to the location of European-based health resources. But government administrators are not the only persons that have caused Belyuen Aborigines to reassess space based on health. If an Aboriginal visitor from another community sickens, is injured, or dies while staying at a camp, his or her relatives can "pay back" any member of that camp. Visitors from communities that Belyuen elders believe are "stronger" in ritual and ceremonial power are closely watched and rarely encouraged to go far from a source of medical aid. Their accidental injury or death could provoke a retributive assault that the community would be unable to deter. Because of their proximity to several mythic sites and burial grounds, Binbinya and other camps are dangerous in this light.

The choices of Belyuen men and women to live at or use a certain place also appear to depend on how they identify themselves in relation to that place historically. The responsibilities attached to *durlg, maroi,* and burial sites are the most obvious ways that people articulate their ties to certain camping spots. For example, a Kiyuk family looks after burial sites on the west coast close to its outstation. Nearby, a Kiyuk-Laragiya sibling set looks after several *durlg* sites related to them. As I already noted, Emiyenggal and Menthayenggal families are looking after a region on the north coast because an important, now deceased, Emi man established an outstation there in the early 1970s and was a "boss" for several ceremonies associated with the area. This Emi clever man protects and "plays fun" with his relations while they are camping in the area. But we must also be careful not to resort to psychological absolutism. The clever man's spiritual presence in the area provides a particularly persuasive way that his surviving family can articulate their rights to the region. But while Emiyenggal and Menthayenggal presently emphasize their association with the north coast, they could select from other possible associations on the southwest, west, and east coasts.

In fact, it would be misleading to present Belyuen Aborigines as driven to camp at any site because of cultural or historical ties to it. The evidence people present for their attachments to a site is selective in several senses: it does not account for everyone's attachments to places (an impossibility since, as discussed in chap. 3, new ones are "growing" all the time), and it reflects Belyuen people's own historical, social, and cultural selectivity. As with their use of Bemandjeli, people select certain relationships among persons and places for sociocultural, psychological, and political-economic ends.[20] But each family has historical and personal ties to a large number of camps on the Cox Peninsula and near the Daly River.

For instance, the sibling set who now have an outstation on the west coast were born on, grew up near, and now regularly visit a site on the northwest coast. And the Emi who live on the north coast also stay on the west and southwestern coasts during different parts of the year. Not only do people change where they live, hunt, and camp, but, as I noted earlier, social groups align and realign themselves throughout the course of a year for personal and practical reasons. Fred Myers notes, "Pintupi people did not always live with the same coresidential group or even within a single territory" (1986, 71). He suggests

> that we should recognize the spatial component of production in hunting-and-gathering societies, rather than envisioning the organization of productive roles as reflecting only the division of labor by sex. . . . Marriage [for instance] establishes not only the immediate relations of production but also, by creating ties between distant people, establishes relations of production and access to land within a larger ecological region (1986, 71).

Rather than an effect of history, the claims that families make for local countries based on sentimental, cultural, and historical ties are better understood as historically rooted discourses used to ground and establish familial rights to a number of places.

CONCLUSION

The Dreaming and Development provide two competing discursive frames for thinking about land spatiotemporally, both what it has been and what it can become. Moreover, each framework offers a way of thinking about the productive potentials of types of human-human and human-land relations (or "modes of production"). In this chapter I discussed how Western notions of development have affected how non-Aboriginal Australians think about the legitimate nature of Northern Territory government's claim that their economic plans are being stifled by southern mismanagement and about the potential uses of the northern landscape for socially liberal land rights projects. The 1976 passage of the Aboriginal Land Rights (NT) Act put a small dent into the discursive power of development's potential. At least through the late 1970s and early 1980s, some voters acknowledged development's limit in the Top End of the Northern Territory of Australia. The historical failure of the Northern Territory government to "develop" northern lands provided some voters with a sense that the Dreaming may better serve northern interests. I also discussed how Belyuen notions of human-human and human-land relations effect how they use various sections of the land and struggle to resist the encroachment of non-Aboriginal people onto them. While Belyuen Aborigines do not focus on how different modes of production effect human-human or human-land relations, they do look at the form of various ethnic groups' actions in the countryside. Indeed, in some ways, they link a form of labor-action to a type of ethnic group (panicked and excessive behavior to white men and women). In any case, Belyuen women use the Dreaming to understand the effects various groups' labor-action have on the changing social and ecological topography of the Cox Peninsula and on the expanding networks of non-Aboriginal private and government-sponsored businesses being run there.

Just because Belyuen Aborigines are able to use the Dreaming as a framework to assess, interpret and understand contemporary events does not mean they are immune to the structural and cultural onslaughts of the nation-state's development policies. Many of seasonal patterns of land use are more influenced by political and economic issues arising from regional trade than by the optimality of the foraging moment. Relatedly, the early history of the Delissaville settlement shows that the state restricts Aboriginal land use in order to provide for even *hypothetical* European development plans in the future. Belyuen Aborigines are quite aware that even the potential of non-Aboriginal economic advancement outweighs the actual benefits they would gain from full possession of local lands. And where some actual resource exists in and around the Cox Peninsula, Belyuen Aborigines often find that the land movers or the pearl-shell divers, backed by state resources, have beaten them to the catch. Because the white men (*bedagut*) want "more and more," Belyuen women say, they ignore the fact that Belyuen men and women use all regions of the Cox Peninsula and that the materials and Dreamings they collect are critical to their health and well-being. Indeed, the same type of criticism Belyuen women leveled at drinkers and shopmen ("they are excessive," "they cannot be satisfied," "they go for more and more"; see chap. 4 above) they level, more generally, at Euro-Australian society—it cannot be satisfied with a well-working world.

The changing nature of non-Aboriginal uses and interests in the Cox Peninsula have affected how Belyuen Aborigines themselves view the potential uses of it. Whereas in the early colonial period, the best strategy for land use was to engage selectively and sporadically in the European-based economy and to abandon places when European settlers intruded, in the contemporary period *being there* has become one of the best strategies for land-based resistance for several reasons. First, being there is compatible with local cultural notions and uses of labor-action. Being in country allows Aborigines to gain Dreamings (*maroi* and *nyoitj* in an immediate way, and *durlg* in the long term), to persuade the country in a positive manner to provide rich and plentiful foods and resources; it also permits Aborigines to nuance their cultural knowledge about the dispositions of the mythic countryside in ways crucial to inter-Aboriginal disputes. Aborigines ensure the well-being of themselves and the countryside by stopping at sites and using them, by telling mythic or personal stories about them, and by providing them physical and legal upkeep. Second, being there also allows Belyuen Aborigines to block non-Aboriginal encroachments onto their land as it allows Aborigines to accumulate rights under Western law (the "bums on sand" test). In short, being there is the best strategy Belyuen Aborigines have found for maintaining their lives within the often contradictory mandates of the Dreaming and Development, both of which can be found on the Cox Peninsula.

6 The Assessment of Cultural Identity and Political Economic Practice
A Conclusion

> Heidegger's attack on the primacy of the "viewpoint" and his alternative, which understands the world of persons and things as produced by prior practices embedded in language in general and speech practices in particular, provides an opening for the old "humanistic" genres that were, until recently, proscribed by those interested in human sciences.
>
> —Michael Shapiro, *Language and Politics*

LABOR'S VALUE: ECONOMIC SIGN-CULTURAL ECONOMY

This book has examined the multiple motivations and lots of Belyuen Aboriginal labor, its ultimate destination (including its trickle up rather than down into multinational corporations and the national GNP in the form of a vibrant and voyeuristic tourism industry) and the values various groups see it as capable of producing. Hunting and gathering provides Belyuen men and women with the intricate knowledge of the physical and mythical landscape that imbues mythic metaphor with meaning as it provides the group with foods (Povinelli 1992); moreover, their food collection practices produce cultural and social identity as they produce their economic and political well-being.

Values associated with hunting and gathering are abilities, not things. Belyuen women and men produce symbolic and political value by linking present action to past action, bodies to landscapes, and economic practices to cultural meanings. For Belyuen Aborigines land use (land-based action) creates political value by indexing the location and quality of human-land relations. The productivity of a place—including not only what foods but also what signs and symbols of relatedness it provides (a bird crying out, stones left on rocks, Dreaming sites cracking asunder)—daily marks the quality of that relationship. But social and political value resides most fully in the ability to associate not in the goods collected or accumulated, though these are essential to the economic health of the community.

Aborigines' cultural economy is found and formed most fully, then, in the interactive moments in which humans and country encounter each other and in the conversational practices in which people narrate (or "plot"; Ricouer 1984) those encounters. Myers notes a similar emphasis among the Pintupi on plotting connections between "historic or mythic events" and their current "situation and . . . events" (1986, 289; see also Williams 1986, 48). For the Belyuen, virtually every event is a possible place of meaning and every place the possible result of a meaningful event.[1] They link events by joining marks found or left in more than one place—on the land (*durlg*) or the human body (*maroi*). Events themselves are a mark (an icon), in that they have a form in their narration that can be associated with another form; for example, a *durlg* site's sudden activity can be linked to the actions and identities of nearby women. The index, the narrative lines, and the processes with which objects are associated, has ultimate value and provides people with cultural identity and social power.[2] As I have shown throughout this discussion, these encounters and conversations, while formative of Aboriginal economic meaning and practice, cannot be separated from the dialectic interethnic processes that have contributed to the identity and shape of human-human and human-land formations in contemporary Australia. Nor are they separable from the historical, cultural, and social associations that gave rise to "the Belyuen mob."

I discuss Belyuen associative practices in terms of metonymic and synechdochial processes because of the critical importance Belyuen Aborigines place on the path ("lines"; see Strehlow 1971) connecting any two end points—thus the importance Belyuen persons place on the direction and order of site names. Belyuen conversational practices, however, are also like the metaphorical "wise words" of the Western Apache (Basso 1976) in that they focus on the shared behavioral attributes of their referents. But they differ in emphasis (there is no necessity that behavioral attributes be undesirable qualities), in focus (on contiguity rather than on analogy; see Friedrich 1991), and in purpose (most often to join two sites, rather than to mediate or to collapse two notions; but cf. Basso 1984, 1988).

Material products like foods and goods obtained during hunting trips, certainly provide Belyuen Aborigines with a critical component of their physical needs (they are valuable "foodways"; Harris and Ross 1987); that is, as things they are important. In fact, it is necessary to look closely at the material conditions of contemporary Aboriginal life in order to understand the economics of hunting and gathering today. Accounts of

Aboriginal social, economic, and cultural systems that do not look at Aborigines' lived environments fail to understand and explain the meanings of Aboriginal practice and belief. But yams, crabs, fish, and mangrove worms once gotten are immediately consumed by a wider system of meaning. They point to the rich relation that exists between human groups and land sites *because* Belyuen persons hunt in places: this is not so much tautological reasoning as it is reasoning by the circularity of relatedness. Foods, therefore, are not simply symbols or materials separable from lived practice; they are reference points in human performances of economic and cultural prowess, even as they are the products of economic and cultural action. Likewise, it is not in economic or cultural action per se that Aboriginal power, identity, and history originate, but in their associations and disassociations in contemporary space and time. Peoples' abilities to link bodies and landscapes, action and meaning, and cultural and economic practices draws them into an "Aboriginality," a moral zone in which value adheres in processes of association as well as in the things associated. It is important to note that mythic ancestors lodged within the countryside are the originators of value as "object of linkage." These ancestors embody cultural and economic value insofar as they are the ultimate source of environmental products and the human corporeal body. But it is not just their nature as objects that "holds" these values; it is their linkages to or differences from other mythic sites and social groups that creates social value most fully. Clever people "follow" their mythic ancestors in their ability to relate and to store value. Thus the oft-noted obligation of Aboriginal men and women to "follow up the Dreaming" (Stanner 1979b; Myers 1986, 157; Bell 1983) may be usefully joined to the necessity of Aborigines to "follow up" the foods and materials associated with sites coming into and going out of season (Gould 1969; Altman 1987a; Meehan 1982).

Central to the interaction between Aboriginal people and country, and to the orientation of Aboriginal conversational practice, is the historical struggle of the Australian nation-state to understand, create, and preserve the coherence of its symbolic and political economic self and of Aboriginal groups to resist, co-opt, and come to terms with that struggle. In other words, Belyuen Aborigines are not the only ones linking human groups, stretches of land, and cultural-economic practices, nor are they only making links between themselves and the countryside. The nation-state's property laws establish criteria for how individuals and groups can use land and how that use will be assessed. Even socially liberal laws (including the Aboriginal Land Rights [NT] Act, 1976, and the Australian Heritage Commission Act, 1974), while recognizing that indigenous traditions evolve, treat them as something that, at any given time, can be found, weighed, and assessed. In law, "tradition," like the Saussurian sign, is theorized as a stable, coherent thing in the unreal world of synchronic time.

To understand Aboriginal practice fully is to map its operation between two levels of signification (the local/Aboriginal and the non-local/non-Aboriginal), even while recognizing that each "level" is trying to constitute the other in a more beneficial relationship to itself.[3] Insofar as customary Aboriginal identity and practice contributes to the nation-state's welfare in international affairs, the economy, and an internal ideation of the self (Bhabha 1990), it is valuable and can be supported. A central part of Aboriginal land-based action in contemporary Australia is, therefore, the values it accrues in a broadly construed notion of regional and national exchange. Within the nation-state, the Aboriginal subject is absorbed as an object of nationalism and political-economic process. Economic uses of customary Aboriginal identity include its role as an anchor in international media campaigns focused on tourism (to define the state as a site on the global tour), in film and musical explorations of national identity, and as prima facia evidence of the legitimate or illegitimate framework of economic progress. Political legislation supports a particular Aboriginal social form: it endorses traditional owners as a certain type of religious and descent formation. In all these instances—the economic, cultural, and political—the state provides limited rights of land and self-determinism in exchange for a form of Aboriginality useful to it as a symbolic moment of national liberal humanism and as a political-economic asset in international relations and trade. Locally, bush foods and crafts have a "social life" as commodities (Appadurai 1986) just as complex, including their use as a symbolic moment of relatedness and autonomy (Myers 1988a, 1986) and their use as an item of exchange in local markets and groceries. Because the social life of Aboriginal action moves across local and regional political-economic relations and symbolic fields, the nation-state's evaluation of Aborigines' cultural economy is not "outside" or on the periphery of Aboriginal action, although it originates in the unfolding of industrial capitalism to late capitalism (Jameson 1991) not in precolonial Aboriginal socioeconomics.

A focus on the institutional underwriting of Aboriginal social and symbolic lifeways cannot proceed, however, to such an extent that we lose the interaction between speakers and the discursive formulations that "*produce* the object about which they speak" (Dreyfus and Rabinow 1982, 61; my emphasis). The state's evaluation is neither in the center nor at the periphery of Aboriginal action and meaning. Rather, as Aboriginal and non-Aboriginal actors and their respective discursive uses of each other move from site to site (courts, groceries, beach side, settlement, classrooms), different articulations of Aboriginal action and meaning arise, as do different understandings each group has of itself and the other. Conversations that occur in each of these sociopolitical contexts are laden with issues of political-economic, discursive, and symbolic power. For example, legal discourses work to produce the object they supposedly simply describe—the patrilineal descent group and its exclusive right to an estate (Muecke 1988b). But Aborigines' relationship with country also intrudes upon Western understandings of self, knowledge, property, and nation and has intruded upon the practice of social legislation, coercive though this legislation might be. We must, therefore, critically examine the practices and criteria of assessment as they change from local to supralocal legal, economic, and cultural contexts. In any given time, where is power located? Is it *in* political institutions, economic structures, and symbolic representations (a group's "moral design") or is it dispersed *through* the technologies and apparatuses that differentiate physical and social bodies and, through this differentiation, allow them to be assessed?

POWER AND KNOWLEDGE

Two parts of Aboriginal and non-Aboriginal discussions about laboraction and its productive potential are, first, how each group knows (evaluates) work and, second, what knowledge about the social group and the environment in which it lives is produced by various cultural understandings of the form of labor-action. At Belyuen those who are considered to know the countryside are those who have the power to assess its actions and other people's descriptions of its actions. Obviously the processes by which someone is considered to have knowledge are important. At Belyuen, a person's sociopolitical power is derived from and legitimized through others' recognition of their knowledge as authentic. In contrast, in Western courtrooms, judges are generally assumed to know the law and are, thereby, granted power from the state to assess other people's actions and arguments in terms of that law. In interethnic land struggles in contemporary Australia, two power/knowledge regimes and the social institutions or "apparata" that enforce these regimes meet. Aborigines use their knowledge to assert claim over land *and over the process of knowledge assessment;* Western justices use their knowledge of Western sovereignty and Western property law, and their unexamined prejudicial predisposition to development, to "contextualize" indigenous knowledge in a state framework. Williams (1986) provides a good example of the pragmatics of this meeting in her lengthy description of the Yolngu's fight for land rights in western Arnhem Land (1968–71).

> In keeping with their epistemological premises, as I understood them, the leaders of Yirrkala during 1970 saw their most crucial task in the land

rights case as ensuring that the "government", all those as having some ability to contribute to the outcome of the case, became knowledgeable in Aboriginal law, especially laws governing Yolngu land tenure. The assumptions that underlay this task were that knowledge implies understanding and understanding entails respect, by which meant recognition of a natural right of existence. (1986, 7)

While Yolngu elders saw their knowledge-ability of Aboriginal law bestowing on them the power of intergroup translation and authority over their lands, ultimate power remained with Mr. Justice Blackburn. Blackburn, the judge who rejected the Yolngu application, re-translated Yolngu legal concepts into Western property law and found it lacking. The unevenness of power shown in the supposedly neutral instances of translation between Western and indigenous law is by now well-known, evidenced in Australia (Williams 1986; Gumbert 1984; Maddock 1983), as well as in Africa (Gordon 1989; Wilmsen 1989a), North America (Asch 1984, 1989; Scott 1988; Feit 1985) and South America (Turner 1979; Smith 1982). Discussing San land rights in colonial South Africa, Gordon pithily reminds us that "in accepting that only the state confers land rights, we reach the peculiar situation that because a petty German official [Mr. Justice de Villiers] reads a strange-sounding document [Chief Justice Marshall's 1831 U.S. Supreme Court decision in *Johnson v. MacIntosh*], which even few of the Germans present could understand, and fired a volley of shots, suddenly all San peoples find their rights to land entitlement have mysteriously been removed without their even knowing" (1989, 150).

Alongside the state's power of final say (final translation) is its power to categorize and differentially weigh the origins of Aboriginal knowledge. While Belyuen Aborigines root a good deal of their mythic knowledge in and derive much of it from land-based action, current state institutions separately weigh and categorize economic and religious knowledges (their acknowledgement of the problematic nature of that division in no way reduces its force). In current land claim legislation, knowledge derived from economic action (as in knowledge derived from anthropological texts rather than one's father's father) is of secondary value to that derived from religious/cultural practice. Economic practice and its knowledges can be valuable in other contexts. Hunting and gathering's role in indexing Aboriginal cultural identity intersects positively, from a non-Aboriginal commercial sense, with the emerging art and tourism industry (see Altman 1990; Myers 1991; Crick 1989; Graburn 1976).

An example from the Kenbi Land Claim serves to highlight the complex workings of power in the legal assessment of Aboriginal knowledges and of compliance and resistance in contemporary Aboriginal Australia. As I mentioned in chapter 1, a land claim is broken into two broad segments: the presentation of traditional evidence and the presentation of arguments for and against a grant of land irrespective of the presence of traditional owners. Part of the traditional evidence includes the presentation of genealogical evidence. In law it is required that a traditional owner be a member of the descent group who has primary spiritual responsibility and common spiritual affiliation for a mythic site on the land. Genealogical charts are used to provide some proof that those who claim to be in the descent group have descended from or been adopted into that group (Smith 1984). As is common, during the Kenbi land claim, claimants gave their genealogical history (how they reckoned their relationship to Laragiya, Wagaitj, or Beringgen ancestors) and their sociocultural identity (Belyuen, Wagaitj, Danggalaba, Laragiya, Banagula, to name but a few). As claimants ran through their family histories, government and land council lawyers, the land commissioner, and various advocates followed along from prerecorded genealogical books. The following is an example of this process.

> MR PARSONS: Thank you, your Honour. Now, Annabelle, can you say your name, and then introduce the people sitting here?
> ANNABELLE BENTON: Annabelle Benton, Suzanne McLean's sister, Rachel Roman's sister, and my daughter, Linda Hill.
> MR PARSONS: All right. Now, if we turn then to genealogy KG5A, your Honour. We will just ask you a little bit about your parents. Now, your mother and father, who were they?
> ANNABELLE BENTON: Mother, Linda Roman; father, unknown.
> MR PARSONS: Yes, and your mother, when was she born?
> ANNABELLE BENTON: Well, I could not put a date on that. She was born at Mindil Beach, and they estimated her age at about 67, 68.
> MR PARSONS: And that was when she past [sic] away.
> ANNABELLE BENTON: A year ago.
> MR PARSONS: Yes, and what mob was your mother?
> ANNABELLE BENTON: Clan?
> MR PARSONS: Yes.
> ANNABELLE BENTON: I believe the Danggalaba clan.
> MR PARSONS: And what group was that, or what do you class yourself as?
> ANNABELLE BENTON: I class myself as Larrakia.
> MR PARSONS: And why do you say you are Larrakia?
> ANNABELLE BENTON: Because I was brought up at Retta Dixon Home, without parents, and the only people that I knew were my Larrakia

people, and they always stressed to me as I was growing up that I was Larrakia. My mother was a Larrakia, my grandmother was a Larrakia.
(Kenbi Transcripts 1989–90, 1163–64)

Of significance here is not the verity of descent as the primary constituent of Aboriginal groups,[4] but the claimants' willingness (or compulsion) to abide by Western legal processes in which someone outside the group is granted (or acknowledged to have) the power to assess membership within it. Other authors have noted that in Aboriginal Australia group membership is decided by the group, and numerous factors influence when someone is considered inside or outside in any given social context. Anthropologists are becoming increasingly aware of the choices and "politicking" necessary to create and maintain any social group (Sutton and Rigsby 1982; Myers 1986). At Belyuen part of this politic is the staunch commitment to a rhetoric that disputes should be settled by the relevant parties for that matter. So, for example, brothers' families might settle matters dealing with the patrilineal "company" property (see also von Sturmer 1978); other people should not "put themselves" into the dispute. People who wish to involve themselves must present their "relatedness" to the issue or group, in terms similar to how they decide who has the right to tell a story (being there, being straight for, being part of).

In the Australian nation-state's rhetoric, law's authority comes from its supposed location outside the disputing groups; its authority is located within a system and canon of objective, and therefore neutral, legal principles. Obviously, indigenous groups with different canons and principles of law may not grant them this authority, though they may recognize the state's power to impose itself irrespective of their leave. Indigenous groups can, therefore, recognize the powerlessness they have to challenge dominant legal structures and make the pragmatic choice of trying to gain back title to their lands through nonindigenous legal mechanisms or of refusing to engage in a process on unequal terms and try to gain back land by other means (such as "buying back the land"; see Palmer 1988). Having grown up within the violence and hegemony of Western sanction and law (at least within Western spaces), Aboriginal persons may not see any dissonance in the movement between decision-making processes and ways of knowing as they occur inside the community and their transformation when taken outside the community (see also Williams 1987). The difference between the first two and the third strategies is not one of "false consciousness," but of place—various laws are seen to have their place. A final strategy on this chain is a radical refusal of the nation-state's claim that it has the right to decide intragroup matters. This is the position that a group of younger Laragiya took during the genealogical evidence. At the point of evidence I examine below, council for the Laragiya, Mr. Parsons, had just elicited genealogical information from Barbara Raymond and her brother David Mills. He then turned to David Mills's son and two daughters, Weslan, Barbara, and June Mills, "I just want to ask each of you about what you know of Larrakia country in particular what your attitudes are about the land claim?" (Kenbi Transcripts 1989–90, 1292). When June Mills stood to answer these questions the following exchange occurred. I quote at length because her statement draws together the complex entanglement of knowledge, power, and assessment and of compliance and resistance in contemporary Australia.

> JUNE MILLS: Well, before I get into my attitude towards the land claim, I would like to say that everyone—the majority of people here would know that we are Larrakia. The only ones that would not know would be the white people, and actually I find it quite offensive that us black Larrakia people who have lived in—in the Darwin area, I find it—I find it extremely offensive that we have to get up here now, in front of all you people, and try to justify who we are and how we got to be here and do we know this and do we know that.
>
> Obviously, we do not know everything that we—we are supposed to know because we have been taken away. We have been subject to genocide. Our—our people have been killed off and we have been brainwashed, and now we—after so many years of genocide, we are expected to know every little thing about the land, and we have got to justify our claim on this land. As far as I am concerned, I find the whole land claim offensive and the attitude—my attitude to it is that if we get back this land claim, which we are now claiming after so many years, I feel that it is only righting a wrong that has been done to us for so many years.
>
> Up until now, I have not been able to be here because of other commitments, but I have heard through the grapevine that there is some question as to our identity—me and my brothers and sisters. There is some question because we have been placed on the Kungarakyn land claim. My mother is Kungarakyn and every black around Darwin area would know that. My father is a Larrakia, and they married and that is traditionally correct because they are neighbouring tribes, and there is nothing wrong with those people marrying, although the way it came about was because they were all bunched up together when the white man collected us and rounded us all together—or all my old people—and they chose to marry and now there is this question about identities.
>
> Now, the question is not coming from the black people. The black people know who we are. My—my mother's people know who we are and my father's people know who we are, but it is the white people who are questioning us and, frankly, I am sick and tired of all this. We have got—we know who we are and we seem to be having to justify all—not

knowing why we know this and why we do not know that. Sure—it is our land, everyone knows it and to all you—all my people that are here . . .

HIS HONOUR: Mr. Parsons, I think the—if you could pursue—the witness has made a point and it is not going to be a political meeting, and there is no . . .

JUNE MILLS: No. But I want this down as evidence, because this is why I . . .

HIS HONOUR: Well, just—just—just take it easy. You have made your point, and we better get on to something relevant.

JUNE MILLS: You have cut my train of thought now. What was the other thing you brought up? Yes. And the other thing is, I am not sure of the other groups who are interested in this land claim who have got a claim to it, but the other thing I find offensive too, is that there are so many groups in this—involved in this land claim. I do not know why it is called just a Larrakia land claim, because it seems as though the people that are going to benefit from this claim is not going to be Larrakia, and once again we are going to get left out. (Kenbi Transcripts 1989–90, 1294–95)

June Mills frames the land claim process as more than a simple and direct process of obtaining peoples' social identity (this question about identity)—who you are based upon descent and belief. Identity is, instead, a locus of struggle for the power to control the epistemological relations between social action and meaning, social identity and practice including, as this book has shown, between economic practice and cultural identity. Control over the meanings and classifications of these relations is internal to the political-economic process in contemporary Australia of which land claims are an important part. In June Mills's case, the land claim process teeters on the ability of the court to maintain its control over the grounds of knowing what is what. The court must frame who you are, how you obtained this identity, and what knowledge and practice is a necessary or sufficient corollary to it. Who agrees with you that you are who you say you are? Who are they? What do they know? What knowledge do you have? Who provided the knowledge? How? In other words, what were the conditions by which your knowledge was produced, in the cultural, economic, or academic realm? Did you come to obtain knowledge through lived experience, a prerequisite for legitimate knowledge only after a division has been made between oral and literate epistemologies? (See Goody 1987.)

All these questions leave aside any strong critique of the conditions through which indigenous knowledge is assessed in an Euro-Australian context. This latter critique, as articulated by June Mills, includes who decides what action is sufficiently Aboriginal or sufficiently non-

Aboriginal. How do they judge? Finally, whose associations of socioeconomic practice and cultural meaning hold in what contexts?[5] June's portrait of the white grotesque, similar to the Belyuen portrait of the *tjeingithut* white man, is reinscribed by Mr. Justice Olney as "political." In his description of her statements as political lie two assumptions: first, that traditional Aborigines are not "activists" (to mark her action as politically motivated is simultaneously to mark her as nontraditional in aspect) and, second, that the political can be opposed to neutral and objective assessments (such as his description of her anger). Therefore, her protest can be judged as irrelevant to the legal task at hand. These assumptions block Olney from seeing the traditional position June is espousing: matters concerning Aboriginal group formation and its relationship to land should be settled by the group, not by someone outside it. Her argument parallels those of other indigenous leaders throughout the world who argue that "tribal authority" lies outside the nation's sovereignty (see Feit 1989); it is, as Wilkinson puts it, both preconstitutional and extraconstitutional (1987, 112). Instead of examining the rich meanings and layers of June Mills's statement, Olney inspects its political source and social associations in order to undermine its power as legal critique, just as the Northern Territory Government Council undermined the statements of Bill Risk and Richard Barnes.

Her statement is itself a complex laying of political challenge, which questions not only the grounds of the court's authority but also the general social associations being made in the court: the socioracial scale that places urban Laragiya between Euro-Australians and Belyuen Aborigines. Similar in many ways to the Belyuen speaking strategies I discussed in chapter 1, June makes a claim that locates antisocial behavior within Euro-Australian practice and then associates other unnamed Aboriginal groups (the other groups "involved in this land claim") with these practices, challenging without naming the other groups to dispute her words in public. June asks, Who is acting untraditionally here by allowing the land commissioner to decide Aboriginal matters? She challenges the strategies Belyuen families have found for manipulating Western law and political economy, just as Belyuen strategies undermine options that Laragiya families have for relating to lands they were historically deprived of. The complexly entangled nature of law, traditional assessment, and performance, and of compliance and resistance in contemporary Aboriginal Australia makes it extremely difficult to challenge the institutions and networks of dominant power without simultaneously undermining other dominated groups.

The critical linkage between power and knowing that this book investigates parallels in many ways recent work in feminist epistemology and in the social study of science.[6] This literature, diverse though it is in its method, examines how Western science derives knowledge of the social group and of nature. My discussion of the dialectical engagement between Aboriginal understandings and organization of the productivity and environments of their labor and Western scientific assessments of the same raises similar questions. Hegemonic ways of knowing and forms of political-economic organization dialectically inform each other. In what ways do the supposedly neutral legal, economic, and ecological methods of apprehending and assessing human action set the conditions for certain social and political relations between ethnic groups in north Australia? In what ways are those methods the products of a historic appropriative process—the ideological justification for the appropriation of Aboriginal land and the transformation of their cultural lifeways? In other words, how are they part of, as Nancy Williams put it, the historical drama by which Western colonists' limited "understanding was replaced by a number of quickly hardening positions that justified any means to appropriate Aboriginal land" (1986, 152). Are science and law *put to the service* of the nation-state's political-economic agenda or are they an inseparable form of it and, therefore, unavailable as an avenue for radical social action? This much at least seems true at this point: current legal practice is still in an additive phase. The indigenous perspective is added to Western law without policymakers critically examining how, in the process, either it or Western law is rearticulated, challenged, or undermined.

The economic and ecological models that the nation-state uses to assess indigenous action may be even more resistant to change than the legal principles upon which they rely. In an increasingly heated discussion of global environmental change, population growth, and limited resources, science—and those disciplines that are most easily able to imitate its underlying principles and assumptions—is turned to as a "dispassionate" observer of factual relations between human actors and the environment (the human species as one of many in the environment) and of the risks and benefits associated with development projects. Social scientific projects with a more humanistic and activist bent are sometimes enrolled to examine the soft side of these discussions; that is, how the science of ecology and development will be "experienced" by human groups. Very little national or international policy has been influenced by non-Western frameworks for assessing human action in the environment, even though these non-Western frameworks have been used to soften the impact of environmental or developmental projects or to to provide an entrance into local thought as a segue for the transformation of "traditional," "customary," or "local" beliefs and practices.

Because of the nation-state's use of the "local" to initiate change compatible with its own ends, this book has focused on the dialogical engagement between an Australian Aboriginal community's understandings of their action and identity and historical and present-day state discourses on hunter-gatherer economy and society. It diverges, therefore, from that literature in the social study of science that privileges—though it is admittedly a tentative privileging—"local knowledge" (cf. Geertz 1983) as an alternative to Western ways of apprehending nature and human action in it. The boundary between local and nonlocal (regional, national, non-Aboriginal) cannot be easily drawn from either a diachronic or synchronic perspective. On one hand, the West's assessment of need, health, and environmental welfare partially engages non-Western social, legal, and political institutions, although Western governments are reluctant to admit to what extent. On the other hand, local knowledge and practice, a previous sure footing of resistant epistemologies (Scott 1990), reveals itself to be more than local and less than reliable as a stable mark of the Other. One path I have tried to clear through this tangle is the mutual structuring, or, in less complementary terms, the mutual begging, borrowing, and coercion of identity within real power hierarchies.

Appendix One

GUIDELINES

Representation of Transcribed Speech

Indicator	Sound	Indicator	Sound
A. *Vowels and dipthongs*			
i	h*ee*d	u	wh*o*'d
I	h*i*d	er	h*er*d
ei	h*ay*ed	>	H*u*dd
e	h*ea*d	ai	h*i*de
æ	h*a*d	ir	h*ere*
a	h*o*d	air	h*ire*
aw	h*ow*	ju	h*ue*
ö	h*oo*d	oi	h*oy*
ow	h*oe*d	ar	h*oa*ry
B. *Consonants*			
:	labinal l,n		
rr	trill r		
—	retroflex r		
ng	thi*ng*		
n.g.	rai*n*god		
(L)	Laragiya		
(E)	Emiyenggal		
(B)	Batjemal		
(Marr)	Marriamu		

Speakers
cb: Catherine Burga (father Marritjaben, mother Marriamu) born circa 1920
en: Emily Nela (father and mother Emi) born circa 1925
gz: Gracie Ziyesta (father Marriamu, mother Mentha) born circa 1929

cm: Claire Mamaka (father Marritjaben, mother Marriamu) born circa 1930
me: Mary Eladi (father Wadjigiyn, mother Emi) born circa 1930
jz: Jean Ziya (father Emi, mother Emi) born circa 1935
je: Joan Ela (father Marritjaben, mother Marriamu) born 1943
ez: Enez Ziyesta (father Kiyuk, mother Marriamu) born circa 1950
dz: Deborah Zirita (father Emi, mother Marriamu) born circa 1950
kn: Karen Nela (father Emi, mother Emi) born circa 1970
bp: Beth Povinelli (Italian-American) born 1962
sm: schoolmaster (Euro-Astralian) born circa 1950

A. AGREEMENT, DISAGREEMENT, AND INDIRECTION

At Belyuen direct address and references such as pointing and naming a recently deceased person are seen as rude and potentially dangerous acts (see Rosaldo 1973; Brenneis 1988). Typically women avoid directing their statements to anyone in particular (Povinelli 1993b). Instead, speakers criticize indirectly, with listeners playing "an active role in the co-construction of situational definitions" (Ochs 1988, 19). A listener can "pick up" or "leave" a suggested course of action without verbal acquiescence or refusal. In the example below, Mary Eladi and Joan Ela, respectively, tell no one in particular: "Just tell them we just camped along there all the time in the olden times" and "Just like how you visit Beth and tell her stories, you tell all these kids." Note that Joan Ela's statement is also an indirect criticism of some senior women's practice: they should spend more time teaching their own children.

1. THE SHADE (6 February 1989)

1 en:	*eleweda (E) sheid sIdawn . . .*
2	shade shade [let's] sit down
	[segment after children talking]
3 bp:	*wat ar wi duwing*
4	what are we doing
5 en:	*now mar langa kaingmerra (E)*
6	not in the sun
7 me:	*j>s tellm wi j>s stap langa der ala taim wuldentaimz*
8	just tell them we just camped along there all the time in the olden times
9 je:	*j>s laik haw yu stap langa bet n tellm stariz yu tel al diz kidz*
10	just like how you visit Beth and tell her stories, you tell all these kids
11 bp:	*yeh yu alweiz tel mi*

12		yeh you always tell me
13	*je:*	*wel haw ala taim tel bet tel dIs mab*
14		well how all the time you tell Beth, tell this mob
15	*jz:*	*tu hat*
16		too hot
17	*dz:*	*yu kIdz kam lIsen*
18		you kids come and listen
19	*jz:*	*kam an yu mab erye*
20		come on you mob here.

The results of indirect speech are, like direct speech, uncertain. No one takes up Mary's suggestion about what to tell the Anglo teacher, and she ends up telling him the story herself (see App. 1, pt. B, no. 4, below). And, earlier, when Joan Ela specifies a little too directly who is to speak ("You tell a story"), Emily states emphatically, "No more looking at me I never been there" (below, line 14). By doing so, Joan risks gaining the reputation of "thinking herself boss."

2. THE BOAT LANDING (6 February 1989)

1	*cb:*	*Im wanna tellm wi, Im ben tellm mi dæt stap st>ri*
2		he wants us to tell them that "stop story"
3		*sæbi ai ben sæbi dæt yu sæbi*
4		You know, I knew that you knew:
5		*M>dpil hnn wulden taim wi ben ala taim der*
6		"In the olden times we stayed at Madpil all the time"
7		*streitfarwerd wei le mitjiti*
8		Talk in a straightforward way to the white woman.
9	?:	*... lending ...*
10		... [boat] landing ...
11	*je:*	*le lending le lending?*
12		at the landing, at the landing?
13	*en:*	*now mar löking et mi ai never ben der*
14		don't look at me, I was never there.

Indirection is also achieved through repetition, which disperses the agency of a statement through the group. Shadow repetition also confirms that speakers and listeners have a similar view of how the conversation is progressing. Three or more people often repeat the same phrase in a round. In this way, people speak as a group rather than as individuals and the story remains the group's rather than the speaker's. A statement, in effect, becomes the production of the group as individuals repeat it.

3. THE BUSH ROAD (6 February 1989)

1 dz: nowb>di kempIn an the bitj then dIdent now this eriya yet
        dæt dhæt dæt dæt pleisez then
2   no one was camping on the beach then, they [white people] didn't
        know this area yet those places then [noise]
3   ownli j>s bösh rowd
4   there was only just a bush road
5 me: bösh rowd
6   bush road
7   mmm traid tu teik dæt gerl awei fr>m mai mather and father
        dæt dei b>t dæt wulmen
8   b>t
9   mmm he tried to take that girl away from my mother and father that
        day, but that old man but
10   Im ben hert Im leig erye lök erye fr>m mai mather lata pip>l
        w>z der dringkin emiyanggel
11   my mother hurt his leg here look here, my mother did it. A lot of
        Emiyenggal people were drinking there.
12 dz: thIs w>z bifar the war ar efta the war
13   this was before the war or after the war
14 me: bifar the war bifar the war.
15   before the war, before the war
16 dz: bifar the war ei yu awl ben muv arawnd, ei, bifar war ben
        hirye
17   before the war huh? you all moved around, huh? before war was
        here.

By repeating words or phrases, speakers can also dispute or confirm the speaker's narrative without directly confronting them. People disagree by withdrawing from these repetitive routines, thereby disagreeing with a narrative without directly confronting the speaker. Without leaving the group—a very strong statement of dissatisfaction—a person disagrees by not repeating key elements of a story. In Western conversations such a person may be considered a "passive listener." If a Western speaker believes that the listener has a different opinion he or she may "pursue a response" but otherwise silence is often interpreted as agreement (Pomerantz 1987). At Belyuen, speakers are far less likely to pursue a particular person's response—another form of direct probing. They may tag a statement with "oh," an indirect and ambiguously oriented interrogative that can sometimes prompt a response from listeners. People do note, however, when a person withdraws from a conversation. They may comment afterward, "I think that old lady thinks another way, she never did say herself."

Below, although disagreeing with the previous statement, a respondant incorporates the previous speaker's words or sentence construction into her own utterance, thereby lessening the impression of difference between the two positions. Everything remains the same except the meaning.

4. DON'T LOOK AT ME (6 February 1989)

1 en:	*now mar löking et mi ai never ben der*	
2	no more looking at me I never been there	
3 me:	*nu mar laik djidje <u>yera-maka</u> nada <u>yera-maka piya</u> (E)*	
4	no more, like teacher, <u>for the children</u>, another, <u>for the children</u> (E)	
5 en:	*now mar sIdawn erye ala taim*	
6	no more I sit down here all time.	

Another verbal strategy is to present competing stances in alternating turns without marking the disagreement until someone in the conversation asks, refers to the repeated statement, or drops the issue. Note in the following, Grace Ziyesta repeats a phrase (lines 11, 15, 19, 33) until Mary Eladi answers (line 35); the place name and place of the site is then negotiated.

WHERE DID WE CAMP (22 March 1989)

1 me:	*der naw wadaa wat Im neim <u>parrapiya</u> (E)*
2	there now, what's what's it's name, <u>rock python snake</u>
3 bp:	*kengaru parr<u>apiya</u> (E)*
4	kangaroo, <u>rock python snake</u>
5 me:	*der naw wulman bla mi ben gedjIm nek*
6	there now, that snake grabbed my husband's neck.
7 bp:	*aiyiye*
8	ah yeh
9 me:	*Im ben getIm erye nek*
10	it [the snake] got him here on the neck
11 gz:	*wer wi ben kemp*
12	where did we camp?

258   Appendix One

13 me: *teigIm awtbet*
14   he unwrapped the snake from his neck.

15 gz: *wer wi ben kemp*
16   where did we camp?

17 me: *dæt wulman wer mibla ben sIdawn*
18   that old man, where did my group camped?

19 gz: *wer wi ben kemp*
20   where did we camp?

21 bp: *wii*
22   wow

23 me: *ahahaaha*
24   ahahaha

25 gz: *ehh anti*
26   ehh auntie

27 bp: *wer*
28   where?

29 gz: <u>*wuta*</u> *(E)*
30   <u>water</u>

31 me: *uuuha*
32   uuuha

33 gz: *wer wi ben kemp*
34   where did we camp?

35 me: *ye yu sæbi*
36   yeh you know

37 gz: *[noise]* <u>*yakarraaa*</u> *(E)*
38   <u>goodness</u>

39 bp: *wer wer wer*
40   where, where, where?

41 me: *thæt eriya naw*
42   that area now

43 gz: *nandjyin nandjyin nandjyin*
44   Nandjyin [place name on one of the Port Patterson Islands] Nandjyin Nandjyin.

The following two exchanges are less confrontational examples of the steering of knowledge and conversation through verbal repetition. In the first conversation women alternate Aboriginal names of Cheeky Yam. At line 13, Emily Nela disputes my response that the relevant Cheeky Yam is *mimi*. In a verbal strategy of inclusion, at lines 25 and 27, Joan Ela is careful to note several linguistic options to Cheeky Yam and to refer her knowledge back to the old women.

6. LIKE A WILD YAM (6 February 1989)

1 dz:	Im laik a a waild laik a	
2	it is like a a wild like a	
3 me:	waild yem yena (E) Im driming tharr>n djiki yem naw	
4	wild yam is there she's Dreaming that Cheeky Yam now	
5 en:	minthene (E) naw	
6	Cheeky Yam now	
7 jz:	wila (B)	
8	Cheeky Yam	
9 bp:	mimi? (E)	
10	pumpkin yam?	
11 me:	wila (B)	
12	Cheeky Yam	
13 en:	now mar dæt n>therwan	
14	no that other one	
15 jz:	minthene (E)	
16	Cheeky Yam	
17 cb:	yeh	
18	yeh	
19 jz:	yu sei m minthene (E)	
20	you say Cheeky Yam	
21 je:	dæt manster dæt wi ben show yu dæt dei, yeh therrawin (E)	
22	that monster we showed you that day, yeh Rainbow Sea Serpent	
23 en:	nat therrawin (E)	
24	not Sea Serpent	
25 je:	hm gata a laika leig thIs mab wulgamen sæbi thei tel yu the wan naw KalIm minthene (E)	
26	it has a, like a leg, this bunch of old ladies know, they can tell you the one, call it Cheeky Yam	
27	ar wila (B)	
28	or Cheeky Yam.	

B. SERIATION, MIXING, AND SOCIAL GROUPS/LANDSCAPES

Seriation. The following conversation is a supplement to the school history lesson. They both show how women challenge one another's knowledge of country by lining up sites in the correct order and the importance of order in local epistemology. Lines 1–42 were previously given in sec. A, no. 5.

1. WHERE DID WE CAMP (22 March 1989)

43 gz:	*nandjyin nandjyin nandjyin*	
44	Nandjyin [place name on one of the Port Paterson Islands] Nandjyin Nandjyin	
45 me:	*dæt eriya naw yu howldImbet*	
46	that area now you keep touching	
47	*nandjyin dIs>n*	
48	Nandjyin this one	
49 me:	*dæt eriya naw dIsaid Im erye naindjin ai think*	
50	that area now, this side, its here, Naindjin, I think	
51 bp:	*ow naindjin*	
52	oh Naindjin	
53 je:	*nai-*	
54	Nai-	
55 me:	*wi ben kemp*	
56	we camped	
57 gz:	*yubela ben kemp der*	
58	your group camped there	
59 me:	*yeh dIs eriya er lök dIs eriya mibela ben dIgImbet*	
60	yeh this area, here look, this area, my group always dug [yams].	
61 gz:	*mmm*	
62	mmm	
63 me:	*erye*	
64	here	
65 gz:	*nha wi ben*	
66	nha we were	
67 je:	*wa pleis abi*	
68	what place Abi [me]	
69 me:	*en wi ben gow arawnd erye <u>parrabiya</u> (E)*	
70	and we went around here, <u>rock python snake</u>	
71 jz:	*<u>parrapiya</u> (E) yeh*	
72	<u>rock python snake</u>, yeh	
73 gz:	NOWMAr Now Mar *dærr>n sneik dærr>n sneik Im tellN Im th*	

74	No More No More, that snake, that snake, its, tell her th-
75 bp:	*yeh ai now*
76	yeh I know
77 me:	*mm parrabiya (E) dærr>n mm ben gldIm*
78	mm, it was a snake that got him [the old man]
79 gz:	*wat pleis dærr>n*
80	what place is that
81 me:	*dæt b>lp>l nawa eintlt*
82	that's Bulpul [another site on the island] now, isn't it
83 bp:	*ow now b>lp>l Im dawn erye*
84	oh no, Bulpul is down here
85 gz:	*Im er b>lp>l*
86	it's here, Bulpul
87 je:	*ee der*
88	ee there
89 gz:	*en naindjyin Im her*
90	and Naindjyin is here
91 bp:	*ye sow yu be yu ben kemp dIswei*
92	yeh, so you you camped this way
93 me:	*yeh*
94	yeh
95 bp:	*yeh*
96	yeh
97 gz:	*now mar wi ben kemp erye naindjyin wer naindjyin*
98	no more, we camped here, Naindjyin, where Naindjyin
99 bp:	*naindyin erye*
100	Naindjyin here
101 gz:	*erye wi ben kemp*
102	here we camped
103 me:	*klows bla wila*
104	close to the Cheeky Yam.

Kinship and Seriation. The sociological meaning of order and mixture depends upon the social strategies of speakers and listeners. Writing of code switching, but of use to us in understanding the multivocality of "mixing" at Belyuen, Monica Heller has noted, "code-switching [read *mixing*] can be seen as a resource for indexing situationally salient aspects of context in speakers' attempts to accomplish interactional goals" (1988, 3).

Seriation is an important motif for the ordering of social relations. In the following conversation, "lining up" names in the landscape and the names of kin are ways of mixing groups; that is, mixing is primarily a method of increasing the linkages and potential alliances between places and social groups.

2. THESE TWO MEN (13 February 1989)

1 gz: *owkei dIs tubela na det tubela na*
2   okay, these two men, now, these two men

3 bp: *oowkei owkei*
4   okay, okay

5 ez: *det bla dIsun neim, Im gana mIxIm up dIsun erye bla dediwan*
6   that is this one's name, she's going to mix them up, this one here is dad's [name]

7 bp: *am owkei am owkei*
8   I'm okay, I'm okay

9 gz: *Im alrait Im mIxIm up na tharrun neim*
10   she's alright, she is mixing-up [linking] that name

11 ez: *neim caan mIxIm up Im dIfrent father*
12   you can't mix-up names, he's a different father

13 bp: *ye Im gata*
14   yeh he's got a

15 gz: *no mor dIfrent father, Im gata Kiyuk neim tu*
16   don't say "different father," he's got a Kiyuk name too.

17   *Im jus seim kuntri, gudnes, seim father hn muther det tubela*
18   they're from the same country, goodness, these two have the same father and mother [i.e., the two "fathers" are brothers]

19 bp: *yeh   okei   Im gatIm Im gatIm seim wei*
20   yeh   okay   he had her [as a mother] he had her too

21 gz: *Im mutha Ngalginbena darrun*
22   His mother was Ngalginbena that man

23   *en Im mathe Bandawarrangalgin hei yu kayan meika dIfrent*
24   and his mother was Bandwarrangalgin. Hey you can't make them different.

25   *detz de al ben djoin up detz de ala kuyuk*
26   they've all been joined up, they're all Kiyuk.

27 ez: *wi neve ben born, wi neve ben bawn fram Mowzez*
28   we weren't born from, we weren't born from Moses.

29 gz:	ye but nyiben meikim frum dIs men wulmen erye, yaa
30	yeh but this old man here [tapping notebook] made them both [i.e. he was both men's father], goodness
31 ez:	na, Im tingking about for the father said dIsun erye
32	no, she is asking for the father's side, this man here [pointing to notebook]
33 bp:	but Im seim? Im seim kiyuk Kiyuk?
34	but are they the same are they both Kiyuk?
35 ez:	but aliya ben father said na det mab
36	but all of them are on my father's side, this group.
37 gz:	Im seim Kiyuk, wat yu gana meigIm dIfrent agen
38	they're the same, Kiyuk, what are you going to do, make them different again?
39 bp:	hn dei gatIm Im dei gatIm
40	and they came from him they came from him
41 gz:	yu kayan meigIm rang, yu gata meigIm, yu gata lainIm up
42	you can't make them wrong, you can't make them, you've got to line them up.

In this next conversation, women "line up" the various relationships that exist between speakers and characters in a story before starting the action. In the course of the exchange, the daughter of the female narrator explores her and my relationship to the actors. In this way we are linked (or mixed into) the fabric of the action: relatedness is established to another person's experiences and thus provides us with a "track" back to other times and landscapes.

3. WHEN WE WERE TRAVELING (17 May 1989)

1 en:	ai ben fullIm b>ket
2	I filled a bucket [with tomatoes from a white man's garden]
3 bp:	ai wudaben item wan wei
4	I would have eaten them nonstop
5 en:	ha ha Im putIm ppp b>ket ei owkei <u>ngamama</u> (E) ai ben tellmIm sister main naw
6	haha, he put them in a bucket ei, <u>we were standing there</u>, I told my sister, mine now
7 kn:	unk>l ari
8	Uncle Harry
9 en:	ye ei Im stillmbet . . . Im sei
10	yeh ei, he stole them . . . he'd say

11		*batjemal Im wadjIgiyn*	
12		batjemal, he's Wadjigiyn	
13 bp:		yeh	
14		yeh	
15		*Im wadjIgiyn*	
16		he's Wadjigiyn	
17 kn:	*bla wi bla wi tjemela dærr>n*		*Im le deili rIva*
18	our, our mother's mother's brother that man [Mission]		he's at Daly River
19 bp:		eeyah	*deili rIva wei yeh*
20		eeyeh	Daly River way yeh
21 en:	*Im wulman, dæt wulman*		
22	he's an old man, that old man		
23 kn:		*mmwulman*	
24		mmm old man	
25 bp:		<u>*yaga*</u> (E)	
26		gosh	
27 kn:		*bla wi grendfather tharr>n*	
28		our grandfather that man	
29 bp:	*ai ben l>kIm ai downt think sow n>thing*		
30	I've never seen him, I don't think, nothing		
31 en:	*Im djainamen wulman*	mm	emm
32	he's Chinaman old man	mm	emm
33 bp:		aiye	
34		oh yeh	
35 kn:	*Im gata het*		
36	he's got a hat		
37 bp:	heha		
38	haha		

Social action and mixed groups. While speakers can track and line up the relations between speakers, countrysides, and events, mixed social activity is itself recognized as creating the tracks between people (Myers 1986; Meggitt 1965). Patrick McConvell (1988) and Maria Brandl and Michael Walsh (1983) have examined the sociolinguistic and social meanings of "mixing" among northwest Aboriginal groups. In a short article on the "mixed" nature of Laragiya and Wadjigiyn groups and ceremonies in the Cox Peninsula-Bynoe Harbour area, Michael Walsh and Maria Brandl have written, " 'Mixing' does not mean 'mixed up' or confused. Rather, it describes the intricate interconnections of all the activities of people in the area claimed" (1983, 154). They argue that the cultural connections between and joint activities of Aboriginal peoples in the Cox Peninsula, Bynoe Harbour, and Daly River areas influenced how groups became mixed during the colonial period. Segments 4 and 5 present a few instances of the way Belyuen speakers embed the mixed nature of social action in their descriptions of social identity and land use.

In the next two segments of talk, Mary Eladi describes life on a site on the northeast of the Cox Peninsula. Mary Eladi is *straight for* stories about this region because she was born at and has a personal Dreaming (*maroi*) from the area. Moreover, and most important for this discussion, although her father was Emiyenggal and mother Wadjigiyn, she was raised by a Laragiya woman who taught her many of the Dreaming stories of foods in the Cox Peninsula region. Mary can, therefore, make claims for her family for these particular sites based on her long association with them; she can do this without excluding the traditional presence and memory of the Laragiya, as others might have had to do, because she was raised by and knew many Laragiya who were living there in the 1930s and 1940s.

4. CALL THIS PLACE MANDORAH, WANGGIGI (6 February 1989)

1 me:	kalIm mænd>ra:	:wanggIgi
2	call [this place] Mandorah	Wanggigi [Aboriginal name for Mandorah]
3 dz:	b>t eberlgln.l neim:	
4	but Aboriginal name	
5 me:	wi uztu lIv er bifar. bIg kemp humpti haws wIth peiperbark en swamp. ai w>z j>s	
6	we use to live here before, there was a big camp, humpy house made with paperbark and a swamp. I was just a	
7	lItt>l gerl laik yu. Mai grendfather and grendmather w>z lerye seim taim. dæt mIlkwöd	
8	little girl like you. My grandfather and grandmother were here at the same time. That milkwood tree	
9	der dæt birriy>l grawnd. Mai grendfather en mai grendmather. uz tu bi ala red ep>l tri	
10	there marks a burial ground. My grandfather and grandmother were buried there. Use to be all the red apple trees	
11	der al alang. Dæt owld leidi nowz Im ben erye. Lats pip>l M>dpil wei, BIbInbiyirrk,	
12	there, all along. That old lady knows. She was here. Lots of people were living Madpil way, Bitbinbiyirrk	

13	al mIkst >p Emi, Mentha, WadjIgiyn mIkst.
14	all mixed up Emi, Mentha, Wadjigiyn mixed.
15 dz:	thru B>lg>l er tu Bainow Harbar tu trænzmIter Laragiya
16	through Bulgul [placename in Daly River] to Bynoe Harbour to transmittor is Laragiya [land]
17 me:	stIl Laragiya. al yuzd tu bi erye k>z bIg mab <u>buliya</u> (B) Is erye mab dei yuzd tu
18	yes, it's still Laragiya. All of these Aboriginal groups use to be here because there was big mob of *relations*. This mob they use to
19	meik a b>sh t>ka, dæt t>ka <u>mada tjuntju</u> (B). yu now wer waitmen stei. wi yuzd tu
20	make a bush tucker, that bush tucker <u>cycad nut</u>, you know where that white man lives, we use to
21	p>t Im en dæt water meik Im kam fresh. kam bek feyu wiks p>tIm In faiyer
22	put cycads in that water, make them come fresh. We would come back in a few weeks and then put them in a fire.
23	<u>miya wardarbu.</u> (E), yuz tu gow dir getIm yem wer dæt waitmen der naw. Howl
24	They use to go there get cycads where that white man lives now. A water hole is
25	der wer Im sIdawn freshwan kam awt laik erye tu.
26	there where he lives: fresh water comes out of it like here too.
27 je:	laik kId grow >p sei now b>sh t>ka b>t lata b>sh t>ka erye. wen grow >p en yer
28	If a kid grows up and says "no bush tucker" but lots of bush tucker here. When you grow up, your
29	parentz show yu und yu j>s waking an the grawnd lata b>sh t>ka der
30	parents show you and you're just walking on the ground, lots of bush tucker there.

5. THAT LIGHTHOUSE PLACE (6 February 1989)

1 dz:	laik a laithaws eriya naw yu gat dæt Laragiya pip>l ben stei-yIn der haws Im gat
2	Like the lighthouse area now, there were Laragiya people staying there. House, does that place have
3	eni haws der?
4	any house there?

5 me:		ye sam pip>l yuz tu bi der bifar ben der >ntll wan waitmen ben der le alidja.
6		Yeh some people use to be there before. They were there until one white man was there with all of them.
7		wan waitmen ben der Im ben growIm >p stak, pi>t, pawpaw hn benene Im ben
8		One white man was there. He raised stock, peanut, pawpaw and banana. He
9 he:		growIm>pbet. watermelan. evrithing Im ben meikImbet. dIs owld leidi ben der
10		always grew watermellon, everything he always made, this old lady was there
11 je:		[faint]
12		[faint]
13 cb:		mItjelmar
14		Mitjelmore [proper name]
15 me:		mIsta mar hn tam eltjelbi. tu pip>l ben der hn al the eberlgin>l pip>l ben werking
16		Mr. More and Tom Echelby, two people were there and all the Aboriginal people always worked
17		far them tu. grow >p garden pinut pawpaw watermelan
18		for them, tending the garden, peanuts, pawpaws, watermelons
19 sm:		haw lang agow w>z thæt
20		how long ago was that
21 me:		bifar the war [pause] yeh [pause] yeh
22		before the war yeh yeh
23 je:		dæt sek>nd werld war [faint]
24		that Second World War
25 me:		yeh [pause] enden yeh b>t dæt ferst wan. wi never si dat ferst werld war
26		yeh and then, yeh, but that first one, we never saw that First World War
27 je:		j>st dæt sekand wan haw kam yInmi never si dæt ferst war?
28		just that second one. How come you and I never saw that first war?
29 me:		ai downt now ai never ben bawn dæt ferst war
30		I don't know, I wasn't born for that first war
31 en:		wi never ben bawn yet
32		we were not born yet
33 me:		le ferst war

268   Appendix One

34   for the first war
35   nathing meit
36   nothing mate
37 bp: dIswan naw ben sIdawn der
38   this woman now lived there
39 me: yeh dIsmab naw wulgamen dei ben sIdawn der
40   yeh this group of old ladies, they lived there.

The following two segments of talk are examples of how shared memory of mixed social action further integrates presentday Belyuen action. The speakers describe groups living and traveling together up and down the Cox Peninsula to Daly River coastline. Note that in the second segment, Grace Ziyesta describes this social action as "straight"; that is, correct in orientation and practice. This type of shared experience is given as the primary constituent of Belyuen social identity and cohesion. Although lines 5 and 9 frame the mixed group as "all the family" and "all the fathers," respectively, this kinship arose not through consanguinity or affinity but through shared practice.

6. TARZAN (31 March 1989)

1 en: ownli ben lök erye lata pip>l erye
2   I only saw here lots of people
3 gz: al mIkz >p
4   all mixed up
5 bp: now ala femIli
6   no, all the family
7 gz: al mIkz >p wi ben trev>l
8   all mixed up we traveled
9 en: beti marin mi ala fatherz
10   Betty Moreen, me and all the fathers.

In this next exchange, shared/mixed ceremonial activity is another method by which groups on the Cox Peninsula were integrated.

7. THE BIG CEREMONIAL PLACE (31 March 1989)

1 gz: ala pip>l bIg mab WadjIgin al mIkz bIg siremowni pleis Daramanggamaning
2   all the people, big mob Wadjigiyn, all mixed, big ceremony place, Daramanggamaning [place name]

3 bp:	ɛn anti hu yuztu sIdown langa dIs pleisez
4	and auntie who use to live along these sites
5 gz:	lata pipl> ben erye
6	lots of people were here
7 jz:	evriwan erye naw eriye
8	everyone was here now, in this area
9 gz:	evriwe naw eriye langa siremowni pleis Daramanggamaning
10	everywhere now they lived in this area, along this ceremony place, Daramanggamaning
11 bp:	yeh dIswan bIgwan siremowni pleis eh
12	yeh this was a big ceremony place, huh
13 gz:	yeh dIswan naw
14	yeh this place now
15 jz:	wer dei ben sIdawn aliya aliya Laragiya ben stap erye
16	where did they camp, all of them, all of the Laragiya lived here as well
17 gz:	dIs>n WadjIgiyn naw wul mIkst>p
18	They were Wadjigiyn now, all mixed up
19 bp:	al mIkst>p endei yuztu sIdawn erye
20	all mixed up and they use to live here
21 gz:	ya al mIkst>p dei ben stap langa erye
22	yeh all mixed up they lived along here
23 bp:	rait e e iven wen yer parentz ben alaiv?
24	right, e e even when your parents were alive?
25 gz:	mai parentz ben laiv erye
26	my parents lived here
27 en:	mi mai grenfa n>ting
28	me, my grandfather didn't
29 bp:	en dir parentz? meibi? iven bek dæt far dei ben sIt her?
30	and their parents? Maybe? Even back that far, they camped here?
31 gz:	dei ben wal mIkst>p ma mai parentz ben lang wei
32	they were all mixed up, my my parents were a long way away
33 jz:	nusens dIswan mab
34	nuisance this group [children]
35 bp:	dei dId yer parentz kam bek fram der
36	they, did your parents come back from there
37 gz:	mmmm
38	mmmm
39 bp:	le Deili RIver wei

40		from Daly River way
41 gz:		*aanaddIdi*
42		aa Naddidi [place name in southern Daly River]
43 bp:		*naddIdi*
44		Naddidi
45 gz:		*dei ben kam dIswei naw streit >p*
46		they came this way now straight up [the coast]
47 bp:		*mm*
48		mm
49 gz:		*langa dIsmab na emiyenggal mab mentheiyenggal mab wi ben mIkst>p dei ben al mIkst*
50		with this group now—Emiyenggal mob, Menthayenggal mob—we were mixed up, they were all mixed
51 bp:	*yeh*	*yeh*
52	yeh	yeh
53 gz:		*en dei ben kam dIswei dei ben lök dIs darwIn naw.*
54		and they came this way, they saw this Darwin now.

The term "mixed" is not unambiguously positive; it can also refer to a variety of social situations. It can indicate a socially tumultuous situation such as at the Katherine "Donkey War Camp" or it can more positively describe how disparate families came to be the "Belyuen mob." Indeed, in the Northern Territory, especially in the Top End where most Anglos settled, the "mixing" of Aboriginal groups—the 'joining up' of two smaller related groups—seems a common strategy for preserving a local Aboriginal identity.[1] If, as Peterson has argued (1983), small groups were already under threat, then the violence and killings of the colonial period increased the likelihood of extinction, and groups increasingly utilized available kinship relations to arrange marriage patterns that would "join up" estates. Even so, people at Belyuen say that not only are they "mixed" but they are also often confused and upset by the mixture. While I agree that people's mixed identities are, at a conscious level at least, a "selection" that is not "distorted nor confused," but rather "a choice from among authentic identification labels of the most appropriate to a given question" (Brandl and Walsh 1983, 152), the inability to choose anything other than the present mixture—a mixture filled with historic competition and strife between language and family groups—fractures the simple positive identity of "mixed."[2]

APPENDIX TWO

Number of Animal and Plant Species Name and Frequency of Use When Encountered

	No. of Species Named by Belyuen Women	Frequency/Infrequency of Use (%)*		
		Never	Occasionally	Regularly
Tubers	31	.548	.226	.161
Flowers	83	.385	.265	.385
Woody	8	.875	.125	...
Honey, clay†	4	.5=m	...	.51=m
Funggi, seaweed	3	1.00	...	...
Land mammals	18	.333	.278	.389
Land worms, snails, and frogs	10	.8=m	.2=m	...
Birds	66	.697	.227	.076
Crustacea, shrimp	11	.091	.545	.364
Insects	15	1.00	...	...
Goanna, crocodile	14	.428	.071	.5=m
Turtles	6	.167	.333	.5=m
Fish	31	.193	.129	.677
Snakes	25	.96=m	.04=m	...
Sea snails, chitons	26	.346	.346	.308
Rays, sharks, sandfish	11	.091	.273	.636
Sea mammals	5	.8=m	...	.2=m

*Because one part of a species may be used and another part not—for instance the fruit but not the tuber although both are considered food—the percentages listed do not always add up to 1.00.

†Two indigenous honeys are regularly collected. The white clay, mentioned in the text, is never now eaten. A honeycomb bee is also avoided because of its "cheeky" sting.

Notes

Introduction

1. The *Belyuen* people referred to in this monograph as the Wagaitj include people identifying with the Kiyuk, Wadjigiyn, Emiyenggal, and Menthayenggal Daly River language groups; the Beringgen include those identifying with the Marriamu and Marritjaben language groups.

2. See di Leonardo (1991) and Mascia-Lees, Sharpe, and Cohen (1989) for feminist theory's contribution to this discussion and its relationship to poststructuralism (most usefully summarized in Clifford [1988]).

3. For informative discussions see Neate (1989), Peterson and Langton (1983), Peterson (1982).

4. In the literature on African hunter-gatherer societies, the turn to a "discursive history of hunter-gatherers" has provoked quite a storm (Lee 1992). In their efforts to situate African groups in regional and world histories, a number of "revisionist" authors have critiqued portrayals of foragers as "isolated and timeless" groups (see Endicott 1988; Headland and Reid 1989; Bird-David 1988; Schrire 1984; Gordon 1989; Wilmsen 1989a). Instead of isolated remnants of our Pleistocene past, so-called foraging groups, revisionists argue, are and have been engaged in a number of economic pursuits including pastoralism, agriculture, and trade. The strong form of the argument is that rather than foraging bands, modern hunter-gatherers are actually marginalized classes (see Wilmsen 1989a; Barnard 1988). Solway and Lee (1990) and Lee (1992), defending the study of "hunter-gatherers," have responded that hunter-gatherers' place in history has long been established (Leacock and Lee 1982), that "cultural contact" does not "automatically" undermine the structures of foraging society, and that, though threatened, foragers remain viable and vital social groups in the postmodern world (see also Woodburn 1988). This debate does not easily translate to the Australian continent where Africa's socioeconomic diversity is not found. Nonetheless, two observations are relevant. First, examining the discursive frames in which Australian groups have been apprehended is critical to understanding their treatment in the early and late colonial period as well as in the contemporary Australian nation-state. Critical to the focus of this project are the discussions of Morris (1989), King and McHoul (1986), and Larbalestier (1990). In particular King and McHoul (1986, 70) note the effects of "changing configurations of power" on Aboriginal identity, the historical discourses or "*accounts* of 'the Aboriginal

problem'" that relate to hegemonic power, and colonial discourses of Aboriginal-European relations. However, these authors do not discuss Aboriginal notions of labor-action and its representations. Second, whether or not Aborigines were always a marginalized group (one would have to ask, to whom?) they certainly have been used as a cheap and expendable labor group, although today the trend is toward long-term Aboriginal "unemployment" (see Altman 1985; Cass 1988). In the past, pastoralists used cheap Aboriginal labor during the dry season and then "dispersed" the Aboriginal group in the monsoon season so as not to have to pay laborers year-round (for ethnographic examples see Morris [1989, 32–49] and Lyon and Parsons [1989]). Today, the Northern Territory government, as I show in detail in chap. 4, continues to depend upon Aborigines' food collection practices to supplement social welfare.

5. Godelier (1986, 84) notes the difficulty of defining *labor* in respect to property, territory, and "forms of action on nature"; Donham (1990, 20) notes the difficulty of defining *work* in noncapitalist societies.

6. R. M. Berndt, another Australianist well known for his portraits of the Australian Dreaming, writes, "All Aborigines, whatever their socio-cultural perspective, were *directly* dependent on the land and what it produced—or, if we want to put it more generally, on nature, with *land as the constant factor,* even though its outward manifestation changed from season to season. But this seasonal fluctuation, notwithstanding drought or flood, famine or plenty, was *on the whole constant and predictable*" (1970a, 1; my emphasis).

7. Ethnographers theorized that the timelessness of myth and the constant and regular progression of seasons formed another people for whom history was meaningless. In his essay "The Dreaming," W. E. H. Stanner writes, "A central meaning of The Dreaming is that of a sacred, heroic time long ago when man and nature came to be as they are; but neither 'time' nor 'history' as we understand them is involved in this meaning. I have never been able to discover any Aboriginal word for *time* as an abstract concept. And the sense of 'history' is wholly alien here. We shall not understand The Dreaming fully except as a complex of meanings. A blackfellow may call his totem, or the place from which his spirit came, his Dreaming. He may also explain the existence of a custom, or law of life, as causally due to The Dreaming" (1979, 23). Eric Wolf's *Europe and the People without History* (1982) should also be read in this context.

8. See Errington and Gewertz (1987) for a similarly argued point about female false consciousness.

9. See Sherzer and Urban's (1991) study for the importance of a discourse-centered approach to ethnography when discussing cultural contact in the context of the nation-state. Also of relevance is Haviland's classic (1977) study of gossip, reputation, and knowledge in Zinacantan and his more recent work in Australia (Haviland 1991), Ridington's discussion of knowledge, power, and the individual in subarctic hunting society (1988a, 1988b), and Lindstrom's (1990) recent investigation of the links between discourse, power, and knowledge in the South Pacific.

10. This data base consists of over two hundred hours of tape-recorded conversations, one-third of which is presently closely transcribed.

NOTES TO CHAPTER ONE   275

11. The purpose of my first trip was to study the changing settlement practices of Belyuen women (Povinelli 1991). Unfortunately I did not record hunting trips as precisely as I now might have liked.

12. See Allen, Altman, and Owen (1991) for a review of the literature. See Fisk (1975, 1985) and Peterson (1977) on Aboriginal involvement in the Australian economy. See Taylor (1977) and D. Turner (1974) for how Aboriginal economies have been adopted into and have adapted to regional and national economies over time. And see Meehan (1977, 1982) and Altman (1982, 1987b) for their ground-breaking economic analyses of eastern Arnhem Land foraging practices. They studied groups who had returned to their traditional country from the larger Maningrida Settlement in the 1970s.

13. See esp. W. E. H. Stanner's work on the Daly River region (1932–34, 1979).

Chapter One

1. See Dyck (1985); Hocking (1988). A focus on these common "problems" can itself be seen as part of the ongoing construction of the group (Conkey 1984; Keene 1986).

2. Fred Myers (1988b) points out the implications of these larger anthropological debates for the study of hunter-gatherers.

3. John Locke ([1690] 1988, 28, 32). For a discussion of social science's discursive use of the "ignoble savage" see Meek (1976). For the effect of this discourse on Australian Aboriginal land rights see Williams (1986, 109–206).

4. In a series of essays, James Woodburn developed the distinction between immediate- and delayed-return societies (1980, 1982, 1988). For other discussions see Testart (1982) and Price and Brown (1985). For Australian responses see Layton (1986) and Altman and Peterson (1988). Briefly, immediate-return societies are those in which activities are oriented to the present and in which people do *not* hold "valued assets which represent a yield," nor do they create dependencies. Delayed-return societies are oriented to the past and the future and do hold valued assets that create dependencies between persons or groups (Woodburn 1988, 32).

5. See, e.g., Hawkes, Hill, and O'Connell (1986); Altman (1987b); Gross (1984); Winterhalder (1987); Lee (1979). See Myers (1982a) for a critique of such socioecological approaches.

6. Nicolas Peterson, who has worked extensively on Australian Aboriginal land rights, insightfully argues that it was indigenous hunter-gatherers' realization in the 1960s that they were not recognized by white governments as "the unquestioned owners of the land on which they lived . . . [that] led to [their] developing legal and political battles for recognition of their rights and [that] has begun to result in legislation: in Alaska the Alaskan Native Claims Settlement Act of 1971; in Quebec the James Bay Agreement as outlined in 1975; in Australia's Northern Territory, the Aboriginal Land Rights (Northern Territory) Act, 1976; and in all three countries continuing negotiations for settlements covering other regions. *It is important to emphasize that these agreements, which are seen as such a positive step by many whites, are in reality a final acknowledgement of*

defeat for the indigenous people. For in every case they consolidate the loss of land to whites and grossly reduce the rights associated with the land they have managed to retain (Paterson, 1982, 441; my emphasis).

7. Territory legislation includes the Conservation Commission Act, 1980, which establishes the Conservation Land Corporation, and the Territory Parks and Wildlife Conservation Act, 1988, which vested park lands in the Conservation Land Corporation. With regard to land conflict in the territory, these acts place land in a "person other than the Crown" (Neate 1989, 138) and, therefore, make it unavailable for a traditional Aboriginal land claim. Another significant piece of territory legislation is the Aboriginal Sacred Sites Act, 1978, which charges the Aboriginal Areas Protection Authority to keep a Register of Sacred Sites and to protect those sites by restricting entry to them by non-Aboriginal inhabitants and, if necessary, to acquire land for their protection. The act was amended in 1989 to give non-Aboriginal landowners the opportunity to make representations before a site is listed. National legislation includes the Australian Heritage Commission Act, 1974. In this act, Aborigines can register sites as components of the "national estate" (Bates 1992, 247). This registration is problematic from a radical critique of the nation-state's authority over indigenous lands. Finally, the Aboriginal and Torres Strait Islander Heritage Protection Act, 1984, was established "to protect areas or objects that are of particular significance to Aboriginals in accordance with Aboriginal traditions" (Bates 1992, 247).

8. Administrative duties include consulting with and acting on behalf of traditional Aboriginal landowners in matters of land use and land development such as mining or tourism and (now voluntarily) compiling and maintaining "a register setting out 'the names of the persons who, in the opinion of the Council, are the traditional Aboriginal owners of Aboriginal land in the area of the Land Council,'" an important function since the "final decision as to traditional ownership of areas of land rests with the local Land Council" (Neate 1989, 17).

9. What "land" is available is complicated in coastal regions like the Cox Peninsula. Land available for claim is "unalienated land or alienated Crown land in which all estates and interests not held by the Crown are held by, or on behalf of, Aboriginals" (Aboriginal Land Rights (NT) Act, 1976 [sec. 50(1)(a)]). But, as Neate notes, "although the Act provides for applications to be made in respect of 'an area of land', and for a grant of title to land, it does not define 'land'. Usually there is no doubt that land is being claimed. However, in some coastal claims there may be a question whether certain reefs, islands, and sandbars constitute land which can be claimed. As title to Aboriginal land is granted to the low water mark, land must be sufficiently exposed and identifiable for the purpose. The Limmen Bight land claim included reefs exposed at low tide, a number of river islands, a sandspit and sandbar, and the Commissioner found these to be unalienated Crown land" (1989, 94–95).

10. See Morphy and Morphy (1984), Keen (1984), Maddock (1983). In his response to the Kenbi Land Claim Mr. Justice Olney wrote, "I do not accept that the inherent justice of a claim of land, however strong the moral basis for the claim may be, can justify the redefinition of the concept of 'local descent group' to accommodate a factual situation which was not within the contemplation of the legislature" (1991, 99). According to Olney one such "redefinition" is that

"the status of traditional Aboriginal owner can be proved merely by the assertion (as counsel would have it), or even the proof, of the fact that individual members of the claimant group have an ancestor who was a member of a language group, which in pre-contact times was associated with and used a substantial area of land, of which the claim area is but a small part" (1990, 100).

11. Keen (1984, 40–42) insightfully analyses the implications of linking knowledge and land rights.

12. When making his report, the land commissioner must "have regard to the strength or otherwise of the traditional attachment by the claimants to the land claimed" [sec. 50(3)].

13. Graham Barker outlines a similar view in the anthropological literature. Discussing Hiatt (1962) and Stanner's (1965a) discussion of the estate and range, Barker writes that both agreed that, "at one extreme, where the estate is sufficiently well endowed with food to support the territorial group within its bounds, estate and range coincide. At the other extreme the estate and the range are all but dissociated—the group is forced to search for food far beyond its estate boundaries, returning only in good seasons to its ritual 'home'" (Barker 1976, 225). Neate supports this reading in the legal context. He notes that the entitlement to forage is the "only economic component" of the act although foraging itself "is not necessarily 'secular' in a sense that Europeans might understand. . . . Whether Aboriginals draw a distinction between things which might be considered spiritual and those which are economic or secular may not be clear . . . [but] *the land ownership/usage distinction has been expressedly recognized in land claim reports*" (1989, 77, 79; my emphasis).

14. The act was first based on claimants' economic or social "needs" but after a constitutional crisis in the Australian nation-state and a subsequent change from Labor to Liberal government the act underwent a revision (see Eames 1976; Neate 1989). Its final version was based on the "rights" of "traditional Aboriginal owners." For an informative discussion of the implications of the distinction between the act's first formulation on the basis of need and its final formulation on the basis of rights, see Basil Sansom's (1985) "Aborigines, Anthropologists, and Leviathan."

15. This and *maroi* are Batjemal terms; *ngirrwat* is used in both languages. The Emi equivalents are *therrawin* and *mirr*, respectively. I use Batjemal for these two terms for consistency since the Kenbi transcripts use the Batjemal, a point that is not insignificant in terms of the politics of regionalism I discuss in chap. 2.

16. Donald Brenneis discusses "indirect speech" in Indian Fijian and Afro-Caribbean societies in a way suggestive for the Belyuen case: "The possibilities they [indirect speech acts] afford for ambiguity, disguise and disavowal help answer the questions posed by the precarious flexibility of egalitarian relations. Beyond their strategic benefits, however, artifices of indirection also offer stylized answers, esteemed for the wit of grace which transforms originally defensive practices into sources of local pride and pleasure" (1987, 507).

17. Brenneis (1984) describes the direct discussion of a conflict producing "hard men."

18. Several fields within anthropology have examined this inequality including feminist approaches (cf. Gal 1991; di Leonardo 1991), Marxist analyses

(Comaroff and Comaroff 1991), and sociolinguistic or language studies (Woolard 1989; Shapiro 1984; Volosinov 1973).

19. I discuss this later in the third section of chap. 2.

20. Capital letters indicate the language from which a particular term originates. In this case, *therrawin* and *durlg* are the Emiyenggal and Batjemal terms for Rainbow Serpent Dreaming. For full list of language "codes," see Appendix Guidelines below.

21. Throughout the nineteenth century and the first half of the twentieth century, it was a common Anglo practice to give Aborigines Western names. "All the Maggies" notes a common situation in which many people ended up with the same Anglo name, often because Euro-Australians could not tell two people apart.

22. See Ridington's (1988a) suggestive discussion of knowledge, power, and the individual in subarctic hunting groups.

23. Although I have mainly discussed mythic creatures who emerge from the water like the Cheeky Yam, Blanket Lizard, and Rainbow Serpent Dreamings, creatures emerge from the ground as well. *Letharrgun,* or predatory giraffes, emerge from beneath towering antbeds or milkwood trees.

24. Others have discussed the relationship between a person's or group's knowledge of the mythic countryside and their "power" or "proprietary rights." For example, Ronald Berndt has pointed out the importance of Aborigines "knowing" the land when they make a claim of ownership for it: "Ownership, therefore, is not ratified simply by making a claim to land, even though substantiating genealogical information may be available. A major issue is *knowing* that particular land—knowing about the sites, their songs and rituals. . . . The land is a living thing, the source of all life, and the mythic deities who symbolize that land and its inherent life-giving properties need to be nurtured" (1982, 7; see also Myers 1982b).

25. Such as the use of community vehicles and some monetary compensation for consultancy work.

26. From transcript of Kenbi hearing, 21 November 1989 (see Kenbi Transcripts 1989–90, 593–94).

27. Several people have discussed the problems the term "owner" creates when discussing concepts of land tenure, human-land relations, and the complex, intersecting duties and rights of various social groups to the same stretch of land (Morphy and Morphy 1984; Maddock 1983; Myers 1986).

28. Cf. Bell (1984–85), and Bern and Layton (1984) on the implications of an Aboriginal division of labor for land claim deliberations.

Chapter Two

1. Written by James Harvey in 1909 on his departure south; published by the *Northern Territory Times and Gazette* (*NTT&G*) on 31 October 1930 after fifty-odd years of interethnic conflict in the Anson Bay region. I have left the original spelling.

2. Augustine's problematic encounter with the a priori nature of time (Ricouer 1984, 15).

3. According to Trigger (1992) Aboriginal time is broken into different seg-

ments roughly corresponding to the Dreaming and the historical arrival of Europeans, the latter upsetting the former's temporal order. Debora Bird Rose similarly discusses how Aborigines in the Victoria River district conceive Captain Cook—the immoral incarnation of the European everyman—to have introduced a temporal and moral break with the Dreaming (cf. Rose 1984). See also Chris Healy's (1990) interesting discussion of the cultural frameworks of Aboriginal histories.

4. George Stocking has, more recently, reinterpreted this model as "one ethnographer/one tribe" (1989, 211).

5. This theory has long since been critiqued. Meggitt ([1965] 1971) demonstrated that, for the Walbiri of central Australia, patriclans were not the basis of the land-using group, a claim supported by L. R. Hiatt's work in Arnhem Land (1962, 1984). While acknowledging the attention Hiatt and Meggitt paid to land use, Myers has more recently critiqued their approach for not exploring "the dialectical relationship between the organization of local groups and the larger structure of which they are a part" (1986, 20).

6. "[I]n particular Foucault, Donzelot, Baudrillard and Deleuze—for whom, in their quite different ways, questions of discourse and power can no longer be clearly separated" (King and McHoul 1986, 22).

7. King and McHoul, it should be noted, repudiate making any "contribution to Aboriginal studies, and still less to Aboriginal anthropology. (It is in fact our shared belief that black Australians are now in the best, and perhaps only, position to do this—should they so wish)" (1986, 22-24). While I agree with the importance they place on "discourse and its operations," I think it somewhat disingenuous to claim such a study will not have an effect on Aboriginal studies within or without anthropology.

8. *Puden* in the "mixture" of Belyuen English.

9. Belyuen Aborigines use this term to refer to transient rural squatters. Many "rebels" are young male Euro-Australians who are subsequently found to be under warrant for arrest. This has led to the general perception among Belyuen women that all white men are "armed and dangerous" and should be avoided.

10. *Bifor thei ben dringk juz watr swit wan frum grawn, meibi mixim up gota tjugerbeig. Thei never ben sik bifor, yu now bedagut ben kom.*

11. Robert Hughes (1986) discusses the strategic importance of Baudin's voyage to the British settlement of South Australia. Already competing with the French for colonies and sea lanes, the British saw the French "scientific" missions as thinly veiled attempts to establish settlements in Australia. This helped encourage the British administration to establish south Australia as its new penal colony.

12. For a discussion of the role that disease played in the "age of exploration" see Crosby (1987) and Cronon ([1983] 1990).

13. For an Aboriginal history of these encounters see Rose (1984).

14. These three social figures have received some attention recently as the ancestors of modern ethnography. George Stocking writes, "Three looming archetypes contest the stage of the disciplinary past: the amateur ethnographer, the armchair anthropologist, and the academically trained fieldworker" (1989, 208). Some government officials and settlers were amateur ethnographers, often undergoing informal training. Clifford (1981) examines one such figure in Melanesia.

15. Curr uses the word "live" to indicate where a group's land lays.

16. Bill Rosser's *Up Rode the Troopers* (1990) is a moving and interesting historical narrative of the atrocities black and white troopers and pastoralists committed against Queensland Aborigines. He notes that the term "dispersal" was a code word for massacre. From the newspaper articles I quote in the following, it is clear the term was similarly used in the Northern Territory.

17. Powell also notes that Spencer showed "more sympathy for traditional blacks then town dwellers." He does not, however, discuss the social or geographic implications of this (1988, 162–63).

18. *Djeraidj* (sherait) is a Batjemal (the Wadjigiyn language) term for belly button and whirlwind or whirlpool. During a mapping trip to the Daly River, senior Belyuen women suggested that earlier ethnologists must have misunderstood their informants who were describing a *djeraidj* Dreaming (*durlg*) in the area but were mistakenly understood to be referring to a human group. Whether or not there were "belly button people," there might have been a Wadjigiyn or Laragiya estate group associated with the now-hypothetical whirlpool Dreaming located somewhere in the Finniss River area. The Djerait may have been "dispersed" in the early 1800s when miners moved into the Finniss River region; see *NTT&G*, 13 October 1888.

19. I am not advocating the use of a "language group model" to describe residence or social organization among precolonial Daly River and Cox Peninsula groups. Bruce Rigsby and Peter Sutton write, "We believe that the phenomenal referents of such concepts [speech community, language community, and the like] are fundamentally social—they refer to groupings of social actors—and that our analyses and descriptions of Aboriginal peoples and languages are obscured when we substitute secondary terms such as speech community for primary social anthropological terms such as land-holding group, local residence group, ceremonial congregation and the like" (1980-82, 8).

20. See Hiatt (1984) and Myers (1986) for a discussion of evolving anthropological understandings of Australian Aboriginal land tenure.

21. These are housed in the University of Sydney archives (Laycock 1982).

22. Basedow confirms part of this view, "The *Larrekiya* and *Wogait* are, so far as my observation went, friendly with one another, and tribal intermarriage is not infrequent" (1906, 4).

23. Richard White (1981, 13) and Bob Reece (1974) describe similarly "cruel and vicious" mockery of Aborigines living in and around the Port Sydney settlement.

24. Basedow, e.g., argued that Aborigines' entrance into the wage labor system could be understood as the rationalization of hunting and gathering society by productive agricultural practices (1932).

25. There have been a number of ethnographic studies that have examined the relationship between Aboriginal men and women vis-à-vis economic, social, and ceremonial activities. See Bell (1980, 1983, 1987), Brock (1989), Gale (1974, 1983), Rowell (1983), Goodale (1980), and Hamilton (1975, 1981).

26. That some such mediation was occurring in the above instance is suggested by Basedow's comment, "The men had excelled themselves in their efforts to win our friendship" (1935, 38).

27. Here Solway and Lee's (1991) "coke bottle in the Kalahari" critique is well taken. Commodity contact is in no simple sense cultural distortion. See also Peterson (1991).

28. Foelsche's complex position in the community is best summarized by the following: "neither Foelsche nor most of his men could escape a degree of association with the 'quietening' of Aborigines; yet Foelsche would never yield to the demands of cattlemen for a native police and it was only the strenuous efforts of the police which enabled Dashwood to collect the evidence he needed to shape his 1899 Bill for the protection of Aborigines" (Powell 1988, 134). "A young trooper fresh from the south, with some influence at his back, had been entrusted with the leadership of a party to the Adelaide River, where an outrage had to be inquired into. He was receiving his final instructions from Inspector Paul, who remarked, by the way, that if he chanced to encounter a native named Dombey he was to call upon him to surrender, and if he refused he was to open fire. One of the troopers, with a keener sense of humour than barrack discipline, asked in an innocent way—'And if, sir, he has his son with him will we call upon Dombey & Son?' The Inspector gave ever such a faint smile, then sternly said: 'What the Dickens are you talking about?' With a hearty laugh the horses' heads were then turned for the road. The young fellow returned all the better for his experiences. When asked by the Inspector if he had knocked over Dombey & Son he smilingly replied that so far as he knew the firm was still intact" (Searcy 1912, 318–19). "When Mr. Foelsche, perhaps the most painstaking and accurate of all investigators in the Territory, was photographing blacks at Port Essington many years ago, he found that his prints came out black and white, and that his plates were piebald. He suspected his plates, his solutions, in fact everything in turn, until it struck him that the shiny skin of the nigger itself was the cause. He tried in several ways to overcome this difficulty but failed, until an old sailor who was assisting him suggested that they should dust powdered charcoal over the subject to be photographed. This was found to be successful, as Mr. Foelsche's beautiful photographs abundantly testify. Cotton-free charcoal has been found to give the best results" (Smith 1924, 142).

29. One of the earliest colonial-era occupations of the Laragiya was as message couriers for colonial administrators and businesses.

30. Theweleit's (1987) discussion of the symbolism of flood imagery in Nazi Germany could be fruitfully applied to colonial discourse of the colonized subject as engulfed by European vices.

31. Belyuen Aborigines use this term as well to describe the joining together of two patrifilial, matrifilial, or language groups for the purpose of ceremony, travel, or residence. See App. 1, pt. B, for a fuller discussion.

32. Basedow presents the "mixing" of Laragiya and Wagaitdj groups during men's ceremony as a traditional form of exchange: "Although the *Larrekiyas* do not circumcise, yet when a performance of this nature is about to take place amongst the *Wogaits,* invitations to be present are sent to the former tribe, and the members of the two hold a joint corroboree [*sic*]" (Basedow 1906, 12). Some members of the anthropological community criticized Basedow for his popular portraits of Aboriginal society and culture. Books such as *Knights of the Boomerang* seemed, according some social scientists, to cast suspicion on his scientific

writings. It is true that Basedow, more than other anthropologists, consciously attempted to glamorize traditional aspects of Aborigines—especially their noble demeanor when they lived and hunted in their traditional countries—in order to change popular opinion about their society. To his credit, however, his scientific articles refrain from judging as authentic or corrupt those Aboriginal practices he observed.

33. My discussion focuses on European descriptions of their own relations with two sets of Aboriginal groups and the contrastive uses they made of them. Jan Larbalestier (1990) has shown a different narrative take in the writings of Aneneas Gunn. She argues that "myths, fictions, and omissions" of the Northern Territory's European/Aboriginal relations produced an "enduring 'fiction'" that both groups could live together in "amity and kindness" (70).

34. *NTT&G*, 21 January 1882, is typical of the play these fights received from local newspapers.

35. The Daly River was named after another Daly, Sr Dominick Daly, governor of South Australia, 1862–68.

36. *NTT&G*, 30 April 1881; my emphasis. See also Goyder (1971, 21–26).

37. In *History of South Australia* Edwin Hodder (1893, 108) writes, "In September, 1884, the blacks attacked and killed a number of whites on the Daly River, and made hostile demonstrations at Rum Jungle, where two of them were shot. Parties were sent out to capture the murderers, one composed of the police and commanded by Corporal Montague. The police report of the matter, ordered by the House, did not make its appearance till the end of 1885. This report gave ground for a suspicion that there had been outrageous and indiscriminate slaughter of the blacks without due regard to innocence or guilt. The public demanded an official investigation, and a board of inquiry was appointed. Corporal Montague declared that his first report was an exaggeration, and the result of the inquiry was that the police were exonerated from the charge of undue severity." One of the members of the "Southport party" sent to revenge Housechildt's death writes, "The country is fast being settled, and Government makes no provision for the clear rights of the blacks, nor does it take any trouble to explain our laws and system to them, nor does it afford any protection to our settlers; consequently outrages may be looked for, similar to the Daly murders. Can the Government raise any objection under the circumstances if club law and Martini-Henri rifles become the order of the day. Let our Government, the Exeter Hall congregation, and the various aborigines' societies ponder this question, and make what they can of it" (*NTT&G*, 20 March 1886).

38. This is not the only reprisal party that Montague led in the Top End. In 1875, Aborigines near the Roper River attacked two miners, killing one, a Mr. Johnston. Montague set out to "investigate," but the South Australian government not wishing for a massacre, sent out another party to meet his. The local press commented, "It is to be hoped that Mr. Little and Corporal Montague have proceeded so far on their journeys that they cannot receive instructions of this party being sent to meet them.... If ... not ... the progress of the expedition will be seriously impeded, and in all probability the object for which it has been sent out frustrated" (*NTT&G*, 24 July 1875). The object was not frustrated. On 18 September 1875, the *NTT&G* reported, "They dispersed them thoroughly;

and as they [Little's party] found remains of natives, no doubt fully avenged Johnston's death." Montague's recommendation of the Martini-Henry was taken up by another agent of the law. In June 1894 Constable Willshire, who worked in the Victoria River Downs region, reported tracking down a group of Bilinara people peacefully camped in the sandstone region. Coming upon them, "They scattered in all directions, setting fire to the grass on each side of us, throwing occasional spears, and yelling at us. It's no use mincing matters—the Martini-Henry carbines at this critical moment were talking English in the silent majesty of those great eternal rocks" (quoted in Rose 1991, 12).

39. Compare, for instance, the United States' civil and military actions against the Western plains groups around this time (Lazarus 1991).

40. Quoted in the *Kenbi Land Claim* (Brandl, Haritos, and Walsh 1979, 116) from H. W. Christie's article "Down on the Daly" (*Adelaide Weekly News* 5 May 1906). In 1897, a reporter for the *NTT&G* (24 September 1897) wrote that the two Charles Point Lighthouse keepers, Christie and Benison, had a large, well-kept garden, but fails to note any Aboriginals who worked in it.

41. Brandl et al. discuss Laragiya employment in the Overland Telegraph Company, Laragiya and Wagaitj employment at the Charles Point Lighthouse, and Aborigines' use as domestics in Darwin (1979, 86–93). They also describe Cox's pastoral activity, European use of the Port Patterson Islands for recreational sailing and camping, P. H. Mitchelmore's lease of Quail and Southern Grose islands, and his later lease of the Point Charles area (81–84).

42. See Frederickson's (1971) discussion of American ideology about the Afro-American's entrance into "civil society."

43. The "rationalization" of the English countryside was likewise achieved through the privatization and enclosure of common lands. "During the eighteenth century one legal decision after another signalled that the lawyers had become converted to the notions of absolute property ownership, and that (wherever the least doubt could be found) the law abhorred the messy complexities of coincident use-right" (Thompson 1975, 241).

44. Gilruth invoked sec. 9 of the Aboriginals' Ordinance of 1911, "Whereby it is declared unlawful for any aboriginal or half-caste to be or remain within such prohibited area unless with the express permission of the Protector or a Police Officer, and also whereby it is declared an offense for any person—(*a*) to induce any aboriginal or half-caste to come within a prohibited area, (*b*) to suffer any aboriginal or half-caste to come within a prohibited area, (*c*) to conceal or harbor any aboriginal or half-caste within a prohibited area (*NTT&G*, 17 February 1916).

45. See chap. 5 below. But briefly, even if the immediate results were unprofitable, the confinement of Aboriginal people onto settlement gardens in order to describe the land from which they were removed as "pristine," has proved useful in the long run to local government. Administrators view crown land as a capital and natural reserve whose resources can be exploited at a later date. The Laragiya's, Wagaitj's, and Beringgen's use of the land as a means of livelihood unsettles this notion of a land held in reserve. Therefore, land alienation and the rationalization of the "roaming" Aboriginal household go hand in hand.

46. Here I would just mention several works of Herbert Basedow (1906,

1935) and Paul Foelsche's writings (esp. 1881–82). In Basedow's earlier writings he employs a then-common ethnological technique of listing Aboriginal technologies with accompanying drawings and the foods and materials Aboriginal groups collect. Foelsche does likewise. Neither provides details of the place or actual organization of a hunting-gathering party, nor can it be supposed that they went on many hunts themselves. In Basedow's later writings, motivated by a concern to represent customary life in a positive vein to his readers (Bonnin 1980), he uses actual hunts (many with the "Wogaits"; 1935, 59–63) to illustrate the "noble" aspects of traditional life.

47. *NTT&G,* 24 February 1883. The older women at Belyuen have often laughed, in the course of recording ethnobiological terms, about their mothers and grandmothers who loved this clay (*pele,* E) and hid it in their petticoats to nibble on when they worked around the West Point and Darwin regions.

48. "The fifteen Chinamen working on the estate at £1 a week have their own galvanized iron quarters, and the blacks—the Port Essington tribes—who do the weeding and such like, have theirs on the opposite side of the creek. These blacks, who have their lubras with them, are fed and housed, but do not receive a stated wage. . . . Mr. De Lissa will allow no communication between them and the tribes round Palmerston. Some of them essayed to break through the ban a few months ago, but Mr. De Lissa gave them such a fright, *by means of rockets and such like,* while not injuring them, that they have not tried to do so since" (Sowden 1882, 86; my emphasis).

49. But in the 1940s at army installations in the Daly River, Belyuen Aborigines saw films that Cook may or may not have thought portrayed the right relationship between the white and black man. Tarzan, e.g., supposedly civilized the African outback by his presence, not as a proper starched English aristocrat, but as a barbarian in scant clothing.

50. For references to the Laragiya or Berringgen-Wagaitj see Harney (1952, 1960, 1961, 1963, 1965; and Harney and Elkin (1968). Harney's *Songs of the Songmen,* co-authored with A. P. Elkin, includes four songs of the Wagaitj that Harney rather fancifully lyricizes, including two "women's songs" (Harney and Elkin 1968, 30, 40–41). One of these women's songs is about men's and women's separate song space ("men make taboos, and so do we/And while we hold ours we are free) and the other is about love magic.

51. For discussions of the discursive intersections and political implications of race, nature, and culture see Gates (1987) and Haraway (1989).

52. For a general discussion of the use of Aborigines in Australian literature see J. J. Healy (1989). M. R. Bonnin examines the advocacy stance of writers like Harney, Idriess, and even Herbert Basedow, the anthropologist. She writes, "These descriptive discussions of the aborigines were considered unsatisfactory by anthropologists writing in the same period, such as A. P. Elkin, W. L. Warner, and W. E. H. Stanner because they were often not specific to dates, locations, and tribes, or to methodology. Some of these anthropologists referred to the paucity of reliable written material on the aborigines, preferring to ignore the mass descriptive books containing material less systematically collected and arranged than that which appeared in their own books" (Bonnin 1980, 246).

53. Bill Harney was married to an Aboriginal woman and so was well aware

of conflicting views that surrounded the social character of Aborigines and the Anglo social context in which these competing portraits arose: "With contact came a changed environment and in it aborigines became 'strong-fellow-face' in the presence of the 'too-white-ones' and their learned friends who came to study the black people and who found them stern dour people ever shrouded in the secret mysticism and taboo rituals. But to the white toilers, in the lower levels of their society, who had always rubbed shoulders with the native men and women, the aborigines were a laughing carefree people full of humour and a curious custom, in that they were only too happy to share their female companions with their friends. Out of these two contacts arose different lines of thought that prevailed in an ever-changing society that slowly weaned the aborigines away from their hunting and tribal customs" (1960, xv).

54. For the effect of missionaries on Aboriginal gender relations, see Bell (1988); for the effect of missionaries on Aboriginal compliance and resistance to white cultural and political hegemony, cf. Trigger (1988) and Attwood (1989). There are several invaluable oral histories of Aboriginal life on missionary and government settlements. See esp. Read (1984) and Labumore (1984).

55. "The Department of Native Affairs in conjunction w/Police & Military have rounded up all Natives around the Darwin town area & further . . . & sent them to Mataranka for their own protection of course. The Department considers the beach area from Severe's Bluff to Point Charles an unsafe one for them. So we would appreciate your cooperation in keeping these beaches free of natives and instructing natives from now on that they *must* keep away from beaches inside the harbour. If there are any natives in your vicinity we would deem it a good favour if you order them off & tell them they *must* keep away. It is the ——— of the Dept. with natives this side, to keep them right back in the bush" (Murray, 5 April 1942).

56. Murray also seems to have believed that by having a central reserve of "natives" he could more easily monitor the arrival of new Aborigines in the area and control the sexual activities of his wards. Note the following two entrees. "Wed Jan 7 [1942]. . . . From my deduction after a conversation with him [Willie Woodie], the natives must be camping somewhere in the vicinity of the soldiers camp near Fosters beach & Talc Head. So have decided to [send] Bull Bull & possibly Jack Mowbery per horse back to find out just where they are and how many" and "Sat May 19th [1942]. . . . Five girls . . . run about to beach Sunday afternoon probably to make contact with soldiers, came back early Monday morning."

57. Older Belyuen women describe white men as always accusing them of seeking sex whenever they left a camp: "Maybe we go for crab, that *bedagut* (white man): 'I know where you're going. You're looking for sex.'"

58. As printed in the *Government Gazette*, published by the authority of the government of the Commonwealth, Northern Territory (N. T.) Archives, Darwin.

59. See Stoler (1991), who discusses similar changes in colonial Asia.

60. See letter addressed to the "Protector of Aborigines" by the Laragiya woman, Kitty Fejo, December 1934 (N. T. Archives, Darwin). See also Powell, "Protectors—mainly the police—sifted through the Aboriginal camps of the Territory, gathering up mixed-blood children and placing them in half-caste homes

in Darwin, Alice Springs and, for a time, Pine Creek. There, girls were trained for domestic work and boys mainly for stock work" (1988, 187).

61. Also, the Northern Territory of Australia, Welfare Ordinance, 1953–1960, pt. 3, 14(1).

62. Foley (1987; n.d.). See also a description of the "black watch" in excerpts from letter 1980/11, green folder of miscellaneous paper, papers 1 & 2 (N. T. Archives, Darwin).

63. This and other excerpts are from letter 1980/11, green folder of miscellaneous paper, papers 1 & 2 (N. T. Archives, Darwin).

64. The same is true of Trigger's (1992) description of the Doomadgee.

65. Dierdre Jordan emphasizes the agency of Aborigines within Western educational settings. She argues that Aboriginal identity is found in "different worlds of meaning.... [The] elements from which these worlds are constructed are drawn from various pasts" and while "in the case of tradition-oriented people, selection from the past for the purposes of schooling is controlled by the people themselves, not white teachers" (Jordon 1988, 126, 122).

66. The assertion that women are symbolic and real exchange articles in the elementary structure of human society has been discussed at length since Levi-Strauss (1969; cf. Hartsock 1983; Chowning 1987; and Strathern 1990).

67. "It was likadjet in the olden days, im still likadjat im-keep going same way."

68. There are several interesting books that examine sorcery and bush magic in modern aboriginal communities (see Reid 1983; Sansom 1980; Elkin 1980). Aborigines have had to deal with the effects of drugs and violence, like other social groups in Australia, for quite a long time. For example, in the *NTT&G*, 6 October 1893, we read of Aborigines smoking opium on Cavanaugh Street in downtown Palmerston, and of a "trio of [Aboriginal] fallen sisters" arrested for being corrupted by the effects of civilization's narcotics. In the *NTT&G* 31 January 1896, an article about the passage of the opium bill notes that narcotics were just one problem Aborigines face; others, such as alcohol and "whites and Chinese" keeping "harems of black girls," were great causes of death and suffering.

69. *Bedagut* foods are still the mainstay of the Belyuen diet and the center of a number of "contact stories" told throughout north Australia (Rose 1984; Kolig 1980). Catherine Burga tells a story in which Captain Cook sails into the Darwin Harbour (according to his travel log, Cook never sailed into the Darwin Harbour), meets the Laragiya, and gives them gifts of rice, flour, sugar, and tea. The Laragiya think that the grains of rice are maggots, the flour is paint, the sugar is sand, and the tea is poison. Enraged that the white man tried to give them useless items and poison, the Laragiya kill Cook and bury him on a knoll in Darwin. The story sometimes ends with Catherine Burga saying, "Then all the other whites came and took the Laragiya country away."

70. Christian missionaries, moral-minded administrators, and upright pastoralists all attempted to instill in Aborigines a sense of shame. Private and church campaigns were focused on efforts to civilize the passions of Aborigines, and a relentless legal campaign was waged against Aboriginal "nudity," in particular, women's "toplessness." It is easy to find in the local papers items such as the following: "Tis bad enough that they [Aborigines] should be allowed to prowl

round the streets in a semi-nude state during the daytime, begging, pandering, and stealing, without being permitted to make the night hideous with their shrieking play or quarrelling" (*NTT&G*, 12 January 1884), and "Sir—As a stranger in your town, it appears to me odd, that the Government authorities should allow gangs of half naked savages to block the roads and footpaths, accompanied by hordes of dogs, which attack Chinese residents, and sometimes show a disposition to go for Europeans" (*NTT&G*, 19 January 1889). A naturalist and ethnographer, W. Ramsey Smith, gives us some insight on how this affected European research. He describes the difficulties he had photographing Darwin Aboriginal women's "body markings" in the early 1900s: "The women are afraid they will be laughed at by others of their tribe; and the aboriginal, who may not or does not mind being half flayed alive, cannot stand ridicule" (1924, 133). Smith does not say at what "others of their tribe" were laughing, perhaps at a woman being the subject of his gaze. The women that Smith was photographing were by this time living on Christian missions, government settlements, or in squatter camps along Darwin beaches.

71. "You gonna *tell-imbet* [keep telling] story, you gonna tell that story straight way *le-im* [to them] maybe they give you and me this country". But Theodor Adorno has a more sour prognosis, "Culture sprang up in the marketplace, in the traffic of trade, in communication and negotiation" and is "reduced to that as which it began, to mere communication" (1988, 25).

72. It is also an old issue. When she was young, Catherine Burga (born ca. 1920) traveled all the way to Adelaide for a tourist performance. She often describes the funny scene when she decided to dance without a shirt and the whites stared at her ("*Bedagut* [E, white man] *im eye dukduk* [E, too big] im-been *meriduk* [open eyed, E] im-been open up now").

73. "Use to be people never think about it.... No body been worry about im, *yingi* [E, breast] been hang outside."

74. "I don't know about that *miya* (plant food) might be *pedagut* been make-im, this man wants that real one, real one black medicine."

75. "All blackfella now this lot *miya* [plant food], mango and the lot, *awa* [animal food], bullocky [cow], let them go *picturepicture* [E, photograph] anything now."

76. "Same thing we doing every time, same piece of this and that, this mob can't get together talk *gidja* (E, to each other)? You now should be tell im baby."

Chapter Three

1. For a discussion of primary and secondary rights see Peterson, Keen, and Sansom (1977), Keen (1984) and Neate (1989, 82–87). Group succession to land is generally accepted to occur, "on or before the death of the last member of a land-owning group, other groups whose members have 'secondary' rights in the estate convert these rights into 'primary' rights" (Keen 1984, 29).

2. For an example of ceremonial transmissions between other groups in the region see Layton and Williams (1980) and Toohey (1982a).

3. The Pintupi, as Myers describes them (1986, 48–51), differently distinguish among the Dreaming, noumenal realm (*tjukurrpa*) and the visible phenomenal realm (*mularrpa*).

4. See Myers's discussion of the value attached to difference expressed in the geography (1986, 66–68).

5. See also Williams's discussion of Yolngu names and land tenure (1986, 57–74, 86–89).

6. I say "generalized" because Belyuen speakers do not usually specify which dreaming in the waterhole children come from. Belyuen himself is sometimes named, but the Kenbi tunnel is also critical to the regional identity of Belyuen children. It seems then that Belyuen adults are maximizing the connections the waterhole provides for the children's identity to the region.

7. The pregnant mother vomits, not Agnes.

8. "Economic history is incorporated into unchanging, ever-present features of the landscape" (Myers 1986).

9. Ingold (1987) similarly bases his distinction between human economic action and non-human action on "intentionality": humans are the selectors of cultural attributes and economic practices not environmental objects. See, however, Myers's (1982a) critique of this approach which does not take into account the "social logic" of local groups, in this case the notion that mythic subjects in the landscape do create human objects as depositories of cultural value (see also Munn 1970). I would like to thank one of the reviewers for pointing to this paper.

10. While most young and old people use the creole form "chuck-im sweat" the Emi verb form is (*kamutpiR*, 3d person singular [3d S]). A different verb form is used, however, for the act of throwing (*karrabaitj*, 3d S) and pushing (*kurren t:unggudu*, 3d S).

11. "No more story, it slips through the belly."

12. Williams discusses the differing levels of foreignness of Malay and Europeans in Yolngu thought. Whereas "in the far distant past when spirit-beings were investing the world with meaning, spirit-Macassans" appeared, "Europeans are sharply differentiated from Macassans" because the former, unlike the latter, attempted to disrupt the moral and spiritual foundations of the Dreaming (1986, 28–29; see also Rose 1991; Healy 1990).

13. Fred Myers has discussed the relationship between "hearing," "thinking," and "understanding" among the Pintupi. He writes, "In the Pintupi view, the concepts 'thinking,' 'understanding,' and 'hearing' are expressed by a single term, *kulininpa*, which means literally 'to hear.' To be *patjarru* (or *ramarama*), they say, is to have one's 'ears closed.' The implication is that young children do not process the available information about who is present and what is happening" (1979, 349). The term *ramarama* is also applied "to those whom they consider insane or 'mad': the person's ears are closed" (1979, 350).

14. Belyuen Aborigines say this is a distinctly local form of English. They distinguish it from, say, Bamiyili Aboriginal English; the two varieties of English differ in lexicality (such as *bla* for *belonga*) and prosody (high versus low pitch).

15. Daly River languages fall within what Barry Blake (1987) has described as part of the non-Pama-Nyungan, prefixing languages of the Kimberleys and the Top End of Australia. He distinguishes these languages from the suffixing, Pama-Nyungan languages of the greater continent.

16. Michael Walsh (1989) has provided a speculative history of how phono-

logical and lexical changes occurred, and so, how Laragiya names were dropped or "Wadjigiynized." Over time, some Laragiya place-names were phonologically adapted to Batjemal. Other place names were switched to the Batjemal language, reflecting, it seems, a new human majority on the Cox Peninsula.

17. Peterson (1983) and Barker (1976) have argued demographically that the estate group (the patrilineal clan) was often in the threat of extinction.

18. A. P. Elkin (1936–37) reports that Aborigines living at the Daly River mission were so frightened of the increased number of sorcerer attacks during this time that they would not travel even a short distance into the bush at night.

19. Women say it is like wars they have seen on television with dead bodies scattered everywhere (*kaiya mirrmirr*).

20. Munn notes similarly for the Pitjantjatjara and Walpiri: "The number of distinctive ancestors is indefinite, and the objects they create constitute, in effect, the total, non-sentient environment as epitomized by the country itself. Transformations which are not directly a part of the topography (such as string crosses or oval boards) are variously linked to the country in Aboriginal thought" (1970, 143). See also Myers's discussion of *ngurra* ("camp," "country") (1986, 54–56).

21. Myers notes similarly of the Pintupi, "Thus, the Pintupi blur the distinctions between range and estate. Talk of 'my country,' 'our [exclusive] country,' and 'their country' denotes a whole panoply of rights, duties, and degrees of substantiality" (1986: 129).

22. "Im join-im up now from that point now that *berlu*."

23. "Im ben want that place again, im ben make-im track, im ben join them twobela."

24. All Belyuen residents call the mythic Belyuen *tjemila,* of fa's mo.

25. "Another controversial aspect of the Land Rights Act is the amount and type of land which is, or could become, Aboriginal land. Schedule 1 of the Act contains descriptions of areas which become Aboriginal land without the need for a land claim hearing. Most of the areas were Aboriginal reserves and are now held by Aboriginal Land Trusts. In 1985 title to land in the Uluru (Ayers Rock-Mount Olga) National Park was also granted to a Land Trust. Schedule 1 land covers approximately 258,000 square kilometres or 19.6 per cent of the 1,345,200 square kilometres of land of the Northern Territory" (Neate 1989, 93).

26. Although there is a site near it.

Chapter Four

1. Data gathered from other Aboriginal communities show that women's economic position has declined even more dramatically as they have been incorporated into the capitalist economy (Bell 1980; Berndt 1980; Gale 1974; Goodale 1974; Hamilton 1975). In Bloomfield, north Australia, an Aboriginal community of approximately 263 persons, Christopher Anderson (1982) reports that thirty-one men are employed in a variety of labor and administrative duties, while only two "young women" are employed full-time in the local store and several others are employed part-time in the kindergarten and as cleaners. Anderson marks the sex of a worker only if she is female. He does not provide the ages of workers. Annette Hamilton (1975) attributes the decline in women's status to a shift in

their relation to the means of production. In the capitalist economy, theoretically, women have a right to sell their labor freely on the market; however, the market is structured to absorb women's labor as less physically and mentally fit than men's and so it receives lower remuneration.

2. See Myers (1986, 39–40) on how the Pintupi have similarly described an initial period of bounty among Anglo-Australians change to one of enforced work with little pay. Hercus and Sutton (1986) is an interesting collection of oral history of Aboriginal stories about the different economic conditions that groups faced.

3. Bagot is a small Aboriginal enclave in the middle of Darwin. It was a settlement for Aborigines in the 1930s when its location was still "out of town." Now people at Belyuen see Bagoteers as unable to move and go hunting, as being swamped by bills and engulfed by the Anglo-dominated city. See Penny Taylor's (1988) photoessay.

4. The Commission into Poverty in 1974 reported that, in Brisbane, only 26 percent of Aborigines and Torres Strait Islander men earned $80 or more per week. No women earned more than this, and 47 percent of the households were below the poverty line. Moreover, one-fourth of all income was derived from government sources (Brown, Hirshfeld, and Smith 1974; Hill 1975).

5. There are approximately two private landrovers, three community landrovers, three sedans, one barge, two private dinghies, and three community dinghies in the Belyuen community, although rarely are all of these vehicles in running order at one time.

6. Rhys Jones has noted for the northern tropical Top End that the "dominant climatic factor controlling vegetation is the seasonal variation in rainfall" (1980, 108; see also Jones and Bowler 1980). David Harris takes a similar approach, noting that the savanna zone "is best defined climatically in terms of the duration of the dry season, despite the fact that the traditional connotation of 'savanna' implies a type of vegetation rather than a type of climate" (1980, 3). With the changing climatic conditions of the late twentieth century, many environmentalists predict that severe seasonal fluctuations will have a serious effect on coastal ecosystems such as the Cox Peninsula (Whitling 1990).

7. John Brock (1988) has written a comprehensive guide to Top End native plants.

8. While there are numerous surveys of the general ecology, fauna, and flora of northern Australia and, more specifically, surveys of mangrove formation and zonation, of floodplain dynamics, and of the interaction between introduced and indigenous fauna and flora, very little research has described or analyzed the ecology of the Cox Peninsula region. One map of Indian Island, prepared in the 1960s, distinguishes four dominant vegetative types on the island: MF (monsoon forest), DVT (dense vine tangle), OF (open forest), and man (mangrove).

9. The exploitation of sea products by foraging groups has also concerned many researchers in economic archaeology. When did human populations turn to the sea and notice the productive forces that lay below its ebb and tide? Is the evolution of a marine economy a turn toward Eden, or away from a ravaged environment reeling from the effects of "big game hunting." Indeed, are mythic Dreamtime creatures the imaginative remnants of earlier Paleolithic plants and

animals? The answers to these and other questions, such as the energetic motives behind the turn to the sea, have been the focus of much of the Australian literature. Roger Lawrence provided a broad survey of the inland and sea-hunting technologies that precolonial Aborigine groups used (1968; see also Thomson 1939; Mulvaney and Golson 1971; Jones 1980). Using more recent quantitative data, Betty Meehan has suggested that shellfish were only a moderate contributor to an otherwise mixed marine and terrestrial diet (1977). Yesner has agreed, suggesting more broadly that "even in those temperate zones where aquatic resources were more prevalent in the diet . . . seafoods rarely appear to have formed the greater part of that diet" (1987, 297–98). Others have discussed the relative energetic returns of sea foods and inland foods and the relative difficulty in changing subsistence technologies from land hunting to sea hunting (Ames 1985; Aschamnn 1975; Yesner 1980).

10. A food bank runs periodically at the Belyuen Women's Centre—these days more off than on (see Povinelli 1991).

11. "Inland *meats*" include honey, reptiles, mammals, and fowl as the local ethnoclassification system stipulates (Povinelli 1990a).

12. The real expenditure of calories might be lower or higher than this average depending upon a person's activity, a highly variable component in the Belyuen community.

13. "The variable pattern of food intake in the Belyuen and Pipalyatjara communities shows up three periods of greatest shortage or crisis in each fortnight, when children wander looking hopefully for food and mothers swallow their pride to ask for food wherever they suspect it to be. (One particular group of widows at Belyuen known well to us, suffered constant headaches during these periods, from hunger, and also from anxiety about finding enough food for the youngsters in their care)" (Coombs et al. 1983, 356).

14. See Altman (1987b, 64–65); see also Bird-David (1992) for an examination of the metaphorical use of "bush as bank" and my (1991) for "bush as store."

15. Those eleven include four fruits, three bush potatoes, one yam, one grass, one vegetable, and one nut.

16. Jon Altman (1987a) does not count child minding in his analysis of productive work. In this and other ways his differentiation of women's labor from productive labor is problematic.

17. "No more listen lei im, you sebi before, *piyawa* (E)."

18. Etienne and Leacock argue that the latter perspective would help to "illustrate the reality of female-male complementary [in small-scale societies] and to document the clash between this egalitarian principle and the hierarchical organization that European colonization brought about in many parts of the world" (1980, 10).

19. The recognition of women's bush knowledge and practices in the Belyuen community was no doubt helped by the importance attached to this cultural knowledge in the wider Australian community over the last twenty years. Over time, male and female researchers, social workers and lawyers have turned and returned to senior women as "those who know their culture." One must keep in mind that there are processual historical reasons why women, rather than men,

now have this knowledge. During his stay at Delissaville in the 1950s, A. P. Elkin worked primarily with senior Wagaidj and Beringgen men, and from his field notes we can assume that these men had extensive knowledge of the male side of the Wagaidj and Beringgen cosmology. But the average life-span of Belyuen men is much lower than women due in large part to the different levels of drinking between the two groups.

20. Present Aborigines and past Western explorers report that Daly River Aborigines used pandanus string nets and lines for fishing in inland swamps.

21. "Maybe that maiyal im findimbet one *airada*, but that wulgamen im finished now, one beiyig full."

22. This is a pseudonym for the store.

23. People are often most unequivocal about Belyuen having no bosses when individuals from families with high incomes and connections to white or Aboriginal sources of power attempt to force social or economic changes onto the community. By galvanizing younger and older people around the rhetoric of "no bosses here," poorer, but often more "traditional" individuals can isolate persons or families attempting to direct the community, but the influence of working, wealthier individuals and families in areas such as community hirings and regional politics is not diminished.

24. There is a certain irony in the inclusion of tea, sugar, flour, and tobacco in this list. As Sidney Mintz (1985) has noted elsewhere, colonial agents used these foods to establish footholds into countries.

25. See also "Parks and People," *Cultural Survival Quarterly* (vol. 9, no. 1 [1985]).

26. I have described elsewhere how close kin play in teams to win money (Povinelli 1991); see also Berndt and Berndt (1947) and Altman (1987b).

Chapter Five

1. See, e.g., The Northern Territory government's proposals: *Cox Peninsula Land Use Structure Plan, 1990* and *Mandorah Land Use Concept Plan, 1990*.

2. H. C. Barclay to the Director of Welfare, memo dated 15 May 1958, quoted in Brandl et al. (1979, 129, my brackets).

3. See, e.g., Sequoyah vs. Tennessee Valley Authority, 620 F.2d 1159 (6th Cir., 1980), cert. denied, 449 U.S. 953 (1980); Badoni vs. Higginson, 638 F.2d 172 (10th Cir., 1980), cert. denied, 452 U.S. 954 (1981); Fools Crow vs. Gullet, 541 F. Supp. 785 (D.S.D. 1982), aff'd., 706 F. 2d 856 (9th Cir., 1983), cert. denied, 464 U.S. 977 (1984); Wilson vs. Block, 708 F.2d 735 (D.C. Cir., 1983), cert. denied, 464 U.S. 956 (1984); Bowen vs. Roy, 476 U.S. 693 (1986). See also Cadwalader and Deloria (1984).

4. There are several reasons for Britain's slow development of the Australian continent that have effected the further development of the Top End of the Northern Territory, including the colony's initial use as a dumping ground for British convicts and poor and its subsequential lack of a large, nonconscripted labor force. A further impediment to early development was the lack of viable trade markets within easy access of the colonies or, for that matter, any local produce to trade, although indigenous seal populations and timber groves did produce some exchange between the colony and world markets. The whaling, sealing,

and timber industries were, however, extractive in nature and, therefore, subject to depletion.

5. McMichael notes, "'Squatting,' initially referring to the illegal occupations of Crown land by landless men of ill fame ('bush harpies') who preyed on others' livestock . . . , achieved social legitimacy as landowning graziers advanced their flocks into the unsettled districts en masse. Responding to land pricing and the constant need for open pasture, the squatters overrode the Colonial Office's attempt to confine settlement within official boundaries" (1984, 89). The class of squatters included, "new emigres, sometimes representing companies floated in Britain (significant in the Port Phillip region), landholders from the settled districts (that is, the colonial gentry), and overseas for absentee flockowners from urban centers" (McMichael 1984, 89).

6. In the editorial of the *NTT&G*, 2 January 1875, is found "complaints which were made in this place as to the difficulty of getting land were not confined to the question of 'Lands beyond Goyder's survey,' but included town and suburban lands."

7. *Northern Miner*, 29 December 1885; subsequent references to this publication are abbreviated *NM*.

8. Bandler's (1984) account of her childhood in *Welou, My Brother* is an interesting portrait of the use of migrant and immigrant labor in Queensland.

9. The colonial discussion of immigration and economic growth tied into current, racial theories about the fitness of different (so-called) races for certain types of work. Federal legislature regulated immigration and employment policies based on these discussions. Chinese were seen as most suitable for the harsh subtropical climate of the north, although some aspects of their "character," including the racist belief that they had a propensity for smuggling and larceny, were seen as major drawbacks as was, ironically, their willingness to engage in hard work for a profit—a possible threat to Anglo-Australian hegemony in the region.

10. Powell (1988) reports that in 1880 the value of gold exported from the Northern Territory was close to 100,000 pounds sterling but rapidly fell to two-thirds this value.

11. White settlers feared that without the large Anglo-Australian owned plantations and mining interests—such as the Queensland settlements–which alienated valuable lands, Asian immigrants might establish their own privately owned small-scale mines, businesses, and pastoral industries. Advocates for a "white Australia" argued that large-scale immigration and the foreign ownership of land and businesses undermined the authority of Anglo-Australians by fracturing the group-who-ruled from the group who-labored and the group-who-ruled and the group-who-owned. So, the argument went, this fracture would have serious political consequences down the road. The large Asian laboring population might call for independence from the distant, southern Anglo-government and for unification with the closer southeast Asian community. In 1901, the new Australian federation legislature enacted a literacy test "with the tacit understanding that it would be so administered as to exclude black, brown, and yellow peoples as permanent settlers" (Gratten 1963, 7). It would be misleading to think that Asian workers were evicted in order for Anglo workers to replace them. Rather, large

numbers of Asian laborers challenged the white northern administration's claim to represent residents in the southern, federal government. And, from a political-economic perspective, a large Asian work force undermined Anglo claims that they were producing the wealth of the state.

12. A current common attitude toward rural squatters is captured in a report prepared for the Northern Territory Department of Environment, Housing, and Community Development on the impact of recreational activities on the natural environment (Foley 1978). Using squatting developments on the southwest corner of the Cox Peninsula as a primary example, the study focuses on the environmental destruction and social problems that arise with rural, residential squatting. The report advises that the government prevent new squatter-shack developments on beaches and other crown lands and that it monitor existing shack areas for damage done to the environment.

13. MacKenzie has attributed northern economic stagnancy to five causes: "The first has been the significant lack of political and economic control in the north. Both the South Australian and Commonwealth Governments maintained a centre-periphery relationship and would not relinquish authority despite this recommendation from several enquiries. Unlike north Queensland, no Territorians have been Cabinet Ministers able to dispense political largesse. The second hindrance was the poor mining and land acts legislated by the South Australian Government. These favoured absentee speculators rather than would-be smallholders as in Queensland, and the Northern Territory is still suffering from this poor land administration. Much of the landscape was permanently damaged from irresponsible use. Thirdly, from 1858 to the present, speculation for rapid profits has been prominent in almost every undertaking. The fourth reason lies in the colonial attitude of southern and local administrators? . . . Social orientation has always been to the south with little of the independence which arose in that other isolated region, south-west Western Australia. Finally, over the total period of European involvement in the Northern Territory, there has been the consistent belief in the ability of capital and technical knowledge gained in other areas, to overwhelm the Territory environment" (1980, 63, 65).

14. A basis of settlement that Mr. Justice Blackburn upheld in the first legal challenge by an Australian Aboriginal group to the state's sovereignty over its lands (see Williams [1986] for a discussion of the case).

15. Literally "they have no ass."

16. I do not give precise locations due to the ongoing nature of the land claim.

17. "Rebels" is a term Belyuen people use to describe any Anglo male bushwhacker.

18. The clever man and clever woman are well-known figures to students of Australian Aboriginal culture. A. P. Elkin (1980) noted that these men and women were persons of exceptional intuition and intelligence who gained the highest degree of initiation and understanding of the mythical-magical aspect of Aboriginal society.

19. I have not been able to confirm this.

20. Indeed, one hallmark of foraging society is its social and physical mobility and flexibility (Young and Doohan 1989; Williams 1982).

Chapter Six

1. This is a common feature of the Aboriginal epistemological stance toward the natural world. As Nancy Williams notes for the Yolngu, "Everything, it is assumed, stands for something else—at least to some people in some place at some time—whether or not particular individuals at a particular time or in a particular context may ever know the further significance" (1986, 48).

2. See Munn's discussion of "relationality" (1986) and Silverstein's discussion of referentiality and cultural process (1976).

3. In Marxist literature in the 1970s, this struggle was discussed as the articulation of modes of production within any social formation. "In this interaction [between capitalism and some other mode of production], the capitalist mode was usually said to be dominant; that is, it subjected the other modes to its own requirements rather than the reverse. In this way it was claimed capitalism could actually preserve so-called precapitalist modes on the periphery of the world system. Articulation became thereby an explanation for underdevelopment" (Donham 1990, 208; see also Wolpe 1980).

4. See Scheffler's (1985) discussion of descent as a particular type of filiation.

5. As I discuss below, these questions parallel others in the social study of science. In a study of risk management and political culture, e.g., Sheila Jasanoff writes, "Different societies also respond differently to questions of political process and institutional design: Who should participate, how much should they know, how should disputes be resolved, and *by what ultimate authority*" (1990, 79; my emphasis).

6. For the former see Harding (1986), Narayan (1989); for the latter, Jasanoff (1990), Latour and Woolgar (1986), Shapin and Schaffer (1985).

Appendix One

1. A variety of authors have described this process. See Sutton (1980), Sansom (1980), and Trigger (1987).

2. Brandl and Walsh note that the timeless framework imposed on Aboriginal groups "denies the members of those groups, as human beings, the ability to adapt and to think their way through the possibilities offered by their culture" (1983, 155).

Works Cited

Adas, Michael. 1989. *Machines as the measure of men: science, technology and ideologies of Western dominance.* Ithaca, N.Y.: Cornell University Press.

Adorno, T. 1988 *Prisms.* Cambridge, Mass.: MIT Press.

Alexander, Peter. 1985. *Ideas, qualities, and corpuscles: Locke and Boyle on the external world.* Cambridge: Cambridge University Press.

Allen, J. 1980. "Head On: The early nineteenth-century British colonisation of the Top End." In *Northern Territory: Options and implications.* Ed. Rhys Jones, 33–40. Canberra: Australian National University Press.

Allen L. M., J. C. Altman, And E. Owen. 1991. *Aborigines in the economy: A select annotated bibliography of policy-relevent research, 1985–1990.* Canberra: Australian National University, Centre for Aboriginal Economic Policy Research.

Altman, Jon. 1982. Maningrida outstations: A preliminary economic overview. In *Small, rural communities.* Ed. E. K. Fisk and E. A. Young, 1–42. Canberra: Australian National Press.

———. 1985. Aboriginal employment in the informal sector: The outstation case. In *Employment and unemployment: A collection of papers.* Ed. D. Wade-Marshall and P. Loveday, 163–173. Darwin: Northern Australia Research Unit.

———. 1987b. *Hunter-gatherers today: An Aboriginal economy in north Australia.* Canberra: Australian Institute of Aboriginal Studies.

———. 1987a. The economic impact of tourism on the Multijulu Community, Uluru (Ayers Rock–Mount Olga) National Park. Working Paper no. 7, Department of Political and Social Change, Research School of Pacific Change, Australian National University.

———, ed. 1990. *Marketing Aboriginal art in the 1980s.* Canberra: Australian Studies Press.

Altman, Jon, and John Nieuwenhuysen. 1979. *The economic status of Australian Aborigines.* Cambridge: Cambridge University Press.

Altman, J., and N. Peterson. 1988. Rights to game and rights to cash among contemporary Australian hunter-gatherers. In *Hunters and gatherers, 2: Property, power, and ideology.* Ed. T. Ingold, D. Riches, and J. Woodburn, 75–94. London: Berg.

Ames, K. 1985. Hierarchies, stress, and logistical strategies among hunter-gatherers in northwestern North America. In *Prehistoric hunter-gatherers: The emergence of cultural complexity.* Ed. T. D. Price and J. A. Brown, 155–80. Orlando, Fla.: Academic Press.

Anderson, B. 1990. *Imagined communities.* New York, Verso.

Anderson, C. 1982. The Bloomfield community, North Queensland, In *Small, rural communities.* Ed. E. K. Fisk and E. A. Young, 89–159. Canberra: Australian National Press.

Appadurai, Arjun. 1986. Commodities and the politics of value. Introduction to *The social life of things: Commodities in cultural perspective.* Ed. Arjun Appadurai, 3–63. Cambridge: Cambridge Univesity Press.

Asad, Talal. 1986. The concept of cultural translation in British anthropology. In *Writing culture: The poetics and politics of ethnography.* Ed. J. Clifford and G. Marcus, 141–46. Berkeley and Los Angeles: University of California Press.

Asche, Michael. 1984. *Home and native land: Aboriginal rights and the Canadian constitution.* Toronto: Methuen.

———. 1989. To negotiate into confederation: Canadian Aboriginal views on their political rights. In *We are here: Politics of Aboriginal land tenure.* Ed. Edwin Wilmsen, 118–37. Berkeley and Los Angeles: University of California Press.

Aschamnn, H. 1975. Culturally determined recognition of food resources in the coastal zone. *Geoscience and Man* 12:43–47.

Attorney General for the Northern Territory 1990. *Kenbi land claim: Submissions on traditional ownership.* Darwin: Northern Territory Goverment.

Attwood, B. 1989. *The making of the Aborigines.* Sydney: Allen & Unwin.

———. 1990. Aborigines and academic encounters: Some recent encounters. *Australian Historical Studies* 24 (94): 123–35.

Baker, S., P. Nicoll, and W. F. Yik. 1985. Aboriginal participation in the Community Employment Program State/Territory elements in the Northern Territory and Australia. In *Employment and unemployment: A collection of papers.* Ed. D. Wade-Marshall and P. Loveday, 83–96. Darwin: North Australian Research Unit.

Bakhtin, M. M. 1986. The problem of speech genres. In *Speech genres and other late essays.* 60–102. Austin: University of Texas Press.

Bandler, Faith. 1984. *Welou, my brother.* Sydney: Redress Press.

Barber, Kim. 1987. A preliminary report on land ownership in the vicinity of the Daly River mouth. Darwin: Northern Land Council.

Barker, Graham. 1976. The ritual estate and Aboriginal polity. *Mankind* 10 (4): 225–39.

Barnard, A. 1988. Cultural identity, ethnicity, and marginalization among the Bushmen of Southern Africa. In *New perspectives on the study of Khoisan.* Ed. R. Vossen, 9–27. Hamburg: Helmut Buske Verlag.

Barnard, Alan, and James Woodburn. 1991. Property, power and ideology in hunting and gathering societies: An introduction. In *Hunters and gatherers, 2: Property, power and ideology,* 4–32. New York: Berg.

Bartells, Barbara. 1988a. Prisoners of assimilation. *Land Rights News.* March. Darwin: Northern Land Council.

———. 1988b. A story that has never been told. *Land Rights News.* January. Darwin: Northern Land Council.

Basedow, H. 1906. Anthropological notes on the western coastal tribes of the Northern Territory of South Australia. *Transcripts of the Royal Society of South Australia* 31:1–62.

———. 1932. The possibilities of the northern territories of Australia, with special reference to development and migration. *Empire parliamentary association*, 3–20. United Kingdom: N.P.

———. 1935. *Knights of the boomerang*. London: Endeavor Press.

Basso, Keith. 1976. "Wise words of the western Apache": Metaphor and semantic theory. In *Meaning in anthropology*. Ed. K. Basso and H. Selby, 93–123. Albuquerque: University of New Mexico Press.

———. 1984. "Stalking with stories": Names, places, and moral narratives among the western Apache. In *Text, play, and story: The construction and reconstruction of self and society*. Ed. E. Bruner, 19–53. Washington, D.C.: American Ethnological Society.

———. 1988. "Speaking with names": Language and landscape among the western Apache. *Cultural Anthropology* 3, no. 2 (May): 99–130.

Baudin, N. 1974. *The journal of Post Captain Nicolas Baudin*. Adelaide: Library of South Australia.

Bates, G. M. 1992. *Environmental law in Australia*, 3rd ed. Sydney: Butterworths.

Beckett, Jeremy. 1964. Aborigines, alcohol, and assimilation. In *Aborigines now: New perspectives in the study of Aboriginal communities*. Ed. Marie Reay, 32–47. Sydney: Angus & Robertson.

———, ed. 1988. *Past and present: The construction of Aboriginality*. Canberra: Aboriginal Studies Press.

Bell, D. 1980. Desert politics: Choices in the "marriage market." In *Women and colonization: Anthropological perspectives*. Ed. M. Etienne and E. Leacock, 239–69. New York: Praeger.

———. 1983. *Daughters of the Dreaming*. London: Allen & Unwin.

———. 1984–85. Aboriginal women and land: Learning from the Northern Territory experience. *Anthropological Forum* 5 (3): 353–63.

———. 1987. The politics of separation. In *Dealing with inequality*. Ed. M. Strathern, 112–29. Cambridge: Cambridge University Press.

———. 1988. Choose your mission wisely: Christian colonials and Aboriginal marital relations in the northern frontier. In *Aboriginal Australians and Christian missions*. Ed. Tony Swain and Deborah Bird Rose, 338–52. Adelaide: Australian Association for the Study of Religion.

Berger, Thomas. 1986. *The rights of indigenous peoples in international law*. Ed. Ruth Thompson. Saskatoon: University of Saskatchewan, Native Law Centre.

Bern, John, and Robert Layton. 1984. The local descent group and the divison of labour in the Cox River land claim. In *Aboriginal landowners: Contemporary issues in the determination of traditional Aboriginal land ownership*. Ed. L. R. Hiatt, 67–83. Sydney: University of Sydney.

Berndt, C. 1954. *Women's changing ceremonies in Northern Australia*. Paris: L'Homme Libraire Scientifique Hermann et Cie.

———. 1965. Women and the "secret life." In *Aboriginal man in Australia*. Ed. R. Berndt and C. Berndt, 238–84. Sydney: Angus & Robertson.

———. 1980. Aboriginal women and the notion of the "marginal man." In *Aborigines of the west: Their past and present*. Ed. R. Berndt and C. Berndt, 28–38. Nedlands: University of Western Australia Press.

Berndt, Ronald. 1970. *The sacred site: The Western Arnhem land example*. Social Anthropology Series no. 4, Australian Aboriginal Studies no. 29. Australian Institute of Aboriginal Studies, Canberra.

———. 1982. Traditional concepts of Aboriginal land. In *Aboriginal sites, Rights, and resource development*. Ed. R. Berndt, 1–12. Perth: University of Western Australia Press.

———. 1987. *The end of an era: Aboriginal labor in the Northern Territory*. Canberra: Australian Instioute of Aboriginal Studies.

Berndt, R., and C. Berndt. 1947. Card games among the Aborigines of the Northern Territory. *Oceania* 17 (3): 248–69.

———. 1964. *The world of the first Australians*. Sydney: Ure Smith.

Bhabha, Homi. 1990. Narrating the nation. Introduction to *Nation and narration*. Ed. Homi Bhabha, 1–7. New York: Routledge.

Biernoff, D. 1978. Safe and dangerous places. In *Australian Aboriginal concepts*. Ed. L. Hiatt, 93–105. Canberra: Australian Institute of Aboriginal Studies.

Bird-David, N. 1988. Hunters and gatherers and other people—a reexamination. In *Hunters and gatherers 1: History, evolution and social change*. Ed. T. Ingold, D. Riches, and J. Woodburn, 17–30. London: Berg.

———. 1990. The giving environment: Another perspective on the economic system of gatherer-hunters. *Current Anthropology* 31, no. 2 (April): 189–95.

———. 1992. Beyond "The original affluent society": A culturalist reformulation. *Current Anthropology* 33, no. 1 (February): 25–34.

Blake, Barry. 1987. *Australian Aboriginal grammar*. Sydney: Croom Helm.

Bonnin, M. R. 1980. A study of Australian descriptive and travel writing, 1929–1946. Ph.D. Dissertation. University of Queensland, Department of English. Brisbane.

Bourdieu, Pierre. 1991. *Language and symbolic power*. Trans. Gino Raymond and Matthew Adamson. Cambridge, Mass.: Harvard University Press.

Brand, J., and V. Cherikoff. 1985. Australian Aboriginal bushfood: The nutritional composition of plants from arid and semi-arid areas. *Australian Aboriginal Studies* 2:38–46.

Brand, J. C., C. Rae, J. McDonnell, A. Lee, V. Cherikoff, and A. S. Truswell. 1983. The nutritional composition of Australian Aboriginal bushfood, vol. 1. *Food Technology in Australia* 35 (6): 293–98.

Brandl, Maria, and Michael Walsh. 1983. Roots and branches, or the far-flung net of Aboriginal relations. In Aborigines, Land and Land Rights. Ed. N. Peterson and M. Langton, 149–59. Canberra: Australian Instioute of Aboriginal Studies.

Brandl, Maria, Adrienne Haritos, and Michael Walsh. 1979. *The Kenbi land claim to vacant crown land in the Cox Peninsula, Bynoe Harbour and Port Patterson areas of the Northern Territory of Australia*. Darwin: Northern Land Council.

Brenneis, D. 1984. Straight talk and sweet talk: Political discourse in an occasionally egalitarian community. In *Dangerous words: Language and politics in the

Pacific. Ed. D. Brenneis and F. Myers, 69–84. New York: New York University Press.
Brenneis, Donald. 1987. Talk and Transformation. *Man* 22 (3): 499–510.
———. 1988. Language and disputing. *Annual Review of Anthropology* 17:221–37.
Brock, John. 1988. *Top End native plants: A comprehensive guide to the trees and shrubs of the Top End of the Northern Territory.* Darwin: Brock.
Brock, P., ed. 1989. *Women, rites and sites: Aboriginal women's cultural knowledge.* London: Allen & Unwin.
Brown, Jill, Roisin Hirshfeld, and Diane Smith. 1974. *Aboriginals and islanders in Brisbane.* Report to the Commission on Inquiry into Poverty. Canberra: Australian Government Publishing Service.
Cadwalader, Sandra, and Vine Deloria, Jr., eds. 1984. *The aggressions of civilization: Federal Indian policy since the 1880s.* Philadelphia: Temple University Press.
Carroll, John, ed. 1982. *Intruders in the bush: The Australian quest for identity.* Oxford: Oxford University Press.
Carter, P. 1987. *The road to Botany Bay: An exploration of landscape and history.* Chicago: University of Chicago Press.
Cass, B. 1988. Social Security review, income support for the unemployed in Australia: Towards a more active system. Issues paper no. 4, 241–53. Canberra: Australian Government Publishing Service.
Certeau, Michel de. 1984. *The practice of everyday life.* Berkeley and Los Angeles: Univesity of California Press.
Chicago Cultural Studies Group. 1992. Critical multiculturalism. *Critical Inquiry* 18 (Spring): 530–55.
Chowning, A. 1987. "Women are our business": Women, exchange and prestige in Kove. In *Dealing with inequality.* Ed. M. Strathern, 130–49. Cambridge: Cambridge University Press.
Clifford, James. 1981. *Person and myth: Maurice Leenhardt in the Melanesian world.* Berkeley: University of California Press.
———. 1988. *The predicament of culture: Twentieth-century ethnography, literature, and art.* Cambridge, Mass.: Harvard University Press.
Collman, Jeff. 1988. *Fringe-dwellers and welfare: The aboriginal response to bureacracy.* St. Lucia: University of Queensland Press.
Comaroff, J., and J. Comaroff. 1991. *Of revelation and revolution: Christiantiy, colonialism, and consciousness in South Africa,* vol. 1 Chicago: University of Chicago Press.
Conkey, M. 1984. To find ourselves: Art and social geography of prehistoric hunter-gatherers. In *Past and present in hunter-gatherer studies.* Ed. C. Schrire, 253–76. Orlando, Fla: Academic Press.
Coombs, H., M. Brandl, and W. Snowdon. 1983. *A certain Heritage.* Centre for Resource and Environmental Studies Monograph no. 9. Canberra: Australian National University.
Coombs, H., B. Dexter, and L. Hiatt 1982. The outstation movement in Aboriginal Australia. In *Politics and history in band societies.* Ed. E. Leacock and R. Lee, 427–40. Cambridge: Cambridge University Press.

Crawford, R. M. (1952) 1961. *Australia*. London: Hutchinson University Library.
Crick, M. 1989. Representations of international tourism in the social sciences. *Annual Review of Anthropology*, 307–44. Palo Alto, Calif.: Annual Review.
Cronon, William. [1983] 1990. *Changes in the land, Indians, colonists, and the ecology of New England*. New York: Hill & Wang.
Crosby, Alfred. 1987. *Ecological imperialism: The biological expansion of Europe, 900–1900*. Cambridge: Cambridge University Press.
Curr, Edward. 1886. *The Australian race: Its origin, languages, customs, place of landing in Australia and the routes by which it spread itself over that continent*, vol. 1. Melbourne: John Ferres, Government Printer.
Daly, Mrs. Dominic D. 1887. *Digging, squatting and pioneering life in the Northern Territory of south Australia*. London.
Davidson, Bruce. 1980. The economics of pastoral and agricultural development in northern Australia. In *Northern Australia: Options and implications*. Ed. R. Jones, 73–84. Darwin: North Australian Research Unit.
di Leonardo, Micaela. 1991. Gender, culture and political economy: Feminist anthropology in an historical perspective. In *Gender at the crossroads of knowledge: Feminist anthropology in the postmodern era*. Ed. M. di Leonardo, 1–47. Berkeley and Los Angeles: University of California Press.
Donham, Donald. 1990. *History, power, ideology: Central issues in Marxism and anthropology*. Cambridge, Cambridge University Press.
Doolan, J. K. 1977. Walk-off (and later return) of various Aboriginal groups from cattle sations: Victoria river District, Northern Territory. In *Aborigines and change: Australia in the 70s*. Ed. R. M. Berndt, 106–13. Canberra: Australian Institute of Aboriginal Studies.
Douglas, Mary. 1966. *Purity and danger: An analysis of concepts of pollution and taboo*. New York: Praeger.
Dreyfus, H., and P. Rabinow. 1982. *Michel Foucault, beyond structuralism and hermeneutics*. Chicago: University of Chicago Press.
Dyck, Noel, ed. 1985. *Indigenous peoples and the nation-state: "Fourth World" politics in Canada, Australia, and Norway*. Social and Economic Papers no. 14, Institute of Social and Economic Research, Memorial University of Newfoundland.
Eades, Dianne. 1991. *Aboriginal English and the law*. Cairns: Queensland Law Society, Continuing Legal Education Department.
Eames, Geoff. 1976. *Land rights or sell-out? An analysis of the Aboriginal Land Rights (Northern Territory) Bill, 1976*. Melbourne: Victorian Fabian Society.
Elkin, A. P. 1936–37. Beliefs and practices connected with death in north-eastern and western South Australia. *Oceania* 7(3):275–99.
———. 1950. Ngirawat, or the sharing of names in the Wagaitj tribe, northern Australia. In *Beitrage zur Gesellungs-und-Volkerwissenschaft*. Ed. I. Tönnies, 67–81. Berlin: Gebruder Mann.
———. 1955–56. Arnhem Land music. *Oceania* 26(2):127–52.
———. 1980. *Aboriginal men of high degree*. St. Lucia: Univesity of Queensland Press.

Endicott, K. 1988. Propety, power, and conflict among the Batek of Malaysia. In *Hunters and gatherers, 2: Property, power and ideology.* Ed. T. Ingold, D. Riches, and J. Woodburn, 110–28. London: Berg.

Engels, Friedrich. 1958. *The conditions of the working class in England.* New York: Macmillan.

Enloe, Cynthia. 1989. *Bananas, beaches, and bases: Making feminist sense of international politics.* Berkeley and Los Angeles: University of California Press.

Errington, Frederick, and Deborah Gewertz. 1987. The remarriage of Yebiwali: A study of domination and false consciousness in a non-Western society. In *Dealing with inequality: Analysing gender relations in Melanesia and beyond.* Ed. M. Strathern, 63–88. Cambridge: Cambridge University Press.

Etienne, Mona, and Eleanor Leacock. 1980. Introduction to *Women and colonization: Anthropological perspectives.* Ed. M. Etienne and E. Leacock, 1–24. New York: Praeger.

Fabian, J. 1983. *Time and the other.* New York: Columbia University Press.

Falkenberg, J. 1962. *Kin and totem.* Oslo: Oslo University Press.

Fanon, F. 1967. *Black skin, white masks.* New York: Grove Weidenfeld.

Feit, H. 1985. Aboriginal rights in Canada: Indigenous strategies for relative autonomy within the Canadian state. In *Native peoples: The Canadian Constitution, civil and minority rights,* 40–65. Cardiff: Canadian Studies in Wales Group.

———. 1989. James Bay Cree self-governance and land management. In *We are here.* Ed. E. Wilmsen, 68–98. Berkeley and Los Angeles: University of California Press.

Fisk, E. 1975. The subsistence component in National Income Accounts. *The Developing Economies* 13 (3): 252–79.

———. 1985. *The Aboriginal economy in town and country.* Sydney: George Allen & Unwin.

Foelsche, P. 1881–82. Notes on the Aborigines of north Australia. *Royal Journal of South Australian transcripts and proceedings* 5:1–18.

Foelsche, P. 1886. Port Darwin, the Larrakia tribe. In *The Australian race,* Vol. 1. Ed. E. M. Curr, 250–59. Melbourne: Ferres.

Foley, Mike. 1978. *The impact of recreational activities on the natural environment of the Top End of the Northern Territory.* Darwin: Department of Environment, Housing, and Community Development.

———. 1987. *Point Chalres Lighthouse and the military occupation of Cox Peninsula.* Darwin: Northern Territory State Reference Library Occasional Papers.

———. N.d. *The history of the Cox Peninsula.* Unpaginated manuscript. Darwin. Northern Territory State Reference Library.

Foucault, Michel. 1973. *The order of things.* New York: Vintage.

———. [1978] 1990. *The history of sexuality: An introduction,* vol. 1. New York: Vintage.

———. 1979. *Discipline and punish: The birth of the prison.* New York: Vintage.

Frederickson, George. 1971. *The black image in the white mind: The debate on Afro-American character and destiny, 1817–1914.* New York: Harper & Row.

Friedrich, P. 1991. Polytropy. In *Beyond metaphor: The theory of tropes in anthropology*. Ed. J. Fernandez, 17–55. Stanford, Calif: Stanford University Press.

Gal, Susan. 1991. Between speech and silence: The problematics of research on language and gender. In *Gender at the crossroads of knowledge*. Ed. Micaela di Leonardo, 175–203. Berkeley and Los Angeles: University of California Press.

Gale, Fay, ed. 1974. *Woman's role in Aboriginal society*. Canberra: Australian Institute of Aboriginal Studies.

———. ed. 1983. *We are bosses ourselves: The status and role of Aboriginal women today*. Canberra: Australian Institute of Aboriginal Studies.

Gates, H. L., Jr. 1987. *Figures in black: Words, signs, and the "racial" self*. New York: Oxford Univesity Press.

Geertz, Clifford. 1983. *Local knowledge: Further essays in interpretive anthropology*. New York: Basic Books.

Gelder, Ken. 1991. Aboriginal narrative and property. *Meanjin* 50, nos. 2/3, 353–80.

Giddens, A. 1986. *The constitution of society: Outline of the thoery of structuration*. Berkeley and Los Angeles: University of California Press.

Gluckman, M. 1955. *Custom and conflict in Africa*. Oxford: Blackwell.

———, ed. 1962. *Essays on the ritual of social relations*. Manchester: Manchester University Press.

Godelier, M. 1986. *The mental and the material: Thought, economy, and society*. Trans. M. Thoms. London: Verso.

Gold, Gerald, ed. 1984. *Minorities and mother country imagery*. Social and Economic Papers, no. 13, Institute of Social and Economic Research. Memorial University of Newfoundland.

Goodale, J. 1974. *Tiwi wives: A study of the women of Melville Island, North Australia*. Seattle: University of Washington Press.

Goody, Jack. 1987. *The interface between the written and the oral*. Cambridge: Cambridge University Press.

Gordon, Robert. 1989. Can the Namibian San stop dispossession of their land? In *We are here*. Ed. E. Wilmsen, 138–54. Berkeley and Los Angelges: University of California Press.

Gould, Richard. 1969. *Yiwara: Foragers of the Australian desert*. New York: Scribner.

———. 1982. To have and have not: The ecology of sharing among hunter-gatherers. In *Resource managers: North American and Australian hunter-gatherers*. Ed. N. Williams and E. Hunn, 69–92. Canberra: Australian Institute of Aboriginal Studies Press.

Goyder, Margaret. 1971. *The surveyors: The story of the founding of Darwin*. Sydney: Rigby.

Gratten, C. Hartley. 1963. *The southwest Pacific since 1900*. Ann Arbor: University of Michigan Press.

Graburn, N., ed. 1976. *Ethnic and tourist arts: Cultural expressions from the fourth world*. Berkeley: University of California Press.

Gribble, E. 1932. *The problem of the Australian Aboriginal.* Sydney: Angus & Robertson.

Grimshaw, A. 1990. *Conflict talk: Sociolinguistic investigations of arguments in conversations.* Cambridge: Cambridge University Press.

Gross, D. 1984. Time allocation: A tool for the study of cultural behavior. *Annual Review of Anthropology* 13: 519–58.

Gumbert, Marc. 1981. Paradigm lost: Anthropological models and their effect on Aboriginal land rights. *Oceania* 52 (2): 103–23.

———. 1984. *Neither justice nor reason: A Legal and anthropological analysis of Aboriginal land rights.* St. Lucia: Queenstand University Press.

Gumperz, J. J. 1982. *Discourse strategies.* Studies in Interactional Sociolinguistics no. 1. Cambridge: Cambridge University Press.

Hamilton, Annette, 1975. Aboriginal women: The means of production. In *The other half: Women in Australian society.* Ed. J. Mercer. Melbourne: Penguin.

———. 1980. Dual social systems: Technology, labour, and women's secret rites in the eastern western desert of Australia. *Oceania* 51 (1): 4–19.

———. 1981. *Nature and nurture: Aboriginal child-rearing in North-Central Arnhem Land.* Canberra: Australian Institute of Aboriginal Studies.

———. 1982. Descended from father, belonging to country: Rights to land in the Australian western desert. In *Politics and history in band societies.* Ed. Eleanor Leacock and Richard Lee, 85–108. Cambridge: Cambridge University Press.

———. 1984. Spoonfeeding the lizards: Culture and conflict in central Australia. *Meanjin* 43 (3): 363–78.

———. 1990. Fear and desire: Aborigines, Asians and the national imaginary. *Australian Cultural History* (July): 14–35.

Haraway, Donna. 1989. *Primate visions: gender, race, and nature in the world of modern science.* New York: Routledge.

Harding, Sandra. 1986. *The science questions in feminism.* Ithaca, N.Y.: Cornell Unviersity Press.

Harker, R. K., and K. R. McConnochie. 1985. *Education as cultural artifact: Studies in Maroi and Aboriginal education.* Palmerston North: Dunmore Press.

Harney, W. E. 1952. Sport and play amidst the Aborigines of the Northern Territory. *Mankind* 4 (9): 377–379.

———. 1960. *Tales from the Aborigines.* London: Robert Hale.

———. 1961. *Life among the Aborigines.* London: Robert Hale.

———. 1965. *Content to lie in the sun.* London: Robert Hale.

Harney, W. E., and A. P. Elkin. 1968. *Songs of the songmen.* Sydney: Rigby.

Harney, W. E., and D. Lockwood. 1963. *The shady tree.* London: Rigby.

Harris, David. 1980. Tropical savanna environments: Defintion, distribution, diversity, and development. In *Human ecology in savanna environments.* Ed. David Harris, 3–27. New York: Academic Press.

Harris, Marvin, and Eric Ross, eds. 1987. *Food and evolution: Toward a theory of human food habits.* Philadelphia: Temple University Press.

Harris, Stephen. 1990. *Two-way aboriginal schooling: Education and cultural survival.* Canberra: Australian Studies Press.

Hartsock, Nancy. 1983. *Money, sex, power: Toward a feminist historical materialism.* New York: Longman.
Haviland, John. 1977. *Gossip, reputation and knowledge in Zinacantan.* Chicago: University of Chicago Press.
———. 1991. "That was the last time I saw them, and no more": Voices through time in Australian Aboriginal autobiography. *American Ethnologist* 18 (2): 331–61.
Hawkes, Kristen. 1987. How much food do foragers need? In *Food and evolution: Toward a theory of human food habits,* Ed. M. Harris and E. Ross, 341–56. Philadelphia: Temple University Press.
Hawkes, Kristen, K. Hill, and J. O'Connell. 1986. Why hunters gather: Optimal foraging and the Ache of eastern Paraguay. *American Ethnologist* 9 (2): 379–98.
Headland, T., and L. Reid. 1989. Hunter-gatherers and their neighbors from prehistory to the present. *Current Anthropology* 30(1):43–66.
Healy, Chris. 1990. "We know your mob now": Histories and their cultures. *Meanjin* 49 (3): 512–23.
Healy, J. J. 1989. *Literature and the Aborigine in Australia,* 2d ed. St. Lucia: University of Queensland Press.
Heller, M. 1988. Introduction to *Code-switching: Anthropological and sociolinguistic perspectives.* Ed. M. Heller, 1–25. Berlin: Mouton de Gruyter.
Hendrickson, C. 1991. Images of the Indian in Guatemala: The role of indigenous dress in Indian and Ladino constructions. In *Nation-states and Indians in Latin America.* Ed. G. Urban and J. Sherzer. Austin: University of Texas Press.
Hercus, Luise. 1989. The status of women's cultural knowledge: Aboriginal society in northeast South Australia. In *Women, rites, and sites: Aboriginal women's cultural knowledge.* Ed. P. Brock, 99–119. Sydney: Allen & Unwin.
Hercus, Luise, and Peter Sutton, eds. 1986. *This is what happened: Historical narratives by Aborigines.* Canberra: Australian Institute of Aborginal Studies.
Hiatt, L. R. 1962. Local organisation among the Australian Aborigines. *Oceania* 32 (4):267–86.
———, ed. 1975. *Australian Aboriginal mythology.* Canberra: Australian Institute of Aboriginal Studies.
———. 1982. Traditional attitudes to land resources. In *Aboriginal sites, rights and resource development.* Ed. R. Berndt, 13–26. Perth: University of Western Australia Press.
———. 1984. Traditional land tenure and contemporary land claims. In *Aboriginal landowners: Contemporary issues in the determination of traditional Aboriginal land ownership.* Ed. L. R. Hiatt, 11–23. Sydney: University of Sydney.
———. 1984. *Aboriginal landowners: Contemporary issues in the determination of traditional Aboriginal land ownership.* Oceania Monograph no. 27. Sydney: University of Sydney Press.
———. 1986. *Aboriginal political life: The Wentworth lecture, 1984.* Canberra: Australian Institute of Aboriginal Studies.
Hill, Kathleen. 1975. *A study of Aboriginal poverty in two country towns.* Report prepared for the Australian Government Commission on Inquiry into Poverty. Canberra: Australian Government Publishing Service.

Hobsbawm, E., and T. Ranger, eds. (1983) 1987. *The invention of tradition.* Cambridge: Cambridge University Press.

Hocking, Barbara. 1988. Colonial laws and indigenous peoples: Past and present law concerning the recognition of human rights of indigenous native peoples in British colonies with particular reference to Australia. *International law and Aboriginal human rights.* Ed. Barbara Hocking, 3–18. Sydney: The Law Book Company.

Hodder, Edwin. 1893. *The history of south Australia from its foundation to the year of its jubilee, with a chronological summary,* 2 vols. London: Sampson Low, Marston & Company.

House of Representatives Standing Committee on Aboriginal Affairs. 1977. *Alcohol problems of aboriginals, final report.* Canberra: Australian Publishing Service.

Hughes, Robert. 1986. *The fatal shore: The epic of Australia's founding.* New York: Knopf.

Ingold, T. 1987. *The appropriation of nature: Essays on human ecology and social relations.* Iowa City: University of Iowa Press.

———. 1988. Notes on the foraging mode of production. In *Hunters and gatherers, 1: History, evolution, and social change,* Ed. T. Ingold, D. Riches, and J. Woodburn, 269–85. London: Berg.

Jacobs, Jane M. 1989. "Women talking up big": Aboriginal women as cultural custodians, a south Australian exmaple. In *Women, rites, and sites: Aboriginal women's cultural knolwdge.* Ed. Peggy Brook, 76–98. Sydney: Allen & Unwin.

Jameson, Fredrick. 1991. *Postmodernism, or, The logic of late capitalism.* Durham, N.C.: Duke University Press.

JanMohamed, Abdul. 1983. *Manichean aesthetics: The politics of literature in colonial Africa.* Amherst: University of Massachusetts Press.

Jasanoff, Sheila. 1990. *The fifth branch: Science advisers as policymakers.* Cambridge, Mass.: Harvard University Press.

Jones, Rhys. 1980. Hunters in the Australian coastal savanna. In *Human ecology in savanna environments.* Ed. David Harris, 107–146. New York: Academic Press.

Jones, Rhys, and Jim Bowler. 1980. Struggle for the savanna: Northern Australia in ecological and prehistoric perspective. In *Northern Territory: Options and implications.* Ed. Rys Jones, 3–31. Research School of Pacific Studies. Canberra: Australian National University Press.

Jordon, D. 1988. Aboriginal identity: Uses of the past, problems for the future. In *Past and present: The construction of Aboriginality.* Ed. J. Beckett, 109–30. Canberra: Aboriginal Studies Press.

Kaberry, P. 1935–36. Spirit-children and spirit centres of the north Kimberley Division. *Oceania* 6(4): 392–400.

———. 1939. *Aboriginal women: Sacred and profane.* London: Routledge.

Kearney, W. J. 1988. *Jawoyn (Katherine area) land claim.* Report by the Aboriginal land commissioner, Justice Kearney, to the minister for Aboriginal Affairs and to the administrator of the Northern Territory. Canberra: Australian Government Publishing Service.

Keen, Ian. 1984. A question of interpretation: The definition of "traditional Aboriginal owners" in the Aboriginal Land Rights (NT) Act. In *Aboriginal landowners: Contemporary issues in the determination of traditional Aboriginal land ownership.* Ed. L. R. Hiatt, 24–45. Sydney: University of Sydney.

Keene, A. 1986. Stories we tell: Gatherer-hunters as ideology. Paper presented at the fourth international conference of the Hunting and Gathering Society. London.

Kelsey, Dudley Evan. 1975. *The shackle.* Adelaide: Griffen Press.

Kenbi Transcripts. 1989–90. *Transcripts of proceedings of the Kenbi land claim to vacant crown land in the Cox Peninsula, Bynoe Harbour and Port Patterson areas of the Northern Territory,* Darwin: Office of the Aboriginal Land Commissioner.

King, D. A., and A. W. McHoul. 1986. The discursive production of the Queensland Aborigine as subject: Meston's proposal, 1895. *Social Analysis* 19: 22–39.

King, Philip Parker. 1827. *Narrative of a survey of the intertropical and western coasts of Australia, performed between the years 1818 and 1822.* London: J. Murray.

Kolig, E. 1980. Noah's Ark revisited: On the myth-land connection in traditional Aboriginal thought. *Oceania* 51 (2): 118–32.

Labumore [Elsie Roughsey]. 1984. *An Aboriginal mother tells of the old and the new.* Harmondsworth: Penguin.

Larbalestier, Jan. 1990. Amity and kindness in the never-never: Ideology and Aboriginal-European relations in the Northern Territory. *Social Analysis* 27: 70–82

Latour, Bruno, and Steven Woolgar. 1986. *Laboratory life: The construction of scientific facts.* Princeton, N.J.: Princeton University Press.

Lattas, Andrew. 1990. Aborigines and contemporary Australian nationalism: Primordiality and the cultural politics of otherness. *Social Analysis,* 27: 50–69. (Special issue: Writing Australian culture, text, society and national identity.)

Lawrence, Roger. 1968. *Aboriginal habitat and economy.* Department of Geography and School of General Studies, Occasional Paper no. 6. Canberra: Australian National University.

Laycock. Jennifer. 1982. The Elkin papers: A brief description and guide to the collection. *Aboriginal History* 6: 139–41.

Layton, R. 1986. Political and territorial structures among hunter-gatherers. *Man* 21 (1): 18–33.

———. 1989. *Uluru: An Aboriginal history of Ayers Rock.* Canberra: Aboriginal Studies Press.

Layton, R., and N. Williams, eds. 1980. *The Finniss River land claim.* Darwin: Northern Land Council.

Lazarus, Edward. 1991. *Black Hills, white justice: The Sioux Nation versus the United States, 1775 to the present.* New York: Harper Collins.

Leacock, E., and R. Lee, eds. 1982. *Politics and history in band societies.* Cambridge: Cambridge University Press.

Lee, R. 1979. *The !Kung San: Men, women, and work in a foraging society.* Cambridge: Cambridge University Press.

———. 1988. Reflections on primitive communism. In *Hunters and gatherers 1:*

History, evolution and social change. Ed. T. Ingold, D. Riches, and J. Woodburn, 252–68 London: Berg.

———. 1992. Art, science, or politics? The crisis in hunter-gatherer studies. *American Anthropologist* 94, no. 1: 31–54.

Lévi-Strauss, C. 1969. *The elementary structure of kinship.* Boston: Beacon Press.

Liberman, K. 1985. *Understanding interaction in Central Australia.* London: Routledge & Kegan Paul.

Lindstrom, Lamont. 1990. *Knowledge and power in a South Pacific society.* Washington, D.C.: Smithsonian Institution Press.

Locke, John. [1690] 1988. *Two treatises of government.* Cambridge: Cambridge University Press.

Lockwood, D. 1977. *The front door.* Sydney: Rigby.

Lyon, Pamela, and Michael Parsons. 1989. *We are staying: The Alyawarre struggle for land at Lake Nash.* Alice Springs: I.A.D. Press.

MacKenzie, Ihian. 1980. European incursions and failures in northern Australia, In *Northern Australia: Options and implications.* Ed. R. Jones, 43–72. Darwin: Northern Australian Research Unit.

Macpherson, C. B. 1962. *The political theory of possessive individualism: Hobbes to Locke.* Oxford: Clarendon Press.

Maddock, K. 1983. *Your land is our land: Aboriginal land rights.* Harmondsworth: Penguin.

Mandorah Land Use Concept Plan, 1990. Northern Territory Department of Lands and Housing. Darwin: Colemans Printing.

Marcus, George, and Michael Fischer. 1986. in *Anthropology as cultural critique,* Chicago: University of Chicago Press.

Marcus, Julie. 1988. Bicentenary follies: Australians in search of themselves. *Anthropology Today* 4 (3): 4–6.

Martin, J. 1983. Optimal foraging theory: A review of some models and their applications. *American Anthropologist* 85 (3): 612–29.

Marx, Karl. [1887] 1987. *Capital. vol. 1: A Critical Analysis of Capitalist Production.* Unabridged. New York: International Publishers.

Mascia-Lees, Frances, Patrica Sharpe, and Colleen Ballerino Cohen. 1989. The postmodernist turn in anthropology. *Signs: Journal of Women in Culture and Society* 15 (1): 7–13.

McConvell, P. 1988. MIX-IM-UP: Aboriginal codeswitching in the mangement of conflict. In *Code-switching, anthropological and sociolinguistic perspectives.* Ed. M. Heller 97–150. Berlin: Mouton de Gruyter.

McGrath, Ann. 1987. *"Born in cattle": Aborigines in cattle country.* Sydney: Allen & Unwin.

McMichael, Philip. 1984. *Settlers and the agrarian question: Foundations of capitalism in colonial Australia.* Cambridge: Cambridge University Press.

Meehan, Betty. 1977. Man does not live by calories alone: The role of shellfish in a coastal cuisine. In *Sunda and Sahul: Prehistoric studies in Southeast Asia, Melanesia, and Australia.* Ed. J. Allen, J. Golsen, and R. Jones, 493–532. New York: Academic Press.

———. 1982. *Shell bed to shell midden* Canberra: Australian Institute of Aboriginal Studies.

———. 1988. Changes in Aboriginal exploitation of wetlands. In *Floodplains research*. Ed. Deborah Wade-Marshall and Peter Loveday, App. 2, 1–23. Canberra: Australian National University Press.
Meek, R. L. 1976. *Social science and the ignoble savage*. Cambridge: Cambridge University Press.
Meggitt, Mervyn. [1965] 1971. *Desert people: A study of the Walbiri Aborigines of central Australia*. Chicago: University of Chicago Press.
Meillassoux, Claude. 1973. On the mode of production of the hunting band. In *French perspectives in African studies*. Ed. P. Alexandre, 187–203. London: Oxford University Press.
Merlan, F. 1981. Land, language and social identity in Aboriginal Australia. *Mankind* 13 (20): 133–48.
———. 1986. Australian Aboriginal conception beliefs revisited. *Man* 21 (3): 474–493.
———. 1988. Gender in Aboriginal social life: A review. In *Social anthropology and Australian Aboriginal studies*. Ed. R. Berndt and R. Tonkinson, 15–76. Canberra: Aboriginal Studies Press.
———. 1991. The limits of cultural constructionism: The case of Coronation Hill. *Oceania* 61 (4): 341–52.
———. 1992. Male-Female separation and forms of society in Aboriginal Australia. *Cultural Anthropologist* 7 (2): 169–93.
Mintz, Sidney. 1985. *Sweetness and power: The place of sugar in modern history*. New York: Viking.
Morphy, H., and F. Morphy. 1984. The "myths" of Ngalakan history: ideology and images of the past in northern Australia. *Man* 19 (3): 459–78.
Morphy, Frances, and Howard Morphy. 1984. Owners, managers, and ideology: A comparative analysis. In *Aboriginal landowners: Contemporary issues in the determination of traditional Aboriginal land ownership*. Ed. L. R. Hiatt, 46–66. Sydney: University of Sydney.
Morris, B. 1982. The family, group structuring and trade among South Indian hunter-gatherers. In *Politics and history in band societies*. Ed. E. Leacock and R. Lee, 171–88. Cambridge: Cambridge University Press.
Morris, Barry. 1989. *Domesticating resistance; The Dhan-Gadi Aborigines and the Australian state*. New York: Berg.
Muecke, S. 1988a. Body, inscription, epistomology: Knowing Aboriginal texts. In *Connections: Essays in black literatures*. Ed. E. Nelson, 41–52. Canberra: Aboriginal Studies Press.
———. 1988b. The children's country: Ethical statements/useful instructions. *Oceania* 59 (2): 143–58.
Mulvaney, D., and J. Golson, eds. 1971. *Aboriginal man and environment in Australia*. Canberra: Australian National University Press.
Munn, Nancy. 1964. Totemic designs and group continuity in Walpiri cosmology. In *Aborigines now: New perspectives in the study of Aboriginal communities*. Ed. Marie Reay, 83–100. Sydney: Angus & Robertson.
———. 1970. The transformation of subjects into objects in Walpiri and Pitjantjatjara myth. In *Australian Aboriginal anthropology*. Ed. R. Berndt, 141–63. Nedlands: University of Western Australian Press.

———. 1973. *Walpiri iconography: Graphic representation and cultural symbolism in a central Australian society.* Ithaca, N.Y.: Cornell University Press.

———. 1986. *The fame of Gawa: A symbolic study of value transformation in a Massim (Papua New Guinea) society.* Cambridge: Cambridge University Press.

Murray, E. J. 1942. Diary letters. Darwin Archives, Northern Territory.

Myers, Fred. 1979. Emotions and the self: A Theory of personhood and political order among Pintupi Aborigines. *Ethos* 7: 343–70.

———. 1982b. Ideology and experience: The cultural basis of politics in Pintupi life. In *Aboriginal power in Australian society.* Ed. Michael Howard, 79–114. Honolulu: University of Hawaii Press.

———. 1982a. Always ask: Resource use and land ownership among Pintupi Aborigines of the Australian western desert. In *Resource managers: North American and Australian hunter-gatherers.* Ed. Nancy Williams and Eugene Hunn, 173–96. Canberra: Australian Institute of Aboriginal Studies.

———. 1986. *Pintupi country, Pintupi self: Sentiment, place, and politics among western desert aborigines.* Canberra: Australian Institute of Aboriginal Studies.

———. 1988a. Burning the truck and holding the country: Property, time and the negotiation of identity among Pintupi Aborigines. In *Hunters and gatherers, 2: Property, power and ideology.* Ed. T. Ingold, D. Riches, and J. Woodburn, 52–74. New York: Berg.

———. 1988b. Critical trends in the study of hunter-gatherers. *Annual Review of Anthropology* 17: 261–82.

———. 1989. Truth, beauty, and Pintupi painting. *Visual Anthropology* 2: 163–5.

———. 1991. Representing culture: The production of discourse(s) for Aboriginal Acrylic paintings. *Cultural Anthropology* 6, no. 1 (February): 26–62.

Narayan, Uma. 1989. The project of feminist epistemology: Perspectives from a nonwestern feminist. In *Gender/body/knowledge.* Ed. Alison Jagger and Susan Bordo. Brunswick, NJ: Rutgers University Press.

Neate, Graham. 1989. *Aboriginal land rights law in the Northern Territory,* vol. 1. Sydney: Alternative Publishing.

Northern Territory Department of Lands and Housing. 1990. *Cox Peninsula land use structure plan.* Darwin: Colemans Printing.

Ochs, Eleanor. 1988. *Culture and language development: Language acquisition and language socialization in a Samoan village.* Cambridge: Cambridge University Press.

O'Malley, Pat. 1983. *Law capitalism and democracy: A sociology of Australian legal order.* Sydney: George Allen & Unwin.

Olney, Maurice. 1991. *Finding and report of the Aboriginal land commissioner, Kenbi (Cox Peninsula).* Darwin: Land Claim Office of the Aboriginal Land Commissioner.

Ortner, Sherry. 1970. Food for thought: A key symbol in Sherpa culture. Ph.D. dissertation. University of Chicago, Department of Anthropology.

———. 1989. *High religion: A cultural and political history of Sherpa Buddhism.* Princeton, N.J.: Princeton University Press.

Palmer, Ian. 1988. *Buying back the land: Organisational struggle and the Aboriginal Land Fund Commission.* Canberra: Australian Studies Press.

Parkhouse, T. A. 1895. Native tribes of Port Darwin and its neighborhood *Australian Association of the Advancement of Science* 6: 638–7.

Peron, Francois. 1809. *A voyage of discovery in the Southern Hemisphere.* London: Richard Phillips.

Peterson, N. 1972. Totemism yesterday: Sentiment and local organisation among the Australian Aborigines. *Man* 7 (1): 12–32.

———. 1977. Aboriginal involvement with the Australian economy in the Central Reserve during the winter of 1970. In *Aborigines and change: Australia in the '70s.* Ed. R. M. Berndt, 136–46. Canberra: Australia Institute of Aboriginal Studies.

———. 1982. Aboriginal land rights in the Northern Territory of Australia. In *Politics and history in band societies.* Ed. E. Leacock and R. Lee, 441–62. Cambridge: Cambridge University Press.

———. 1983. Rights, residence and process in Australian territorial organisation. In *Aborigines, land and land rights.* Ed. N. Peterson, M. Langton, 134–48. Canberra: Australian Institute of Aboriginal Studies.

———. 1985. Capitalism, culture and land rights: Aborigines and the state in the Northern Territory. *Social Analysis* 18: 85–103.

———. 1991. Cash, commoditisation and authenticity: When do Aboriginal people stop being hunter-gatherers? In *Cash, commoditisation and changing foragers.* N. Peterson and T. Matsuyama, 67–90. Osaka: National Museum of Ethnology.

Peterson, Nicolas, and Marica Langton, eds. 1983. *Aborigines, land and land rights.* Canberra: Australian Institute of Aboriginal Studies.

Peterson, Nicolas, Ian Keen, and Basil Sansom. 1977. Succession to land: Primary and secondary rights to Aboriginal estates. In *Hasard of Joint Select Committee on Land Rights in the Northern Territory.* Canberra: Government Printer.

Pietsche, B. A., and B. A. Simons. 1986. *Bynoe 5072 geological map series: Explanatory notes.* Department of Mines and Energy. Darwin: Government Printer of the Northern Territory.

Pomerantz, Anita. 1987. Pursuing a response. In *Structures of social action: Studies in conversational analysis.* Ed. J. Maxwell Atkinson and John Heritage, 152–64. Cambridge: Cambridge University Press.

Povinelli, Elizabeth, 1989. The ecological and economic use of the Cox Peninsula by Darwin Larragiya and Belyuen Aborigines. Darwin: Northern Land Council.

———. 1990b. Quantitative analysis of Wagaidj and Larragiya's collection of foods and materials in the Cox Peninsula. Darwin: Northern Land Council.

———. 1990a. Emiyenggal and Batjemal folk classifications, Cox Peninsula, Northern Territory: "Figuring" continuity and contigency. *Australian Aboriginal Studies* 2: 53–59.

———. 1991. Organizing women: Rhetoric, economy and politics and process among Australian Aborigines. In *Gender at the crossroads of knowledge: Feminist anthropology in the postmodern era.* Ed. M. di Leonardo, Berkeley and Los Angeles: Univerity of California Press.

———. 1992. "Where we gana go now?" Foraging practices and their meanings among the Belyuen Australian Aborigines. *Human Ecology* 20 (1).

———. 1993a. "Might be something": The language of indeterminacy in Australian Aboriginal land use. *Man*, In Press.

———. 1993b. The shopman and us: Indexing action and identity in Aboriginal Australia. Manuscript. Cornell University.

Powell, Alan. 1988. *Far country: A short history of the Northern Territory*. Melbourne: Melbourne University Press.

Price, T., and J. Brown, eds. 1985. *Prehistoric hunter-gatherers: the emergence of cultural complexity*. Orlando, Fla.: Academic Press.

Radcliffe-Brown, A. 1930. The social organization of Aboriginal tribes. *Oceania* 1 (1): 34–63.

———. 1952. *Structure and function in primitive society*. London: Cohen & West.

Ranger, Terence. [1983] 1987. The invention of tradition in colonial Africa. In *The invention of tradition*. Ed. E. Hobsbawm and T. Ranger, 211–62. Cambridge: University of Cambridge Press.

Read, Peter, ed. 1984. *Down there with me on the Cowra mission*. Rushcutters Bay: Pergamon Press.

Reece, R. 1974. *Aborigines and colonists: Aborigines and colonial society in New South Wales in the 1830s and 1840*. Sydney: Sydney University Press.

Reid, J. 1983. Sorcerers and healing spirits. Canberra: Australian National Univerity Press.

Reynolds, H. 1982. *The other side of the frontier*. Victoria: Penguin Books.

———. 1987. *Frontier*. London: Allen & Unwin.

Ricoeur, Paul. 1984. *Time and narration*, vol. 1. Chicago: University of Chicago Press.

Ridington, R. 1988a. Knowledge, power and individual in subartic hunting societies. *American Anthropologist*. 90 (1): 98–110.

———. 1988b. *Trail to heaven: knowledge and narrative in a northern Native community*. Iowa City: University of Iowa Press.

Rigsby, Bruce, and Peter Sutton. 1980–82. Speech communities in Aboriginal Australia. *Anthropological Forum*. 5 (1): 8–23.

Rosaldo, Michelle. 1973. I have nothing to hide: The language of Ilongot oratory. *language and Society* 2: 193–223.

Rose, D. 1984. The saga of Captain Cook: Morality in Aboriginal and European law. *Australian Aboriginal Studies* 2: 24–39.

———. 1991. *Dingo makes us human: life and land in an aboriginal Australian culture*. Cambridge: Cambridge University Press.

Roseberry, William. 1983. *Coffee and capitalism in the Venezuelan Andes*. Austin: University of Texas Press.

———. 1989. *Anthropologies and histories: Essays in culture, history, and political economy*. New Brunswick, N.J.: Rutgers University Press.

Roseberry, W., and J. O'Brien. 1991. Introduction to *Golden ages, dark ages: Imagining the past in anthropology and history*. Ed. J. O'Brien and W. Roseberry, 1–18. Berkeley and Los Angeles: University of California Press.

Ross, Eric. 1987. An overview of trends in dietary variation from hunter-gatherer to modern capitalist societies. In *Food and evolution: Toward a theory of human food habits*. Ed. M. Harris and B. Ross, 7–56. Philadelphia: Temple University Press.

Rosser, Bill. 1990. *Up rode the troopers: The black police in Queensland*. Brisbane: University of Queensland Press.

Rowell, M. 1983. Women and land claims in the Northern Territory. In *Aborigines, land and land rights*. Ed. N. Peterson and M. Langton, 256–67. Canberra: Australian Institute of Aboriginal Studies.

Rowley, C. D. 1970a. *The destruction of Aboriginal society*. Canberra: Australian National University Press.

Rowley, C. D. 1970b. *The Remote Aborigines*. Sydney: Penguin.

Rubin, G. 1975. Traffic in women: Notes on the 'political economy' of sex. In *Towards an anthropology of women*. Ed. R. Rieter, 157–210. New York: Monthly Review Press.

Sahlins, Marshall. 1968. Notes on the original affluent society. In *Man the hunter*. Ed. R. Lee and I. DeVore, 85–89. Chicago: Aldine.

———. 1972. *Stone Age economics* Chicago: Aldine-Atherton.

———. 1985. *Islands of history*. Chicago: University of Chicago Press.

Said, Edward, 1983. Opponents, audiences, constituencies and community. In *The politics of interpretation*. Ed. W. J. T. Mitchell, Chicago: University of Chicago Press.

Sansom, Basil. 1980. *The camp at Wallaby Cross: Aboriginal fringe dwellers in Darwin*. Canberra: Australian Institute of Aboriginal Studies.

———. 1982. The Aboriginal commonality. In *Aboriginal sites, rights and resource development*. Ed. R. Berndt, 117–38. Perth: University of Western Australian Press.

———. 1985. Aborigines, anthropologists, and leviathan. In *Indigenous peoples and the nation-state: "Fourth World" politics in Canada, Australia and Norway*. Ed. N. Dyck, 67–94. Social and Economic Papers no. 14, Institute of Social and Economic Research. Memorial University of Newfoundland.

———. 1988a. A grammar of exchange. In *Being black: Aboriginal cultures in "settled" Australia*. Ed. Ian Kenn, 159–78. Canberra: Australian Institute of Aboriginal Studies.

———. 1988b. The past is a doctrine of person. In *Past and present: The construction of Aboriginality*. Ed. Jeremy Beckett, 147–60. Canberra: Aboriginal Studies Press.

Scheffler, H. W. 1985. Descent and filiation. *Man* 20 (1): 1–21.

Schrire, C. ed. 1984. *Past and present in hunter gatherer studies*. Orlando, Fla.: Academic Press.

Scott, Colin. 1988. Property, practice and aboriginal rights among Quebec Cree hunters. In *Hunters and gatherers, 2: Property, power and ideology*. Ed. T. Ingold, D. Riches, and J. Woodburn, 35–51. Berg: New York.

Scott, James C. 1985. *Weapons of the weak: Everday forms of peasant resistance*. New Haven, Conn.: Yale University Press.

———. 1990. *Domination and the arts of resistance: Hidden transcripts*. New Haven, Conn.: Yale University Press.

Searcy, Alfred. 1912. *By flood and field: Adventures ashore and afloat in North Australia.* London: G. Bell & Sons.

Shapin, Steven, and Simon Schaffer. 1985. *Leviathan and the air-pump: Hobbes, Boyle and the experimental life.* Princeton, N.J.: Princeton University Press.

Shapiro, Ian. 1982. Realism and the study of the history of ideas. *History of Political Thought.* 3 (3): 535–78.

———. 1986. *The Evolution of Rights and Liberal Theory.* Cambridge: Cambrdige University Press.

Shapiro, Michael. 1983. *The sense of grammar: Language as Semeiotic.* Bloomington: Indiana University Press.

Shapiro, Michael ed. 1984. *Language and politics.* New York: New York University Press.

Sherzer, Joel, and Greg Urban, eds. 1991. *Nation-states and Indians in Latin America.* Austin: University of Texas Press.

Silverstein, Michael. 1976. Shifters, linguistic categories, and cultural description. In *Meaning in anthropology.* Ed. K. Basso and H. Selby, 11–55. Albuquerque: University of New Mexico Press.

Smith, Diane, 1984. That register business: The role of the land councils in determining traditional Aboriginal owners. In *Aboriginal landowners: Contemporary issues in the determination of traditional Aboriginal land ownership.* Ed. L. R. Hiatt, 84–103. Sydney: University of Sydney Press.

Smith, W. Ramsey. 1924. *In Southern seas: Wanderings of a naturalist.* London: John Murray.

Smith, Richard Chase. 1982. Liberal ideology and indigenous communities in post-independence Peru. *Journal of International Affairs* 36, no. 1 (Spring/Summer): 73–83.

Sowden, William J. 1882. *The Northern Territory as it is.* Adelaide: W. K. Thomas & Co.

Solway, Jacqueline, and Richard Lee. 1990. Foragers, genuine or spurious? Situating the Kalahari San in history. *Current Anthropology* 31 (2): 109–46.

Spencer, Baldwin. 1914. *Native tribes of the Northern Territory of Australia.* London: Macmillan & Co.

———. 1928. *Wanderings in wild Australia.* London: Macmillan & Co.

Spillett, Peter. 1972. *Forsaken settlement: An illustrated history of the settlement of Victoria, Port Essington, North Australia, 1838–1849.* Melbourne: Landsdowne Press.

Stanner, W. E. H. 1933. The Daly River tribes: A report of fieldwork in North Australia. Parts 1, 2. *Oceania* 3, 4: 377–405, 10–29.

———. 1937. Aboriginal modes of address and reference in the north-west of the Northern Territory. *Oceania* 7 (3): 300–315.

———. 1965a. Aboriginal territorial organisation: Estate, range, domain, and regime. *Oceania* 36 (1): 1–26.

———. 1965b. Religion, totemism, and symbolism. In *Aboriginal man in Australia: Essays in honour of emeritus professor A. P. Elkin.* Ed. R. Berndt and C. Berndt, 207–237. Sydney: Angus & Robertson.

———. 1966. *On Aboriginal religion.* Oceania Monograph no. 11. Sydney: University of Sydney.

———. 1979. *White Man Got No Dreaming.* Canberra: Australian National University Press.

Stanton, John. 1983. Old business, new owners: Succession and "The Law" on the fringe of the western desert. In *Aboriginal land and land rights.* Ed. N. Peterson and M. Langton, 160–71. Canberra: Australian Institute of Aboriginal Studies.

Stocking, George. 1989. *Romantic motives: Essays on anthropological sensibility.* Madison: University of Wisconsin Press.

Stokes, J. Lort. 1846. *Discoveries in Australia,* vol. 2. London: T. & W. Boone.

Stoler, Ann L. 1985. *Capitalism and confrontation in Sumatra's plantation belt, 1870–1979.* New Haven, Conn.: Yale University Press.

———. 1991. Carnal knowledge and imperial power: Gender, race and morality in colonial Asia. In *Gender at the Cross Roads of Knowledge: Feminist Anthropology in the Postmodern Era.* Ed. M. di Leonardo, 51–101. Los Angeles: University of California Press.

Strathern, Marilyn. 1990. *The gender of the gift.* Berkeley and Los Angeles: University of California Press.

Strehlow, Theodore. 1971. *Songs of central Australia.* Sydney: Angus & Robertson.

Stubbs, Michael. 1983. *Discourse analysis: The sociolinguistic analysis of natural language.* Chicago: University of Chicago Press.

Sutton, Peter. 1980. Aboriginal groups and aboriginal land ownership. Paper prepared for Australian Institute of Aboriginal Studies. Biennial Conference, Canberra, May.

———. 1988. Myth as history, history as myth. In *Being black: Aboriginal culture in "settled" Australia.* Ed. Ian Keen, 251–68. Canberra: Australia Studies Press.

Sutton, Peter, and Bruce Rigsby. 1982. People with "politicks": Management of land and personnel on Australia's Cape York Peninsula. In *Resource managers: North American and Australian hunter-gatherers.* Ed. N. Williams and E. Hunn, 155–72. Canberra: Australian Institute of Aboriginal Studies.

Taylor, J. C. 1977. Diet, health and economy: Some consequences of planned social change in an Aboriginal community. In *Aborigines and change: Australia in the '70s.* R. M. Berndt, ed. Pp. 147–58. Canberra: Australia Institute of Aboriginal Studies.

Taylor, Penny, ed. 1988. *After 200 years: Photographic essays of Aboriginal and Islander Australia today.* Canberra: Aboriginal Studies Press.

Terdiman, Richard. 1985. Introduction to *Discourse/counter-discourse: The theory and practice of symbolic resistance in nineteenth-century France.* 25–84. Ithaca: N.Y.: Cornell University Press.

Testart, A. 1982. The significance of food storage among hunter-gatherers: Residence patterns, population densities, and social inequalities. *Current Anthropology* 23 (5): 523–37.

Theweleit, Klaus. 1987. *Male fantasies.* vol. 1: *Women, floods, bodies, history.* Minneapolis: University of Minnesota Press.

Thomas, S., and M. Corden. 1977. *Metric tables of the compositon of Austrlian foods,* rev. ed. Canberra: Australian Government Publishing Service.

Thomson, Donald. 1939. The seasonal factor in human culture. Paper no. 10. Reprint from the *Proceedings of the Prehistoric Society* for 1939 (July-December).

Thompson, E. P. 1975. *Whigs and hunters: The origin of the black act.* New York: Pantheon Books.

Toohey, John 1982a. *Daly River (Malak Malak) land claim.* Report by the Aboriginal Land Commissioner, Mr. Justice Toohey, to the Minister for Aboriginal Affairs and to the Administrator of the Northern Territory. Canberra: Australian Government Publishing Service.

———. 1982b. *Warlmanpa, Warlpiri, Mudbura and Warumungu land claim.* Report by the Aboriginal Land Commissioner, Mr. Justice Toohey, to the Minister for Aboriginal Affairs and to the Administrator of the Northern Territory. Canberra: Australian Government Publishing Service.

Trigger, D. 1987. Languages, linguistic groups and status relations at Domadgee, an Aboriginal settlement in north West Queensland, Australia. *Oceania* 57 (3): 217–38.

———. 1988. Christianity, domination, and resistance in colonial social relations: The case of Doomadgee. In *Aboriginal Australians and Christian missions.* Ed. Tony Swain and Deboarh Bird Rose, 213–35. Adelaide: Australian Association for the Study of Religion.

———. 1992. *Whitefella comin': Aboriginal responses to colonialism in nothern Australia.* Cambridge: Cambridge University Press.

Tryon, D. T. 1974. *Daly River family languages, Australia.* Pacific Linguistic Series C, no. 32. Canberra: Australian National University.

Tully, James. 1980. *A discourse on property: John Locke and his adversaries.* Cambridge: Cambridge University Press.

Turnbull, C. 1965. *The Mbuti Pygmies: An ethnographic survey.* New York: Anthropological Papers of the American Museum of Natural History.

Turner, David. 1974. *Tradition and Transformation: A study of Aborigines in the Groote Eylandt Area.* Canberra: Australian Institute of Aboriginal Studies.

Turner, T. 1979. Anthropology and the politics of indigenous people's struggles. *Cambridge Anthropology* 5: 1–43.

———. 1991. "We are parrots," "Twins are birds": Play of tropes as operational structure. In *Beyond metaphor: The theory of tropes in anthropology.* Ed. J. Fernandez, 121–58. Stanford, Calif.: Stanford University Press.

Turner, Victor. 1969. *The ritual process: Structure and anti-structure.* Chicago: Aldine.

Volosinov, V. N. 1973. *Marxism and the philosophy of language.* Cambridge, Mass.: Harvard University Press.

von Sturmer, J. R. 1978. *The Wik Region: Economy, territoriality and totemism in western Cape York Peninsula, north Queensland.* Ph.D. thesis. St. Lucia: University of Queensland.

———. 1981. Talking with Aborigines. *Australian Institute of Aboriginal Studies Newsletter* 15: 13–30.
Walsh, M. 1989. *The Wagaitj in relation to the Kenbi land claim area.* Darwin: Northern Land Council.
Watson-Gegeo, K. and G. White, eds. 1990. *Disentangling: Conflict discourse in Pacific societies.* Stanford, Calif.: Stanford University Press.
Weaver, Sally. 1984. Struggles of the nation-state to define Aboriginal ethnicity: Canada and Australia. In *Minorities and mother country imagery.* Ed. Gerald L. Gold, 182–210. Social and Economic Papers no. 13, Institute of Social and Economic Research, Memorial University of Newfoundland.
Weber, Max. 1958. *The Protestant ethic and the spirit of Capitalism.* Trans. Talcott Parsons. New York: Scribner.
White, Richard. 1981. *Inventing Australia: Images and identity, 1688–1980.* Sydney: Allen & Unwin.
Whitling, Richard. 1990. *Comment on the Darwin regional land use structure plan, 1990.* Darwin: Environment Centre.
Wilkinson, C. 1987. *American Indians, time and the law: Native societies in a modern constitutional democracy.* New Haven, Conn.: Yale University Press.
Williams, Nancy. 1982. A boundary is to cross: Observations on Yolngu boundaries and permission. In *Resource Managers: North American and Australian Hunter-Gatherers.* N. Williams and E. Hunn, eds. 131–154. Canberra: Australian Institute of Aboriginal Studies.
———. 1986. *The Yolngu and their land: A system of land tenure and the fight for its recognition.* Stanford, Calif.: Stanford University Press.
Williams, R. 1973. *The country and the city.* New York: Oxford University Press.
Wilmsen, Edwin. 1983. The ecology of illusion: Anthropological foraging in the Kalahari. *Reviews in Anthropology,* 10: 9–20.
———. 1989a. *Land filled with flies.* Chicago: University of Chicago Press.
———. 1989c. Those who have each other: San relations to land. In *We are here: Politics of Aboriginal land tenure.* Edwin N. Wilsem, 43–67. Berkeley: University of California Press.
———. 1989b. Introduction to *We are here: Politics of Aboriginal land tenure.* Ed. Edwin Wilmsen, 1–14. Berkeley and Los Angeles: University of California Press.
Winterhalder, Bruce. 1987. The analysis of hunter-gatherer diets: Stalking an optimal foraging model. In *Food and evolution: Towards a theory of human food habits.* Ed. M. Harris and E. Ross, 311–40. Philadelphia: Temple University Press.
Woenne, Susan Tod. 1977. Old country, new territory: Some implications of the settlement process. In *Aborigines and change: Australia in the '70s.* Ed. R. M. Berndt, 54–64. Canberra: Australian Institute of Aboriginal Studies.
Wolf, Eric. 1982. *Europe and the people without history.* Berkeley and Los Angeles: University of California Press.
Wolpe, Harold, ed. 1980. *The articulation of modes of production: Essays from economy and society.* London: Routledge & Kegan Paul.
Woodburn, James. 1980. Hunters and gatherers today and reconstruction of the

past. In *Soviet and Western anthropology.* Ed. E. Gellner. London: Duckworth.

———. 1982. Egalitarian societies. *Man* 17 (3): 431–51.

———. 1988. African hunter-gatherer social organization: Is it best understood as a product of encapsulation? In *Hunters and gatherers, I: History, evolution and social change.* Ed. T. Ingold, D. Riches, and J. Woodburn, 31–64. London: Berg.

Woolard, Kathryn. 1989. *Double talk: Bilingualism and the politics of ethnicity in Catalonia.* Stanford, Calif.: Stanford University Press.

Yesner, David. 1980. Maritime hunter-gatherers: Ecology and prehistory. *Current Anthropology* 21 (6): 727–50.

Yesner, David. 1987. Life in the "Garden of Eden": Causes and consequences of the adoption of marine diets by human societies. In *Food and evolution: Towards a theory of human food habits.* Ed. M. Harris and E. Ross 285–310. Philadelphia: Temple University Press.

Young, Elsbeth, and Kim Doohan. 1989. *Mobility for survival: A process analysis of Aboriginal population movement in Central Australia.* Darwin: North Australia Research Unit.

INDEX

aboriginal freehold land, 23, 166
aboriginal heritage: as cultural repository, 123; and educational process, 107, 109
aboriginal identity: appropriation of, 91–92; and hunter-gatherer practice, 27; and nation-state, 13, 23, 28, 53, 66, 137, 217, 241–42; symbols of, 2–3
Aboriginal Land Rights (Northern Territory) Act, 1976: anthropologists' influence on, 10; assessment of Aboriginal action, 3, 53–54, 79, 241; and development, 236; and land appropriation, 166; and land tenure, 135, 205, 276n, 289n; and mining, 201; and nontraditional owners, 58; and outstation movement, 207; and sociocultural mandate, 28; and tourism industry, 218. *See also* land rights legislation
Aboriginal Ordinance of 1918, 101
Aboriginal Sacred Sites Act, 1978, 276n
Aboriginal and Torres Strait Islander Heritage Protection Act, 1982, 276n
aboriginal traditions, definition of, 54–55
addiction, 199, 194, 200; race and gender, 100–101
African hunter-gatherers: land appropriation, 8; land rights, 244; colonial violence, 83. *See also* indigenous groups
Alaskan Native Claims Settlement Act, 275n
alchemy, and understanding of nature, 6
alcoholism: and aboriginal identity, 128; cultural notion of, 198–201; and descriptions of the past, 67, 119–20; expenditure on, 185, 191, 193–95; and social disturbance, 207–8, 223–24, 292n
alienation, 156; of workers from goods, 215

Altman, Jon: conversion tables, 18, 178; economy, 274–75, 292; population figures, 169; saving strategies, 60, 291; seasonal round, 233, 241; social stress, 207–8; tourism, 201, 217–18, 244; work-leisure ratios, 185–86
Anderson, Benedict, 66
animism, 6
Anson Bay, 64, 160; history of, 71–74, 81–84, 98
Appadurai, Arjun, 1, 242
articulation: of Aboriginal action and meaning, 168–69, 242–43; of comparative laws, 250; of human-land relations, 138, 167; of modes of production, 295n; of world landscapes, 137
Asad, Talal, 125
Asche, Michael, 244
Asians: effect on Aboriginal culture, 75; and ethnic violence, 70, 216; as immigrant labor pool, 216; and land rights orientation, 220; Northern Territory economic ties, 220; and "white Australian" policy, 216–17, 293–94n
Augustine, Saint, 278n
Australian Heritage Commission Act, 1974, 276n
Australian Workers Union, 217
autonomy: and ethnic relations, 197–98; and foods, 242; and gender, 189; ideology of, 172, 197–98; and outstation movement, 208

Bakhtin, M. M., 133
Barker, Graham, 23, 135–36, 140, 143, 147, 277, 289
Basedow, Herbert, 72–73, 75–76, 79, 160, 280, 283–84

Basso, Keith, 240
Beckett, Jeremy, 2, 28, 55, 106, 194
bedagut, 129, 190, 221, 237, 285–87n
being greedy, 178–80, 195, 197, 199. *See also* principles for speaking
being satisfied, 196–97, 199–200, 205, 237. *See also* principles for speaking
Bell, Diane, 5, 189, 241, 278, 280, 289
Belyuen Kenbi Corroboree Crew, 233
Berndt, Catherine, 15, 29, 170, 189, 289, 292
Berndt, Ronald: dreaming, 10, 109, 274; traditional aboriginal owner, 29; Aboriginal economy, 97, 170, 292; rights to land, 134, 157–58, 278
Bhabha, Homi, 28, 242
Biernoff, David, 153, 187
Bird-David, Nuit, 26, 185, 273, 291
birthmarks, 141. *See also* conception; *maroi*
body: cultural conception of, 141; and cultural value, 160, 239, 241; health of, 152; and mythic landscape, 140, 146–47, 151–52, 165–66; social history embedded in, 143
boiya, 161
Bourdieu, Pierre, 1
Boyle, Robert, 6
Brandl, Maria: Belyuen cosmology, 73, 134, 150, 264, 270, 295n; Belyuen economy, 60, 178; Belyuen history, 88, 205–6; Belyuen politics, 2, 46
Brennis, Donald, 34, 110, 196, 254, 277
British Association for the Advancement of Science, 75
bulpul, 148

capitalism, 196; development in Australia, 211–12; industrial to late, 242
Carter, Paul, 80
cash: flow, 196; royalties, 201; supply, 180; surplus, 200–201; tax rebates, 201
Certeau, Michel de, 169
Clifford, James, 17, 77, 273, 279
code-switching: and human-land interaction, 151; metacommentary on ethnic relations, 53; and politics of land claims, 54. *See also* ways of speaking
coercion: cultural, 105, 251; economic, 196; labor, 204. *See also* domination; hegemony

coincident use rights, 283n
collateral, 194
colonial violence: history of, 2, 65, 80–84, 135; and mythic relations, 151
Comaroff, Jean, 13–14, 278
Comaroff, John, 13–14, 278
commercial fishing, 2, 174, 222
commercial products: Aborigines as, 66, 217; and colonization, 76; purchase of, 185, 193–94; social costs of, 207
commodities: Aborigines as, 218; cultural, 14; definition of, 25; discursive use of, 86, 192, 213, 215, 220; and landscapes, 212; and labor congealed in, 25–26, 137, 152; orientation of urban Aborigines to, 55
common spiritual affiliation, 29–30, 245
Community Employment Program, 171
comparative law: in social anthropology, 9–10; and Aboriginal dialogue with nation-state, 238, 246, 250
complex division of labor, 7. *See also* labor-action; modes of production; work
conception: cultural construction of, 31, 73, 136, 139–47, 149, 151; and gender, 16; and land rights legislation, 29, 58, 166. *See also maroi*
convict labor, 211–12, 216
convicts and colonial violence, 83
Cook, C. E., 88
Country Liberal Party, 218
Cox Peninsula Land Use Structure Plan, 1990, 205, 292n
credit, 195, 200–201
Cronon, William, 212, 279
cultural ecology, 13
cultural editing, 126–28
cultural encyclopedia, 47, 56
cultural identity: and authenticity, 1, 4–5, 74–84, 106, 127; and the body, 74, 194; and difference, 123–24, 127–29, 191, 201, 218, 227; and economic practice, 26–27, 66, 84, 106, 133–67, 176, 181, 186, 190–91, 197–98, 225–27, 232, 240, 282n; and history, 65–129, 176, 286n; legal implications of, 27–28, 63, 72, 78–80, 103–4, 139; and nation-state, 1–3, 11–12, 14, 23–24, 65–66, 91–92, 209, 217, 241–43; per-

formance of, 2, 3, 74–80, 106–29; and power, 3, 24, 125, 239, 273n; and talk, 34–53, 75, 188; and urban Aborigines, 55, 120. *See also* speech acts
cultural mediation, 13, 124; and knowledge/power, 76, 176; and the nation-state, 56
cultural studies, 24
cultural topography, 47, 51; and the body, 67, 78, 135–36; and hunting action, 155; and mythic sites, 161; plotting, 147

Daly, Harriet, 81–82, 215–16
Daly River: Aborigines and labor practices, 86, 154–55; cultural systems, 147, 151; history of, 40, 68, 91, 100, 110, 198, 212; language groups, 2, 23, 134; representations of groups, 65, 70–74; royalties from, 201; violence in, 79–84, 161–62
Daly River Mission, 161, 289n
danggalaba, 44, 54, 140, 161, 164, 171
debt, 194, 197–98; and repayment, 200–201
delayed return societies, 25, 186, 275n
De Lissa, M., 84, 87, 89, 205, 220, 284n
demand sharing, 198
Department of Lands, 207
Department of Native Welfare, 91, 93, 106, 205
dependency: economic, 24, 35, 86; and gender relations, 76, 189; of Northern Territory on south Australia, 214, 219, 294n; positive function in human-land relations, 197
detriment hearings, in Aboriginal land claims, 58, 60
development: of Cox Peninsula, 192, 203, 205, 207–21, 224, 292–93n; as discursive framework, 4, 27, 83, 166, 192, 203, 224, 236–38, 250; and land claim process, 59–60, 62
dialectics: of action and identity, 1; of knowledge, 56, 240, 279n; and productivity, 250
dialogical nature: of Aboriginal action, 5; of contemporary Aboriginal society, 137, 250–51
dialogue: Aboriginal and nation-state, 9, 27; and cultural association, 14
di Leonardo, Micaela, 273, 277

dispersal, 71, 83, 274n, 280n, 282–83n
domination, 1, 12, 14, 105; cultural, 125. *See also* coercion; resistance
Donham, Donald, 7, 14, 274, 295
Dreaming: cultural construction of, 133–67, 234, 274n; and cultural performance, 125; historical locations of, 73; historical portraits of, 9–11; and politics of speech acts, 45–47. *See also durlg; maroi; therrawin;* totemic relationships
durlg: cultural meanings of, 139, 143, 147–52, 240, 278n, 280n; and descent totems, 31, 68, 73, 235; and narrative, 37, 114; and time, 167, 237; tracks, 160–61, 165, 221

ecological knowledge: of Belyuen Aborigines, 134, 144; and gender power, 187–88; and mythic knowledge, 187; and politics, 166
ecology, of Cox Peninsula, 173–75, 180, 290n
economic policy, 12, 171–73, 205–6, 210–21
economic practice: discursive uses of, 11–12, 75, 133, 176, 192; and dreaming, 136, 142–67; and social regulation, 14, 65, 84–103, 106, 198, 200, 205–6, 283n; and the traditional aboriginal owner, 28–30; and world system, 27, 127, .195, 232. *See also* cultural identity; labor-action
efficiency: of labor, 6, 224; and mode of transportation, 234
Elkin, A. P.: Daly River totemism, 31, 73, 139, 141, 147–49, 156, 160–62, 284n, 286n, 289n, 292n, 294–95n; and Bill Harney, 89; territories of Daly River groups, 72 73, 84, 161–62
embodiment: of economic practice, 139; of *maroi* into fetus, 142–43; and social history, 145, 152; and spirits of the dead, 152, 162–63
empathy, 157
Engels, Friedrich, 7
Enloe, Cynthia, 195, 217
epistemology: definition of, struggle over, 248–49; divergent, 13; feminist, 249–50; resistant, 251; Yolngu, 295n. *See also* feminist epistemology; social study of science

ethnicity: cultural evaluation, 243, 250; and economic practice, 191; and land conflict, 168, 204, 208; and mythic reaction, 154; and violence, 216, 234, 278n

evaluation: cultural, 11–12, 30, 35, 55, 66, 78–86, 103–29; and gender, 124, 188; of historical origins, 3–4, 70–103; of knowledge, 243–52; legal, 3–4, 6–8, 14, 24, 35, 103, 239–51; and legislation, 78–80, 124–29; and resistance, 14, 27; socioeconomic, 3–4, 7, 11–12, 30, 168–69, 176, 204–5, 210–11, 237, 250–51. *See also* measurement; work

exegesis, of mythic texts, 10

exogamy, 29

Fabian, Johannes, 160
Falkenberg, J., 31, 141, 143
false consciousness, 246
family history, 36, 105
Fanon, Franz, 125
feminist epistemology, 249
feminist theory, 189, 249, 273n, 277n. *See also* gender
fifth branch of government, 205
Finniss River, 90
Finniss River Land Claim, 58
Fischer, M., 17, 23
Foelsche, Paul, 71, 74, 77–78, 281, 284
food preference model, 180–81
forage as of right, 29–30, 277n
Foucault, Michel, 13, 70, 279
four stages theory, 7, 9–10
Fourth World: property and human rights, 8, 24, 28; resistant knowledges, 12–13. *See also* indigenous groups
framing devices, 147. *See also* ways of speaking
freedom of the market: on Cox Peninsula, 194–95; and labor, 290. *See also* markets
Friedrich, Paul, 26, 240

Geertz, Clifford, 251
gender: cultural texts, women's, 15, 119, 156, 199, 284n; and drinking, 199–200; perceptions of labor-action, 14–17, 151, 156–59; and race, 15, 76, 101, 199; and welfare, 170–71; and work, 35, 100–101, 143, 183–85, 188–92, 196, 280n, 286n, 289–91n

genealogy, 36, 145; and land claim process, 245–49
Giddens, Anthony, 127
Gluckman, Max, 9
Godelier, Maurice, 274
Goodale, Jane, 181, 280, 289
Gordon, Robert, 217, 244, 273
greed. *See being greedy*
Gumbert, Marc, 29, 244
Gumperz, John, 34, 146

Hamilton, Annette: Aborigines and Asians, 70, 215; cultural appropriation, 2, 66, 85; gender, 15–16, 189, 280, 289–90; land ownership and conception, 29, 143; land politics, 137
Harney, Bill, 73, 89–93, 100–101, 198, 209, 231, 284–85
Haviland, John, 34, 274
Healy, J. J., 91, 284, 288
hegemony, 8, 246, 293n; economic, 12; and knowledge, 13, 250; and sociocultural practices, 125, 274n, 285n. *See also* evaluation; domination
Hercus, Luise, 15, 76
Hiatt, L. R.: myth, 142; land ownership, 9, 29, 277, 279–80; outstation movement, 207; politics, 27, 33–34, 134, 197–98
historical anthropology, 13–14
Hobbes, Thomas, 6
Hobsbawm, Eric, 106
Hocking, Barbara, 24, 55, 214, 275
Hughes, Robert, 70, 83, 211, 279
human-land relations: and gender, 15, 32; signs of, 135–36, 138, 140–67, 186, 236, 239–40; and talk, 43–47. *See also* hunter-gatherers; labor-action; signs; work
hunter-gatherers: class model, 5, 273n; foraging model, 5, 11, 146, 160, 185–86, 210, 273n, 294n; and Fourth World, 8, 24; and law, 28, 30–31, 58–63, 222, 251, 283n; portraits of, 1, 3–4, 9–14, 23–24, 26–27, 85–86, 126–29, 165, 189, 212–13, 242, 273–74n, 284n; and productivity, 23, 25–27, 60, 176–92; subsistence economy, 3, 5, 60, 175, 210; supplemental economy, 86, 103, 204, 274n; surplus production, 190; technology, 173, 175, 234. *See also* human-land relations; hunting band; labor-action

INDEX   325

hunting and gathering: spatial aspects, 203–4, 219, 221–38; temporal aspects, 181–92, 224, 227
hunting and gathering discourse: and cultural identity, 127; and dreaming, 139, 143–44, 166; and land claim, 59–63; and mediation of land conflict, 34, 210, 215, 217; and politics, 28, 31, 52–53, 219, 251
hunting band: flexible nature of, 136, 165; Northern Territory economy as, 220

ideology of land use: and land claim hearings, 28, 62; political entanglements, 164, 208; prescriptive nature of human-land relations, 142; and working for country, 135–36, 143–44, 223
ignoble savage, 70, 76, 275n
immediate return societies, 25, 186, 275n
indexicality: and conception dreamings, 140; in interpretive process of human-land relations, 135, 158; and land-management, 46; of person and event, 36, 192; and value, 240
indigenous groups: and African and American dreamings, 138, 150; and international conflicts, 1, 13, 211, 220, 275–76n; and law, 246, 248–51
indigenous practice: contemporary motivations of, 229; evaluation of, 213, 241–44; and identity, 24; and meaning, 1–2, 13
indigenous property law, 9
infrastructure: and economic development, 208–10; outstation, 223–24
Ingold, Tim: intentionality, 8, 25, 137, 141, 288n; subsistence economy, 3, 26
ingyarainy, 161
institutions, educational, 105–20; and evaluation, 12, 243; and gender, 15
integrated system, 27
intentionality: and the dreaming, 47, 138, 140–41, 150; and labor-action, 1, 6–7, 26, 137, 141, 145–46, 288n; and manufacturing, 12; and property, 7–8, 25–26; and reproduction, 142
intentional making, 7–8, 25, 146
interpretation: of event and meaning, 1, 6, 154, 192, 237; of human-land relations, 135–36, 146–47, 158; of identity, 77; and mythic process, 140; of social geography, 204

interpretive anthropology, 5, 10–13
invented traditions, 106

James Bay Agreement, 275n
Jameson, Fredrick, 242
JanMohamed, Abdul, 125
Jasanoff, Sheila, 14, 205, 295
Jawoyn, 30, 55
Johnson v. MacIntosh, 244
join-up, 164–65, 262, 281n

Kaberry, P., 140, 143, 189
Kakadu National Park: and royalties, 201; and tourism, 225
kanggalang, 44
Katherine Gorge: and royalties, 201; and tourism, 218, 225
Keen, Ian, 29, 276–77, 287
kenbi, 48, 54, 165, 176
Kenbi Land Claim, 28, 35, 46, 52, 54–57, 79, 104, 106, 125, 134, 140–41, 144–45, 150, 153–54, 175, 183, 187, 191, 203, 205, 210, 244–50, 276–78n
Ku Klux Klan, 119
knowledge: and authenticity, 57, 66–84, 103, 127; and context, 51; cultural performance of, 51, 75, 201–2; and experience, 187; and power, 1–4, 13–14, 33–34, 44–46, 51, 66–84, 109, 181, 187–89, 243–51, 274–78n; processual nature of, 148–49; and property, 1, 29, 31, 34, 44, 46, 51–53, 80, 134, 157, 181, 218, 237–38, 277–78n; and talk, 31–53, 103–29. *See also* cultural identity; speech acts
koinme, 48
kugon, 161
kunaberruk, 233
kurraguk, 161

labor-action: applied hermeneutics of, 25; cultural discourses of, 6, 12–14, 26, 94, 133–67, 186–92, 203, 237, 241–43, 291n; definition of, 27, 274n; forced, 173, 221, 231, 274n, 290n; historical records of, 86–87, 92–103; in hunter-gatherer discourse, 4, 6–7, 25–26, 154; and legislative frameworks, 11, 24, 243–44; and market, 194–202; productive power of, 26, 168–69, 186; and property, 16, 25–26, 74; and value, 4.

labor-action (*continued*)
  See also human-land relations; hunter-gatherer; productivity; value; work
land: blocked, 223, 229–30; closed, 224; empty, 203, 210
land appropriation, 173–74, 208–9; and Aboriginal settlements, 89–90, 166–67, 222–23; and agriculture, 85; and colonization, 220; and cultural cohesion, 124; discursive use of, 199; and law, 227, 250, 283n
land claims: and cultural cohesion, 51, 104, 137; and developmental discourse, 205, 220; Kenbi, 35, 57; international, 24, 211, 244; structure of, 28–30, 145. *See also* Kenbi Land Claim; Finniss River Land Claim
land commissioner: evaluative function of, 28–30, 56, 79–80, 248–49, 276–77n; Kenbi, 35, 52, 54, 62–63, 245
land councils, 28–29, 46, 54, 60, 62, 188, 201, 276n
land ownership: and Aboriginal Land Rights (Northern Territory) Act, 1976, 28–30, 218; and corporate group, 2–3, 15–16, 29, 36, 53, 136, 139–40, 277n, 289n; and gender, 15–16; interethnic discussions of, 1–3, 28, 104, 133–35; and managers, 125, 172, 186, 197; orthodox model of, 29, 72, 74; and rights and duties, 148
land rights legislation: and evaluation of indigenous practice, 27–28, 127, 220; and Fourth World, 24; and state domination, 1, 3–4, 11, 63, 204, 222, 275–76n; and tourism, 218
land sentiment: influence on action, 166, 172, 198, 234–35; and land appropriation, 78, 208; and land claims, 62–63; sociocultural meanings of, 91, 100, 138, 146, 157, 163; and speech practice, 30, 43–44, 114
land succession, 134–35, 287n
land tenure, 14, 29, 66, 208; primary and secondary rights, 134, 238, 287n
land use, 11, 24, 33, 119, 135, 205
land use and cultural meaning, 74, 110, 134–36, 139–67, 174, 186, 203–5, 233, 239
land users: bands and hordes, 29, 279; of Cox Peninsula, non-Aboriginal, 203–4, 210–21

language: and conception, 140; group, 29, 54, 58, 72, 157, 161, 186, 201, 232, 270, 277n; and group identity, 31–32, 43, 46, 88, 127–28; and proprietary rights, 33–34, 53, 66, 72–73, 153, 172; and sentient landscape, 16, 45–46, 147, 151–60, 174, 218. *See also* speech acts; ways of speaking
Latour, Bruno, 295
Lee, Richard, 3, 26, 135, 273, 275, 281
legisign, 135
leisure, meaning of, 11, 26, 63, 169, 185–92, 203
letharrgun, 59, 278n
liberal state, 24, 242
Liberman, Kenneth, 34, 110
life-style, 53–58, 74–75, 91–92, 208–9
linguistic competence: Belyuen Aborigines', in Daly River, 154–55; Belyuen and *nyoitj*, 163; country's, 44
local descent group, 29, 58, 63, 79, 245, 276n
local knowledge, 109, 251
Locke, John, 6, 25, 214, 275

Maddock, Kenneth, 29, 125, 244, 276, 278
mal, 33, 53, 114, 147, 152
malarritj, 158
malnutrition, 178, 207
Mandorah Land Use Structure Plan, 1990, 292n
Maori, colonial violence, New Zealand, 83
Marcus, G., 17, 23
markets, 168; contribution to Belyuen diet, 176, 178–79; relationship to hunting, 185–86, 233; use of, 192–202, 242
maroi, 31; historical records of, 73; and labor-action, 134, 139–47, 149–52, 165–67, 237; and land-use, 235, 265, 277n; and value, 240. *See also* conception
Marxism, 13, 277n; and bodies of commodities, 25; and hunting and gathering, 210, 295n; and labor value, 7–8, 215
measurement, of hunter-gatherer productivity, 27, 168–69, 185–92. *See also* evaluation; work
medawok, 233–34
mediation: Aboriginal self-knowledge and nation-state, 56; commercial, 76; cul-

tural meaning and action, 13, 133; economic, 10–11, 200; human relations by land, 43; of social violence, 160–61; and speech acts, 4; totemic knowledge and history, 148–49
Meehan, Betty, 18, 177, 233, 275, 291
Meggitt, M., 143, 264, 279
Meillassoux, Claude, 7, 26
memoradjamul, 161
menggin, 41, 43
Merlan, Francesca, 2, 137; assessment of Aboriginal action and identity, 5, 28–29, 133; conception, 140–43; and gender, 189; language and land, 32, 66, 137, 153
merrumerru, 161
metaphor: and body, 166; for cultural economy, 26, 32; for hunting and markets, 176–77, 189; and metonymy, 140, 240; and spirits of the dead, 163; for value, 148, 239
metonymy: and conception, 140; and cultural economy, 26, 240; and naming practices, 240; and narrative, 120
migrants: and land claim, 58; and cultural history, 163. *See also* squatting
mining: economic importance to Northern Territory, 214, 216–17; and effect on hunting, 174; media campaign, 220; and tourism, 217
Mintz, Sidney, 8, 292
mirr, 277n
missionaries: and cultural hegemony, 125, 286–87; and ignoble savage, 76
missions: conditions on Aboriginal, 207; versus government settlements, 92
mixing: ceremonies, 72–73, 78–79, 264, 268–70, 281n; people and practices, 3, 19, 67, 72, 74, 101, 164, 261, 263–70; land appropriation, 78–80, 279n
miya, 181
mode of transportation, 183, 197, 207, 223, 230; and "seasonal round," 234–35
modes of production: advanced, 6; articulation of, 295; discursive use of, 143–44, 165, 236; foraging, 3, 5–6, 25, 60, 62; precapitalist, 8; and property, 11, 25, 135. *See also* hunter-gatherers
moiyin, 161
monetary system, 195
Montague, George, 83, 282–83

Morphy, Francis and Howard, 276, 278
Morris, Barry, 3, 135, 274
Muecke, Stephen, 51, 243
mungarra, 59
munggul, 119, 162, 230
Munn, Nancy, 289n, 295n; conception, 141; country as subject, 26, 133, 137, 148, 288n; land orientation, 43–44; sign-function, 135
Murray, Jack, 90, 92–93, 100, 102–3, 209
Myers, Fred: autonomy, 197, 242; conception, 141; emotions, 156, 287–88n; history, 144; hunter-gatherer studies, 5, 24–29, 186, 244, 275n; land ownership, processual nature of, 16, 43–44, 52, 134–38, 240, 245, 264, 278–80n, 289n; metaphors of value, 148; property, 177, 224, 236; tourism, 171; value, 241, 290n

name-sharing, 31, 43, 73, 149, 151. *See also ngirrwat;* nicknames; placenames
narrative: and the body, 140, 144–45; and colonial land appropriation, 80; and the dreaming, 138, 140, 147, 186, 240; and history, 65, 92, 98, 103–29, 144–45, 176, 186, 204, 235–36, 282n; and law, 104–5, 110, 165, 187–88, 241; and sexuality, 100–101; and social context, 78, 104–29; and socioeconomic relations, 86, 92–103, 157, 164, 187, 199, 204; and time, 105–6, 117–29, 147, 187. *See also* speech acts
national symbolic, 28, 242; and imagery, 3
Native American: land rights, 211, 244; violent relations with U.S. government, 83, 283n. *See also* indigenous groups; land rights legislation
need-based land claims, 29, 277n; limited, as discursive frame, 199; production of, 198, 200. *See also being satisfied*
neoclassical economics, 8–9, 186, 210
New Science, 6, 12
ngapa, 115
ngirrwat, 31, 43, 73, 277n. *See also* name-sharing
nicknames, 148
no more like, as framing device, 196–97. *See also* principles of speaking
Northern Territory Education Department, 171

Northern Territory (Self Government) Act, 1978, 218
nyoitj, 162–63, 237

Olgas, and tourism, 218
ontology: and orientation of speech, 52; and people's relation to sites, 44, 187; and politics of dreaming, 138, 143
open land, 203, 224
optimal foraging moment, 237
original affluent society, 26, 185
original man, 25
origins: Aborigines and nation-state, 14, 66, 242; of Belyuen groups, 4, 134–36; of knowledge, Belyuen, 47, 164, Aboriginal, 55, 57–58, 137, 244, 249; land, as origin of value, 241; and succession, 134
Ortner, Sherry, 13, 187
outstations, Belyuen, 227–37; and cultural identity, 129; maintenance of, 221–24; movement, 207

palimpsests, and history, 65
pastoral policy, 204, 215–17, 219
pederra, 158, 162, 230
perrk, 233
Peterson, Nicholas: commodity orientation, 55, 170–71, 218, 281n; delayed-return society, 186; Fourth World, 24, 28, 244; land rights, 273n, 275n; land-use, 146; politics of locality, 133–35, 137, 143, 289n
place-names: appropriation of, 209–10; and history, 176; local practice, 148; and trauma, 231
Pleistocene foragers, 10
plot, Aboriginal economy, 233; and narrative, 147; and social history, 144–47; and value, 43, 240. *See also* narrative; ways of speaking
political-economic anthropology, 5–6, 8–9, 11–14
political economy: of Aboriginal and nation-state interaction, 239–43; of cultural exchange, 124–25, 202; cultural underpinning of, 12, 211, 217; and knowledge/power, 2, 76, 127–29; and land appropriation, 221, 229; and models of hunter-gatherer productivity, 5–14, 25, 85, 87, 103, 169, 186, 215, 217; of Northern Territory, 210, 220; and violence, 83. *See also* labor-action; productivity
politics of locality, 137, 277n; country versus sacred site, 164; and land claims, 246; and orientation in space, 143, 145.
population: of Belyuen community, 169–70; of Northern Territory, 216–17; increasing pressure of, 222
Powell, Alan, 89, 101–2, 204, 211, 213–14, 280–81, 293
pragmatics, 10, 29, 47, 220
primary spiritual responsibility, 29–30, 136, 245
principles for speaking: *being straight for,* and disputes, 246;—, and turn-taking, 36; *being part of,* and disputes, 246;—, and turn-taking, 36; *being there,* and "bums on sand" test, 222;—, and disputes, 246;—; and politics of locality, 147, 225;—; and turn-taking, 36; *no more like,* as framing device, 196–97. *See also being greedy; being satisfied*
private speculators, in Northern Territory, 212–14, 216
productivity: assessment of, 30–31; of body, 30, 60, 165; cultural framework of, 1–2, 134–67, 170, 185–92; economic, 4–5, 31, 60, 156, 159, 168, 170, 234; and proprietary rights, 25, 134; signs of, 135–37; of speech and sweat, 133–67, 172, 174, 218; symbolic, 13, 85, 239; western models of, 12. *See also* evaluation; measurement
property: evolution of, 9; historical model of Aboriginal, 71–74; indigenous and nation-state, 8, 210, 241, 243–44; and intentional labor, 7, 214;
proprietary interest, 10–12, 24
public access, 169

Radcliffe-Brown, A., 9, 29, 66
Rainbow Snake, 147
Ranger, Terence, 106, 125
reciprocity, human and land, 46
Reece, R., 66, 101, 280
relatedness: circularity of, 241; of humans and land, 138, 147, 242, 295n; manipulation of, 198; and value, 239
rent, 14, 172, 196
residence, 134–35, 146, 149, 172, 197, 220

resistance: and accommodation, 106–7, 204, 245–49; colonial, 102; and domination, 14, 35–36; of nation-state's definition of labor, 241; of white encroachment, 222–23, 236–37. *See also* domination
resource allocation, 223–24, 234, 237
resource availability, 110, 221
revisionists, 273n
Reynolds, Henry, 66, 70
Ricardo, David, 215
Ricouer, Paul, 240
Ridington, Robin, 274, 278
Rose, Deborah Bird, 279, 283, 286, 288
Roseberry, William, 3, 8, 65, 77, 106
Rowley, C. D., 92, 97, 204
Rubin, Gayle, 171

sacred site registration, 31, 42, 158
Sahlins, Marshall: original affluent society, 26, 160, 185; *Stone Age Economics*, 160; structural history, 13–14, 67, 186
Said, Edward, 17
Sansom, Basil, 47; land rights, 277n, 287n; narrative, 147; shared experience, 43, 103, 120; siege, 162, 286n; ways of speaking, 34, 110;
satisfied. *See* principles for speaking
Saussure, Ferdinand de, 242
saving, 178–80, 200–201
Scott, James, 35, 251
seasonal round, 233–36
sentient landscape: and labor-action, 1, 4–5, 8–9, 11–12, 31–33, 133–67, 189–91; and sweat-language, 45, 52–53, 133–67; and tourism, 217–18; versus western notions of land, 7, 155–57, 217. *See also* labor-action; language; sweat; work
settler cosmology, 2, 220–21
sex, 193; and land politics, 33, 154, 157–59
sex-gender system, 171
sexuality: and dreaming process, 142, 157–59; and racial discourse, 100–102, 199, 285n; and racial violence, 119, 173, 231
Shapiro, Michael, 135, 239, 278
sharing, 178–80, 200–201. *See also being satisfied*; *being greedy*
shell midden, and social memory, 246

signs: of Aborigines, 68; of cultural appropriation, 209; of cultural authenticity, 190; of cultural purchase, 77; of cultural transformation, 88; environmental, 233; of land intentionality, 33, 134–35, 137, 139–40, 145–48, 156–57, 163, 186, 188; and value, 240, 242
Silverstein, Michael, 295
sing: and mythic action, 10; and sorcery, 43, 158; and *walakantha*, 163
sinsign, 135
small-scale communities, 18, 34
Smith, Adam, 215
Smith, Ramsey W., 75, 124, 281
social change, 119, 149
social geography: and cultural action, 159; and land appropriation, 89; and land use strategy, 203, 208, 211, 225, 237; and resistance narratives, 103–4. *See also* cultural topography; social history
social history: and the body, 143, 145; and cultural identity, 176; discursive use of, 65, 198; and ideology of work, 144; and narrative, 144–47, 164; of non-Aborigines in Northern Territory, 204; and totemic process, 135–37, 142
social relations of production, 223
social security benefits, 60; distribution of, 170–71. *See also* unemployment benefits; welfare
social stasis, 149
social study of science, 205, 249
sovereignty, 249
special rights, 55
speech acts: and gender, 15–16; 191–92; and history, 17, 104–29, 173, 233; and identity, 4, 17, 75, 176, 186, 242–43; interethnic, 25, 104–29, 167, 241; and knowledge, 31–53, 104, 125, 167, 187–89; and land interaction, 144, 151, 163, 166, 240; and law, 104–5, 243; narrative principles, 36, 94. *See also* code-switching; framing devices; narrative; ways of speaking
Spencer, Baldwin, 71–72, 78–79, 145, 280
squatters: and development of the Northern Territory, 208–212, 214–17, 220–221, 293–94n; and land appropriation, 174, 222, 224, 232, 279n; and land claim, 58. *See also* migrants
stagnation, 205

Stanner, W. E. H.: the Dreaming, 133, 141, 241, 274n; land ownership, 2, 29, 66, 136, 277n; land use, 145, 233, 275n; sign-function, 33, 135, 137, 141; social regulation, 9–10; social transformation, 76, 106; speech practices, 110
Stocking, George, 279
Stokes, J. L., 68, 70, 80
Stone Age people, 87; rites of, 11; traditions of, 210
straight: and economic practice, 190; and land politics, 136, 143; narrative device, 47, 50–51, 164, 265, 268; and sharing, 179. *See also* principles for speaking
Strehlow, T., 143, 240
strength of attachment, 30, 62, 220, 277n
structural-functionalism, 210
subaltern knowledge, 12–13
subjectivity: commodification of Aboriginal, 75, 85, 105, 115; and hunter-gatherers, 8–9, 47, 143; human and nonhuman, 7, 26, 137; and intentionality, 7, 137; and property, 8–9, 11
Sutton, Peter: identity, politics of, 23, 27, 78, 135, 246, 295n; land ownership, 16, 43; history, 105, 134, 144, 290n; political structure, 197, 280n
swallowing and regurgitating, and economic practice, 142–43
sweat: and group identity, 31–32; and proprietary rights, 33–34, 172; and sentient landscape, 45–46, 52, 54, 62, 140, 151–60, 174, 218, 227. *See also* labor-action; sentient landscape; work
sweeten, 32, 194–96, 198, 218, 227
synecdochy, 240; and corporeal and cultural decay, 74; and ethnic relations, 175

Taylorism, 6
Terdiman, Richard, 17
terra nullius, 9, 11, 214, 220
Territory Parks and Wildlife Conservation Act, 1988, 276n
theft, 232
therrawin, 37, 42, 44, 149, 176, 259, 277–78n
Theweleit, Klaus, 281n
Thompson, E. P., 283
tjeingithut, 35, 43, 153, 156–57, 199, 249
totemic descent, 16, 147; and Land Right (NT) Act, 1976, 30; patrilineal and matrilineal, 31, 134, 145
totemic relationship, 10–11, 31, 134; among Belyuen families, 161; and conception, 134, 142, 149; and prefiguring will, 163–64; and transfer of rights and duties, 136, 151
totemic site, 140, 144
totemic tracks, 136, 160–61
tourism: appropriation of Aboriginality, 2, 127, 217–19, 242, 244; Belyuen engagement in, 171, 173, 194–95, 201, 225–26, 233, 287n; and Land Councils, 276n; and Northern Territory economy, 208, 211, 217–19, 239
trackers, 102–3
traditional Aboriginal owner, 60, 62, 73, 172, 277n; definition of, 28–30, 58; politics of, 23, 44, 53, 136, 144, 208, 242, 245, 278n
traditional evidence, in Aboriginal land claims, 58, 60, 245
trauma: of country by foreigners, 153–54, 156; embedded in landscapes and names, 231; of people, 156, 234–35
travel narratives, 80–84
tricksters: Aboriginal, 68; European, 70
Trigger, Bruce, 3, 66, 278–79, 285–86, 295
Turner, Terry, 140, 244
Turner, Victor, 19

Uluru (Ayers Rock): and national identity, 2, 218; and royalties, 201; and tourism economy, 217–18
unemployment benefits: distribution of, 170–71; and extension of credit, 200; and gender discourse, 191

value: and association, 4–5, 14, 32–33, 143, 239, 241; cultural constructions of, 6–8, 11–12, 138, 186, 218, 239, 242, 244; and cultural knowledge, 75; and intentionality, 8; and labor, 75, 97–98, 136–67, 215, 288n; metaphors of, 148; and property, 7, 210, 212, 214, 220
video, 124
Volosinov, V. N., 278

Wadeye (Port Keats), 2, 23, 144
wagaitj, 209

Wagait Residential Development, 117, 172, 194, 198, 209
wage labor, 211, 280n; Belyuen engagement in, 14, 85–87, 170–71, 173; effect on hunting, 185, 234; and notion of labor, 26
Walsh, Michael: succession, 134, 295n; language, 159, 288–89n; land ownership, 2, 73, 264, 270
wangga, 161
Wariyn, 52, 148, 154, 176
ways of speaking, 34, 43, 104–5, 196, 240; agreement-disagreement, 254, 256; code-switching, 151, 261; direct-indirect, 34, 110, 188, 249, 254–56, 277n; hard talk, 34, 38, 110, 113, 123, 196; modal, 187–88; repetition, 123, 255–59; seriation, 259–63. *See also* narrative; speech arts; principles for speaking
Weber, Max, 196
welfare, 170, 191, 193, 207, 217
Welfare Ordinance, 102, 286n
White, Richard, 66, 280
wila, 174, 176
Williams, Nancy, 240; foreignness, 288n; four-stage theory, 7; Fourth World property, 8–9, 275n; land appropriation, 250; land claims, 58; land tenure, 135, 139, 243–44, 246, 287n, 294–95n
Williams, Raymond, 77
Wilmsen, Edwin, Fourth World property, 8, 24; hunter-gatherer studies, 5, 8, 27, 185–86, 210, 273n
winga, 148
Wolf, Eric, 274
World War II: Aboriginal involvement in, 92–93, 120; and dreaming, 156, 172; effect on Aboriginal practice, 65, 97, 205
Woodburn, James, 3, 26, 186, 275
work: alternate ideologies of, 13, 26, 136–37, 185–86, 196–202, 243; capitalist ethic, 85, 196; and intentionality, 1; measurement of, 11–12, 26–27, 203, 274n. *See also* evaluation; labor-action; human-land relation; hunter-gatherers
wulgamen, 44, 46
wutwut, 52, 61–62, 154

Yolngu, 243–44, 288n, 295n